P9-ASG-287

OKLAHOMA TRAVEL HANDBOOK

Sailboats on Fort Gibson Reservoir.

OKLAHOMA TRAVEL HANDBOOK

BY KENT RUTH

University of Oklahoma Press : Norman

By Kent Ruth

Colorado Vacations (New York, 1959)
Great Day in the West: Forts, Posts, and Rendezvous Beyond the Mississippi (Norman, 1963)
Touring the Old West (Brattleboro, Vt., 1971)
Trip Teasers (Oklahoma City, 1977)
Oklahoma Travel Handbook (Norman, 1977)
Window on the Past: Historical Sites in Oklahoma (Oklahoma City, 1974; Norman, 1978)

Library of Congress Cataloging in Publication Data

Ruth, Kent.
  Oklahoma travel handbook.

  1. Oklahoma—Description and travel—1951–
—Guide-books. 2. Oklahoma—Gazetteers. I. Title.
P693.3.K46   917.66'04'5   76-62517
ISBN: 0–8061–1539–4

Copyright © 1977 by the University of Oklahoma Press, Norman, Publishing Division of the University. Manufactured in the U.S.A. First edition, 1977; second printing, 1980; third printing, 1985.

To Helen,
who has shared all aspects of this project,
from initial on-site inspection
to final in-print proofreading.

University of Oklahoma football (photograph courtesy OU Photo).

Downtown Oklahoma City at night (photograph courtesy OKC Tourism Center).

Overholser Mansion, in Oklahoma City, restored by the Oklahoma Historical Society.

ACKNOWLEDGMENTS

There's a quaint custom in rural Oklahoma (and elsewhere) that allows the overwhelmed recipient of many favors, large and small, to make a single public pronouncement of gratitude. This "Notice" in the local newspaper usually costs fifty cents and says, in effect, "God bless all of you who have done so many nice things for me recently." As a bargain, it compares favorably with the storied $24 purchase of Manhattan Island. And we'd be tempted to run such a Notice, if only we could arrange for all who have made this book possible to read the same local paper! Alas, since that is impossible, we fall back on the traditional listing of thank-yous. And the just-as-traditional apology to those who are invariably overlooked.

George H. Shirk, long-time president of the Oklahoma Historical Society, rates the first nod of appreciation. To his *Oklahoma Place Names* we are indebted for many dates and many word origins. To Angie Debo, who edited the original edition of *Oklahoma: A Guide to the Sooner State*, we are indebted for the countless bits of history and legend with which we have tried to make this volume both valuable as a reference work and readable as a less formal travel guide.

Then we would thank—for many, if unspecified, favors—Joe Lawhead, Susan Sam, Oscar C. Cornut, Gene Provolt, Harry Wilson, Clyde C. Cole, Jr., Marty Hagerstrand, Charles E. Engleman, Bonnie Hiler, Linda Sullivan, and many more.

The book as you now hold it in your hands was a real pleasure to research and write. It would not have been without the help of "all of you who have done so many nice things for us recently." Thank you!

Geary, Oklahoma   *Kent Ruth*

Gilcrease Museum, Tulsa, houses the world's largest collection of paintings by Thomas Moran, famed painter of the American West.

Philbrook Art Center in Tulsa, which houses notable collections of American Indian baskets and pottery, Italian Renaissance paintings and sculpture, and Chinese jades (photograph courtesy Public Relations Department, Tulsa Chamber of Commerce).

Sculpture by Frederic Remington in the Gilcrease Institute, Tulsa, which has the largest collection of works by Remington and by Charles Russell.

OKLAHOMA
TRAVEL
HANDBOOK

Rodeo at Guthrie's '89ers Day Celebration (photograph by Fred W. Marvel, courtesy Oklahoma Tourism Department).

 **INTRODUCTION**

An explanation of what follows would seem to be an attempt to gild the lily. To explain the arrangement of a dictionary, so to speak! Few books indeed are as honest and as forthright as a dictionary. First there is Aa, then Ab, and so on, right through to Zz.

Oklahoma Travel Handbook is presented just as forthrightly. Everything is arranged alphabetically, by proper place names. It is assumed that every traveler, by auto or armchair, has a map and the desire for more information. It follows then that he (or she) has only to spot **Achille** (the first entry in the book) or **Yukon** (the last) on the map and look up that name in the book. The reader should find an entry here for *every* proper place name one can find on the most generous map of Oklahoma—be it city or near-ghost town, lake or river, county or mountain range, state park or major tourist attraction.

When he finds that particular entry, he will also find, in most cases (data presented varies, understandably, with the nature of the entry itself), such information as location, access by highway, population, derivation of name, date of establishment, historic development, and any other such *curiosae* pertaining thereunto as the author considered, in what passes for his wisdom, might be of interest to the reader.

Because he is a frustrated historian, the author has included far more history than is included in most popular travel guides. Because he is also a frustrated humorist, he has put in far more of the off-beat details than are found in most histories. The result, more than likely, is neither fish nor fowl, neither travel guide nor history. And, candidly, that was the intention! That the world's greatest collection of western art is in Tulsa is obviously not on the same plane as the fact that the world's largest peanut is in Durant. Both facts, however, can help to make one's travels a bit more enjoyable.

There is a section of maps which includes eight state and area maps showing each entry in the book and also several historical maps of general interest. Unless

3

otherwise noted, all photographs used in the book are from the Oklahoma Tourism Department.

If the reader desires more information, there is an appendix at the back of the book containing names and addresses of sources for same. There is also an index for such non-place names as Will Rogers, Coronado, Jesse Chisholm, Stand Watie, Redd Foxx, and others who are in some way or another, a part of the Oklahoma story.

The book is easy to use. We hope it is equally helpful. And entertaining.

Young Indian dancer, State Fair of Oklahoma, Oklahoma City (photograph courtesy OKC Tourism Center).

 **MAPS**

In order to help the reader locate the various entries in this book, we have divided the state into seven sections and mapped each section separately, in detail. Map Number 1 shows the entire state, with county names and section divisions indicated. Maps 2 through 8 are the section maps.

Following the present-day maps we have included eight historical maps, all from the *Historical Atlas of Oklahoma*, Second Edition, Revised and Enlarged, by John W. Morris, Charles R. Goins, and Edwin C. McReynolds, which show many of the historical places and locate many of the events mentioned in this book.

Neustadt Wing of the University of Oklahoma's Bizzell Memorial Library (photograph courtesy OU Photo).

The '89ers Day Celebration parade at Guthrie (photograph by Fred W. Marvel, courtesy Oklahoma Tourism Department).

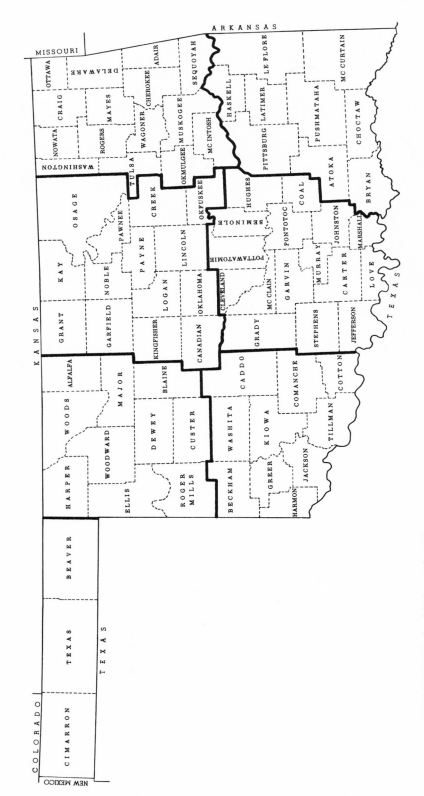

MAP NUMBER 1—*Oklahoma Counties*
© 1977 by the University of Oklahoma Press

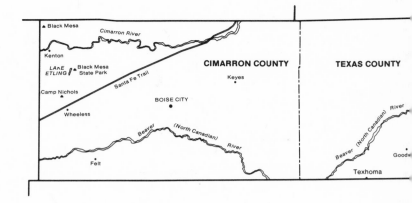

MAP NUMBER 2—*Panhandle of Oklahoma*
© *1977 by the University of Oklahoma Press*

MAP NUMBER 3—*Northwestern Oklahoma*
© *1977 by the University of Oklahoma Press*

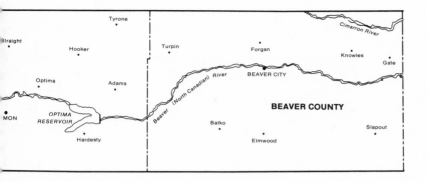

Straight •   • Tyrone

• Hooker   • Turpin   • Forgan   • Knowles   • Gate

• Optima   • Adams   BEAVER CITY

MON

OPTIMA RESERVOIR   Beaver (North Canadian) River

• Balko

BEAVER COUNTY

• Hardesty   • Elmwood   • Slapout

Cimarron River

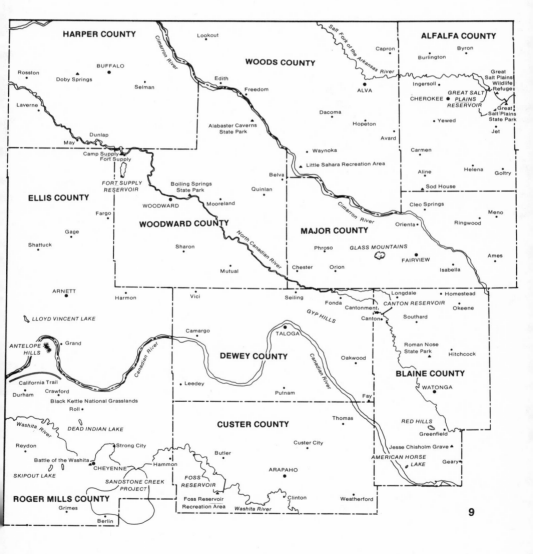

HARPER COUNTY

• Lookout

WOODS COUNTY

ALFALFA COUNTY

• Rosston   ▲ BUFFALO

• Doby Springs

• Selman   • Edith   • Freedom

• Capron   • Byron

• Burlington

Salt Fork of the Arkansas River

Great Salt Plains Wildlife Refuge

• Ingersoll

CHEROKEE ●   *GREAT SALT PLAINS RESERVOIR*

Great Salt Plains State Park

• Laverne   • ALVA

• Dacoma   • Yewed

• Jet

• Dunlap

• May   Camp Supply Fort Supply

• Hopeton   • Avard   • Carmen

FORT SUPPLY RESERVOIR

Boiling Springs State Park

• Waynoka   • Aline   • Helena   • Goltry

▲ Little Sahara Recreation Area

ELLIS COUNTY

• Fargo   WOODWARD   • Mooreland

Belva   • Quinlan   • Sod House

Cimarron River

• Cleo Springs

• Gage

• Shattuck

WOODWARD COUNTY

• Sharon

North Canadian River

• Meno

• Orienta   • Ringwood

MAJOR COUNTY

• Phroso   *GLASS MOUNTAINS* 🗲   • Ames

FAIRVIEW

• Mutual   • Chester   • Orion   • Isabella

• ARNETT   • Harmon   • Vici   • Seiling

• Longdale   • Homestead

• Fonda   • Cantonment   *CANTON RESERVOIR*   • Okeene

🪶 *LLOYD VINCENT LAKE*

GYP HILLS

Canton ●   • Southard

ANTELOPE HILLS   • Grand   • Camargo

TALOGA

• Roman Nose State Park   • Hitchcock

Canadian River

DEWEY COUNTY

• Oakwood

BLAINE COUNTY

• California Trail

• Durham   • Crawford   • Leedey   • Putnam   • Fay

• WATONGA

• Black Kettle National Grasslands

• Roll

Washita River   𝄐 *DEAD INDIAN LAKE*

CUSTER COUNTY

• Thomas

RED HILLS

• Greenfield

• Reydon   • Strong City   • Butler   • Custer City

• Jesse Chisholm Grave ▲

• Battle of the Washita ▲   CHEYENNE ●   • Hammon   • ARAPAHO

AMERICAN HORSE LAKE   • Geary

SKIPOUT LAKE

SANDSTONE CREEK PROJECT

FOSS RESERVOIR

ROGER MILLS COUNTY

• Grimes   Foss Reservoir Recreation Area   • Clinton   • Weatherford

Washita River

• Berlin

9

MAP NUMBER 4—*North Central Oklahoma*
© *1977 by the University of Oklahoma Press*

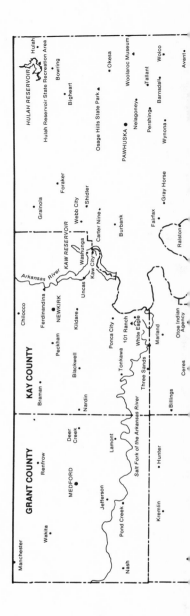

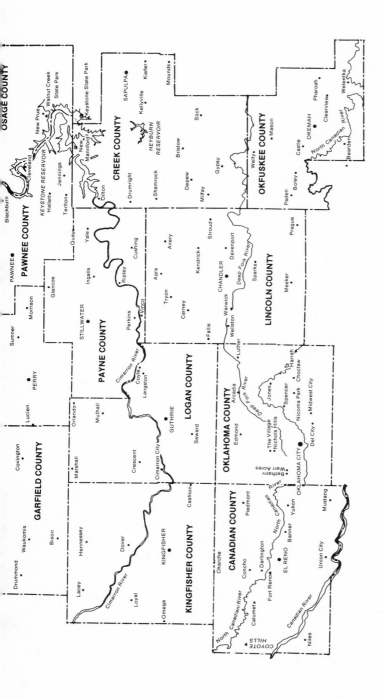

11

Successful fisherman on an Oklahoma lake (photograph courtesy Oklahoma Department of Wildlife Conservation).

A favorite sport in Oklahoma (photograph courtesy Oklahoma Department of Wildlife Conservation).

MAP NUMBER 5—*Northeast Oklahoma*
© *1977 by the University of Oklahoma Press*

13

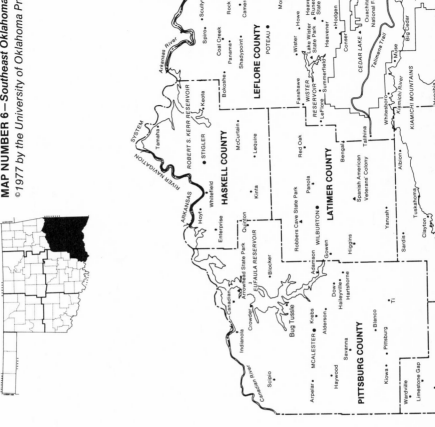

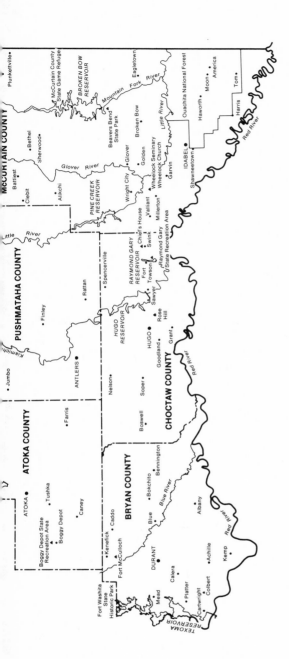

15

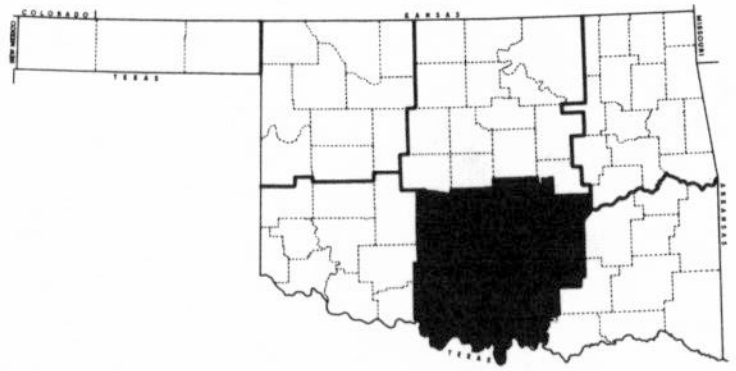

MAP NUMBER 7 – South Central Oklahoma
© 1977 by the University of Oklahoma Press

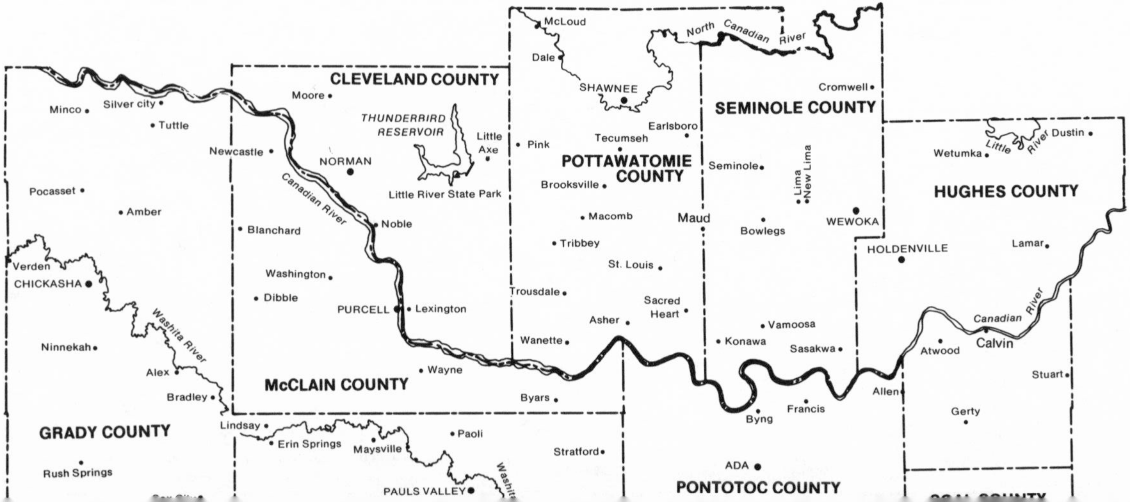

CLEVELAND COUNTY

Moore •
• Tuttle
Silver city •
Minco •
Pocasset •

Newcastle •
• Amber
Verden •
CHICKASHA •
Ninnekah •
Rush Springs •

GRADY COUNTY

Washita River

NORMAN •
THUNDERBIRD RESERVOIR
Little Axe •
Little River State Park
Noble •
Canadian River
Blanchard •
Washington •
• Dibble
Alex •
Bradley •
Lindsay •

McCLAIN COUNTY

PURCELL •
• Lexington
• Wayne
Erin Springs •
Maysville •
• Paoli
PAULS VALLEY •
Washita River

McLoud •
North Canadian River
Dale •
SHAWNEE •
• Pink
Tecumseh •
Brooksville •
• Tribbey
• Macomb
Earlsboro •
Maud •
St. Louis •
Trousdale •
Wanette •
Asher •
Sacred Heart •
Byars •
Stratford •

POTTAWATOMIE COUNTY

Cromwell •

SEMINOLE COUNTY

Seminole •
Bowlegs •
Lima •
New Lima •
WEWOKA •
Konawa •
Vamoosa •
Sasakwa •
Francis •
Byng •
ADA •

PONTOTOC COUNTY

Wetumka •
Little River
HUGHES COUNTY
HOLDENVILLE •
Lamar •
• Dustin
Canadian River
Calvin •
Atwood •
Gerty •
Allen •
Stuart •

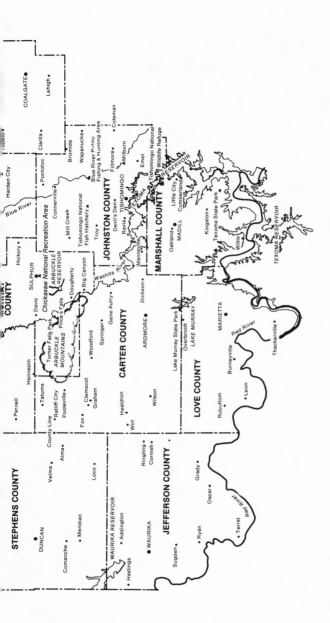

STEPHENS COUNTY

• Pernell

• Comanche   • Velma   • County Line
DUNCAN   • Alma   • Ratliff City
                                    • Pooleville
• Meridian   Fox • • Clemscot
        • Loco   Graham

WAURIKA RESERVOIR
        • Addington
• WAURIKA   • Ringling
• Hastings   • Cornish
Sugden •
                JEFFERSON COUNTY
        • Ryan   • Grady
              • Oscar •
                    • Terral

COUNTY

• Davis
SULPHUR   Chickasaw National Recreation Area
        ARBUCKLE
• Hickory   RESERVOIR
                    Washita River
Hennepin   • Dougherty
Turner Falls Park   • Big Canyon
• Tatums   ARBUCKLE   Price's Falls
              MOUNTAINS
        • Woodford   • Springer
        • Gene Autry •
                    • Dickson
CARTER COUNTY
        • Healdton   ARDMORE •
Wilson •   Lake Murray State Park
• Wirt   Overbrook •
                          LAKE MURRAY
              LOVE COUNTY
        • Leon   • Burneyville
RubuItom •   • MARIETTA
                    Red River
                          • Thackerville

Mill Creek •
Tishomingo National
Fish Hatchery ▲
        JOHNSTON COUNTY
Troy •
        Devil's Den •
Mannsville •
        MARSHALL COUNTY
        Oakland • MADILL
                    Kingston •
                          Willis •
                    Marietta

Blue River
Harden City
• Pontotoc   • Clarita
        • Bromide
        Wapanucka •
Blue River Public
Fishing & Hunting Area
        • Coleman
Connerville •
        Fillmore •
                • Milburn
        Ravia • TISHOMINGO
                    Emet •
        • Tishomingo National
                Wildlife Refuge
Little City •
Cumberland •
        Texoma State Park
TEXOMA RESERVOIR

TISHOMINGO
RESERVOIR

COALGATE •

• Lehigh

Tupelo •

Young girl admiring costumed dolls at the Czech Festival in Yukon.

At the annual Festival of the Arts in Oklahoma City (photograph courtesy Oklahoma Tourism Department).

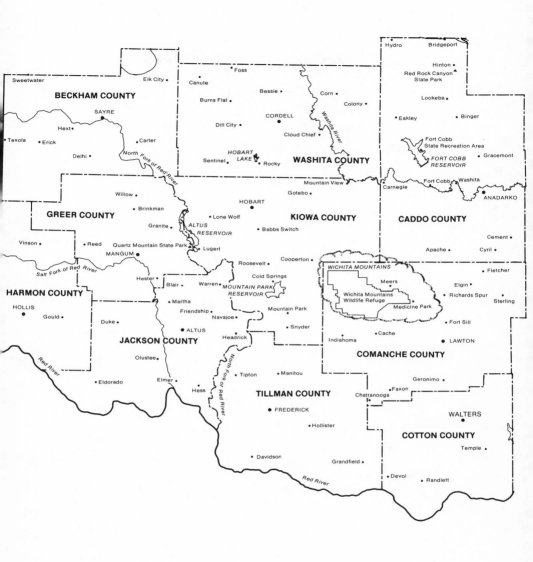

Sweetwater

Elk City •
• Canute

• Foss

BECKHAM COUNTY

Bessie •

Corn •

Colony •

Burns Flat •

Hydro •

Bridgeport •

Hinton •

Red Rock Canyon
State Park

Lookeba •

SAYRE

Hext•

• Carter

Delhi •

CORDELL
•

Dill City •

Cloud Chief •

• Eakley

• Binger

• Texola

• Erick

North Fork of Red River

HOBART
LAKE

Sentinel •

WASHITA COUNTY

Fort Cobb
State Recreation Area

*FORT COBB
RESERVOIR*

• Gracemont

Rocky

Mountain View •

Fort Cobb • Washita

Willow •

Gotebo •

Carnegie •

ANADARKO

• Brinkman

HOBART
•

KIOWA COUNTY

CADDO COUNTY

GREER COUNTY

• Lone Wolf

Granite •

ALTUS
RESERVOIR

• Babbs Switch

Cement •

Vinson •

• Reed

Quartz Mountain State Park

• Lugert

MANGUM •

Roosevelt •

Cooperton •

Apache •

Cyril •

Salt Fork of Red River

Hester •

Blair •

Warren •

Cold Springs •

*MOUNTAIN PARK
RESERVOIR*

WICHITA MOUNTAINS

Meers •

• Fletcher

Elgin •

HARMON COUNTY

HOLLIS
•

Gould •

Duke •

• Martha

Friendship •

Navajoe •

Mountain Park •

Wichita Mountains
Wildlife Refuge

Medicine Park •

Richards Spur •

Sterling •

• Snyder

• ALTUS

• Cache

• Fort Sill

JACKSON COUNTY

Headrick •

Indiahoma •

• LAWTON

Olustee •

COMANCHE COUNTY

Red River

• Eldorado

Elmer •

Hess •

• Tipton

• Manitou

Geronimo •

WALTERS

North Fork of Red River

TILLMAN COUNTY

Chattanooga •

• Faxon

• FREDERICK

COTTON COUNTY

• Hollister

Temple •

• Davidson

Grandfield •

• Devol

• Randlett

Red River

MAP NUMBER 8—*Southwestern Oklahoma*
© 1977 by the University of Oklahoma Press

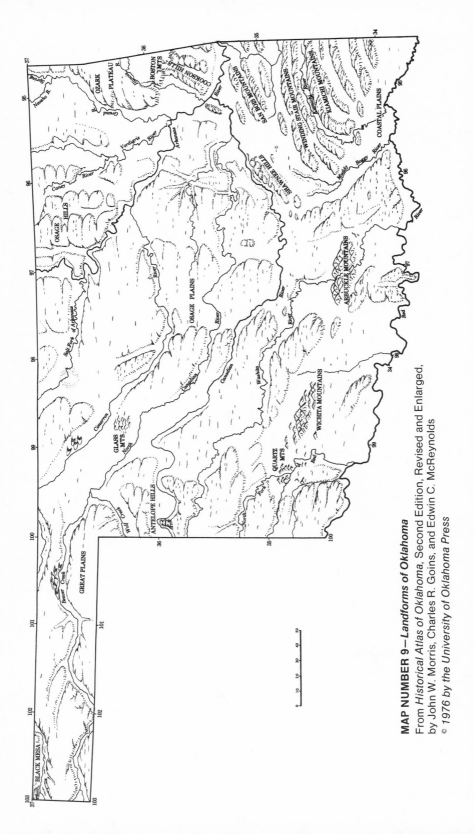

MAP NUMBER 9—Landforms of Oklahoma

From *Historical Atlas of Oklahoma*, Second Edition, Revised and Enlarged,
by John W. Morris, Charles R. Goins, and Edwin C. McReynolds.
© 1976 by the University of Oklahoma Press

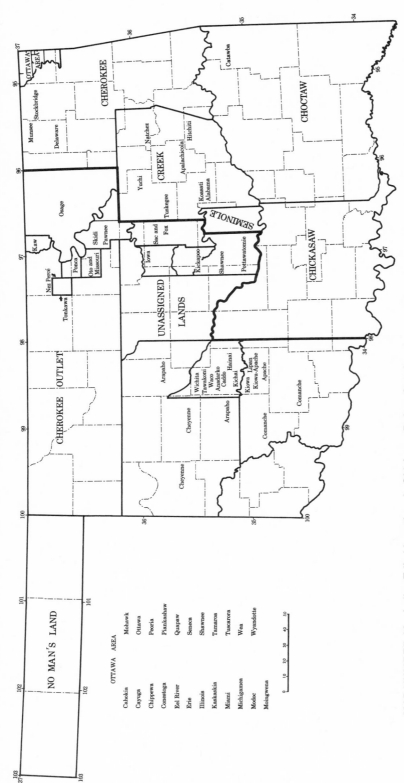

MAP NUMBER 10—*Indian Tribal Locations in Oklahoma Before Statehood*
From *Historical Atlas of Oklahoma,* Second Edition, Revised and Enlarged,
by John W. Morris, Charles R. Goins, and Edwin C. McReynolds
© 1976 by the University of Oklahoma Press

OTTAWA AREA

Cahokia
Cayuga
Chippewa
Conestoga
Eel River
Erie
Illinois
Kaskaskia
Miami
Michigannea
Modoc
Moingwena

Mohawk
Ottawa
Peoria
Piankashaw
Quapaw
Seneca
Shawnee
Tamaroa
Tuscarora
Wea
Wyandotte

0 10 20 30 40 50

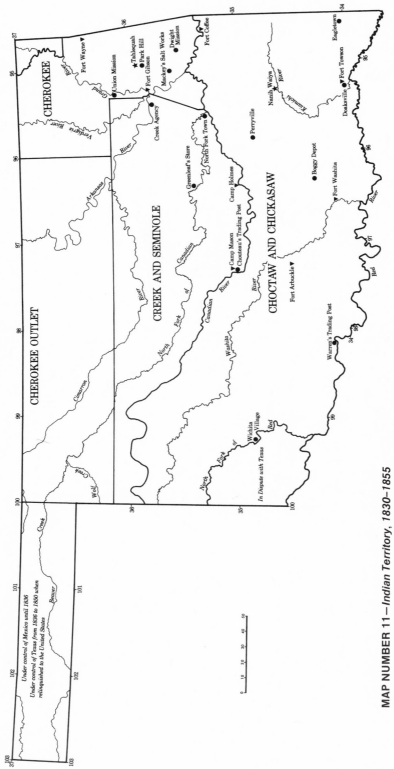

MAP NUMBER 11—Indian Territory, 1830–1855

From *Historical Atlas of Oklahoma*, Second Edition, Revised and Enlarged,
by John W. Morris, Charles R. Goins, and Edwin C. McReynolds
© 1976 by the *University of Oklahoma Press*

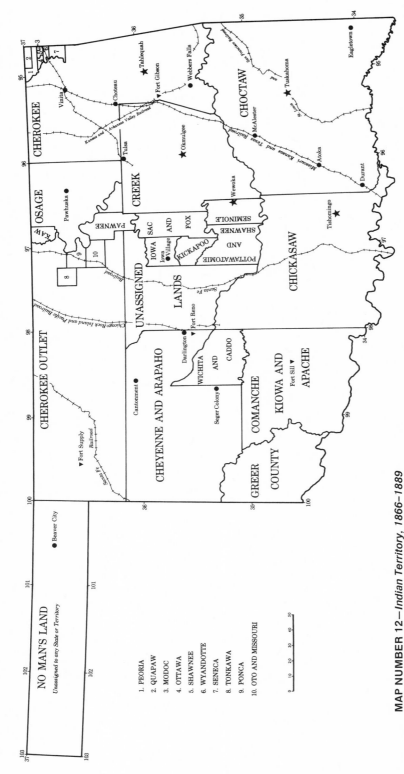

MAP NUMBER 12 – Indian Territory, 1866–1889

From *Historical Atlas of Oklahoma*, Second Edition, Revised and Enlarged, by John W. Morris, Charles R. Goins, and Edwin C. McReynolds

© 1976 by the University of Oklahoma Press

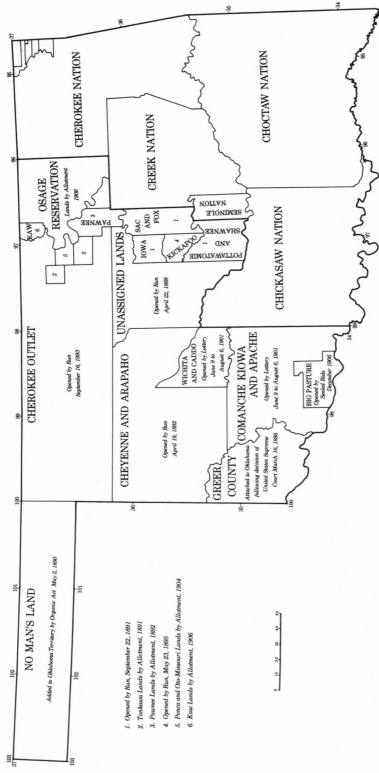

MAP NUMBER 13—Land Openings in Oklahoma

From *Historical Atlas of Oklahoma*, Second Edition, Revised and Enlarged,
by John W. Morris, Charles R. Goins, and Edwin C. McReynolds,
© 1976 by the University of Oklahoma Press

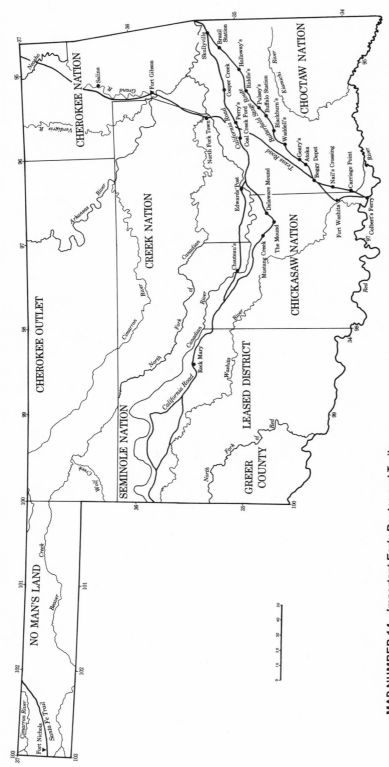

MAP NUMBER 14—Important Early Routes and Trails

From *Historical Atlas of Oklahoma*, Second Edition, Revised and Enlarged,
by John W. Morris, Charles R. Goins, and Edwin C. McReynolds.
© 1976 by the University of Oklahoma Press

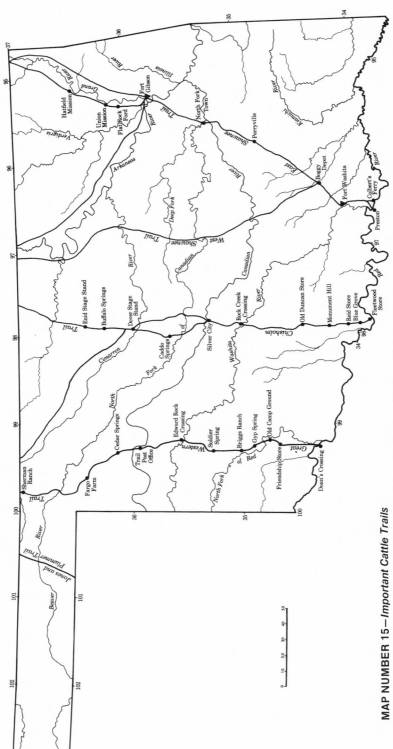

MAP NUMBER 15—*Important Cattle Trails*

From *Historical Atlas of Oklahoma*, Second Edition, Revised and Enlarged,
by John W. Morris, Charles R. Goins, and Edwin C. McReynolds

© *1976 by the University of Oklahoma Press*

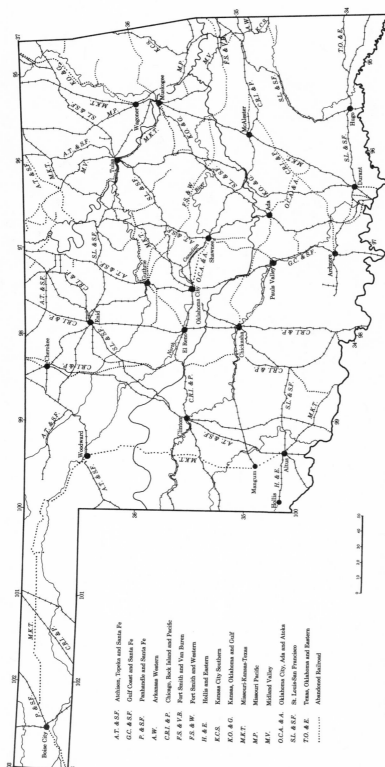

MAP NUMBER 16—*Railroads in Oklahoma, 1870–1958*

From *Historical Atlas of Oklahoma*, Second Edition, Revised and Enlarged,
by John W. Morris, Charles R. Goins, and Edwin C. McReynolds

© *1976 by the University of Oklahoma Press*

A.T. & S.F.	Atchison, Topeka and Santa Fe
G.C. & S.F.	Gulf Coast and Santa Fe
P. & S.F.	Panhandle and Santa Fe
A.W.	Arkansas Western
C.R.I. & P.	Chicago, Rock Island and Pacific
F.S. & V.B.	Fort Smith and Van Buren
F.S. & W.	Fort Smith and Western
H. & E.	Hollis and Eastern
K.C.S.	Kansas City Southern
K.O. & G.	Kansas, Oklahoma and Gulf
M.K.T.	Missouri-Kansas-Texas
M.P.	Missouri Pacific
M.V.	Midland Valley
O.C.A. & A.	Oklahoma City, Ada and Atoka
S.L. & S.F.	St. Louis-San Francisco
T.O. & E.	Texas, Oklahoma and Eastern
....	Abandoned Railroad

Alabaster Caverns.

A

Achille (Bryan Co., pop. 382, on OK 78, 12 mi. S of **Durant,** see Map 6). A dwindling community established in 1910 on a now abandoned section of the Kansas, Oklahoma & Gulf Railroad (present Missouri Pacific). The name (pronounced ACH-uh-lee) is neither classical nor misspelled, but a corruption of the Cherokee "atsila," meaning "fire." This arose, according to historian George H. Shirk, because a group of Cherokee refugees settled in this area during the Civil War.

About 3 miles south of Achille (on private property, inquire locally) is the site of Bloomfield Academy. One of the Chickasaw Nation's most important educational institutions, Bloomfield was established in 1852, lasted until 1914, when it was destroyed by fire. Only a neglected cemetery—headstones scattered among the trees—marks the site today.

Ada (Pontotoc Co. seat, pop. 14,859, at junc. of OK 1, 3, 13, & 99, see Map 7). What **Enid** is, with four letters, Ada is with three—the crossword puzzle worker's favorite "Town in Oklahoma." The two county seats are similar in other ways, too. Both quickly outlived early periods of violence to become sedate college towns. Today, both are seeing diversified small industry supplement agriculture and petroleum to keep local economies strong.

Jeff Reed started Ada in 1890 with a log structure that served as both store and dwelling. When he acquired a post office the next year, he named it for his daughter. Coming of the Frisco Railroad in 1900 brought rapid growth, and the town soon acquired a well-deserved reputation for lawlessness. In 1908 there were thirty-six murders in and around Ada. Finally a particularly spectacular ambush slaying aroused the indignation of the townspeople. Vigilantes broke into the jail one April night in 1909, took the four men charged with the killing to a nearby livery stable, and strung them up from convenient rafters. The quadruple lynching, still a record for Oklahoma, had the desired salutary effect on local law and order.

Perhaps coincidentally, it was also in 1909 that the state legislature created present East Central Oklahoma State University, originally as a two-year, teacher-training school. Degree granting authority came, with a four-year college curriculum, in 1919. Today the thoroughly modern campus (east end of Main Street) accommodates some 3,000 students. Most unusual new building is the $2 million Robert S. Kerr Activities Center, its gold geodesic dome enclosing 50,000 square feet of physical education space on three levels.

No coincidence at all is the name of the activities center. The late millionaire oil man and former governor of Oklahoma and United States senator was born about nine miles southwest of Ada (inquire locally). The birthplace cabin is carefully preserved in a small park, with the senator's grave. Nearby is an interesting old Chickasaw cemetery. Located in Ada is the Robert S. Kerr Environmental Research Laboratory, an agency of the Federal Water Pollution Control Administration. Its research and training programs, administered by some 150 technicians, focuses primarily on pollution problems in the Southwest as they pertain to agriculture.

Other points of interest in Ada include a giant Callixylon (at the entrance to the East Central campus), the fossilized stump of a tree, 5 feet in diameter, that dates back 350 million years to the Devonian period; the East Central Oklahoma State University Museum (library, Mon.–Fri. 8–5) with important exhibits in the fields of geology, paleontology, anthropology, zoology and history; Wintersmith and Glenwood parks, municipal properties with swimming pool and other sports and recreation facilities; the Ada Chamber of Commerce building (west end of Main Street), an impressive renovation of the town's old Frisco passenger depot.

Oil is still important in Ada, providing some 500 jobs. The county itself has more than 2,300 producing wells. But other industries have long been important, too. The town's first feed mill was established in 1902. Ideal Cement Company, started four years later, now employs over 200 persons. Its principal limestone quarry is at **Lawrence.** Other important manufactured items include glass, brick, modular homes, meat products, and work clothes.

Biggest annual event is an I. R. A. rodeo in early August. East Central provides a year-round calendar of sports, concerts, art, and cultural events. Well known, too, is fishing in the Ada area, especially on such rivers as the **Blue** and Little Blue, and on Pennington, Mill, Clear Boggy, and Jack Fork creeks.

Adair (Mayes Co., pop. 459, on US 69, 9 mi. N of Pryor, see Map 5). Like **Adair County,** the town honors the prominent Cherokee Indian family, one of the best known of whom was William Penn Adair. Here in July, 1892, the notorious Dalton gang staged one of their more daring robberies. A shipment of $17,000 in currency was taken from the express car of an M-K-T train at the Adair station, despite the fact authorities had been tipped off, and a lively gun battle preceded the successful getaway.

Adair County (east-central Oklahoma on the Arkansas border, see Map 5). Area, 569 sq. mi.; pop., 15,141; county seat, **Stilwell.** This is the heart of the area first settled by the immigrant Cherokees in the 1830's and Adair County—for a prominent Cherokee family—still claims a higher percentage of Indian population than any other in the United States.

With the Cherokee Hills on the north and the Cookson Hills on the south, the county has a natural beauty that at least partially masks its very real poverty. Small farming, fruit growing, and lumbering are the economic mainstays, and in recent years strawberry raising, centered on Stilwell, has become a million-dollar industry.

Top travel lures: **Bitting Springs Mill,** Cookson Hills sightseeing.

Adams (Texas Co., pop. 200, on paved county road 15 mi. SE of **Hooker,** see Map 2). An isolated farm agricultural community established in 1930 after the Rock Island built a secondary north-south line through the county. It has received an economic boost in recent years from extensive oil and gas activity immediately to the southwest.

Adamson (Pittsburg Co., pop. 160, on county road 10 mi. E of **McAlester,** see Map 6). Another dwindling coal mining community, established in 1906 and named for Peter Adamson, local mine owner. A white granite monument—near the abandoned Adamson school and overlooking an arm of **Eufaula Reservoir**—memorializes the area's greatest tragedy. Standing within a few feet of the sealed-off entrance to the old Union Coal Company's No. 1 mine, it pays tribute to the fourteen men entombed about 1,600 feet underground in a massive cave-in the afternoon of September 4, 1914.

Addington (Jefferson Co., pop. 123, on US 81, 6 mi. N of *Waurika*, see Map 7). A fading community that dates from 1896. James P. Addington was its first postmaster. Three miles east of the town is sprawling Price Ranch, established by J. C. Price in 1886. Across it, from 1867 to the middle 1880's, ran the storied Chisholm Trail. (Evidences of the trail are still visible here and about 5 miles east of *Waurika*, where it is now crossed by US 70.)

Price himself drove herds of Kansas-bound Texas cattle through this area before settling down to ranching. On his ranch is one of the few landmarks of the trail—so-called Monument Hill. A spring nearby and its position a day's drive north of *Red River* made it a popular camp site for the drovers. Rocks were added to the "hill" over the years until by 1893 a sizeable monument had been created.

Afton (Ottawa Co., pop. 1,022, on US 60 and US 66, see Map 5). A coal-shipping point on the Frisco Railroad that has benefitted in recent years from recreational development on nearby *Grand Lake of the Cherokees.* The town began in 1886 and was named for Afton Aires, daughter of railroad surveyor Anton Aires, who had named her for the Afton River of his native Scotland.

Agra (Lincoln Co., pop. 335, on OK 18, 12 mi. N of *Chandler,* see Map 4). A dwindling agricultural community, started in 1902 and named, presumably, for the city of that name in India.

Alabaster Caverns State Park (off OK 50, 6 mi. S of *Freedom,* see Map 3). A 200-acre natural preserve featuring what is said to be the world's largest gypsum cave and one of the state's few natural bridges. The 200-million-year-old cavern is traversed by a 2,300-foot-long trail through tunnels of gleaming white stone and pink alabaster, highlighted by sparkling, transparent crystals of selenite. In many areas of the cave bats hang in clusters from the ceil-ing. Occasionally, at dusk the bats may be seen leaving the cave. Eight species in all can be found in the park area.

Entrance to the cave is in a rock cliff facing picturesque Cedar Canyon, which the visitor may also explore. In the park itself is the Natural Bridge, just northwest of the entrance. It rises 150 feet above the floor of Cedar Canyon, was formed by stream erosion undercutting the gypsum. A once distinctive, long-familiar landmark of the caverns area, banded, multicolored, 50-foot-high Chimney Rock, was reduced to a nondescript stub in 1973 by persistent rains and a strong wind.

Alabaster was one of the first stones to be carved by man. It was used to decorate some of the pyramids of Egypt. Oklahoma alabaster varies in color from dark gray and deep rust to pink and gleaming white. Alabaster items are featured in the park's gift shop.

Facilities: playground, picnic and camping areas, swimming pool. Horses are available nearby. For a nominal fee, conducted cave tours are available 8 to 5 daily. Address: Freedom, OK 73842.

Albany (Bryan Co., pop. 150, on US 70-E, 11 mi. S of *Bokchito,* see Map 6). A sprawling roadside community established in 1894 and named for New York's capital city. It serves a rich farming area between *Blue River* and Island Bayou.

Albion (Pushmataha Co., pop. 186, on US 271, 9 mi. SW of *Talihina,* see Map 6). A lumbering town dating from 1887 when the Frisco Railroad built its Fort Smith–Paris (Texas) line through here.

Alderson (Pittsburg Co., pop. 215, on US 270, 5 mi. SE of *McAlester,* see Map 6). A pioneer coal producing community, established in 1890 with arrival of the Choctaw Coal and Railway Company and believed to have been named for an official of that line (the present Rock Island). Both town and railroad featured in a unique labor dispute in 1894 that involved the coal companies and the Choctaw Nation. In a decision that was approved ultimately by President Cleveland himself, some 200 miners from this area, together with their families, were loaded on boxcars and "exiled" to Arkansas.

Alex (Grady Co., pop. 492, off OK 19, 15 mi. SE of *Chickasha,* see Map 7). One of the older county communities, first settled in 1885. A farming community in the rich *Washita River* valley, it was named for William V. Alexander, its first postmaster.

Alfalfa County (northwestern Oklahoma bordering on Kansas, see Map 3). Area, 867 sq. mi.; pop., 7,224; county seat, *Cherokee.* Organized in 1907, the county was named for William H. (Alfalfa Bill) Murray, president of the Constitutional Convention and later governor of the state. Farming and ranching are the leading economic mainstays. Alfalfa ranks generally among the top twenty counties in the United States in wheat production.

Top travel lures: *Salt Plains National Wildlife Refuge,* selenite crystal digging near *Jet, Great Salt Plains State Park,* bird hunting on *Great Salt Plains Reservoir,* Homesteader's Sod House near *Cleo Springs.*

Alikchi (McCurtain Co., on unnumbered county road, 18 mi. N of *Wright City,* see Map 6). A scattered Choctaw community dating back to 1850 when Apukshunubbee District Court (of the Choctaw Nation) was established here. The name means "to doctor" and apparently alludes to nearby Sulphur Spring.

Here in the ruggedly isolated forestlands between the *Little* and *Glover* rivers the last tribal execution of an Indian in McCurtain County took place, in July, 1899. Tonaka (William Going), tried by a jury of fellow Choctaws, was convicted of murder. Then, according to tribal custom, he was allowed to return to his home. On the day set for execution he turned himself in and was shot to death.

Aline (Alfalfa Co., pop. 260, just W of OK 8, 19 mi. S of *Cherokee,* see Map 3). Small agricultural community in the southwest corner of the county, established in 1894, a year after the Cherokee Outlet was opened to settlement. Name honors Marie Aline Hartshorn, daughter of a prominent early settler.

Allen (Pontotoc Co., pop. 1,974, on OK 1, 18 mi. NE of *Ada,* see Map 7). Bucking the trend of most small, non-county-seat towns in agricultural Oklahoma, Allen is growing modestly, largely on the strength of a camper manufacturing concern that employs about 100 area residents. Ironically, it occupies at least part of the site once used by a refinery, closing of which some twenty years ago threatened to kill the town.

Settlement began in 1892. The name honors Allen McCall, son of a deputy U.S. marshal. Oil and ranching continue to be important in this northeastern corner of *Pontotoc County.*

Alma (Stephens Co., pop. 80, off OK 7, 6 mi. SE of *Velma,* see Map 7). A scattered rural community dating from shortly after the turn of the century and named for an early-day resident, Alma Peoples. It is best known today for the large Velma-Alma consolidated school district that gives both communities a sense of identity.

Altus (Jackson Co. seat, pop. 23,302, at junc. of US 62, US 283, and OK 44, see Map 8). Many towns are flooded out of existence. But Altus, it seems, was flooded *into* being. Settlement in this area began in 1885. The following year the town of Frazier was born with the first post office in old *Greer County.* But a flood on Bitter Creek in 1891 drove the settlers out, and most of the refugees moved two miles east, to a "high place" they called Altus.

A bustling city today, the new settlement has come a long way from its humble beginnings. But it hasn't forgotten the past. A granite marker in the city square designates the spot where the community pump once stood. And the Museum of the Western Prairie (Tues.–Fri. 9–5, Sat.–Sun. 2–5), dedicated to preserving "the historical artifacts, papers, and remnants of southwest Oklahoma," is strikingly designed as a half dugout, like the first homes of many of the pioneer settlers in this region.

It was lush "short grass" rangeland that first brought Texas ranchers into old **Greer County** in the 1880's, and Altus has been the center of a rich agricultural area ever since. But cotton, the first major crop, now shares honors with wheat and alfalfa. Diversity and a certain stabilization of farm income followed construction of **Altus Reservoir,** which has made irrigation possible. With hundreds of additional deep irrigation wells, agriculture has now grown into a $20 million industry.

An even greater "industry" perhaps is the U.S. government. Altus Army Field was established on east edge of the city in 1942 as an advanced flight training facility. Shut down after World War II, it was re-activated in 1953 as Altus Air Force Base, under first the Tactical Air Command and then the Strategic Air Command. Since 1968 the sprawling base has been run by the Military Airlift Command (MAC) as a primary training facility for Air Force pilots and flight engineers handling the military's largest jumbo jet transports (C-5, C-141).

Altus has kept pace in other fields, too. In 1956 it was named an "All-Amer-

Quartz Mountain State Lodge, at Quartz Mountain State Park on Altus Reservoir, offers year-round swimming under a plexiglass dome.

ican City," the first in Oklahoma to win that designation. Its crude one-room schools have expanded now to include fully accredited Western Oklahoma State College, with an enrollment of over 1,000 students. The school moved in 1976 to a new facility 2 miles north of downtown Altus.

The city maintains 187 acres in parks and recreation areas. Unusual features: a lighted 9-hole golf course, an old Frisco steam locomotive in South Park. A lingerie maker is the town's largest private employer (300). Primary annual events include a Junior Livestock Show (early March), the Miss Altus Pageant (mid-April), and Armed Forces Day salute to Altus AFB (May).

Altus Reservoir (20 mi. N of **Altus,** in Greer and Kiowa Counties, see Map 8). A 6,260-acre reservoir created by the Bureau of Reclamation in 1943 with construction of a 94-foot-high dam on the **North Fork of Red River.** Set in a colorful notch of the Quartz Mountains, it creates a highly scenic playground

The Museum of the Prairie, in Altus (photograph courtesy Museum of the Prairie).

in a relatively arid section of the state. Resort accommodations are available near the dam in **Quartz Mountain State Park**. The state also provides the 3,100-acre Lugert Public Hunting Area. A special hunting feature of the Altus Reservoir area is crow hunting (see **Fort Cobb Reservoir**).

Facilities (on the SW shore above the dam): lodge, cabins, picnic and camp areas, swimming pool, boat ramps and docks, golf course. Address: Bureau of Reclamation, Altus, OK 73521.

Alva (Woods County seat, pop. 7,440, at jct. US 64 and US 281, see Map 3). One of the four designated land-office towns at the opening of the Cherokee Outlet in 1893, Alva today is a pleasant, prosperous little college town. Its name honors Alva B. Adams, attorney for the Santa Fe Railroad, whose main east-west line serves the town. (Adams later became governor of Colorado.)

Alva is built around a spacious courthouse "rectangle." The Cherokee Strip Museum is at 901 14th St. (Sat., 2–4, Sun., 2–5, free). There is also a museum in Jesse Dunn Hall on the campus of Northwestern State University.

Northwestern, founded in 1897, is the state's second oldest normal school. Its first building, constructed the following year at a cost of $110,000, was underwritten by citizens of the new town, itself only five years old. This so-called "Castle on the Hill," designed by Joseph Foucart of **Guthrie**, the territorial capital, was destroyed by fire in 1935. Of strong interest in the library today is a forty-page brown leather brand book. It contains some 600 listings for about 300 ranches registered with the Cherokee Strip Livestock Association for the roundup of 1886.

Amber (Grady Co., pop. 200, on OK 92, 11 mi. NE of Chickasha, see Map 7). A scattered farming community that dates from 1903 with arrival of the Frisco Railroad. The name was probably inspired by the song, America the Beautiful, with its "fields of amber grain."

America (McCurtain Co., off OK 3, 18 mi. SE of Idabel, see Map 6). A virtual

ghost today, although the town, settled in 1903, once had upwards of 2,000 inhabitants when cotton and lumber were important booming local industries. Still standing, though abandoned, is the home of William Spencer, one-time storekeeper and self-styled "richest man in America." Curiously, the town was named for America Stewart, wife of area resident Tom Stewart—for whom was named the nearby near-ghost town of **Tom**.

American Horse Lake (10 mi. W of **Geary**, from US 270 & 281, 1 mi. N of Geary, W on paved farm-market road, follow markers, see Map 3). A deep-water fishing lake in the red-canyon area, managed by the Oklahoma Department of Wildlife Conservation.

Facilities: picnic areas, campgrounds, boat ramp.

Ames (Major Co., pop. 227, NE of **Okeene**, see Map 3). An isolated farming community on the Frisco Railroad and named, in 1902, for rail financier Harry S. Ames of St. Louis.

Anadarko (Caddo Co. seat, pop. 6,682,

At Indian City, near Anadarko, visitors can see reconstructions of typical villages of seven different tribes.

at junc. of US 62 & 281 and OK 8 & 9, see Map 8). Its unique name a corruption of that of a Caddoan tribe, Na-da-ko, Anadarko was Indian reservation land until August 6, 1901, when it was opened to white settlement. In a very real sense, however, it has remained Indian land, if not in ownership, then in appearance and mood. In spirit (color and excitement) as well as in substance (agencies, schools, museums, and shops) Anadarko is the Plains Indians capital of Oklahoma.

Roots of the Anadarko Area Office go back almost a century. The Kiowa, Apache, and Comanche agencies were consolidated here with the Wichita office in 1878. The welfare of some 26,000 Indians in Western Oklahoma and all of Kansas is directed now by the various bureaus and agencies headquartered here.

Indian culture and history dominate Anadarko's visitor attractions. The Southern Plains Indian Museum and Crafts Center (Tues.–Sat. 9–5, Sun. 1–5) is located on US 62 at the east edge of the city. It exhibits displays of Indian life, sells authentic hand-made Indian crafts. Adjacent to it is the National Hall of Fame for Famous American Indians, an outdoor display of bronze busts of great Indian leaders (Sacajawea, Chief Joseph, Pocahontas, Black Beaver, Sequoyah, many others), together with documents and artifacts concerning their lives. Black Beaver was long buried near Anadarko, but recently was reinterred on Chief's Knoll at Fort Sill.

In the rolling Tonkawa Hills immediately southeast of the city is Indian City, U.S.A. (daily 9–6 summer, 9–5 winter), an imaginative series of reconstructions of seven Indian villages (Caddo, Kiowa, Apache, Pueblo, Navajo, Pawnee, Wichita) providing an insight into the daily life, religion, and social life of the Plains tribes. Indian guides conduct forty-five-minute tours through the villages. Indian dances are presented daily in summer. The complex also includes a crafts shop (pottery, jewelry, beadwork).

Other points of Indian interest in the area include the Philomathic Museum in the one-time Rock Island Depot (open

Dancer at Anadarko's American Indian Exposition.

daily, 1–5), displaying Indian artifacts, pioneer relics; Riverside Indian School, off US 281 just north of town, dating from 1871 and still enrolling 300–400 students a year; the Federal Building downtown, featuring murals by such famed Kiowa artists as Mopope, Asah, and Auchiah.

The Anadarko special events calendar, too, is dominated by Indian events, particularly the American Indian Exposition (third week in Aug.) one of the nation's top Indian ceremonials and perhaps its most prestigious dancing competition. Dating back to the 1930's, the six-day affair draws up to 4,000 Indians from three dozen tribes across the country, up to 40,000 non-Indian spectators for the day-long fair and nighttime grandstand programs. A cultural show-

Antelope Hills, in northern Roger Mills County northwest of Cheyenne (photograph courtesy Cheyenne Chamber of Commerce).

case for arts, crafts, and life styles, the Exposition is planned and staged exclusively by and for Indians, with visitors welcomed as paying guests. Other annual events include a two-day Kiowa Veterans Day Celebration (Oct.), Kiowa-Apache Ceremonials (mid-June), junior and adult rodeos (June).

In recent years Anadarko has developed several industrial payrolls to augment agricultural and governmental employment. Visitors may now tour the Sequoyah Carpet Mills and the Gold Kist Peanut Plant.

Antelope Hills (in extreme northern Roger Mills Co., W of US 283 and N of OK 33, see Map 3). Six conspicuous, irregular peaks rising from a level plain inside a giant horseshoe of the *Canadian River*. The mile-wide, sandy stream, fringed with scattered trees and sparse vegetation, "fences in" the hills on the east, north, and west, and makes this one of the most isolated and picturesque ranching areas in the state. And explains why this part of the county is referred to as the Snaky Bend community.

A few cattle-guarded, trail-like roads serve the scattered ranches. From the hilltops they provide panoramic views of much of both *Ellis* and *Roger Mills* counties. The Antelope Hills were once a prominent landmark for the international boundary between the United States and Mexico. They were also well known to travelers on the *California Trail* that crossed this region for a time in the middle of the nineteenth century.

Antlers (Pushmataha Co. seat, pop. 2,685, at junc. of US 271 & OK 2 and OK 3 & 7, see Map 6). Though owing its start as a town to the arrival of the Frisco Railroad in 1887, Antlers was well known in pre-Civil War days as a camping area originally called Beaver's Station. The spring there, according to Indian custom, probably had been marked with a set of antlers fastened to a nearby tree. From this feature the town is thought to have acquired its name.

Lumbering remains the principal industry, although ranching has become increasingly important in recent years. As evidence of this trend a local drugstore displays (for sale) one of the state's most complete lines of livestock branding irons. Rodeos and livestock shows figure prominently in the town's annual events.

Apache (Caddo Co., pop. 1,421, at junc. of US 62 & 281 and OK 19, see Map 8). Yet another agricultural community, established in 1901 when the Kiowa-Apache-Comanche Indian lands were thrown open to white settlement. The Rock Island Railroad arrived the following year, and the little town was well on its way. Handsome relic of these early boom days is the one-time Apache State Bank. Now on the National Register of Historic Places, and restored by the Apache Historical Society, it now houses the town's library and museum.

Arapaho (Custer Co. seat, pop. 531, on US 183, 4 mi. N of Clinton, see Map 3). This next to smallest of Oklahoma's seventy-seven county seats (see *Taloga*) has begun to grow modestly in recent years. But it is apparently far too late for it to regain either its former importance as a freighting center or its turn-of-the-century population of 1,500. Nor, for that matter, will it ever catch up with its arch-rival, Clinton, although it has been able to fend off all attempts of west-central Oklahoma's largest city to take away from it the county seat itself.

Arapaho was surveyed in 1891 as the designated seat of county "G" when the Cheyenne and Arapaho Indian lands were opened the following year. Some 2,000 persons made the run, and about 400 of them staked out lots in the town-to-be by nightfall of April 19, 1892. A tent city sprang up (in one tent the *Arapaho Arrow* appeared, the area's first newspaper) and for the next ten years it was the traditional pioneer town, raucous and violence-prone. Freight wagons and stages passed through its dusty streets on the main trail between *El Reno* on the east and *Cheyenne* on the west. A branch led north to *Taloga*.

Then in 1901 the present Rock Island Railroad, building westward for Texas, missed Arapaho on the south. In 1903 nearby *Clinton* was established, a crippling blow from which the town never recovered. Despite this injury, a modern courthouse, school, and municipal building, along with many new homes, attest to Arapaho's unfailing optimism and determination.

Rock strata exposed by highway cut in the Arbuckle Mountains.

Arbuckle Mountains (Murray Co., traversed by I 35 and US 77, see Map 7). If not the most extensive, then perhaps this is the best known and most striking range of mountains in Oklahoma. The name honors Brigadier General Matthew Arbuckle, for whom nearby Fort Arbuckle was named (see *Davis*).

The east-west trending Arbuckles contain some of the earth's oldest rock formations, from the Pennsylvanian and Mississippian to the Ordovician and Cambrian periods. The range, exposed by uplift and erosion, is remarkable for the dramatic way its many formations provide a veritable index to the geological makeup of south-central Oklahoma. As an exposed mountain-top geology textbook, the Arbuckles have long drawn students on field trips from the University of Oklahoma and other schools. At various vantage points the different formations are identified for the visitor.

Until recently the only major road to serve the mountains was US 77. A slow but highly scenic route (completed in 1928, largely with convict labor from *McAlester*), it passes access roads to *Price's Falls* and *Turner Falls Park* before topping out on a rugged, cactus-studded flat. From here up-ended rock strata stretch away as far as the eye can reach, much like the row-upon-row of identical memorials in a National Cemetery. I 35, by contrast, is such a smooth, even-grade highway that the unwary motorist is often through the mountains before he realizes their significance. This can be remedied by watching for two marked scenic turn-offs serving exceptionally advantageous observation points, complete with helpful informational material.

Visitor accommodations for the Arbuckles can be found in **Davis** on the north and **Ardmore** to the south. The mountains also shelter a number of youth camps of state, church, fraternal, and civic organizations.

Arbuckle Reservoir (Lake of the Arbuckles, SW of **Sulphur,** in Murray County, see Map 7). One of the state's newer major lakes, this 2,350-acre empoundment was created in 1967 with a 142-foot-high dam across Rock Creek, a tributary of the **Washita River.** It lies on the east flank of the rugged **Arbuckle Mountains,** in a heavily wooded, highly scenic area. Recreational development is still relatively light. The Oklahoma wildlife department maintains the 1,260-acre Arbuckle Public Hunting Area. In 1976 the playground was merged with **Platt National Park** to form the **Chickasaw National Recreation Area.**

Facilities: picnic and camping areas, boat ramps. Address: Chickasaw National Recreation Area, Sulphur, OK 73086.

Arcadia (Oklahoma Co., pop. 400, on US 66 just NE of Oklahoma City, see Map 4). A still largely "arcadian" settlement in the wooded hills just beyond the capital city's limits. Arcadia was established a year after the Run of 1889, opening Old Oklahoma to settlement. A historical marker calls attention to a Washington Irving camp site near here in 1832 (see **Jones**).

Ardmore (Carter Co. seat, pop. 20,881, at junc. of US 60 & 77, see Map 7). From log ranch house to modern industrial city in less than a century—that is Ard-

more's record of progress. The traditional double cabin with open "dog-trot" (part of the old "700 Ranch" and dating from around 1880) was the only structure on the site when the Santa Fe Railroad arrived in 1887 and erected a station. An official of the line named the station for his home town in Pennsylvania, a fashionable Philadelphia suburb. The ranch house itself, now restored, serves as a pioneer museum in Fair Park.

Oil was first discovered in this area in 1905, but it was not until 1913, with opening of the vast **Healdton** field, that production was significant enough to trigger a boom. Since then Ardmore has grown steadily in size and importance. And oil men who made their money in the region have proceeded to pour it back into notable cultural and economic projects. These include the Charles B. Goddard Cultural Center in downtown Ardmore and the Samuel Robert Nobel Foundation on US 70, 4 miles to the east (established in 1945 by the late Lloyd Noble to carry out biomedical and agricultural research).

Despite the glamor that surrounds the discovery and production of oil, agriculture remains important economically in this section of the state that Ardmorites refer to as the Sunny Side of the **Arbuckle Mountains.** Two of southern Oklahoma's largest commercial dairies are located in Ardmore. Visitors to the Noble Foundation (see above) discover how much of its research work is geared to bettering farm and ranch life by improving the region's crops and livestock. Visitors are also welcomed at Oak Hill Farm (off US 70, 9 miles northeast of Ardmore), a large breeding and training facility for fine saddle horses.

World War II significantly changed Ardmore. An Air Force Base (see **Gene Autry**) brought considerable growth to the area. Then in 1959 the surplus facility was turned over to the city for use as an industrial park, and Ardmore began the expansion that gives it today an industrial employment of about 3,500 and a total payroll of more than $25 million. Biggest employer is the newly established $75 million Uniroyal tire plant. But the city also boasts payrolls in such fields as plastics, electronics, sportswear, food processing, refining, and petroleum products. Many of the plants offer tours. For details on these and other information, write the Chamber of Commerce, Ardmore, OK 73401.

Cultural and recreational activities center around the Goddard Center (art shows, little theater, concerts, lectures, films), the YMCA and YWCA, the Hardy Murphy Coliseum (annual Shrine Rodeo in early Apr., horse shows, bull-riding competition, mid-Oct.), Ardmore City Lake (rental boats, fishing fee required), and sprawling *Lake Murray State Park* on the city's southern doorstep. Also noteworthy: the Ardmore Public Library's Eliza Cruce Hall Doll Museum, displaying over 300 dolls collected by a niece of Oklahoma's second governor, Lee Cruce, and an Ardmore resident since 1897. Carter Seminary, on the north edge of Ardmore, was established in 1917 as the third and final location of Bloomfield Academy (see *Achille*), a Chickasaw institution dating back to 1852.

Important visitor attractions in the area include *Fort Washita* (extensive reconstruction of which has been supported by another Ardmore oilman, Ward S. Merrick), *Turner Falls Park, Platt National Park,* and *Texoma State Park.*

Arkansas River. The state's most important river system, draining all of northern Oklahoma and much of the central section. The stream heads high in the Rocky Mountains of Colorado and crosses half of Kansas before entering Oklahoma north of *Ponca City.* In its 328-mile, southeasterly course across the state, to the point where it enters Arkansas at Fort Smith, it fills *Kaw* and *Keystone* reservoirs and operates five separate lock-and-dam facilities of the *Arkansas River Navigation System.*

Trappers, fur traders, explorers, and adventurers all used the Arkansas in the eighteenth and nineteenth centuries. Steamboats plied its waters, after a fashion, through much of the last century. Sections of the Arkansas served as boundaries of the Indian nations and, with sections of *Red River,* were used in defining boundaries established by the Adams-Onís Treaty of 1819 that defined the limits of Spanish and American territory.

Arkansas River Navigation System. This 440-mile-long waterway was completed by the U.S. Corps of Engineers in 1971 at a cost of $1.2 billion (four times that of the Panama Canal). It connects the Port of *Catoosa* near *Tulsa* with the seaports of the world via the *Verdigris River* (for 50 miles), the *Arkansas,* and the Mississippi. Seventeen lock-and-dam structures, five in Oklahoma and twelve in Arkansas, provide the total lift of 420 feet required to maintain the 9-foot channel.

Five primary ports are served by the waterway, three in Arkansas and two in Oklahoma—*Catoosa* and *Muskogee.* Ten reservoirs complete the navigation system, including *Gibson, Wash Hudson, Grand, Wister, Tenkiller, Keystone, Oologah,* and *Eufaula.*

The system is known officially as the McClellan-Kerr waterway, for the two U.S. senators, John McClellan of Arkansas and the late Robert S. Kerr of Oklahoma, who were its principal Congressional supporters. For maps, facilities, and other information write U.S. Corps of Engineers, Box 61, Tulsa, OK 74102.

Arnett (Ellis Co. seat, pop. 711, at junc. of US 60 and US 283, see Map 3). The town dates back to territorial days—a post office was established in 1902, named for A. S. Arnett, a Fayetteville (W. Va.) minister—and has at least one building to prove it, a hut of hand-hewn cedar logs near the courthouse. Otherwise its appearance is clean, alert, and progressive. As in most parts of western Oklahoma, over-population of the semi-arid farmland that resulted from homesteading has long since given way to consolidation of holdings and far more efficient and productive procedures. Dairying and purebred cattle raising are now economic mainstays of the county. Some of the larger ranches are private wildlife refuges, stocked with quail, prairie chickens, turkeys, and buffalo. The area is a favorite with state hunters.

"Tree House" rental cottages are available at Arrowhead State Park.

Arpelar (Pittsburg Co., pop. 150, on US 270, 12 mi. W of McAlester, see Map 6). Community dating from the turn-of-the-century. Name honors Aaron Arpelar, county judge of Tobucksy County in the old Choctaw Nation. Tobucksy Courthouse still stands in *McAlester.*

Arrowhead State Park (off US 69, 1 mi. E of Canadian, see Map 6). The scenic sister park to *Fountainhead* on the south side of sprawling *Eufaula Reservoir.* The rough-hewn rock surfaces of handsome Arrowhead Lodge contrast sharply with the light, flowing lines of multi-story Fountainhead Lodge. But its 2,459 acres of wooded shoreline offer much the same blend of water and land-based sport and recreational opportunities. One unusual feature: the so-called Tree Houses—deluxe rental cottages gracefully projected into the air to resemble the stilted affairs that are featured in some of the wild animal parks in Africa.

Facilities: 104 lodge rooms and 100 cottages and tree houses, extensive camp and picnic areas, trailer hookups, 3,500-foot airstrip (asphalted, lighted),

9-hole golf course, pro shop and driving range, stable, boat ramps and docks, enclosed fishing dock, boat rentals and fishing guide service, swimming pool, beach and bathhouse, water skiing, lake excursion cruises. Address: Box 57, Canadian, OK 74425.

Asher (Pottawatomie Co., pop. 437, at junc. of US 177 & OK 59 and OK 39, see Map 7). Settlement in this *Canadian River* area began in 1891 with opening, by run, of the Pottawatomie/Shawnee Indian lands. The town began as Avoca, changed its name to honor townsite developer G. M. Asher when the Choctaw, Oklahoma and Gulf Railroad (present Rock Island) ran a branch line to this point from *Tecumseh* in 1902.

Two miles east of Asher, on the north side of OK 39, are the remains of a trading post established by Jesse Chisholm in 1848. Chisholm Spring still flows and is used by the present owner of the site. Four miles farther east and a mile and a half north is the impressive *Sacred Heart* Church.

Atoka (Atoka Co. seat, pop. 3,346, at junc. of US 69 & 75 and OK 3 & 7, see Map 6). The Rev. J. S. Murrow, a Baptist missionary, founded Atoka in 1867. There he established the Atoka Baptist Academy, eventually absorbed into the Murrow Indian Orphans' Home on the Bacone College campus at *Muskogee.* The name, like that of the county, honors the Choctaw subchief, Captain Atoka, who lived near present-day *Farris.*

Atoka has long thrived on its status as not only the seat of county government, but the county's only trade center as well. Recently, a small women's wear factory has added its payroll to the agriculture-oriented economy. (Atoka high school claims the state's largest Future Farmers of America chapter.)

Of particular visitor interest in Atoka is the Chuck Wagon Musical Museum (on US 69 & 75 downtown), a notable collection of antique mechanical music makers. It is free except for the coins needed to operate the machines. A Trailriders Rodeo is scheduled each year in July. Each May the Atoka Historical Society presents "Journey's End," a dramatization of the removal of the Choctaws from the Southeast to Indian Territory.

Civil War buffs will want to hunt up the state's only Confederate Cemetery (just east of US 69 on the north bank of Muddy Boggy north of Atoka). It marks the 1864 Muddy Boggy battle site. Area recreation centers around **Atoka Reservoir** north of town.

Atoka County (southeastern Oklahoma, see Map 6). Area, 992 sq. mi.; pop., 10,972; county seat, **Atoka.** Although not organized until 1907, with statehood, the county was long a center of Choctaw Indian trade and culture. Captain Atoka, for whom the town and county were named, was a prominent Choctaw leader. Best known early-day town was **Boggy Depot,** home of chief Allen Wright, governor of the Choctaw Nation who suggested the name **Oklahoma.**

Top travel lures: **Boggy Depot Recreation Area, Atoka Lake,** hunting and fishing.

Atoka Reservoir (off US 69 north of Atoka, see Map 6). This 5,500-acre reservoir was constructed by **Oklahoma City** as a municipal water supply. (The water is pumped to the capital city in giant conduits, being raised nearly 700 feet along the way.) The lake area provides hunting and fishing. The Oklahoma Department of Wildlife Conservation manages the Stringtown Public Hunting Area, embracing 90 water acres and 5,500 acres of land.

Facilities: picnic areas and campgrounds.

Atwood (Hughes Co., pop. 200, at junc. of OK 1 & 68, 11 mi. S of **Holdenville,** see Map 7). A scattered, schoolless community on the Kansas, Oklahoma and Gulf Railroad (now Missouri Pacific) that began before the turn of the century as Newburg, changed its name to honor townsite owner C. C. Atwood in 1909.

Avant (Osage Co., pop. 439, on OK 11, 10 mi. SE of **Barnsdall,** see Map 4). A

Arrowhead Lodge, on Eufaula Reservoir at Arrowhead State Park.

small community, started in 1906 and named for a well-known local Osage, Ben Avant.

Avard (Woods Co., pop. 59, 10 mi. SW of **Alva,** see Map 3). A small community on the main east-west line of the Santa Fe in a generally prosperous farming/ranching area. It was established in 1895, two years after the Cherokee Outlet was opened to settlement, and named for the wife of the first postmaster, Isabell Avard Todd.

In 1973 the Frisco Railroad completed a $4 million up-grading of a former secondary line from **Tulsa** to this point. The result is a new trans-continental freight route between Virginia (via the Seaboard Coast line) and California (via the Santa Fe).

Avery (Lincoln Co., pop. 25, on county road 7 mi. S of **Cushing,** see Map 4). A railroad-siding community, platted in 1902 as Mound City. However, its post office, until closed in 1957, was Avery, for Santa Fe official Avery Turner. That post office, incidentally—window, lock boxes, official sign and all—may be seen today in the Lincoln County Historical Society Museum at **Chandler.**

Babbs Switch (Kiowa Co., on US 183, 6 mi. S of **Hobart**, see Map 8). Only a granite historical marker beside the road notes the site of this one-room frame school that burned to the ground December 24, 1924, taking the lives of thirty-six men, women, and children. A modern brick schoolhouse replaced the destroyed one and served the area until 1943. Now it, too, is gone.

The fire started from a candle on the decorated cedar tree at the height of the Christmas Eve party. Most of the deaths resulted from the fact that the doors, which opened into the schoolroom were quickly blocked in the panicky stampede to escape. Ironically, the tragedy led to design changes and new laws that made schools safer all across the nation.

Bald Hill (Okmulgee Co., near junc. OK 16 & OK 52, 17 mi. NE of **Okmulgee**, see Map 5). Now but a name on the more generous road maps, this tiny rural community is perhaps best known for the expensive home of Enos Wilson, who died in 1937. With Jackson Barnett, Wilson was among the world's richest Indians—because of oil and gas income from the 160-acre allotment given him in 1899, when the Creek Nation lands were being assigned prior to statehood.

Balko (Beaver Co., pop. 100, at junc. US 83 and OK 3, see Map 2). A scattered community—so scattered, indeed, that its consolidated school sits beside Ok 3 more than 2 miles east of its post office, churches, and handful of stores. It serves an area of fertile farmlands and, in recent years, highly productive oil and gas wells.

Banner (Canadian Co., just N of US 66, 5 m. W of **Yukon**, see Map 4). An elevator, a church, and a scattering of houses marks this railroad-siding community that began as Cereal around the turn of the century, became Banner in 1911.

Barnsdall (Osage Co., pop. 1,579, on OK 15, see Map 4). The typical Osage

The Nellie Johnstone No. 1, Oklahoma's first commercial oil well, near Bartlesville.

country town, in name and appearance. Started soon after the turn of the century as Bigheart, for the Osage chief James Bigheart, it changed its name to honor the Barnsdall Oil Company in 1921, when the Osage boom was at its height. And oil is still the town's economic mainstay, as pointedly demonstrated by the neatly pipe-fenced pumping jack beside the highway in the center of town. The sign above it: "America's Only Main Street Oil Well." Completed in 1914, it is still producing.

The Bareco Wax Division of the Petrolite Corporation in Barnsdall is the world's largest producer of petroleum wax and accounts for 22 per cent of the world's production.

Baron (Adair Co., pop. 100, on US 59, 5 mi. S of **Westville**, see Map 5). A small community on the Barren Fork of the *Illinois River* (from which it apparently got its name). A large charcoal kiln is the economic mainstay of the area. US 59 in this area, through the heavily wooded Cherokee Hills, is one of the state's most scenic highways.

Bartlesville (Washington Co. seat, pop. 29,683, at junc. of US 60 and US 75, see Map 5). Of Oklahoma's 77 counties, Washington is simultaneously next to the smallest (Marshall) and next to (i.e., adjacent to) the largest (Osage). It is also the wealthiest, having passed *Tulsa County* in the latest census to boast the highest per capita income. As its seat and principal contributor to its economic well being, Bartlesville comes close to being the model of what a prosperous and progressive small city should be.

The settlement began as a crude gristmill established on Caney River in 1868 by Nelson Carr. He was bought out in 1875 by Jacob Bartles, who built a trading post on the site and gave the embryo town his name (and, some years later, founded nearby *Dewey*). Bartles promptly hauled a dynamo in to produce Oklahoma's first electricity. A pattern for progressiveness and prosperity had been set.

In 1897 a new element was added to the area's economy, heretofore dependent primarily on farming and stock raising. On April 15 the Nellie Johnstone No. 1 came in, at 1,320 feet, to give Oklahoma its first "commercial" oil well. (Now restored, the no longer producing well is a feature of Johnstone Park, beside Caney River on the city's north side.) Oil-related commerce and industry have shaped the city ever since.

An extensive shallow oil field soon developed eastward to the *Verdigris River*. In 1901, H. V. Foster established the famed Indian Territory Illuminating Oil Co., now Cities Service. And in 1917 Frank and L. E. Phillips founded Phillips Petroleum Co. The Frank Phillips home (1107 Cherokee Avenue) is now owned by the Oklahoma Historical Society and is open to the public (Tues.–Fri. 9–5, Sat.–Sun. 2–5).

Both oil companies played a strong role in developing the area, and Phillips influence is apparent everywhere in the city today. Its vast research laboratory—with an assist from the U.S. Bureau of Mines Petroleum Research Center—helps substantiate Bartlesville's claim to having the largest percentage of college graduates of any city in Oklahoma. Most striking landmark in Bartlesville is the nineteen-story Price Tower, designed by Frank Lloyd Wright.

Bartlesville offers a well-balanced blend of entertainment, cultural, and recreational features. Bartlesville Wesleyan College has over 400 students. There's a Little Theater, Art Center, and symphony orchestra, a well developed park system, and the magnificent *Woolaroc Museum*, 14 miles to the southwest. Also of interest to the Bartlesville visitor: *Osage Hills State Park*, 12 miles west.

Battiest (McCurtain Co., pop. 50, 6 mi. NW of *Bethel*, see Map 6). A virtually non-existent community on the picturesque *Glover River*—with one of the state's more unusual names. It is not, however, a superlative, but rather the name of a respected Choctaw jurist, Byington Battiest—which the settlement adopted in 1928, after spending its first two decades as Ida, for an early resident, Ida Griffin.

Battle of the Washita (site just N of OK 47 on W edge of *Cheyenne*, see Map 3). In the bitter winter of 1868 then Colonel George A. Custer led his cavalry some 70 miles from *Camp Supply* to the *Washita River* here and, just at dawn, attacked Chief Black Kettle's encampment of Cheyennes from three sides. Scattering the completely surprised and unprepared Indians, Custer's troopers killed or wounded some 200 men, women, and children. His own losses were negligible. The battle has long been controversial, largely because of the number of women and children killed (although precise figures have never been agreed upon). Indians, and some whites, have always referred to it as the Black Kettle Massacre.

The battle has interested historians

THE BATTLE OF THE WASHITA
1868

BLACK KETTLE   GEORGE A. CUSTER

THE BATTLE OF THE WASHITA, A MAJOR ENGAGEMENT IN THE PLAINS INDIAN WAR WHICH ESTABLISHED THE WESTERN EXPANSION OF THE UNITED STATES WAS FOUGHT ON THIS SITE. COL. GEORGE A. CUSTER'S COMMAND OF 500 TROOPERS FROM THE 7TH CAVALRY, AND A DETACHMENT OF SCOUTS INCLUDING THE FAMED BEN CLARK AND THE OSAGE, HARDROPE, DESTROYED CHIEF BLACK KETTLE'S CHEYENNE VILLAGE HERE ON NOV. 27, 1868.

BLACK KETTLE, PEACE LEADER OF THE SOUTHERN CHEYENNES, HAD SOUGHT MILITARY ASSURANCE THAT HE WOULD NOT BE ATTACKED HERE. THERE WERE IN HIS CAMP, HOWEVER, YOUNG MEN WHO HAD TAKEN PART IN WAR PARTIES RAIDING IN KANSAS.

CUSTER'S COMMAND LEFT CAMP SUPPLY ON NOVEMBER 23. HIS SCOUTS LOCATED THE CHEYENNE VILLAGE ON THE NIGHT OF NOVEMBER 26. AFTER A FORCED MARCH THROUGH A BITTERLY COLD BLIZZARD AND DEEP SNOW, CUSTER DEPLOYED HIS COMMAND TO SURROUND THE VILLAGE, AND AT DAWN, WITH THE REGIMENTAL BAND PLAYING "GARY OWEN," SWEPT IN TO ATTACK THE SLEEPING CHEYENNES.

THE NUMBER OF INDIANS KILLED IN THE FIGHTING IS A POINT OF CONTROVERSY. CUSTER CLAIMED 103 WARRIORS. IN THE REPORT TO THE SECRETARY OF THE INTERIOR (1869-70) CHEYENNES SET THE TOTAL AT 13 MEN, 16 WOMEN, AND 9 CHILDREN, INCLUDING BLACK KETTLE AND HIS WIFE.

CAPTAIN LOUIS HAMILTON, GRANDSON OF ALEXANDER HAMILTON, WAS ONE OF TWO OFFICERS KILLED. MAJOR JOEL ELLIOTT AND A SQUAD OF TROOPERS IN PURSUIT OF FLEEING CHEYENNES WERE TRAPPED ON SERGEANT MAJOR CREEK BEYOND A MILE FROM THE VILLAGE AND KILLED TO THE LAST MAN.

THE CHEYENNE LODGES AND WINTER SUPPLIES OF FOOD AND BUFFALO ROBES WERE BURNED, WHILE 875 OF THEIR HORSES WERE SLAUGHTERED. AT NIGHTFALL, THE CAVALRY RETURNED TOWARD CAMP SUPPLY, WITH 53 WOMEN AND CHILDREN CAPTIVES.

Marker on the Washita battlefield northwest of Cheyenne (photograph courtesy Oklahoma Department of Wildlife Conservation).

over the years for yet another reason. The flamboyant Custer's attack plan here was strikingly similar to that he was to use eight years later on the Little Big Horn. In both battles he ignored the warnings of his scouts and took unnecessary risks to attack vastly superior hostile forces. On the Washita he was successful; only Major Elliott and his unit got caught. In Montana it was Custer himself who paid the price—with 264 of his men. It is for this reason that the Battle of the Washita has been called a "Dress Rehearsal for Disaster."

The site is a National Historic Landmark. Several informational signs recreate the battle for the visitor, who should also visit the Black Kettle Museum in *Cheyenne*.

Bearden (Okfuskee Co., pop. 150, on OK 48, 11 mi. SW of *Okemah*, see Map 4). One of the oldest communities in the county, established in 1896 and named for a local resident, J. S. Bearden.

Beaver City (Beaver Co. seat, pop. 1,853, on US 270 & OK 23, see Map 2). A lively, progressive community whose interest in and respect for its heritage in no way diminishes its enthusiasm for one of the state's most colorful "heritage" events—the annual mid-April Cimarron Territory Celebration, featuring the world championship Cow Chip Throwing competition. The latter—using the real McCoy, though well dried for aerodynamic as well as esthetic purposes—is contested in two classes: Politicians and All Others. Record fling to date: 152 feet.

The unlikely event is deeply rooted in the town's colorful history. "Chips," of course, is a euphemism for dung. And the cow is, perforce, a surrogate for the buffalo, whose "chips"—and bones—did indeed serve the Panhandle pioneer well (see *Oklahoma Panhandle*). As for Beaver City—officially just Beaver, according to the post office, established in 1883 and named for nearby *Beaver River*—it is the one-time capital of the "Territory of Cimarron." An elaborate stone plaque on a downtown pharmacy marks the site of the two-story Capitol and tells the story of the abortive attempt at self-government for the true No Man's Land.

Also telling part of the pre-statehood story of Beaver City are two National Register sites. The modest frame Presbyterian Church, built in 1887 and still in regular use, is one of the oldest in Oklahoma. A two-room sod house, though now incorporated into a six-room stucco affair, is even older. It was built by Jim Lane in 1880 as a home and store on the Jones and Plummer Trail between Tascosa, Texas, and Dodge City, Kansas. Now a private home, it is open to visitors (Mon.–Sat. 11–5, Sun. 2–5) as the Beaver City Museum.

Frustration of its attempt to become capital of the entire Panhandle in no way diminished Beaver's self-reliant ambition. In 1910, when the present M-K-T Railroad built into the Panhandle and established its own town at *Forgan*, thereby cutting off the county seat, Beaver City citizens built their own Beaver, Meade and Englewood Railroad. And, after trying in vain to give it to the M-K-T, they operated it long enough—and profitably enough—to sell the line eventually to its rival for $2 million! Both lines were finally abandoned in 1973.

Beaver County (easternmost of the three Panhandle counties, see Map 2). Area, 1,793 sq. mi.; pop., 6,282; county seat, *Beaver City*. Both county and town are named for *Beaver River*, which farther downstream becomes the *North Canadian*. Beaver was part of a notorious No Man's Land before statehood, and for a time the residents, fearful of the lawlessness, attempted to organize an independent "Territory of Cimarron."

Boating at Beavers Bend State Park (photograph courtesy OKC Tourism Center).

In 1900 the Territorial legislature organized the county, including all the Panhandle. The division into three counties was made in 1907.

Top travel lures: museum, historic buildings in *Beaver City*.

Beaver River, see *North Canadian River*.

Beavers Bend State Park (3 mi. E of US 259 from a point 7 mi. N of *Broken Bow*, see Map 6). Tall pine and hardwood forests, impressive mountains, a swift-flowing stream, and an abundance of wildlife and colorful wildflowers make this 5,135-acre preserve a favorite of nature lovers. Completion of 14,240-acre **Broken Bow Reservoir** has given the area all the traditional big-lake advantages. But a small dam on scenic *Mountain Fork River*, below the big dam, creates a pleasant little

Fishing in Mountain Fork River at Beavers Bend State Park.

lake within easy walking distance of park accommodations.

Facilities: 35 cottages, cafe and store, picnic, camp, and trailer areas, 2 youth camps, swimming beach and bathhouse, boat ramps and rentals, hiking trails. Address: Box 10, Broken Bow, OK 74728.

Beckham County (west-central Oklahoma along the Texas border, see Map 8). Area, 898 sq. mi.; pop., 15,754; county seat, *Sayre*. Organized in 1907, with statehood, it was named for Governor J. C. W. Beckham of Kentucky.

Top travel lures: Bee City near *Erick*, salt making operations, City Museum and Old Town at *Elk City*.

Beggs (Okmulgee Co., pop. 1,107, at junc. US 75 Alt. and OK 16, see Map 5). Established in 1900 with the building of the Frisco Railroad, and named for C. H. Beggs, an official of the line, Beggs boomed from 1910 to 1915 as the rich Glenn Pool oil field spread south and west from *Kiefer*. Three miles NW of Beggs (inquire locally) is the curious "Giants' Highway" near Checkerboard Creek, a section of symmetrically laid limestone blocks, roughly two

feet in thickness. They are so even that early settlers, using them as part of the "Checkerboard Crossing" of the muddy creek, thought them man-laid. The interesting highway-like formation is considered by geologists to be a freak of nature.

Beland (Muskogee Co., pop. 40, S of US 62 & 64, 8 mi. SW of *Muskogee*, see Map 5). A tiny one-time railroad-siding town that began in 1903 as Chase, took its present name five years later.

Belva (Woodward Co. about 12 mi. SW of *Waynoka*, see Map 3). An isolated community in rolling, picturesque ranch country south of the *Cimarron River*. Started in 1900 as a stop on the Santa Fe Railroad, it was named for the daughter of a section foreman.

Bengal (Latimer Co., pop. 80, on unnumbered county road 10 mi. S of *Red Oak*, see Map 6). Isolated community on the north slope of the *Winding Stair Mountains*, established in 1890 and presumably named for the Indian state. A recently completed U.S. Forest Service road vaults the Winding Stairs, creates a new scenic byway route to *Talihina*.

Bennington (Bryan Co., pop. 288, S of junc. of US 70 and OK 70-E, see Map 6). An old Choctaw settlement that grew up around a church organized in 1848. Though considerably altered, the church is still standing, with its interesting burying ground. When the town won a post office in 1873, a descendant of General John Stark gave it a name recalling the Revolutionary War battle of Bennington. Today it is a dwindling farm community, bypassed by US 70 on the north.

Berlin (Roger Mills Co., pop. 50, just E of US 283, 10 mi. N of *Sayre*, see Map 3). A small agricultural community, formerly called Doxey, that changed its name in 1896 for that of the then German capital.

Bernice (Delaware Co., pop. 189, on OK 85-A, 14 mi. E of *Vinita*, see Map 5).

Established as Needmore in 1894, Bernice took its present name in 1913. Today it lives largely off recreation seekers in the Horse Creek area of *Grand Lake*. Nearby Mockingbird Hill cemetery contains the graves of family members of famed Cherokee Indian General Stand Watie (see *Jay*).

Bernice Recreation Area. See *Grand Lake of the Cherokees.*

Bessie (Washita Co., pop. 210, off US 183, 8 mi. S of *Clinton*, see Map 8). The only town in Oklahoma named for a railroad. Known as Boggy from 1895 to 1899, and then as Stout, the settlement adopted its present name in 1903 upon arrival of "The Bess Line," popular monicker of the Blackwell, Enid and Southwestern Railroad (BES, now a Frisco branch). Like *Corn*, the Bessie area attracted many German/Russian farmers, and a large Lutheran church and towering grain elevators dominate the tiny community.

Bethany (Oklahoma Co., pop. 21,785, on US 66 & 270 at NW edge of *Oklahoma City*, see Map 4). As its name implies, Bethany is a stoutly religious community, although tremendous suburban growth since World War II has considerably diluted the influence of the Nazarene Church. Bethany Nazarene College, the sect's fully accredited four-year liberal arts institution, still dominates the compact business district, however. And the school is itself dominated by the 3,000-seat First Church of the Nazarene, a strikingly modern structure featuring 60-foot-high stained glass windows. It is the conservative denomination's largest church building.

The town began in 1908 when Oklahoma Holiness College moved here from *Oklahoma City*, where it had been established two years before. Local "blue laws" long forbade theaters and poolhalls, the sale of beer and cigarettes. (It is still bone-dry.) Best symbolizing Bethany's gradual transition to a prosperous suburban community are Wiley Post Airport, a World War II facility on its north side, and a sprawling Aero Commander (jet airplane) plant.

Bethel (McCurtain Co., pop. 200, on OK 144, 2 mi. E of US 259, see Map 6). A trading point for scattered farm families and timber cutters, this long-isolated little community was established in 1900. Its setting, on a wooded branch of the beautiful *Glover River*, obviously moved the founding fathers to choose the Hebrew word for "House of God" as its name. Today it is a popular rendezvous for fishermen, floaters, and, in the fall, deer hunters.

Big Cabin (Craig Co., pop. 198, on US 69, 9 mi. S of *Vinita*, see Map 5). A tiny settlement astride the M-K-T Railroad, best known today for two Civil War battles fought in the vicinity of Big Cabin Creek to the south. The one-time bustling business district is across the tracks on the east, marked by several picturesque abandoned brick buildings. One, a bank, is broken open to reveal an old vault gaping skyward from its roofless shell.

The Texas Road passed through here before the railroad arrived. Planche Cabin—because it had been built of planking, rather than the more common logs—stood beside the road, gave its name to the creek and, later, the town. Confederate General Stand Watie, a Cherokee, made an unsuccessful attack on a southbound Union supply train in July 1-2, 1863, where the Texas Road crossed the creek. The following year, on September 19, he tried the same maneuver with more success. Some 295 wagons were captured, along with goods valued at $1.5 million. A historical marker beside US 69 notes the events.

Big Canyon (Murray Co., 4 mi. S of *Dougherty*, see Map 7). Little more than a name on generous maps, this scattered community began in 1904 as Crusher, for the nearby rock crusher (see *Dougherty*) that sustains it down to the present. In 1911 it became Arbuckle, and acquired its present name in 1922, for the nearby canyon of the *Washita River*.

Big Cedar (LeFlore Co., at junc. of US 259 and OK 63, see Map 6). Though the

Bitting Springs Mill was the state's last water-powered gristmill to produce stone-ground meal, before it burned in 1983.

community it once represented has pretty well disappeared, Big Cedar is familiar today as the crossroads site of a monument to President John F. Kennedy. Here on October 29, 1961, two years before his assassination, he spoke at a highway dedication, as a guest of the late Senator Robert S. Kerr, whose palatial mountain home is nearby (see *Poteau*).

Bigheart (Osage Co., just off OK 99, 12 mi. N of *Pawhuska*, see Map 4). One-time Indian trading town named for the Osage chief, James Bigheart. This region of upland limestone is one of the finest native grass pasturelands in the state.

Billings (Noble Co., pop. 618, on OK 15, 6 mi. W of I 35, see Map 4). A small agricultural community established in 1899 with the arrival of a Rock Island branch line and given the family name of the wife of the line's townsite agent. Today it is best known as the home town of former governor and present U.S. Senator Henry Bellmon, whose wife operates a small dress manufacturing plant on the main street. Though wheat and cattle are the area's economic mainstays, a powdered metals manufacturing plant on the north edge of Billings employs forty persons.

Binger (Caddo Co., pop. 730, at junc. of US 281 & OK 8 and OK 152, see Map 8). A bustling agricultural community settled in 1901, when the Kiowa-Apache-Comanche lands were opened. Binger Hermann was then commissioner of the General Land Office, which supervised the giant land lottery. Arrival of a Rock Island branch line the following year established the town. Cotton, peanuts, and cattle raising undergird the economy. Binger is best known in recent years as the home town of Cincinnati baseball star Johnny Bench. Logically enough, it has a strong Little League baseball program. The town is in the center of a highly scenic, canyon-laced area of red slick rock and heavy native woods. To the southwest is *Fort Cobb Reservoir*. Salyer Lake (off OK 152, 12 mi. E) is a privately developed family recreation area in a picturesque red-walled canyon.

Many Indians still live in this area, and Indian influence is strong. An historic Caddo Indian cemetery can be found 6 miles southeast of Binger. The town itself hosts Caddo Indian dances from time to time in the summer.

Bison (Garfield Co., pop. 70, off US 81, 15 mi. S of *Enid*, see Map 4). A small agricultural community in the heart of the state's richest wheat growing region. The town was established in 1901, taking its name, after a fashion, from nearby Buffalo Springs, a well-known stopping place on the *Chisholm Trail*. Actually, the town namers were more accurate than those who named the watering place, for the famed "walking commissary" of the American Indian is indeed a bison rather than a buffalo.

48

Surrounding countryside as seen from Black Mesa.

Bitting Springs Mill (off OK 51—watch for local signs—9 miles NW of **Stilwell**, see Map 5). The state's only surviving water-powered mill. Established before the Civil War, it still produces cornmeal, ground with the original French burrs turned by a wooden water wheel. Visitors are welcomed.

Bixby (Tulsa Co., pop. 3,973, at junc. of US 64 and OK 67, see Map 5). Like **Jenks**, Bixby is a pleasant suburban community on the south bank of the **Arkansas River**. It was established in 1899 and named for Tams Bixby, chairman of the Dawes Commission, which supervised the merging of the five separate Indian nations (Cherokee, Choctaw, Chickasaw, Creek, and Seminole) into Indian Territory.

Although surrounded by rich river bottomlands (small truck farms, extensive pecan groves), and calling itself the Garden Spot of Oklahoma, the town looks largely to **Tulsa** for jobs for its citizens. Nearby Lake Bixhoma provides fishing, general recreation. Best known annual event is the early June Green Corn Dance, a significant testimonial to its rich Creek Nation heritage.

Black Kettle National Grasslands (in central **Roger Mills County**, see Map 3). A public hunting area operated cooperatively by the U.S. Forest Service (Hot Springs, Arkansas) and the Oklahoma Department of Wildlife Conservation. It offers the visitor 30,826 acres of land and 400 water acres for hunting, fishing, boating, skiing, picnicking, and camping (limited facilities). Principal lakes are **Dead Indian** and **Skipout**. In all, the county offers anglers about 3,000 lakes of various shapes and sizes. The area is also well known to hunters for its quail, prairie chicken, turkey, and water fowl.

Black Mesa (in extreme NW Cimarron Co., see Map 2). A striking landmark that towers above the isolated com-

Rock formations and petrified wood in Black Mesa State Park.

munity of **Kenton** and is Oklahoma's highest point. Atop the plateau (access difficult for passenger automobile) an 11-foot-tall, four-sided obelisk of rose-colored granite from a quarry at **Granite** gives the altitude as 4,972.97 feet above sea level. The flat mesa was formed by the eruption of a prehistoric volcano in what is now New Mexico. From it a layer of black lava, up to 70 feet in thickness, flowed eastward into this area. Subsequent stream erosion has cut away the softer surrounding formations to leave the black-capped plateau standing some 600 feet above a ruggedly beautiful ranching country.

Black Mesa State Park (30 mi. NW of **Boise City** on un-numbered, mostly paved roads, see Map 2). A change-of-pace park with 200-acre Carl Etling Lake taking second billing to a rugged volcanic setting. The park's lava formations feature dinosaur pits and Indian pictographs, caves, and peculiarly shaped rock formations. The 269-acre preserve has yielded dinosaur bones, fossils, and petrified wood. This valley

of S. Carrizzo Creek, a **Cimarron River** tributary, is believed to have been occupied by man as far back as 10,000 B.C. Immediately south of the park are eroded ruts of the old Santa Fe Trail. Eight miles north of the park is **Black Mesa** itself, the lava-tipped headland that, at 4,973 feet above sea level, is Oklahoma's highest point.

Facilities: camp and picnic areas, playground, boat ramps. Address: Boise City, OK 73933.

Blackburn (Pawnee Co., pop. 88, off US 64, 15 mi. NW of **Cleveland**, see Map 4). A dwindling rural community that began with opening of the Cherokee Outlet in 1893 and is perhaps best known today for the natural calamity that struck it eight years later. Until recently, as many as 200 hardy pioneers and their descendents met in June each year to maintain the life and spirit of the Drought Survivors of 1901, organized by those who had refused to abandon their hard-won homesteads.

Blackwell (Kay Co., pop. 8,645, at junc. of US 177 & OK 11, see Map 4). Beginning life with the opening of the Cherokee Outlet in the Run of September 16, 1893, Blackwell (for townsite developer Andrew J. Blackwell) based its prosperity from the first on the fertility of the rich Chickaskia River farmlands that surround it. Kay has long been considered one of the state's richest agricultural counties. And as its second largest city, Blackwell has always reflected this wealth with elevators, flour mills, meat packinghouses, feed and fertilizer plants, implement dealerships, and other land-oriented businesses.

Oil, of course, and industry have added balance to the area's economy over the years. But the city's largest payroll and its most obvious landmark—the tall-stacked Blackwell Zinc Company smelter, employing up to 1,000 persons—closed down in 1973. As nearby oil fields gradually become depleted the town's primary dependence will thus again turn to the surrounding farm and ranchlands.

The Kay County Fairgrounds just

south of the main business district are among the state's most impressive. Memorial Park contains a large swimming pool that hosts the annual Olympic tryouts. The Blackwell Public Library has notable collections of paintings by Oklahoma Indian artists and autographed books by Oklahoma writers. Lake Blackwell, 12 mi. NW of the city, is a 300-acre municipal empoundment that offers fishing, camping facilities, and general recreation. User fees are collected.

Blaine County (northwestern Oklahoma, see Map 3). Area, 911 sq. mi.; pop., 11,794; county seat, *Watonga*. Organized in 1892, when the 3 million-acre Cheyenne and Arapaho Indian Reservation was opened to white settlement, it was named for James G. Blaine of Maine, speaker of the United States House of Representatives and Republican candidate for president in 1884.

Top travel lures: *Roman Nose State Park*, *American Horse Lake*, *Left Hand Spring*, *Canton Reservoir*, hunting and fishing.

Blair (Jackson Co., pop. 1,114, at junc. of US 283 and OK 19, see Map 8). A farming community that began in 1893 as Dot for the daughter of B. B. Zinn, who operated a store a short distance to the southeast. When the Kansas City, Mexico and Orient Railway (the storied "Orient," now the Santa Fe) arrived in 1901, the town changed location and name, thereby honoring John A. Blair, one of the line's officials.

Blair has had its ups and downs, including a devastating tornado in 1928 and the bitter Dust Bowl days of the 1930's. It survives today largely on the strength of irrigation from nearby *Altus Reservoir*.

Blanchard (McClain Co., pop. 1,580, at junc. of US 62 & 277 and OK 9 & 76, see Map 7). A fast-growing "bedroom" community some 30 miles southwest of *Oklahoma City*. Laid out in 1906 by developer W. G. Blanchard, the town stirred in the 1950's on the strength of

a modest oil discovery in the area. Proximity to *Norman* and the Will Rogers World Airport/Federal Aviation Administration complex has stimulated recent growth.

Blanco (Pittsburg Co., pop. 150, on OK 63, 10 mi. NE of *Kiowa*, see Map 6). Scattered community established in 1901 on a branch of the now abandoned Rock Island Railroad. The name honors Ramon Blanco & Erenas, governor general of Cuba at the outbreak of the Spanish-American War.

Blocker (Pittsburg Co., pop. 100, on OK 31, 15 mi. NE of *McAlester*, see Map 6). A now nearly vanished coal mining community, settled around the turn of the century and named for a local coal dealer, Eads Blocker.

Blue (Bryan Co., pop. 150, on US 70, 9 mi. E of *Durant*, see Map 6). A scattered community on the Frisco Railroad. Started in 1874, it takes its name from nearby *Blue River*.

Blue River. A 150-mile-long tributary of *Red River* that angles southeasterly through *Pontotoc*, *Johnston* and *Bryant* counties in south-central Oklahoma. This is a generally wooded, pleasantly scenic area, a favorite of both the fisherman (for trout especially) and the history buff. *Tishomingo* was the capital of the Chickasaw Nation. Butterfield stages crossed the Blue near present *Kenefick*.

Blue River Public Fishing and Hunting Area (Johnston Co., 9 mi. NE of *Tishomingo*, see Map 7). A 923-acre facility opened by the Oklahoma Department of Wildlife Conservation (1801 N. Lincoln, Oklahoma City, OK 73105) in 1967 on one of the state's best-known fishing streams. Although best known for channel cat, brim, and bass, it is also one of the few areas in Oklahoma where trout can be taken.

Originally this new recreation tract was part of the allotment of a Chickasaw woman married to a white man. The adventurous visitor can still find traces of the mile-long flume he cut to divert water from the spring-fed river to power the water wheel that, in turn, ran a mill, cotton gin, and sawmill. Remains of the wheel are near the main parking area. Camping facilities are available in the park.

Bluejacket (Craig Co., pop. 234, on OK 25, see Map 5). Small community on the M-K-T Railroad in a rolling area of small farms and ranches. Started in 1882, its name honors the Rev. Charles Bluejacket, the town's first postmaster.

Boatman (Mayes Co., pop. 50, just S of OK 20, 8 mi. SE of *Pryor*, see Map 5). A small rural community that took its name in 1922 from Joe P. Boatman, a local merchant.

Boggy Creek. A meandering, 243-mile-long stream that, with its Clear, Muddy, North, and other branches, drains a sizeable chunk of south-central Oklahoma. Much of the history of the old Choctaw Nation was written on or near the Boggy (see *Boggy Depot, Atoka*).

The word came from early French traders who called these streams *Vazzures* (*vaseuse* means miry or boggy). It was used as early as 1805 by Dr. John Sibley, who reported arriving ". . . at the mouth of the *Vazzures*, or Boggy River. . . ."

Boggy Depot (Atoka Co., pop. 50, on country road 14 mi. SW of *Atoka*, see Map 6). One of the state's oldest towns, although the site of the present dwindling community is a mile and a half south of the original settlement. "Old" Boggy Depot began as an Indian log cabin in 1837, became a flourishing trade center and Civil War army post. The name recognizes the various branches of Boggy Creek that drain virtually all of the county. The French traders gave them the name "Vazzures" ("vaseuse," for miry or boggy) and Dr. John Sibley in 1805 referred to them as "the Vazzures, or Boggy River. . . ."

The "Depot" was added in 1837 when annuities from the government to the emigrating Chickasaws were paid at the "depot on the Boggy." When a postal route was established in 1849, Boggy Depot became an official post office.

Located at the junction of the Texas Road and one of the trails west from Fort Smith to California, it soon grew into an important town. In 1858 it served briefly as capital of the Choctaw Nation. During the Civil War, Confederate forces occupied it, and there is a row of Confederate graves in the old cemetery. When the M-K-T Railroad built through this area in 1872, however, it missed Boggy Depot, which declined sharply thereafter.

The town's best-known citizen was Chief Allen Wright. And his impressive two-story home, built in 1860, was its last important landmark. It was destroyed by fire in 1952, and today only traces of the town's streets are still visible. These and the location of once-important structures have been marked by the state, which preserves the site as Boggy Depot Recreation Area. Of interest to the visitor is the cemetery with its many old monuments, including that of Chief Wright (1826–95). He served two terms as the Nation's principal chief, translated several books into the Choctaw language. In 1866 he suggested the name "Oklahoma" for the proposed Indian territory.

"New" Boggy Depot, the present settlement of that name, took the post office from the older town in 1872. The "New" was dropped in 1883, and the office itself was lost in 1944.

Boiling Springs State Park (8 mi. NE of *Woodward* via OK 34 and OK 34-C, see Map 3). A true oasis on the plains, with hundreds of shade trees and numerous cold springs that "boil up" through white sands here along the *North Canadian River*. Wild turkeys are common in the 820-acre park, which contains a 7-acre lake.

Facilities: 4 rental cabins, camp and picnic areas, playgrounds, swimming pool and bathhouse, hiking and motorcycle trails, stable. Address: Woodward, OK 73801.

Boise City (Cimarron Co. seat, pop. 1,993, at junc. of US 56, 64, 287 & 385 and OK 3, see Map 2). Despite the fact it was designated county seat in 1908— at which time it changed its name from

Cimarron—Boise City was only a village of some 350 in 1925 when the Santa Fe Railroad built, southwestward across the county, what was to have been a mainline "cutoff" to California. The project finally floundered in New Mexico, and tracks were pulled back to Boise City in 1942, but the town has maintained its growth. The Santa Fe built lines north and south of Boise in the 1930's, and railroad buffs still bemoan the dismantling of the old stone roundhouse on the south edge of town.

Boise City (for Idaho's capital, although the "Boise" is pronounced as in "voice") is something of a geographic anomaly. At the far western end of the **Oklahoma Panhandle**, it is only 35 miles from Kansas, 18 miles from Colorado, 27 miles from New Mexico, and 15 miles from Texas. It is closer to the capitals of the first three of these (Topeka, Denver, Santa Fe) than it is to Oklahoma City. Its school district of 450 square miles is Oklahoma's largest, and its football teams regularly play a five-state schedule.

Nearly everything else about Boise is an Oklahoma superlative. It and **Keyes** are the only two incorporated towns in **Cimarron County**, itself the only one in the nation that touches five states. It boasts the state's coolest average daily temperature (55.3 degrees), lowest average minimum (40.3 degrees) and most meager annual rainfall total (an average of only 16.51 inches). Most prominent single feature of the town is the imposing, two-story red brick courthouse, built in 1928. Highways entering the city from all four directions deadend at the courthouse square, around which huddle most of its business establishments.

County special events include the now-traditional Easter Pageant near **Kenton**, a Little Hombre Rodeo (July) and the Cimarron County Fair (mid-September).

Bokchito (Bryan Co., pop. 607, at junc. of US 70 and OK 22, see Map 6). This has been an important Choctaw area from the earliest years of the Choctaw Nation. Two miles northeast of the present farming center, Armstrong Academy was established 1844. With a two-decade interruption caused by the Civil War, the institution served the Indian people, young and old alike (in its early years it carried on an active adult education program), until 1921, when it was destroyed by fire. From 1863 to 1883 the academy site was renamed Chata Tamaha (meaning Choctaw Town), and it served as capital of the Nation (see **Tuskahoma**). Only an overgrown cemetery and crumbling piles of brick and stone mark the grounds today, on private property and virtually inaccessible.

The town itself grew up in the early 1890's. Bokchito is the Choctaw word for "big creek." Bokchito Creek runs a mile east of town.

Bokoshe (LeFlore Co., pop. 588, on OK 31, 7 mi. W of US 59 & 271, see Map 6). A coal-mining town that has grown in recent years with the revival of that fuel industry (see **McCurtain**). Established in 1886, it took its name from the Choctaw word for "little creek." The underground coal from this area is of high quality and much of it is shipped by rail to steel mills in Houston and Daingerfield, Texas.

Boley (Okfuskee Co., pop. 514, on US 62, 12 mi. W of **Okemah**, see Map 4). A symbol, albeit a somewhat fading one, of a noble experiment. At the time of the division of Indian lands much of this area was allotted to Negro freedmen listed on the rolls of the Creek tribe. And in 1903, when the Fort Smith & Western Railroad was being built westward toward **Guthrie**, officials promoted the idea of all-Negro communities that would give the black man a chance to prove he was capable of self-government. **Clearview**, **Rusk**, and **Chilesville** were three such communities. Boley, the fourth, was the most successful.

This location was then the heart of a rich cotton producing area. (The county once had 27 gins.) Availability of cheap land attracted many residents, as did the idea of a town free of white-man discrimination. Every train brought new settlers, and by 1905 the town had a population of 2,000. But a gradual decline set in shortly after statehood. Many factors contributed: electoral pressure from white neighbors, the decline of cotton and the growing importance of economic interdependence. Mainstay today is the State Training School for Boys (originally established solely for Negro youths) at the southeast corner of town. Biggest annual event is the Boley Rodeo, a traditional homecoming celebration held late in May.

Boley was named for W. H. Boley, the FS&W roadmaster who was largely responsible for implementing the road's all-Negro-town idea. The line itself was abandoned in 1939. The railroad's nickname, interestingly enough, was the Foot Sore & Weary.

Following the lead of *Taft*, another of Oklahoma's black towns, Boley was recently "adopted" by comedian Flip Wilson, who was named honorary police chief.

Boswell (Choctaw Co., pop. 755, on US 70, see Map 6). S. C. Boswell, a merchant, gave his name to this settlement when the Arkansas and Choctaw Railroad (now the Frisco) built through this area in 1902. But the community is older than the rail line by half a century.

Mayhew Post Office, one of the state's oldest, appeared in 1845 and existed until 1902, when it was moved two miles south to become Boswell. Two adjacent sites were occupied by the town (named for the Mayhew Presbyterian Mission in Mississippi), but today neither has more than a handful of houses. Gone is the one-room Mayhew Courthouse, where the Choctaws held tribal court. Mayhew Cemetery, however, is interesting for its graves dating from the 1850's.

Present-day Boswell remains strongly Indian in character. Beside US 70 just west of town is a modest country church. In the nearby cemetery are three Choctaw burials protected by traditional grave houses. Annual events include an Old Settlers Day get-together and an FFA Rodeo.

Bowlegs (Seminole Co., pop. 300, on OK 3 & 99, 5 mi. S of *Seminole*, see Map 7). A by-product of the *Seminole* oil boom, Bowlegs came into being in 1927, on the allotment of a Seminole Indian of that name. The name itself is the white man's corruption of the tribal family name "Bolek." Chief Billy Bowlegs fought long and valiantly against removal of the tribe from Florida. He is buried in the National Cemetery near *Fort Gibson*. A tintype of him hangs in the lobby of the Bowlegs post office. The Bowlegs Field east of town was discovered in 1922, has since produced over 135 million barrels of oil.

Bowring (Osage Co., pop. 100, on OK 10, see Map 4). A tiny community in the northeast corner of the rolling Osage ranch country. Established in 1923, its name honors two area ranchers, Mart BOWhan and Richard WoodRING.

Boynton (Muskogee Co., pop. 522, on US 62, 20 mi. E of *Okmulgee*, see Map 5). A small agricultural community that began shortly after the turn of the century when the Shawnee, Oklahoma and Missouri Coal and Railway Company laid track through here. E. W. Boynton was chief engineer of the line. Later a part of the current Frisco system, it was only recently abandoned. A once impressive three-story hotel still anchors the business district and recalls happier days.

Bradley (Grady Co., pop. 247, off OK 19, 20 mi. SE of *Chickasha*, see Map 7). An old county community, settled in the early 1890's and named for a local cattleman, Winters P. Bradley. In 1953 it got a new lease on life with production from a nearby "wildcat" oil well that heralded extension of the rich Golden Trend (see *Lindsay*) northwestward across *Grady County*. Subsequent development of highly productive wells in the *Chickasha* area has made this one of the state's latest major fields.

Braggs (Muskogee Co., pop. 325, on OK 10, 12 mi. SE of *Muskogee*, see Map 5). A small community near the entrance to *Greenleaf Lake State Park*. It began in 1886 as Patrick, became

Braggs two years later to honor a local landowner.

Braman (Kay Co., pop. 295, on US 177, see Map 4). A small "elevator" town on the Santa Fe Railroad in the heart of a rich wheat-producing area. It was established in 1898, named for railroad developer Dwight Braman.

Bray (Stephens Co., pop. 100, on OK 29, 8 mi. E of *Marlow*, see Map 7). A scattered rural community served only by a post office, established in 1908 and named for its first postmaster, Thomas W. Bray.

Breckinridge (Garfield Co., pop. 70, off US 64, 10 mi. NE of *Enid*, see Map 4). A small, wheat-rich community on a branch line of the Rock Island. The town was established in 1901 and named for a railroad official, Breckinridge Jones.

Briartown (Muskogee Co., pop. 100, on OK 2, 3 mi. N of the *Canadian River*, see Map 5). A now almost non-existent railroad-siding community that dates back to 1882. The railroad name for the siding was McMurray, but the post office opted for the more picturesque—and truthfully descriptive—name.

Bridgeport (Caddo Co., pop. 142, 2 mi. W of junc. of I 40 & US 66 and US 281, see Map 8). Little remains today to suggest the one-time size and importance of this crossing-point on the south shore of the *South Canadian River*. Substantial bluffs here on either side restrict the broad, often treacherous stream, making early-day bridge building feasible. And it was here in 1898 that the Rock Island, then pushing westward, built its bridge to start the town. Before that, and for many years afterward, the site was familiar to those waiting to ford the river, when low water permitted, or using one of a succession of crude wooden wagon bridges.

Bridges have figured prominently in the town's history—making it to begin with and then, ironically, killing it. The flood of 1914 destroyed the Rock Island bridge, taking four lives. Most famous Bridgeport span, however, was a 900-foot suspension bridge, opened in 1921 as the last link in the Postal Highway through Oklahoma. It was a toll bridge—$1 for automobiles, $1.50 for trucks; this in a day when that amount represented a day's wages for many working men. When US 66 was established several years later, as the so-called "Main Street of America," pressures began to build to make it a free bridge. This was done, finally, in 1930. But a few years later a 3,940-foot steel-and-concrete span was opened a few miles downstream. US 66 was rerouted, and Bridgeport began to fade. The opening of I 40 in the 1960's further isolated and depressed the town.

Brinkman (Greer Co., pop. 7, off US 283 & OK 34, 10 mi. N of *Mangum*, see Map 8). A now almost vanished community, established in 1910 with arrival of the Wichita Falls and Northwestern Railway (later M-K-T and only recently abandoned). John Brinkman was a business associate of townsite developers Joe Kemp and Frank Kell, who also built the railroad. This is one of the county's better wheat producing areas.

Bristow (Creek Co., pop. 4,653, at junc. of I 44, US 66, and OK 16 & 48, see Map 4). Started as a Creek Nation trading post, Bristow was founded as a town in 1901, taking the name of Kansas Senator Joseph L. Bristow. Development of highly productive oil fields from 1916 to 1922 brought considerable growth, set the tone of business and social life in the town that persists today.

Between Bristow and *Stroud*, though unseen by visitors, is one of the state's more unusual storage facilities. It is an underground "tank farm," a depleted gas field into which Oklahoma Natural Gas Company injects gas from other fields during periods of low consumption. The largest of several such facilities in the state, it has a peak storage capacity of 75 billion cubic feet of gas.

Broken Arrow (Tulsa Co., pop. 11,787, on OK 51 at SE corner of *Tulsa*, see Map 5). A manufacturing suburb of *Tulsa* that dates back to 1881. The name recalls a post-Civil War ceremony in which the Creek Indians sought to unite factions created by that conflict.

A score of generally small industries provide employment, although in recent years the town has attracted an increasing number of commuting *Tulsa* workers. Curiously, the oldest (1924) and largest (500) local employer is Braden Industries, maker of such things as winches, towers, pumps—and windmills. (Only a handful of U.S. companies still produce these dependable, and economical, water pumps.)

Memorial Indian Museum (8 a.m. to 9 p.m. May–Sept., 8–5 rest of the year) contains Indian artifacts, prehistoric to modern, pottery, fossils, and rocks. Special events include spring and fall horse shows, a late August rodeo, and Rooster Day, a mid-May gala now more than thirty years old.

Broken Bow (McCurtain Co., pop. 2,980, at junc. of US 70 & 259 and OK 3 & 7, see Map 6). In the center of Oklahoma's finest commercial timberlands, Broken Bow was established in 1911 by the Dierks brothers, pioneer lumbermen, and named for their Nebraska home. Their lumber mill, erected in 1912 and expanded over the years, is still one of the town's largest employers. In 1966 all Dierks operations were merged with the Weyerhaeuser corporation (see *Wright City* and *Valliant*) and a new mill was constructed. Smaller independent lumber operators are also active in the area. A large poultry processing plant provides additional jobs.

The Choctaws came to present *McCurtain County* in the 1830's. But Caddoan Indians lived in the area for centuries before that. And much of this culture is recreated for the visitor in the Memorial Indian Museum (daily May–Sept. 8 a.m. to 9 p.m., rest of year 8–5, fee).

As focal point for *McCurtain County* roads, Broken Bow has traditionally been headquarters for sport and recreation seekers. Thousands of deer hunters each year roam the county's nearly one million acres of timberland. Floaters have long been drawn to the *Glover* and upper stretches of the *Mountain Fork* rivers (see *Smithville*). These two and the *Little River* attract fishermen the year round. Additional recreation facilities are to be found at *Beavers Bend State Park* and recently completed *Broken Bow Reservoir*.

Broken Bow Reservoir (off US 259, 5 mi. N of *Broken Bow*, in *McCurtain County*, see Map 6). One of the state's newest major lakes. This 14,200-acre reservoir was created in 1969 when the Corps of Engineers completed the state's highest dam (225 feet) across the scenic *Mountain Fork River*. It is a rough, heavily wooded area, a favorite of state fishermen and hunters. Just below the reservoir lies *Beavers Bend State Park*. The McCurtain County Wilderness Area (14,078 acres) and a 5,420-acre state game preserve lie just above it.

Facilities: camping and picnic area, boat ramps and docks, beach, playgrounds. Cabins and a cafe are available at the state park. Address: U.S. Corps of Engineers, Box 61, Tulsa, OK 74102.

Bromide (Johnston and Coal Cos., pop. 231, on OK 7-D, 7 mi. NW of *Wapanucka*, see Map 7). Empty, picturesquely vine-covered brick business buildings, wide sidewalks serving weed-grown vacant lots, and a scattering of residences in a pleasant cliff-side setting are all that remain today to remind the visitor of what was, from 1913 until the early 1920's, one of Oklahoma's most popular spas.

Press agents sent out reports of springs gushing "35 million gallons of healing waters daily" and excursion trains brought in guests from Texas to a resort that boasted four hotels, a bathhouse, pool, and other businesses. Little remains today but the beauty of its natural setting.

Brooksville (Pottawatomie Co., pop. 75, 4 mi. SW of *Tecumseh*, see Map 7). A dwindling agricultural community on a Santa Fe Railroad branch line built just after the turn of the century and abandoned in 1963. Known originally as

Sewell, it was renamed in 1909 when Alfred H. Brooks became the postmaster.

Bryan County (southeastern Oklahoma along the **Red River**, see Map 6). Area, 891 sq. mi.; pop., 25,552; county seat, **Durant**. Organized in 1907, with statehood, and named for William Jennings Bryan of Nebraska, unsuccessful three-time Democratic candidate for the presidency.

Top travel lures: **Lake Texoma, Fort Washita**.

Buffalo (Harper Co. seat, pop. 1,579, at junc. of US 64 and US 183, see Map 3). Shaggy buffalo—the "walking commissary" of the nomadic Plains Indians—roamed this area long before the white man arrived. Buffalo wallows, buffalo skulls, and the arrows used to kill the American bison dotted the prairies when the Cherokee Outlet was opened to settlement in 1893. Buffalo Creek was thus named. And in 1907, with statehood, **Harper County** came into existence and Buffalo became its seat.

Curiously, the town was often called "Stone City" because all buildings in its business district had to be of fireproof construction. Consequently, Buffalo maintains an air of dated permanence to this day. Wheat and cattle are its economic mainstays. The region is well known to sportsmen for its small game—quail, doves, and pheasants. Top scenic attraction in the area: **Doby Springs**.

Buffalo Ranch (Ottawa Co., off I 44 at junc. of US 59 and US 60, 66 & 69, 2 mi. E of **Afton**, see Map 5). A crossroads complex of visitor accommodations and services that includes a modest zoo. Featured are buffalo, longhorns, and a brahmalo, a cross between a buffalo bull and a white brahma.

Bug Tussle (Pittsburg Co., 9 mi. NE of **McAlester**, see Map 6). A rural community more formally known as Flowery Mound. The colloquial Bug Tussle is pure rural Americana. That it is better known than Cracker Box, Buzzard

Roost, Gouge Eye and other imaginatively named Oklahoma communities can be credited to the fame of its most famous native son, the Hon. Carl Albert, Speaker of the U.S. House of Representatives, 1971-77.

Bunch (Adair Co., pop. 30, on an improved county road 14 mi. SW of **Stilwell**, see Map 5). An old settlement in the ruggedly beautiful Cookson Hills. Its post office, established in 1886, was named for the prominent Cherokee, Rabbit Bunch.

Burbank (Osage Co., pop. 188, on US 60, 24 mi. W of **Pawhuska**, see Map 4). Little pertaining to Burbank's humble origins or depressed latter years hints at the soaring height of its oil boom in the 1920's. The town began in 1903, primarily as an Osage settlement, taking its name—according to legend—from the profusion of cockleburs in the area. At the opening of the Burbank Field in 1920, nearby leases were still selling for less than $10 an acre.

With the field proven and production climbing, however, lease prices jumped to $10,000 an acre. Land that previously sold for as little as $800 a quarter-section demanded fantastically high prices. Two lease sales in 1922, at the height of the boom, brought what is believed to be the top individual prices: $1,335,000 and $1,160,000.

Burlington (Alfalfa Co., pop. 188; OK 8, 13 mi. N of **Cherokee**, see Map 3). Though only a tiny trading community now, Burlington recalls an important aspect of history in northwestern Oklahoma. It was founded in 1906, with arrival of the Santa Fe Railroad, and named Drumm, for Major Andrew Drumm (1828-1919). One of the first cattlemen to graze herds on the leased Indian lands of the Cherokee Outlet, Major Drumm established his 150,000-acre U Ranch on the rich native grassland of present **Alfalfa County** in 1874 and was the first president of the Cherokee Strip Livestock Association. With the rest of the 6 million-acre Outlet, it was opened to settlement in 1893. The name Burlington (for the Iowa city) was that of a nearby settlement, established in 1900. Drumm took the name in 1907, and the original Burlington disappeared.

Burneyville (Love Co., pop. 60, on OK 96, 12 mi. W of *Marietta*, see Map 7). A scattered Chickasaw Nation community dating from 1879. The name honors David C. Burney, the prominent Chickasaw for whom Burney Academy, a girls' school established in 1859, was named.

Near Burneyville is Falconhead, a $12 million residential and recreational community being developed on the rolling grounds of what was formerly the private country club of *Ardmore* oilman Waco Turner.

Burns Flat (Washita Co., pop. 988, on OK 44, 7 mi. S of I 40, see Map 8). A "Phoenix" community with a fate now tied rather closely to the U.S. military departments. Development of Clinton-Sherman Air Force Base during World War II mushroomed this flat prairie into a town of 2,280 (1950 census). The base had "revived" the long defunct settlement of Burns (for Sarah Burns, the first postmaster), which existed here briefly at the turn of the century. But withdrawal of the Strategic Air Command from Clinton-Sherman in 1971 reduced the reborn town to fourteen persons. An Industrial Park has since been established, along with an area vocational-technical school. The town's rejuvenation—spurred in no small measure by the availability of nearly a thousand modern housing units—continues apace.

Bushyhead (Rogers Co., on US 66, 6 mi. SW of *Chelsea*, see Map 5). A now almost non-existent farming community that was founded in 1898, named for Dennis W. Bushyhead, chief of the Cherokee Nation 1879–87.

Butler (Custer Co., pop. 315, at junc. of OK 33 & 44, see Map 3). Like *Arapaho*, the county seat, Butler bloomed early, then faded quickly. Although nearby *Foss Reservoir* has helped attract residents in recent years, the town has never regained its one-time importance.

Known first as Hatcher's Store, just southwest of its present site, Butler was given its official name—honoring Matthew C. Butler, a Civil War general and U.S. senator from South Carolina—by the Post Office Department in 1898. Ten years later the town bloomed briefly with the building of the Clinton, Oklahoma and Western Railroad. But the so-called COW line (now a Santa Fe branch) never lived up to its promoters' expectations. A devastating tornado in 1911 further depressed the town. Most of its brick business buildings survived the storm, but many of them are now empty.

Byars (McClain Co., pop. 247, on OK 59, see Map 7). A dwindling town, founded in 1903 and named for a local rancher, Nathan H. Byars. Both the California Road (1849) and the Fort Sill to Fort Smith Military Road (1869) passed nearby, and a mile northwest of the village are a number of old houses and scattered foundation stones which mark the remains of several important settlements. Fort Arbuckle (see *Davis*) was first established here. When the post was abandoned it was occupied by Delaware Indians under Black Beaver (see *Anadarko*) and was known for a time as Beaverville. Chickasaw leader Judge T. B. Johnston later built a home here, and the settlement existed as Johnson and Johnsonville from 1876 until Byars was established on a now abandoned Santa Fe branch line.

Byng (Pontotoc Co., pop. 75, on OK 3 & 99, 6 mi. N of *Ada*, see Map 7). A scattered community on the Santa Fe Railroad that was named—in 1917, when it acquired a post office—for Sir Julian Byng of the British Army. The town lost its post office in 1957, but it has definitely not lost its consolidated school—and the ability of its basketball teams to claim winter-time newspaper headlines with their performance in state play-off tournaments.

Byron (Alfalfa Co., pop. 72, on OK 11, 14 mi. NE of *Cherokee*, see Map 3). One of the oldest settlements in the county—it was started in 1894, a year after the opening of the Cherokee Outlet—and now best known for the Byron Fish Hatchery. Established in 1929, the state-owned facility covers 80 acres. Artesian wells supply twenty-five culture ponds with water at an average temperature of 60° F.

Cache (Comanche Co., pop. 1,106, at junc. of US 62 and OK 115, 14 mi. W of *Lawton*, see Map 8). A town with a French name (meaning underground storage pit) and a population perhaps a fourth Indian, Cache was established in 1902 on the banks of Cache Creek, a tributary of *Red River*. The creek was so named for the persistent legends of lost Spanish gold discoveries in the *Wichita Mountains* to the north.

Cache the town has been in the family entertainment business for half a century. In 1924 the late Frank Rush, Sr., and his wife established Craterville Park in a large natural amphitheatre in the hills three miles to the north. Here was organized the first All-Indian Fair and Exposition, which was moved to *Anadarko* in 1935. Over the years, the modestly Disney-like amusement park grew into a popular southwestern Oklahoma playground, until 1957, when expansion of the *Fort Sill* firing ranges (see *Indiahoma*) forced its closing.

Eagle Park, on the north edge of Cache, carries on the Craterville tradition, with a good bit more emphasis on the history and cultural heritage of the region. The 250-acre preserve offers such recreational facilities as skating rink, miniature railroad, bridle trails, and other traditional midway amenities. A kind of frontier Greenfield Village section contains a number of genuine structures from this area, brought here and restored so as to resemble an early-day village. These include a "picket house" erected at nearby *Fort Sill* in 1872; the Saddle Mountain Mission school (1896) and church (1903); the Frisco Railroad depot (1902) from Cache itself; and a representative church and country schoolhouse. In addition, the recreated village contains several authentic replicas (clearly labeled as such) of area structures with strong historic significance. These include the original Red Store (built in 1886 as a commercial forerunner of *Lawton*), the Violett Livery Stable (1901), and the Cache *Journal* newspaper office (1902–36).

Most interesting Eagle Park structure, however, is the so-called Star House, the two-story, twelve-room home of Comanche chief Quanah Parker. Built about 1890 on a site just west of Craterville Park, it was moved here when the Fort Sill firing range expanded in 1957. It is now listed in the National Register of Historic Places.

Cache the town and Eagle Park cooperate to provide one of the state's most crowded special events calendars. Starting in May with a high school rodeo and an Indian arts and crafts fair, it includes powwows, old settlers' reunions, Indian dances, all-night hymn sings, and fairs. An unusual October event that attracts participants and spectators from a wide area is the buffalo auction, held to keep within manageable bounds the animal population of the nearby *Wichita Mountains Wildlife Refuge.*

Caddo (Bryan Co., pop. 886, at junc. of US 69 & 75 and OK 22, see Map 6). A town that began in 1872 with arrival of the M-K-T Railroad, taking its name from the Caddo Indians who occupied this region even before the arrival of the Choctaws. As a Choctaw court town, the new settlement grew rapidly. According to Historian Angie Debo, it was "the largest cotton market in the Indian Territory in 1890." The town's first federal census, taken that year, showed a population of 2,170. In the 1880's the town was the second largest community, after *Muskogee*, in all Indian Territory.

If Caddo is smaller today, it is also quieter. In 1873 and 1874, a crusading local newspaper reported, there had been fifteen murders—most of them unsolved and some not even investigated—within a 30-mile radius. The town's second century has begun on a more law-abiding note.

Caddo County (in the southwest, see Map 8). Area, 1,275 sq. mi.; pop.,

28,931; county seat, **Anadarko**. Organized in 1901 when much of southwestern Oklahoma—with the exception of the Big Pasture—was thrown open to settlement with a giant land lottery. Named for the Caddo Indians, one of several tribes previously living here.

Top travel lures: **Red Rock Canyon State Park**, **Fort Cobb Reservoir**, and **Indian City U.S.A.**, and the Southern Plains Indian Museum, City Museum, and National Hall of Fame for Famous American Indians, all in **Anadarko**.

Calera (Bryan Co., pop. 1,063, on US 69 & 75, 6 mi. SW of **Durant**, see Map 6). Started in 1889 as Cale, honoring railroad official George W. Cale, the town took its modified name in 1910. In 1899 it was one of the first townsites in which white men could purchase lots and get titles for the land directly from an Indian tribe, in this case the Choctaws. (The boundary line between the Choctaw and Chickasaw Nations, cutting off the extreme western section of **Bryan County**, runs just west of Calera.)

Long a small farming community, the town has grown substantially in recent years on the strength of the increasing industrialization of nearby **Durant**.

California Trail. An early-day trail blazed east-west across much of present Oklahoma in 1849 by California-bound gold seekers. For some years afterward the route, generally following the **Canadian River**, was used by emigrants moving west and it was usually referred to as the California Trail. Two of the better-known landmarks along the way were **Rock Mary** in **Caddo County** and the **Antelope Hills** in **Roger Mills County**. The military escort accompanying the initial California party was commanded by Captain R. B. Marcy.

Calumet (Canadian Co., pop. 386, on US 270, see Map 4). Progressive little agricultural community begun in 1898 when the Choctaw, Oklahoma & Gulf (the present Rock Island) reached this point on its way west across Oklahoma. Calumet post office, for the ceremonial pipe of the Indians, dates back to 1893, the year after this area was opened to

settlement. The town is surrounded by rich **North Canadian River** valley farmlands.

Camargo (Dewey Co., pop. 236, on OK 34, see Map 3). Named for a town in Illinois, Camargo was established in 1892, when the Cheyenne and Arapaho Indian Reservation was opened to white settlement. It is perhaps best known for the "free ferry" that for many years assisted traffic across the always treacherous **Canadian River** ford just south of town. Although nearly a mile wide here, and containing dangerous pockets of quicksand, the Canadian at times carries little or no water. Until the highway bridge was finally built in the 1950's, horses and later tractors were kept on the bank to haul out motorists stuck in the sand. Ironically, when it was extremely dry, sprinkling wagons often hauled water to the river bed to keep the roadway passable!

Cameron (LeFlore Co., pop. 311, on OK 112, 8 mi. NE of **Poteau**, see Map 6). A Frisco Railroad community, established in 1880 and named for a local mining superintendent, William Cameron. On the east edge of town is Reynolds Castle, an impressive stone house built about 1890 by James E. Reynolds, a Confederate captain who came to Indian Territory in 1867. Long a Choctaw Nation showplace, it is now privately owned and closed to the public.

Camp Nichols (Cimarron Co., 25 mi. W of **Boise City**, see Map 2). Now a National Historic Landmark, though marked by mounds of crumbled stone that merely outline its dimensions, this U.S. military outpost was established by Kit Carson in 1865 to protect the Cimarron Cutoff of the famed **Santa Fe Trail**. It was not an elaborate fort and it experienced no violence. During its brief existence, however, it played an important, if undramatic, role in the development of the frontier.

Road to the ruined camp (on private land; owner's permission must be obtained) crosses the **Santa Fe Trail**. Similar stretches of deeply eroded parallel ruts in the virgin prairie sod mark almost the

Ruins of Fort Nichols, established in 1865 by Colonel Kit Carson (photograph by Paul Lefebvre Studios).

entire length of the trail across the county. At Flagg Springs, Autograph Rock, and other points along its north-east/southwest course are hundreds of names and dates scratched onto convenient canyon walls.

Camp Supply (just N of US 270 at town of *Fort Supply*, see Map 3). Only a few old buildings remain—on the northeast edge of the sprawling Western State Hospital complex—to remind the visitor of this once important frontier outpost. It was established in November, 1868, as a supply base for U.S. Army operations against the Plains Indians, especially the Cheyennes and Arapahos. At different times it was field head-quarters for Generals Nelson A. Miles, Philip H. Sheridan, Alfred Sully, and George A. Custer. Custer was based here when he engaged Black Kettle in the celebrated *Battle of the Washita*.

The post was abandoned by the army in 1893 and the following year the reservation was given to the Territory of Oklahoma. The state mental facility was established in 1903. Early-day

buildings still standing include the original Guard House, later used as a commissary; the Custer House, now a residence; and a two-room Teamster's Cabin of so-called picket construction, that is, of logs set vertically and chinked.

Canadian (Pittsburg Co., pop. 304, on US 69, see Map 6). On the important Texas Trail, this settlement near the *South Canadian River* was an important supply point during the Civil War. It acquired a post office in 1873 with the name South Canadian, but the "South" was later dropped. A one-room brick jail dating back to territorial days and a nearby livery stable were incorporated in a reconstructed frontier town in 1972 to serve as a setting for a pair of Holly-wood movies. The complex is now used as a summer youth camp. Across US 69 from Canadian is *Arrowhead State Park* on sprawling *Eufaula Reservoir*.

Canadian County (west-central Okla-homa, see Map 4). Area, 885 sq. mi.; pop., 32,245; county seat, *El Reno*. Organized in 1889 when Old Oklahoma was opened to white settlement. Name was taken from the *North* and *South Canadian* rivers that slice through the county from northwest to southeast.

Top travel lures: *Fort Reno, Darling-ton* Game Farm, historical museum at *El Reno*.

Canadian River. Western Oklahoma's most important stream. It heads high in the mountains of New Mexico, flows across the Texas Panhandle and 411 miles of Oklahoma before emptying into the *Arkansas River*. In Oklahoma it is generally referred to as the *South Canadian* to distinguish it from its prin-cipal tributary, the *North Canadian*, which joins it in Eastern Oklahoma near *Eufaula*. Generally it has a mile-wide bed, often pocked with patches of quicksand. Until quite recently it could boast only a handful of bridges.

Caney (Atoka Co., pop. 200, off US 69 & 75, 12 mi. SW of *Atoka*, see Map 6). A community dating from the arrival of the M-K-T Railroad in 1872. The original town was Caney Switch, a mile north of

Ruins of building at Cantonment, temporary military post established in 1879 by Colonel Richard I. Dodge. This building has now been restored.

present Caney, named for nearby Caney Creek. Both names apparently recognize the prevalence of cane brakes along these streambeds.

Canton (Blaine Co., pop. 844, at junc. of OK 51 and OK 58, see Map 3). An agricultural community, established in 1905, that serves the thousands of visitors to nearby **Canton Lake**. Name probably comes from nearby **Cantonment**, the one-time military camp that later became an Indian sub-agency and school. However, it could also honor Frank Canton, an early adjutant general of Oklahoma. Many Cheyennes and Arapahos live in and around Canton.

Biggest annual events: the Walleye Rodeo on **Canton Lake** in early May and a Cheyenne and Arapaho Indian Powwow in August.

Canton Reservoir (off OK 51 and OK 58 NW of **Canton**, see Map 3). This 7,500-acre lake was formed in 1948 when the army engineers constructed 14,300-foot-long Canton Dam across the **North Canadian River**. A flood control and irrigation project by design, it is now northwestern Oklahoma's primary playground. The state maintains an 11,413-acre public hunting area along the northern perimeter of the reservoir. Under development in the **Cantonment**

area, by the Cheyenne and Arapaho business council, is a recreation facility that will, in time, include a lodge, craft shop, museum, and commercial catfish farm.

Facilities (on the south shore near the dam): picnic and camping areas, trailer park (private), swimming beach, airstrip, and hanger. Address: Corps of Engineers, Box 61, Tulsa, OK 74102.

Cantonment (off OK 51, 3 mi. NW of **Canton**, see Map 3). A temporary military post established in 1879 by Colonel Richard I. Dodge. Roughly midway between **Fort Reno** and **Fort Supply**, it served as a supply cantonment until 1882, then was abandoned. Its buildings were later used as a Cheyenne and Arapaho sub-agency and, until 1918, as an Indian school. The last whole building, partly destroyed by fire in 1970, has now been restored by the Cheyenne and Arapaho business council as part of a tribal recreation facility (see **Canton Reservoir**).

Canute (Washita Co., pop. 420, off I 40 & US 66, 8 mi. E of Elk City, see Map 8). Small farming community established in 1901 upon arrival of the westward-building Rock Island Railroad. Named for the ancient King of Denmark, the town is best known for its Catholic Cemetery (on old US 66 at E edge of Canute) with its Crucifixion Scene—the bronze figure of Christ on the cross, two kneeling Marys below—and hillside sepulcher.

Capron (Woods Co., pop. 80; on OK 11, 13 mi. NE of **Alva**, see Map 3). A small trade center in the extreme northeastern corner of the county. If short on people, it is at least long on names under which it has existed since its founding, as Sterling, in 1894. The name of the post office was changed to Virgel the following year. The town was subsequently known as Warren and Kermit before becoming Capron in 1899, for Capt. Allyn K. Capron, commander of territorial troops in the Spanish-American War.

Cardin (Ottawa Co., pop. 800, immediately SW of **Picher**, see Map 5). A now near-ghosted mining town tied to its parent **Picher** by rusted rail lines and eroding chat piles. Started as Tar River (for nearby Tar Creek) in 1915, it changed its name to Cardin (for town-site owner W. Oscar Cardin) in 1920.

The town boomed briefly in 1932 with construction of what was then the world's largest and most modern facility for handling lead and zinc. The Eagle-Picher Central Mill replaced more than 250 of the smaller and less efficient mills that once dotted the Tri-State area. Today the mill is an impressive ruin, only a fraction of its buildings and railroad tracks used in a chat-selling operation.

Carl Blackwell Reservoir (off OK 51, 7 mi. W of **Stillwater**, in Payne County, see Map 4). A 3,264-acre lake formed in 1940 by damming Stillwater and Cimarron creeks to provide Stillwater with a municipal water supply. Much of the 100 miles of shoreline is wooded. Since 1955 the lake has been owned and supervised by Oklahoma State University.

Facilities: cabins, camping and picnic areas, playgrounds and concessions, swimming beach, boat ramps and water skiing take-off. User fees are collected. Address: Oklahoma State University, Stillwater, OK 74074.

Carl Etling Lake. See **Black Mesa State Park**.

Carmen (Alfalfa Co., pop. 519, on OK 45, see Map 3). A small trade center for the surrounding ranching/farming country. The town was founded in 1901 and named for Carmen Diaz, wife of the president of Mexico, probably because of the Kansas City, Mexico and Orient Railway (now a part of the Santa Fe), then building south across western Oklahoma.

Carnegie (Caddo Co., pop. 1,723, at junc. of OK 9 and OK 58, see Map 8). Established in 1901 when the Kiowa-Apache-Comanche Indian lands were opened to settlement and thought to be named for Andrew Carnegie, the

philanthropist. It's a prosperous agricultural community with the payrolls and special events to prove it. But for a small furniture factory, most of its businesses (elevators, feed mills, fertilizer plants, fuel suppliers) are soil related. Peanuts alone are a 2 million-dollar cash crop. Also soil related are its annual Junior Livestock Show (early May), Roundup Club Rodeo (late July), and Tri-County Free Fair (early Sept. and one of the state's oldest).

But Carnegie's Indian heritage is strong, too. And the annual July 4 Kiowa Gourd Clan Ceremonials have long drawn Indian and white visitors from all over the Southwest. And related to nothing—except perhaps the desire to have a good time—is the annual World Championship Domino Tournament (last Fri. in Feb.) at the fairgrounds. It dates from 1945 and draws some 200 contestants.

Carnegie Park is open to visitors year-round. One non-recreational feature: the American Forestry Association's national champion Western Soapberry (or Chinaberry) tree—some 60 feet high and nearly 6 feet in circumference. Additional sport and recreation facilities nearby are at **Fort Cobb Reservoir** to the northeast and the sprawling **Wichita Mountains** to the south.

Carney (Lincoln Co., pop. 396, on US 177, see Map 4). A small agricultural community, established in 1892 and named for Carney Staples, the townsite developer.

Carrier (Garfield Co., pop. 150, on OK 45, 12 mi. NW of **Enid**, see Map 4). A small "elevator town" on a branch of the Frisco in a rich wheat-producing area. Established in 1897, it honors an early merchant, Soloman Carrier, whose family has been influential in the county down to the present.

Carter (Beckham Co., pop. 311, at junc. of OK 34 & 55, 12 mi. SE of **Sayre**, see Map 8). A dwindling farm community (cotton, cattle, feed grains) dating back to 1900, when it obtained a post office named for William G. Carter, an area settler. It did not exist as a townsite, however, until six years later, when a religious group platted it as Beulah. The older name persisted.

Carter County (south-central Oklahoma, see Map 7). Area, 829 sq. mi.; pop., 37,349; county seat, **Ardmore**. Organized in 1907 when Indian Territory joined Oklahoma Territory to become a single state. Named for a prominent early-day family of which Charles D. Carter, a U.S. congressman, was perhaps the best known.

Top travel lures: *Lake Murray State Park*, Ardmore and Mountain lakes near *Ardmore*.

Carter Nine (Osage Co., on OK 18, 2 mi. S of *Shidler*, see Map 4). A once bustling oil camp, established in the late 1920's when the Osage boom was at its peak. It is of interest today primarily for its name, which notes both its developer—the Carter Oil Company (now Exxon)—and its location—Section 9 (Township 26 North, Range 6 East).

Other Osage communities named for the companies that gave them birth are *Wolco* and *Barnsdall*. Another one-time oil camp "suburb" of *Shidler* was Denoya, just west of Carter Nine. It was named for a prominent Osage, Joseph F. DeNoya, but it lives in Oklahoma oil patch folklore as Wizzbang.

Cartwright (Bryan Co., pop. 200, on OK 75-A, 16 mi. SW of *Durant*, see Map 6). A construction camp, established in 1940, that served as headquarters for work on the $65 million Denison Dam. Completed in 1944, the 15,200-foot-long dam formed sprawling *Texoma Reservoir*, the state's most popular recreation area. Named for Wilburn Cartwright, U.S. congressman for this district when work on the dam began, the camp-turned-town is now an elongated highway service center for sportsmen. OK 75-A turns south from the town, runs across the dam itself, the *Red River*, and into Texas.

Cashion (Kingfisher Co., pop. 329, off OK 33, 21 mi. E of *Kingfisher*, see Map 4). A small agricultural community established in 1900 and named for Roy V. Cashion, the first Oklahoma Territory soldier to lose his life in the Spanish-American War. An impressive monument to him stands on the main street of *Hennessey*.

A town with a business district anchored by two banks in the 1920's, Cashion lost its railroad in the 1930's, along with much of its population and most of its businesses. Only in recent years has it begun to grow again, modestly.

Castle (Okfuskee Co., pop. 212, on US 62, 7 mi. NW of *Okemah*, see Map 4). Rural community established in 1903 by the now-abandoned Fort Smith & Western Railway (see *Boley*) and named for an area landowner, Mannford B. Castle.

Catoosa (Rogers Co., pop. 970, on US 66, see Map 5). An old Cherokee town that was founded in 1882 when it was briefly the terminus of the present Frisco Railroad. It was named for nearby Catoos Hill. Today this area is rapidly assuming a position of extreme economic importance to Oklahoma as *Tulsa*'s Port of Catoosa, head of navigation for the 440-mile *Arkansas River Navigation System*. Arrival at the new $20 million port (several miles north of the town) of a barge carrying 650 tons of Tennessee newsprint in January, 1971, heralded completion of the $1.2 billion project that gives inland Oklahoma access to the sea.

Transportation has long figured prominently in the Catoosa area's economy. The old Texas Cattle Trail ran through here in 1867. With the arrival of the railroads it was for a time one of the largest shipping points in Indian Territory. Nearby I 44 and the Will Rogers Turnpike have added yet another carrier to the picture. At the Catoosa interchange is the Cherokee Nation Arts and Crafts Center with display and gift items from all tribes in the state.

Cayuga (Delaware Co., E of OK 10 about 8 mi. NE of *Grove*, see Map 5). A

Splitlog Church, at Cayuga in Delaware County.

now ruined town that was developed almost entirely by the remarkable Wyandotte Indian, Mathias Splitlog. Born in Canada and the possessor of considerable wealth as a flour miller and real estate dealer, Splitlog came to Oklahoma with his tribe and proceeded to develop Cayuga on the banks of Cowskin Creek just above its mouth in Elk River.

In time, he had a flour mill, sawmill, wagon-building works, and other enterprises. And it was to further serve these that he entered (unwisely, as it turned out) into partnership with promoters to build the so-called "Splitlog Railroad." He was badly swindled, and by the time he died in 1893 much of his wealth had disappeared. Principal monument remaining, to the town and the man, is the still-handsome stone Splitlog Church. Nearby in a grove of ancient oaks is the cemetery where Splitlog and his wife are buried. The church—now on the National Register of Historic Places—

was still unfinished when he died. His funeral service was the first meeting held in it.

Cedar Lake (LeFlore Co., 4 mi. W of US 59 & 270 from point 7 mi. S of *Heavener*, see Map 6). A 93-acre reservoir off the highly scenic Holson Valley Road (see *Summerfield*) that offers excellent fishing and fine recreational facilities in a rugged, forrested setting. The U.S. Forest Service provides two developed areas (camping, picnicking, boating, and swimming). Write: Supervisor, *Ouachita National Forest*, Heavener, OK 74937.

Cement (Caddo Co., pop. 892, on US 277 & OK 19, see Map 8). A town that began in 1902 and took its name from nearby quarrying operation. A small gypsum plant still provides some employment, but the town depends largely on agriculture and, with development of the sizeable Cement Field in the early 1920's, on oil. The elongated field stretches from east of Cement on west to beyond *Cyril*, which shared the boom.

Centrahoma (Coal Co., pop. 155, on OK 3, 9 mi. NW of Coalgate, see Map 7). Settlement began here in 1907 when the community of Owl, dating from 1892, moved from its site a few miles to the southwest in order to be on the then-new Oklahoma City, Ada & Atoka railroad. The line is now abandoned, the town nearly so.

Centralia (Craig Co., pop. 155, on County road 22 mi. NW of *Vinita*, see Map 5). Tiny community in rolling ranch country, began life as Lucas in 1892, changed its name to that of the Illinois town in 1899.

Ceres (Noble Co., pop. 10, on US 77, 13 mi. N of *Perry*, see Map 4). A virtually non-existent community that began life as McKinney, within weeks of the opening of the Cherokee Outlet to settlement in 1893, changed its name in 1897 to Ceres, for the Roman goddess of the harvest. Though Oklahoma continues to be an important grain producing state, and this central section is indeed the state's "breadbasket," no Oklahoma place name properly recognizes the fact. Ceres ceased to be even a postmark in 1915. And the town of Cereal, some miles to the north, changed its name in 1911 to *Banner*.

Chandler (Lincoln Co. seat, pop. 2,529, off I 44 at junc. of US 66 & OK 18, see Map 4). Platted on a series of low hills, Chandler was founded in 1891, named for Kansan George Chandler, President Harrison's assistant secretary of the interior. There, six years later, fourteen persons were killed and every structure but the Presbyterian Church destroyed by a devastating tornado.

Central Oklahoma has many native pecan trees, and Chandler has a sufficient number of growers, buyers, and processors to proclaim itself the Pecan Capital of the World. A Lincoln County Pecan Show is staged each fall. Operating since 1957 near Chandler is a professional baseball camp for boys 8–18, run by Roscoe "Bo" and Tom Belcher. Biggest employer in the town is a maker of knitted underwear.

This is one-time Sac and Fox country, and Indian artifacts share space with pioneer items in the Lincoln County Historical Museum (Mon.–Sat. 1–5, free). Of particular interest: early-day drug store fixtures, a dentist's office of 1908, the post office of ghosted *Avery*, and the telephone switchboard that once served nearby *Sparks*.

Chattanooga (Comanche Co., pop. 302, on OK 36, 23 mi. SW of *Lawton*, see Map 8). A dwindling agricultural community, started in 1903 on a now-abandoned branch line of the Rock Island from *Lawton* to *Grandfield*. It was presumably intended to "honor" the Tennessee city of that name.

Checotah (McIntosh Co., pop. 3,074, off I 40 at junc. of US 69 & 266, see Map 5). This tourist-minded trade center for a broad farming/ranching area seems at long last to have bested its rival, the county seat of *Eufaula*. The rivalry began as one of several Oklahoma county seat "wars," this in prestatehood days, and in it Checotah apparently mounted

a charter-train invasion. But *Eufaula*, tipped off by a sympathetic railroad telegrapher, surprised the plotters before they could steal the county records, turning them back, with the reported loss of at least one life. Today, however, Checotah has finally capitalized on its strategic highway location to surpass *Eufaula* and become the county's biggest town.

A post office was established here in 1886 and named for Samuel Checote, the last fullblood chief of the Creek Nation. He had served three terms before his death in 1884. There is a large Odd Fellows Home off US 69 on the north edge of Checotah. Anchor of a new industrial park off I 40 at the south edge of town is a new Indian Arts Center and pottery manufacturing facility, owned by the Creek Nation.

Checotah has been a transportation hub for more than a century now. From the time *Fort Gibson* was established in 1824 the Texas Road to the south was an important frontier trail. Over it in the 1830's rumbled as many as a thousand wagons a week as settlers and freight moved from the East into Texas and the Southwest.

In 1872 this wagon road was retired by the steel rails of the Missouri-Kansas-Texas Railroad (the so-called Katy), first to cross then Indian Territory. When highways were built in turn, US 69 was laid out roughly parallel to the rail line. Fittingly enough, I 40 through eastern Oklahoma, crossing the Katy at Checotah, was completed in 1972, to dramatize a century of progress in transportation.

At the junction, Creek Nation Crafts Inc. provides another blending of the old and the new. The recently opened pottery manufacturing plant, sponsored by the tribe, uses Creek people for its labor force and draws on Creek talent and artistry in its design and production.

Chelsea (Rogers Co., pop. 1,622, at junc. US 66 and OK 28, see Map 5). Will Rogers and oil have long been associated with this town, established in 1882 and named by Charles Peach, a railroad official, for his home in England. One of the earliest oil wells in Indian

Territory was discovered west of Chelsea about 1889. The well was drilled only 39 feet into the earth, and shallow-well production is still economically important to the area, as is strip coal mining. As a boy, Will Rogers was a frequent visitor to the town.

Cherokee (Alfalfa Co. seat, pop. 2,119, on US 64, see Map 3). An attractive little town settled in early 1894 and taking its name from the Cherokee Outlet, which was opened to white settlement the year before. Wheat, alfalfa, and cattle are the economic mainstays of the area, although recreation centering on the vast *Great Salt Plains* stretching away to the east of the town is becoming increasingly important. Convenient access to the western section of this playground can be gained by driving four miles east on Fifth Street in Cherokee. An observation tower here affords an excellent panorama of the desolate flats. Mrs. Walter Ferguson, well-known state newspaperwoman and columnist, formerly lived in Cherokee, publishing, with her husband, the *Cherokee Republican*.

Cherokee County (northeast Oklahoma, see Map 5). Area, 782 sq. mi.; pop. 23,174; county seat, *Tahlequah*. Home of the Cherokee Indians from the time they first arrived in present Oklahoma in 1828 to the present. First *Park Hill* and then, after 1839, *Tahlequah* served as capital of the Cherokee Nation until statehood in 1907. Cherokee is one of fifteen Oklahoma counties (77 in all) that honor Indian tribes.

Top travel lures: *Sequoyah State Park*, *Gruber Public Hunting Area*, *Fort Chickamauga*, Murrell Home, Tsa-La-Gi Village at Park Hill, old Cherokee National Capitol at *Tahlequah*, *Illinois River* float trips, hunting, and fishing.

Cherokee-Disney Recreation Area. See *Grand Lake of the Cherokees*.

Chester (Major Co., at junc. US 60 and US 281, 6 mi. N of *Seiling*, see Map 3). Tiny crossroads settlement established in 1895 and named for U.S. Senator Chester Long of Kansas.

Interior of the Murrell Home in Park Hill (photograph by Paul E. Lefebvre).

Chewey (Adair Co., pop. 30, off OK 10, 7 mi. S of Kansas, see Map 5). A small community on the *Illinois River* in the rolling Cherokee Hills. This is the heart of the Illinois float trip country, and numerous small ranches along the river provide boats and guides.

Cheyenne (Roger Mills Co. seat, pop. 892, at junc. US 283 and OK 47, see Map 3). This pleasant little short-grass community was a creation of the federal government. Uncle Sam designated it the seat of a county somewhat larger than present *Roger Mills County*—and established its post office—a week before throwing open to white settlement the vast, 3 million-acre Cheyenne and Arapaho Indian Reservation. The government also laid out the town and gave away lots with a "Run for Homes."

In Cheyenne is the state-maintained Black Kettle Museum (daily 9–5, free) with exhibits of Indian and cavalry relics, early pioneer articles, and a fine diorama on the *Battle of the Washita,* the state's most significant Indian battle, fought just northwest of the present town. Scenic and recreational points of interest in the area are the *Antelope Hills* to the northwest, the *Sandstone Creek Project* (a significant break-

Black Kettle Museum in Cheyenne and marker showing map of the Battle of the Washita area nearby.

through approach to upstream flood control), and **Black Kettle National Grasslands.** The various lakes and public lands surrounding them, that make up this preserve, provide some of western Oklahoma's finest fishing and hunting.

Chickasha (Grady Co. seat, pop. 14,194, at junc. of US 62, 81 & 277, OK 9 & 92, and the H. E. Bailey Turnpike, see Map 7). Rich **Washita River** valley soil—and the perhaps even greater wealth of oil and gas beneath that soil—have combined to make Chickasha pretty much

what she claims to be: the Queen City of the Washita Valley.

Arrival of the Rock Island in 1892 started things off. Arrival of the Frisco about ten years later assured the county seat the kind of transportation facilities needed for it to develop into a service and supply center for a wide area and to nourish the small industries that now number over two score, giving the city its healthy, diversified economic base. Establishment in 1900 of the Chickasha Cotton Oil Company began the industrialization process. (Although cotton is no longer as all-important as it once was—now wheat, dairying, and cattle are agricultural bellwethers, too—the company has since grown to become a national concern.) Founding in 1908 of Oklahoma College for Women (now the co-educational University of Science and Arts of Oklahoma) assured the infant community a social and cultural base that persists to the present day.

Oil development in the area has come in periodic spurts. A gas field was developed in 1941. In 1953 an oil discovery near *Bradley*, to the southeast, heralded more important things to come. And in recent years a rash of 1000-barrel-a-day oil wells has given the immediate Chickasha area the latest—and "hottest"—of the state's major fields. But local industry continues to reflect the area's agricultural base. A frozen waffle concern, started in 1951, now employs about 135. And over a dozen makers of horse and stock trailers employ some 400. (Over 70 per cent of all such trailers produced in North America are manufactured here.) A mobile home manufacturer employs another 230 persons.

Concerts, plays, lectures, art exhibits, and other cultural events in Chickasha center on the USAO campus. There is an annual art show. Dating back to the 1930's is the annual Chickasha R. C. A. Rodeo, a four-day affair in mid-July. Shannon Springs Park has a zoo, lake, and Kiddy-Park, along with routine sport and recreation facilities.

Two nearby lakes offer additional facilities: Louis Burtschi (200 acres, 8 mi. SW), a Department of Wildlife Conservation reservoir open to free year-round use for fishing, hiking, general recreation; and Chickasha (on Spring Creek, 1,900 acres, 15 mi. NW), a municipal reservoir open (user fee) to hunting, fishing, and water sports.

Chickasaw National Recreation Area (Murray County, see Map 7). Authorized by Congress in 1976 to combine under single National Park Service jurisdiction 912-acre *Platt National Park*, established in 1902, and the much newer 7,003-acre Arbuckle National Recreation Area surrounding *Arbuckle Reser-*

voir. Also included is a 1,170-acre section of woods that connects them.

Chilocco (Kay Co., pop. 400, 1.5 mi. W of US 77, 1 mi. S of the Kansas Line, see Map 4). A non-reservation boarding school was established here by act of Congress in 1882 for the Plains Indian tribes of the western part of Indian Territory. After statehood, which broke up their tribal governments and thus their separate educational systems, the Five Tribes also began to send their children to Chilocco. In the 1970's enrollment, which had ranged from four or five hundred to well over a thousand, represented tribes from all over the country. Called "The School of Opportunity," Chilocco stressed vocational as well as academic training and was considered one of the outstanding institutions of its kind before it closed in 1980.

An extensive building program begun in the early 1970's will give the campus a distinctly modern look and will remove many of the picturesque old cream-colored limestone structures built in the 1890's of stone quarried nearby.

The school has a small Museum. Visitors are welcomed to it and, with permission of the superintendent, to the school's other facilities. Although there are several explanations for the name, historian George H. Shirk believes it stems from the Creek Indian term "tci lake," meaning "big deer," a name often given the horse.

Chisholm Trail. Best known of all the storied cattle trails, this many-branched route across Central Oklahoma left few physical reminders of its two decades of use. But its fame and importance are attested to in a dozen museums, from *Red River* south of *Addington* to the Kansas border north of *Medford*. Best of these are to be found in *Waurika*, *Kingfisher*, and *Enid*. Best-known town associated with the route was Silver City, where the herds were driven across the treacherous *South Canadian River*. The settlement is remembered today only by a cemetery (see *Tuttle*). Jesse Chisholm himself is buried near *Geary*.

A trader rather than a rancher, Chisholm blazed much of the trail for use of his supply wagons, this in 1865. First use of the trail for Texas cattle herds driven north to a succession of railheads in Kansas came in 1867. Some 35,000 head were sent up the trail that year. The number rose year by year until the 1880's, when more than 500,000 a season passed through Oklahoma. In all, an estimated 10 million cattle used the Chisholm Trail before settlement of the land caused its abandonment.

Chockie (Atoka Co., on US 69, 8 mi. NE of *Stringtown*, see Map 6). An old Choctaw village that has now virtually disappeared. First named Chickiechockie in 1891, to honor the two daughters of Captain Charles LeFlore of nearby *Limestone Gap*, it became Chockie alone in 1904. Chickie became the wife of Lee Cruce, governor of Oklahoma, 1911–15.

Choctaw (Oklahoma Co., pop. 4,750, on US 62 & 270 E of *Oklahoma City*, see Map 4). Prosperous trading center and, in more recent years, suburban community on the east edge of the sprawling capital city. It started as Choctaw City in 1890, the year following the opening of Oklahoma Territory to settlement. The "City" was dropped in 1896, after arrival of the Choctaw Coal and Railway Company (present Rock Island).

Choctaw County (southeastern Oklahoma along the *Red River*, see Map 6). Area, 784 sq. mi.; pop. 15,141; county seat, *Hugo*. Named for the Indian tribe that has lived in southeastern Oklahoma since the 1830's.

Top travel lures: *Fort Towson*, Chief's House near *Swink*, *Raymond Gary Recreation Area*.

Choska (Wagoner Co., on OK 104, 10 mi. SW of Porter, see Map 5). The small town that once stood here—established in 1890 and long since disappeared—can still be found on some maps. Some recognition is deserved for the flat, incredibly fertile Choska Bottom, some 90 sections of the state's richest farmland, that stretches along the north bank of the Arkansas River from here to *Porter*. The latter town is the center of

peach production in the state. Choska Bottom pecans are well known. Spinach and other garden produce is also grown here, along with cotton. The word Choska means "post oak."

Chouteau (Mayes Co., pop. 1,046, on US 69, 9 mi. S of *Pryor*, see Map 5). A trading center named for the well-known Chouteau family (see *Salina*) that sprang up in the early 1870's with the building of the Missouri-Kansas-Texas Railroad, Oklahoma's first rail line. A number of conservative Amish farmers live in this area, and their wagons and buggies can often be seen in the town.

Five miles southeast of Chouteau (inquire locally) is the site of Union Mission, established by the Presbyterian missionary Rev. Epaphras Chapman in 1820. Only a few foundation stones remain of the twenty or so buildings that once comprised this initial missionary effort in the state. But a monument notes that Rev. Samuel A. Worcester installed Oklahoma's first printing press here in 1835. In the Union Mission Cemetery is the grave of Mr. Chapman, who died in 1825.

Christie (Adair Co., pop. 50, off US 62, 8 mi. SW of *Westville*, see Map 5). A small community in the rolling Cherokee Hills. It was named for John Christie, owner of the townsite.

Cimarron City (Logan Co., on OK 74, 5 mi. S of *Crescent*, see Map 4). Oklahoma's newest town currently taking shape on a thousand acres of virgin woodland on the north bank of the *Cimarron River*. The $50 million development envisions 1,600 homesites. Nearby is Cedar Valley, a posh new twenty-seven-hole golf course.

Cimarron County (westernmost of the three making up the *Oklahoma Panhandle*, see Map 2). Area, 1,832 sq. mi.; pop. 4,145; county seat *Boise City*. Organized in 1908 and named for the *Cimarron River*, it is the only county in the United States that borders on four states: Texas, New Mexico, Colorado, and Kansas.

Top travel lures: **Fort Nichols, Santa Fe Trail** ruts near **Boise City, Black Mesa State Park**, public hunting areas.

Cimarron River. A principal river of northwestern Oklahoma that heads in New Mexico, runs the length of the **Oklahoma Panhandle** (with occasional digressions into Kansas), then cuts a meandering easterly course across nearly two-thirds of the state before flowing into the **Arkansas River** 15 miles west of **Tulsa**. It is sometimes called the Red Fork of the Arkansas.

The Cimarron is typical of most western Oklahoma streams in that shifting sands in its broad bed allow a usually meager channel to change course frequently. Gypsum deposits give the banks an added air of barrenness and desolation in its middle course. Farther upstream, near **Waynoka**, the sands are plentiful enough to create **Little Sahara Recreation Area.**

In all its 395 miles it has not been dammed. The name Cimarron is Spanish for "outcast," which the river certainly is when it goes on one of its periodic rampages.

Claremore (Rogers Co. seat, pop. 9,084, at junc. of US 66 and OK 20 & 88, see Map 5). The town Will Rogers made famous began before 1830 as the village of Cherokee Chief Black Dog. (Curiously enough, the name honors the well-known Osage chief Clermont or Clermos. He moved his people into this area, from Missouri, in 1802.) Elijah Hicks established a trading post on the site in 1842, and it acquired a post office in 1874. As late as 1890, however, the village still had less than 200 inhabitants.

Medicinal waters were discovered in 1903, and for a time the town flourished as a health spa. In 1907 Claremore boasted one of the region's few "prep" schools, and in 1920 it was taken over by the state to become Oklahoma Military Academy. Today, as Claremore Junior College, it is co-educational, with an average enrollment of 900–1,000 students. The school library contains a notable collection of books and other materials pertaining to Gen-

J. M. Davis Gun Museum in Claremore.

eral Dwight D. Eisenhower.

The name most closely associated with the city, however, is that of Will Rogers. Many people over the world believe the famed humorist was born in Claremore, largely because he himself always claimed he was born "halfway between Claremore and **Oologah** before there was a town at either place." He also referred more to Claremore than *Oologah* because he insisted "nobody but an Indian could pronounce Oologah."

Be that as it may, it is in Claremore that he was buried, following the tragic plane crash in Alaska that claimed his life in 1935. On a low hill about ten blocks west of the business district the Will Rogers Memorial, built and maintained by the state, contains the tombs of Will, his wife, and their infant son, and a notable collection of Rogers materials. Half a million people a year visit this memorial (daily 8–5, free). In front of the impressive stone building stands the familiar Jo Davidson bronze of the slouched, hands-in-pockets humorist, the pedestal inscribed with his famed, "I never met a man I didn't like." Beyond the three galleries, behind the memorial, are the tomb and an attractively terraced garden area.

Claremore has had other well-known native sons. It was the home of Lynn Riggs, author of *Green Grow the Lilacs,* from which was made the long-run Rodgers and Hammerstein musical *Oklahoma!* The Lynn Riggs Memorial on the Rogers State College campus contains the famed surrey with the fringe on top, photographs, and original manuscripts (Mon.–Sat. 9–5). The late J. M. Davis, long-time owner of the Mason Hotel, filled it over the years with 20,000 guns, 7,500 steins, 70 saddles, thousands of animal horns and trophy heads, musical instruments, swords and knives, Indian artifacts, and other items. These are now housed in the new, state-owned J. M. Davis Gun Museum at 333 North Lynn Riggs Blvd. (Mon.–Sat. 9–5, Sun. 1–5, free). Also of interest is Long's Historical Museum of coins, guns, wax figures, other items (daily 9–6, summer months, 8–9; nominal fee).

Fittingly enough, Claremore's biggest annual event is the four-day Will Rogers Rodeo in late June. Northwest of the city off OK 88 are **Oologah Reservoir** and **Will Rogers State Park**, where the humorist's birthplace is preserved.

Clarita (Coal Co., pop. 100, off OK 48, 10 mi. S of **Tupelo**, see Map 7). A scattered community that began around the turn of the century as Kittie, adopted its present name in 1910 to honor the wife of an official of the Kansas, Oklahoma & Gulf (present Missouri Pacific), which served the area.

Clarksville (Wagoner Co., pop. 200, on unnumbered county road SE of **Porter**, see Map 5). An agricultural community, established in 1894, in the fertile Choska Bottom (see **Choska**) on the Arkansas River. Once a rival of **Porter**, its offer of $1,000 to the M-K-T Railroad promoters to build through their town was refused, and the settlement soon died on the vine. The area, however, is still a producer of some of the state's finest peaches.

Clayton (Pushmataha Co., pop. 718, on US 271 and OK 2 at junc. with OK 144,

Sod house near Cleo Springs, preserved by the Oklahoma Historical Society.

see Map 6). Yet another town owes its founding to the coming of the Frisco railroad in 1887. A rival town by the name of Dexter sprang up across the tracks. The post office became Clayton officially in 1907, although there is no agreement as to why. Along with the Missouri town of the same name, credit is suggested to Jerome Clayton, a railroad construction superintendent; to Judge William H. H. Clayton, who served the federal courts in Indian Territory; and to a local cotton gin owner named Clayton.

Whatever the origin of its name, Clayton today is synonymous with hunting, fishing, and all manner of sports and recreation. This eight-county corner of the state has been called Oklahoma's last wildlife frontier. And Clayton is at its heart. **Clayton Lake Recreation Area** is off US 271 south of town. Also curiously interesting, though much more difficult of access (inquire locally), is so-called Rock City, an isolated area jumble of giant rock formations ten miles west of Clayton.

Clayton Lake Recreation Area (off US 271, 30 mi. NE of *Antlers*, in southeastern Oklahoma, see Map 6). In the highly scenic *Kiamichi Mountains*, this 595-acre state playground in central *Pushmataha County* includes 95-acre Clayton Lake itself, offers extensive picnic and camping areas, with trailer hookups, four equipped playgrounds, swimming beach, and bathhouse. The fishing is said to be some of the best in the state. Address: Clayton, OK 74536.

Clearview (Okfuskee Co., pop. 300, off US 62, 8 mi. SE of *Okemah*, Map 4). Another of the all-Negro communities established in this area in 1903, largely through the efforts of the now-abandoned Fort Smith & Western Railroad (see *Boley*). An unsuccessful attempt was made in 1904 to change the name to Abelincoln.

Clebit (McCurtain Co., pop. 200, 11 mi. W of *Bethel*, see Map 6). A scattered community in the rugged, virtually uninhabited woods between the *Glover* and *Little* Rivers.

Clemscot (Carter Co., pop. 150, on OK 53, 11 mi. SE of *County Line*, see Map 7). A scattered oil camp that grew up in the 1920's with development of the vast *Healdton* field. The name, according to historian George H. Shirk, grew from that of two local residents, Clem Brooks and Scott Sparks.

Cleo Springs (Major Co., pop. 344, just N of junc. of US 60 and OK 8, see Map 3). A small agricultural community that, like *Ringwood*, is best known for its watermelons. Established in 1894, it was known as Cleo until 1917, when Springs was added. Name comes from nearby Cleo Springs, which were in turn named, according to tradition, for an Indian maid, Cle-oh-i-to-mo. Nearby points of interest: *Sod House*, 5 mi. north of town, and the *Glass Mountains*, west across the *Cimarron River*.

Cleveland (Pawnee Co., pop. 2,573, at junc. US 64 and OK 99, see Map 4). Townsite owner Willis H. Herbert lost out to the president of the United States

Oklahoma rose rock, prized by lapidarists, a barite formation found in scattered locations in Cleveland County.

shortly after *Pawnee County*'s largest town was platted with the opening of the Cherokee Outlet in 1893. As Cleveland, it has gone through three separate boomlets.

Possession of the only *Arkansas River* bridge between *Tulsa* and the Kansas Line made it "Gate City" in its early years. Then much of its commercial activity stemmed from the Osage country across the river to the north.

In 1904 oil was discovered in the area and "Cleveland Sand" was added to the Oklahoma oilman's lexicon. Some 1200 wells were producing for a time, justifying a "Pioneer Oil City of Oklahoma" claim. And oil production is still important.

Completion of *Keystone Reservoir* in 1964 gave the area's economy yet another turn. Its waters now ring the town on three sides. Boats and trailers are being manufactured. Jolly Roger Water Festival is the biggest special event on the calendar. Serving the increasing recreational needs and pleasures of the traveler has become Cleveland's principal business.

Cleveland County (central Oklahoma, see Map 7). Area, 547 sq. mi.; pop. 81,839; county seat, *Norman*. Organized in 1889, when Old Oklahoma was opened to settlement by run, and named for President Grover Cleveland. Between 1960 and 1970 its population increased 72 per cent, greatest gain of any county in the state. Each town in the county also grew (see *Moore*) as the area became something of a sprawling bedroom community for *Oklahoma City*.

Top travel lures: *Little River State Park*, University of Oklahoma museums and art galleries, at *Norman*.

Clinton (Custer Co., pop. 8,513, at junc. of I 40 & US 66 and US 183 & OK 73, see Map 3). West-central Oklahoma's business and commercial center began with a big town lot sale June 3–5, 1903. Boosters had platted the townsite as Washita Junction (the newly arrived Frisco Railroad crossed the Rock Island just north of the town-to-be), but the Post Office Department changed the name to honor Federal Judge Clinton F. Irwin. Of three buildings standing on the site then, one remains: the old First National Bank building on the southwest corner of Fourth and Frisco.

Building of the so-called COW Line (see *Butler*) and another Santa Fe branch made Clinton an important early-day rail hub, established it as center for wholesale houses and soft goods manufacturers. Plant tours now available include the Acme Brick Co., the Clinton Cotton Oil Mill, Weston Instruments (aircraft), and a turkey processor.

Clinton is also a regional health center. In addition to its municipal facility it has the Clinton Indian Hospital, on the east edge of town, opened by the federal government in 1933. From 1919 until 1972 the Western Oklahoma Tuberculosis Sanatorium operated beside US 183 just south of Clinton. It is now a nursing-home facility operated by the State War Veterans Commission.

Clinton's museum and special events fare features "Indians and cowboys" in almost equal proportions. With its notable pioneer exhibits, the Western Trails Museum (daily 9–5, free) offers extensive Indian artifacts and relics from the famed Cheyenne and Arapaho

Cattle Ranch. Established in 1893 and covering more than a million acres in four counties, it was the largest ever to operate in the state. Special events include Cheyenne and Arapaho celebrations in late April and mid-June, rodeos and horse shows in July and September, and the annual Custer County Fair in mid-September.

Cloud Chief (Washita Co., pop. 25, off OK 54 near junc. with OK 152, see Map 8). Little more than a post office remains of this seat of H County, Oklahoma Territory, established in 1892 when the Cheyenne and Arapaho Reservation was opened to white settlement. (The original townsite name was Tacola, for an Arapaho sub-chief, but it was soon changed to its English equivalent of Cloud Chief.)

Cordell was also established in 1892 (although several miles east of its present location) and a bitter county seat fight between the two towns soon broke out. One pro-Cordell county attorney fled the Cloud Chief area permanently, while an assistant who remained behind was tarred and feathered by irate citizens. But an election in 1900 moved the county seat to *Cordell*, and statehood in 1907 made the move permanent.

Coal County (south-central Oklahoma, see Map 7). Area, 526 sq. mi.; pop. 5,525; county seat, *Coalgate*. Named, of course, for its extensive coal fields, which were opened in 1882 under lease from the Choctaw Nation. County was organized in 1907 when Indian Territory became part of the State of Oklahoma.

Coal Creek (LeFlore Co., on US 59 & 271, 11 mi. N of *Poteau*, see Map 6). No town, actually, but a railroad station and extensive rail yards surrounding the junction of the Fort Smith & Van Buren with its parent line, the Kansas City Southern. The 21-mile branch— the state's shortest, least known, and most profitable!—runs west from here to serve the rich coal producing area around *Bokoshe* and *McCurtain*.

Coalgate (Coal Co. seat, pop. 1,859, at junc. of US 75 and OK 3, see Map 7). The transition from coal to overalls may not be glamorous, but it has saved this small, agriculturally oriented town from possible near-ghosthood. (A Bluebell factory now employing about 200 persons was opened in 1957.) The first coal mine in this area was opened in 1882 within a few feet of present Main Street. The beds were shallow and plentiful; town and county were soon thriving and prosperous.

The town itself began in 1889 as Liddle, assumed its present name the following year. The town's hospital and nursing home are benevolences of the county's best-known citizen, the late Patrick J. Hurley, who was born near **Lehigh** in 1883. Perhaps its best visitor attraction today is the sprawling Hudson's Big Country Store. Established in 1900, it claims to be "the state's largest country department store." Although it stocks everything from galvanized iron bath tubs and cane-bottom rockers to coal oil lamps and can-can petticoats, the old-fashioned emporium is innovative, too. Two distinct firsts for Oklahoma are claimed: complete refrigerated air-conditioning (1937) and merchandise packaging (coffee, beans, and sugar, in 1919). In the early 1920's Hudson's attracted large crowds with an annual tossing of $500 in dimes from the top of the store. The gimmick was abandoned when the scrambling of men allegedly resulted in the injury of too many women and children!

Colbert (Bryan Co., pop. 814, on OK 75-A just E of US 69 & 75, see Map 6). A farming community in the fertile **Red River** valley that preserves the name of one of the best-known and most successful of Chickasaw Indians, Benjamin Franklin Colbert. Coming to this rich Red River valley from Mississippi in 1846, Colbert soon operated a 500-acre plantation, a sawmill, gristmill, and cotton gin. In 1853, when the town of Colbert acquired a post office, he inaugurated ferry service on the Red. Colbert's Station, about three miles south of the town (inquire locally), was a stage stop on the Butterfield Overland Mail route from 1858 to 1861. The B. F. Colbert home has long since disappeared, but his impressive grave marker, with those of other members of the Colbert family, stands in a weed-grown cemetery just north of the old river crossing. A dusty road drops down to the water's edge where the historic ferry ran. In 1875, after completion of the M-K-T Railroad into Texas had seriously curtailed ferry business, Colbert built a 577-foot-long, $40,000 wagon bridge across the river. This and subsequent toll bridges operated here until 1931, when a free bridge (half of the present twin-span crossing US 69 & 75) was completed. Today only two piers and the crumbling toll house mark the picturesque, and highly historic, site.

Near the Colbert turn-off on US 69 & 75 is a state-operated tourist information center.

Colcord (Delaware Co., pop. 438, on OK 116, 4 mi. E of OK 10, see Map 5). A small trading center in extreme eastern Oklahoma that honors one of Oklahoma City's best-known pioneer residents, Charles F. Colcord. It took that name in 1930, when the post office of **Row** was moved there from its previous location a mile to the north.

Cold Springs (Kiowa Co., pop. 30, off US 183, 5 mi. S of **Roosevelt**, see Map 8). Granite and gall both contributed to the early prosperity of this now almost vanished town. It was established in 1903 with arrival of the "Bess Line" (Blackwell, Enid and Southwestern Railroad, now Frisco) and was soon a widely-known real estate development— due in part, according to historian George H. Shirk, to the shrewdness of developers who boosted the sale of lots by placing ice in a nearby spring.

More substantial growth resulted when a Swede named Nordstrum recognized the commercial importance of nearby red, gray, and black granites in this area and imported stonemasons from his homeland to develop them (see **Mountain Park**). Some stone is still quarried in the area (see **Snyder**), but only an elevator on the railroad and a few houses remain of the town. Completion of **Mountain Park Reservoir** will back water eventually to the town's edge.

Coleman (Johnston Co., pop. 160, at junc. of OK 48 & 48-A, 7 mi. S of **Wapanucka**, see Map 7). A scattered community that began life in 1895 as Ego, changed its name in 1910. The loss of "ego" has obviously done it no good.

Collinsville (Tulsa Co., pop. 3,009, at junc. of US 75 & 169 and OK 20, see Map 5). A north-side Tulsa suburban community that was incorporated in 1899 in anticipation of the building of a Santa Fe Railroad line through this area. The original name was Collins (for Dr. H. H. Collins, a prominent local citizen), the original site a mile to the east. A nearby shallow oil and gas field adds to the basically agricultural economy (the Tri-County Fair is held in early August), as does the newly opened **Arkansas River Navigation System**.

Colony (Washita Co., pop. 201, on OK 69, 16 mi. S of **Weatherford**, see Map 8). Known originally as Seger Colony, this dwindling community owes its founding and name to John H. Seger, a Union veteran who came to the Darlington Indian Agency in 1872 and became one of the best friends the Cheyennes and Arapahoes ever had. In 1885 he was sent to this area with some 500 of them to establish an experimental agricultural colony. Something of a jack-of-all-trades, Seger built a sawmill and a brick kiln, taught the Indians to make the materials with which they constructed the five main buildings of the original school.

Land was broken, cattle herds built up. Seger Indian School was opened in 1893, and Seger served as superintendent until 1905. The school and mission, founded by the Dutch Reformed Church in 1895, finally closed in 1941. Two of the old buildings are now a part of the Colony public schools. The handsome main building burned

recently, but the curious brick water tower remains. Indians still use the area for summertime powwows. The handsome brick church on the grounds replaced the historic mission, a frame affair dating from the 1890's, that burned in 1968.

Comanche (Stephens Co., pop. 1,862, at junc. of US 81 and OK 53, see Map 7). In at least several respects Comanche is a cliche—a stereotype of what all Oklahoma small towns should be. Dating from 1892, with the arrival of the Rock Island Railroad, it was named for one of the fiercest of the Plains Indian tribes that roamed the Southwest. Laid out beside the Chisholm Trail, it has always depended heavily on farming and ranching. Native son Clyde Burk was five times World's Champion Calf Roper and is a member of the Oklahoma Hall of Fame. And Comanche's modern livestock auction barn is one of the biggest and best such small-town facilities in the state.

Then there is oil. The Stephens County discovery well was drilled on the north edge of Comanche in 1919. It came in a gusher and is still being produced by pumper. Suitably marked, it stands in a landscaped triangle beside US 81 on the north approach to town. And two miles farther north stands a sprawling, modern refinery (see **Meridian**).

Finally, in 1972, Comanche made yet another move to confirm the out-of-stater's picture of the typical Oklahoma small town: it recognized the prevalence of tornadoes on the Plains by beginning construction of an underground school facility (see **Seiling**, **Duke**).

The Clyde Burk Memorial Rodeo is an annual June event. Recreation centers on 200-acre Comanche Lake (on OK 53-A, 4 mi. E, fishing, 9-hole golf course, picnic and camping facilities). Newly completed **Waurika Reservoir** is to the southwest.

Comanche County (southwestern Oklahoma, see Map 8). Area, 1,088 sq. mi.; pop. 108,144; county seat, **Lawton**.

Another of Oklahoma's counties to be named for an Indian tribe. (There are 14 others.) Organized in 1901 when 3.5 million acres of Indian land in southwestern Oklahoma were opened to settlement by lottery.

Top travel lures: *Fort Sill*, *Wichita Mountains Wildlife Refuge*, *Holy City*, Museum of the Great Plains at *Lawton*, Eagle Park at *Cache*.

Commerce (Ottawa Co., pop. 2,593, on US 66, 3 mi. N of *Miami*, see Map 5). One-time financial hub of the Tri-State mining area, Commerce has now turned to small industry to counter the effect of the almost complete halt in recent years of lead and zinc activity. Sprawling mountains of chat, inside and outside the city limits, characterize Commerce, as they do the nearby towns of *Picher* and *Cardin*.

The town began in 1913 with increased mining activity in the area—the Turkey Fat Mine operated inside the city limits until recently—and took the name of North Miami. Apparently conscious of an identity problem, it changed its name to Commerce the following year. Its best-known hometown-boy-who-made-good is Yankee slugger Mickey Mantle.

Concho (Canadian Co., 2 mi. W of US 81, 5 mi. N of *El Reno*, see Map 4). Now the Cheyenne-Arapaho Area Field Office, Concho was established here at Caddo Springs in 1897 because the Cheyennes no longer wanted to share with the Arapahoes the agency and school at nearby *Darlington*. Ironically, Darlington itself was abandoned in 1909, and the two tribes were again united here.

A score of frame and brick buildings make up the agency today. But the old school buildings that once faced the agency across the canyon-bottom spring to the west have all been torn down. They were replaced by a $3 million complex immediately south of the agency before the school was closed in 1984. In a small cemetery nearby is the grave of Quaker Brinton Darlington, the Cheyennes' and Arapahoes' first, and greatly respected, agent.

Connerville (Johnston Co., pop. 200, on OK 99, 14 mi. N of *Tishomingo*, see Map 7). Like *Pontotoc*, a once prosperous trading center for a rich ranching area. Now a scattered community, it was established in 1897, taking its name from George B. Conner, the first postmaster.

Conser (LeFlore Co., off US 59 & 270, 6 mi. SW of *Heavener*, see Map 6). The little town, established in 1894 and named for Jane Conser, first postmaster, has now virtually disappeared. It is best known today (and still to be found on some maps) for the Peter Conser House. The two-story frame home of the well-known Choctaw lighthorseman of the 1880's has been restored by the Oklahoma Historical Society and is open to visitors (Tues.–Fri. 9–5, Sat.–Sun. 2–5) as a memorial to the Indian police. A small front yard plot contains the graves of several members of the Conser family.

Cookson (Cherokee Co., pop. 25, on OK 82, 15 mi. S of *Tahlequah*, see Map 5). Long an isolated little hill country settlement—its post office was established in 1895 and named for the first postmaster—Cookson has only recently begun to stir, with construction of *Tenkiller Reservoir* and the resulting recreational development. The storied Cookson Hills have given Oklahoma some of its finest scenery, its most dependable deer hunting—and some of its best-known outlaws.

Cooperton (Kiowa Co., pop. 55, near junc. of OK 19 and OK 54, 9 mi. E of *Roosevelt*, see Map 8). A now almost-vanished town, established in 1902 and named for Captain George Cooper, an early settler. A few miles to the southeast is the Cutthroat Gap area of the *Wichita Mountains* where, in 1833, a Kiowa camp was attacked and destroyed by a large Osage war party in the so-called Copper Kettle Massacre.

Copan (Washington Co., pop. 558, at junc. of US 75 and OK 10, 8 mi. S of the Kansas line, see Map 5). A small trade center for a rolling farming/ranching area. It had its beginnings in the 1880's as a trading post popular among the Delawares, Osages, and Cherokees. Arrival of the Santa Fe Railroad in 1898 spurred growth, as did subsequent development of several small, shallow-well oil fields in the vicinity. In recent years recreational use of nearby **Hulah Reservoir** has also contributed to its economy.

The word Copan—replacing Lawton (1900-1901) and Weldon (1909-1904)—comes from a town in Honduras.

Cordell (Washita Co. seat, pop. 3,261, at junc. of US 183 and OK 152, see Map 8). The government of **Washita County** was not "seated" without some difficulty. When the county was formed in 1892, upon opening of the Cheyenne and Arapaho reservation, the seat was awarded **Cloud Chief**. But Cordell, established a few miles east of its present location, began an immediate fight for the courthouse, winning it finally—courthouse and county seat—in a special election in 1900.

Even then there was controversy. Two farmers wanted the honor of providing land for the courthouse square. They compromised, and the section line separating their respective quarters runs through the square—and the courthouse—today. That courthouse, incidentally, was built in 1910 to replace the original two-story frame affair, removed from **Cloud Chief**, that had burned mysteriously in 1909 after statehood had made permanent the removal to Cordell.

Cordell Academy was established in 1906 under auspices of the Dutch Reformed Church, which was also active in **Colony**. The site, just east of City Park, has been marked. Wayne W. Cordell, for whom the town was named, was an employee of the Post Office Department. A downtown historical marker recognizes the original Gosselin variety store, founded by E. L. "Les" Gosselin, the "G" in T.G.&Y., when that Oklahoma-born variety chain was put together. The original "T" store was in **Frederick**, the "Y" in **Kingfisher**.

Corn (Washita Co., pop. 409, on OK 69, 14 mi. S of **Weatherford**, see Map 8).

Like **Meno** and **Bessie**, Corn is a small farming community with a strong German Mennonite heritage. Settlement of these Cheyenne and Arapaho Indian lands began in 1892. The town appeared—as Korn—in 1896. Anglicization of the German word, coming in 1918 just before the end of World War I, was typical of many such patriotic name changes (see **Loyal**) of that period.

Despite the cosmetic change, however, the face and mannerisms of modern Corn retain many indications of its distinctive heritage. The "skyline" is dominated by a grain elevator and the stolid bulk of the Mennonite Brethren church. Corn Bible Academy is an M. B. parochial school. And town businesses run heavily to feed and seed stores, locker and fertilizer plants, machine shops, and a small cafe where neighbors greet one another in voices that betray, more often than not, a thick German accent.

On Monday evenings the restaurant is likely to be crowded with those coming for the regular "Verenika Supper." Occasionally "cracklings" are offered the breakfaster, and "Schnatky" and "Roll-kuchen" are usually available for coffee breaks. Special German Suppers are held at various times through the year as fund-raising events, in Corn and also in nearby **Weatherford**.

Cornish (Jefferson Co., pop. 90, on OK 89, 1 mi. S of **Ringling**, see Map 7). An old settlement, dating from 1891 and taking its name from John H. Cornish, an area rancher. Best known for over half a century for its orphans' home—a private philanthropy that existed from 1903 to 1956—the town itself virtually ceased to exist in 1916, when most of its residents moved north a mile to the then-booming oil camp of **Ringling**.

Cotton County (extreme southern Oklahoma along the **Red River**, see Map 8). Area, 629 sq. mi.; pop. 6,832; county seat, **Walters**. Oklahoma's "youngest" county, organized in 1912 when the voters of southern **Comanche County** approved the setting up of a separate jurisdiction. Name recognizes one of its economic mainstays.

Council Hill (Muskogee Co., pop. 135, on OK 72, 10 mi. NW of *Checotah*, see Map 5). A railroad-siding community that began in 1905, taking its name from a mound some 5 miles to the west, long used for ceremonial purposes by the Creek Indians.

County Line (Carter & Stephens Cos., pop. 500, on OK 7, see Map 7). Like *Ratliff City*, *Fox*, *Wirt*, and many other smaller communities in the western section of the county, County Line owes its existence to development of the vast *Healdton* oil field. Its post office was not established until 1928. Although activity is considerably more restrained today, the town still maintains much the appearance of a boom oil camp.

Unusual attraction for OK 7 motorists approaching from the east is County Line Zoo. Developed on his farm as something of a hobby by the conservation-minded Charley L. Leflars, the 155-acre preserve boasts buffalo, longhorn cattle, deer, and a number of rare, exotic game animals (mouflon, Barbados sheep, European and Japanese deer). The informal Leflars zoo, to which visitors are always welcome, also offers protection to quail, wild turkey, and waterfowl.

Covington (Garfield Co., pop. 605, on US 64, 20 mi. SE of *Enid*, see Map 4). Towering grain elevators rising from flat, fertile farmlands mark this town and certify its location in one of the state's most productive wheat-growing sections. The settlement began as Tripp in 1902, acquired its present name the following year when John H. Covington, an early settler with no sons and the desire to see his name perpetuated, persuaded the newly-arrived Arkansas Valley & Western Railroad (now the Frisco) to so honor him.

Development of the *Garber* oil field after 1916 has given the town's economy additional strength. But one of its landmarks for a third of a century recalls the history of a town some miles to the northeast (see *Marland*). For more than thirty years now a downtown diner has served snacks and plate lunches from the converted Officers'

and Advance Publicity car of the world-famed 101 Ranch Wild West Show of Colonel George W. Miller and his three sons, Joe C., George L., and Zachary Taylor Miller.

Coweta (Wagoner Co., pop. 2,457, at junc. of OK 51 and OK 73, 12 mi. SE of *Broken Arrow*, see Map 5). A predominantly white community dating from the turn of the century that gradually replaced the older Coweta Town, which was settled by the Creek Indians when they first moved into the Arkansas River valley here in the 1840's. The name perpetuates their homeland town on the Chattahoochee River in Alabama. A mile north of town is the now-abandoned site of Koweta Mission (1843), first of three founded in the Creek Nation by Rev. Robert M. Loughridge.

Cowlington (LeFlore Co., Pop. 751, off US 59, 12 mi. NW of *Spiro*, see Map 6). A town dating back to 1884 that had dwindled to the three-score-and-ten mark by the mid-1960's, when construction began on nearby *Robert S. Kerr Reservoir*, a part of the *Arkansas River Navigation System*. A. F. Cowling was a prominent early-day settler whose white frame house, built in the late 1870's, still stands. Area landmark (just off US 59) is the graciously handsome fifteen-room home erected in 1890 by Thomas George Overstreet, who developed a 3,000-acre plantation here, overlooking the Arkansas.

Cox City (Grady Co., pop. 40, on county road 16 mi. SE of *Rush Springs*, see Map 7). A scattered oil camp, dating from 1927, that owes both its name and its existence to an *Ardmore* oilman, Edwin B. Cox.

Coyle (Logan Co., pop. 303, on OK 33, 13 mi. NE of *Guthrie*, see Map 4). A small agricultural community near the *Cimarron River*. Founded in 1899 as Iowa City, it took its present name the following year to honor William Coyle of Guthrie. Near Coyle, on a 290-acre, blackjack-studded site overlooking the river, is Camp Cimarron, a summer recreation facility for Camp Fire Girls.

Coyote Hill (N of US 270, 3 mi. E of *Geary*, see Map 4). A low, twin-humped, red dolomite hill. The flat, mesalike hill-top was the scene of much activity during the Ghost Dance fervor of the 1890's, when many of the Plains Indian tribes looked forward to a messiah who would banish the white man, bring back the buffalo, and restore the Indian way of life.

Craig County (northeastern Oklahoma along the Kansas border, see Map 5). Area, 764 sq. mi.; pop. 14,722; county seat, *Vinita*. Created at statehood, in 1907, and named for the prominent Cherokee Indian, Granville Craig.

Crawford (Roger Mills Co., pop. 40, 1 mi. N of OK 33, see Map 3). A small community serving the needs of isolated farmers and ranchers in the *Antelope Hills* to the north. Louis Crawford was an early-day rancher.

Creek County (east-central Oklahoma, see Map 4). Area, 972 sq. mi.; pop. 45,532; county seat, *Sapulpa*. Oil-rich county named for the Creek Indians, who began arriving here from the southeastern United States in the 1830's. It was organized in 1900.

Top travel lures: fishing at *Heyburn Reservoir*, tour of Frankhoma pottery plant at *Sapulpa*, Oilfield Museum at *Drumright*.

Crescent (Logan Co., pop. 1,568, on OK 74, see Map 4). A bustling trade center for a prosperous farming area in the *Cimarron River* valley. Founded shortly after the opening of Old Oklahoma to settlement in 1889, it took its name, presumably, from a stand of oaks that then rimmed it. Near Crescent is a nuclear research facility established by Kerr-McGee, evidence of the far-sighted diversification of all of Oklahoma's larger oil companies. A traditional July 4 celebration is the town's biggest annual event.

Cromwell (Seminole Co., pop. 287, near junc. of OK 56 & OK 99A, see Map 7). Surrounded by bobbing pumpers and oil-smeared storage tanks, this fading town is yet another product of the Greater *Seminole* Field boom. It was founded in 1924, named for oilman Joe I. Cromwell.

Crowder (Pittsburg Co., pop. 339, on US 69, 15 mi. N of *McAlester*, see Map 6). A little recreation-minded community on *Eufaula Reservoir*. "Women's lib" would seem to have won and lost in the naming of the town. Born in 1902 as Juanita, it became Crowder two years later, honoring the prominent local physician, Dr. W. E. Crowder, husband of Juanita Harlan Crowder!

Cumberland (Marshall Co., pop. 250, 2 mi. SE of *Little City*, see Map 7). A sprawling settlement on the west side of the *Washita River* arm of *Texoma Reservoir*. Established in 1894, it takes its name from the Presbyterian Church branch active in mission work in this area.

The Cumberland Oil Field was discovered in 1939, and an unusual sight is that of pumping wells entirely surrounded by water. Also of interest to the visitor is Cumberland Cut (see *Little City*).

Cushing (Payne Co., pop. 7,529, at junc. of OK 18 & 33, see Map 4). Incorporated in 1894 and named for the secretary to then Postmaster General John Wanamaker, Cushing was just another struggling agricultural community until April 11, 1912. Then the Wheeler No. 1 blew in, 12 miles to the north, and within months it became the brawling, boisterous boom town of legend.

By the end of 1915 it was ringed by a forest of derricks. Over 700 wells were producing more than 300,000 barrels of oil a day. Soon the area was dotted with a dozen refineries, sprawling "farms" of storage tanks, and the nucleus of a far-spreading network of pipelines.

The town has settled down considerably since those rambunctious days. But largely because of those pipelines it has been able to avoid the boom-and-bust cycle of most oil camps. Although down to a single refinery today, Cushing is the "Pipeline Crossroads of the World," served by more than a dozen major crude oil pipelines and half that number of pumping stations, including terminal points for some of the nation's largest pipeline systems. With oil-related small industries, petroleum is still the city's economic mainstay.

A plaque on the front of the downtown Anthony building notes that it was here that Horatio Alger-like C. R. Anthony opened his first successful clothing store in 1922. The department store chain now has some 325 outlets in 21 states.

Custer (Custer Co., pop. 486, on OK 33, 9 mi. SW of *Thomas*, see Map 3). An agricultural community that began as Graves in 1892 when Phillip Graves opened a post office in his dugout home. In 1902, when the Frisco Railroad arrived and laid out the townsite, Graves moved his office into a nearby building and changed the name to Custer, for the famed general. ("Custer City" exists primarily on railroad maps.) Population reached 1,000 the first ten years, has declined since then as the rich farmlands have become increasingly mechanized.

Custer County (west-central Oklahoma, see Map 3). Area, 999 sq. mi.; pop. 22,665; county seat, *Arapaho*. Named for General George A. Custer, who won the celebrated *Battle of the Washita* some miles to the west in 1868. Part of the Cheyenne and Arapaho Indian Reservation until 1892, the county was organized in 1908.

Top travel lures: *Foss Reservoir*, Western Plains Museum in *Clinton*.

Cyril (Caddo Co., pop. 1,302, at junc. of US 277 & OK 19 and OK 8, see Map 8). An agricultural community, started in 1906 and named for Cyril Lookingglass, owner of the townsite. Development of the *Cement* oil field in the early 1920's led to the establishment of a refinery here that is still the area's largest employer.

Dacoma (Woods Co., pop. 226, off US 281 S of *Alva,* see Map 3). A small agricultural community on the Frisco railroad. It began life as Zula in 1894, a year after the Cherokee Outlet was opened to settlement, changed its name to Dacoma in 1904—coined from the words Dakota and Oklahoma.

Dale (Pottawatomie Co., pop. 100, on US 270 & OK 3, 7 mi. NW of *Shawnee,* see Map 7). A somewhat ambulatory settlement that began in 1891 as King (for John King, the Indian allotment holder), moved a few miles east in 1893 and changed its name (to honor Territorial Judge Frank Dale, nemesis of Territorial badmen). Buildings were loaded on wagons for a third, and final, move in 1895, when the present Rock Island laid track through the northern end of the county.

Darlington (Canadian Co., 2 mi. W of US 81, 3 mi. N of *El Reno,* see Map 4). A beautiful, tree-shaded spot beside the *North Canadian River,* where Darlington Agency was established by the government in 1869 to care for the Cheyennes and Arapahoes, then occupying a vast reservation that stretched west and north across present Oklahoma to the Texas border. Brinton Darlington, a Quaker, was appointed the first Indian agent. He was greatly loved by the Indians, and his grave is in a small cemetery at nearby *Concho.*

Darlington, the community, soon became one of the most important settlements in the area. It had a post office in 1873. Stage lines and freight wagons connected it with Texas and Kansas and other western Oklahoma outposts. A school and a Mennonite mission were established. In 1879 the *Cheyenne Transporter* was Indian Territory's first newspaper.

Darlington Agency was moved to *Concho* in 1909, and only two residences remain of its original buildings. The interesting Moorish chapel and fortress-like dormitory date from the 1910–22 period when Oklahoma Masons operated Darlington as a boarding school for orphans and a home for

D

Ruins of Fort Arbuckle, west of Davis.

elderly lodge members. Since 1932 the 95-acre preserve has served as the State Game Farm. Expansion has made it today one of the world's largest quail-pheasant hatcheries—some 100,000 birds hatched and shipped annually. Visitors are welcomed to the administrative buildings and display pens.

Davenport (Lincoln Co., pop. 831, at junc. of US 66 & OK 140, see Map 4). Founded in 1892 and soon a bustling trade center and rival of nearby **Stroud,** Davenport moved to its present location in 1898, with the arrival of the Frisco Railroad. The name honors an early-day merchant. In 1903 a Kentucky colony headed by seven Methodist ministers bought up most of the townsite and redeveloped it. Oil brought further growth in the 1920's.

Davidson (Tillman Co., pop. 515, on US 70 & 183, 3 mi. N of **Red River,** see Map 8). A dwindling farming community, known variously as Texawa and Olds after its founding in 1901 with opening of the Kiowa-Comanche lands. Its present name came in 1903 with arrival of the Frisco Railroad, of which A. J. Davidson was a director. Cotton gins in and around the town indicate the area's eco-

nomic mainstay, along with extensive native rangelands. Three miles south of town is the 5,460-foot Davidson Bridge across **Red River** into Texas. Of concrete, it is the state's longest.

Davis (Murray Co., pop. 2,223, at junc. of US 77 and OK 7, see Map 7). Settlement began here on the east bank of the **Washita River** in 1887 when the Santa Fe Railroad built north-south through this region. Samuel H. Davis was a prominent early-day resident. The town serves as northern gateway to the **Arbuckle Mountains;** the sprawling Chickasaw National Recreation Area; and the Arbuckle Wilderness, a drive-through wild animal park.

Chickasaws began settling this area in the 1830's, and Indian influence is still strong. The two-story Nelson Chigley House (private), a gracious colonial structure set amid fine old trees on the northeast edge of Davis, is an example of the better homes built by prosperous Chickasaws in Territorial days.

The site of old **Fort Arbuckle,** established in 1851 to protect the Chickasaws from the hostile Plains Indian tribes on to the west, is on a private ranch off OK 7, seven miles west of Davis. The post was abandoned in 1869, and only a few stone chimneys now mark its location.

A mile south of the fort is the crude stone post that marks Initial Point, the spot from which all post-Civil War surveys of Oklahoma, with the exception of the Panhandle, were made. The north-south line through the point is called the Indian Meridian, the east-west line, the Base Line.

Dead Indian Lake (just W of US 283, 10 mi. N of **Cheyenne,** see Map 3). A long, narrow lake running back into a couple of side canyons and offering fishing, hunting, other recreation facilities. Maintained by the U.S. Forest Service (Hot Springs, Ark.) as part of **Black Kettle National Grasslands.** Dam was built in 1959 as a flood control project.

Deep Fork River. A 230-mile-long tributary of the **Canadian River.** It heads inside the corporate limits of **Oklahoma**

Stone post marking Initial Point, near old Fort Arbuckle west of Davis.

City, meanders eastward to join the **Canadian's North** and **South** forks in forming octopus-like **Eufaula Reservoir.**

Deer Creek (Grant Co., pop. 203, on OK 11, see Map 4). Established as Orie in 1894, a year after the opening of the Cherokee Outlet, the town changed its name five years later to Deer Creek, for the nearby tributary to the **Salt Fork of the Arkansas River.** It lies in a rich, wheat-producing area and has a sizeable number of German Mennonite farmers, who moved here from Kansas when the Cherokee Outlet was opened to settlement in 1893.

Delaware (Nowata Co., pop. 534, on US 169, see Map 5). Like **Lenapah,** 5 mi. to the north, this little community, established in 1898, recognizes the fact that this area was originally settled by Delaware Indians, who used tribal funds in 1867 to purchase equal rights with the Cherokees in the Cherokee Nation.

The town boomed briefly, after 1907, with development of an extensive shallow-well oil field. It followed the classic pattern of boom towns everywhere. For a time one business block boasted fourteen saloons and gambling houses—all illegal—and brawls and killings were not uncommon.

Delaware County (northeastern Oklahoma, bordering on both Arkansas and Missouri, see Map 5). Area, 720 sq. mi.; pop., 17,767; county seat, **Jay.** Created in 1907, with statehood, and named for the Indian tribe that was moved to this area from Kansas in 1867.

Top travel lures: **Grand Lake of the Cherokees,** Hildebrand Mill near **Flint,** Splitlog Church at **Cayuga.**

Del City (Oklahoma Co., pop. 27,133, on I 40 and OK 3 & 77-H, see Map 4). One of the state's newest, fastest growing cities, Del City is largely a bedroom

Hildebrand Mill, on Flint Creek in Delaware County.

community, snuggled cozily between **Midwest City** and sprawling Tinker Air Force Base on the east and the state capital, **Oklahoma City,** on the west. It sprang from a wheat field in 1946, the creation of Kansas land developer George Epperly, who named it to honor his daughter Delephene.

Delhi (Beckham Co., pop. 35, off US 283, 10 mi. S of **Sayre,** see Map 8). A scattered community, dating from 1893, that has failed to grow despite its unusually distinguished name.

Depew (Creek Co., pop. 739, on US 66, 8 mi. W of **Bristow,** see Map 4). An agricultural community, laid out along the Frisco Railroad just after the turn of the century and named for the well-known New York senator, Chauncey M. Depew.

Devils Canyon, see **Lugert.**

Devil's Den (Johnson Co., off OK 99, 2 mi. N of **Tishomingo,** see Map 7). Although this well-developed family recreation area was long a popular playground, it is now closed to the public. It was located in a scenic natural park on Pennington Creek. The rugged, boulder-strewn canyon boasts such descriptive features as Devil's Chair (a balanced rock), Deadman's Cave (perhaps in deference to prevalent Territorial days legends of outlaws and U.S. Marshals), and the Witch's Tomb. A mile to the west is Bullet Prairie, where a Spanish explorer is said to have battled with the Indians. Besides the viewing of those attractions, park activities included fly fishing, swimming, and hiking.

Devol (Cotton Co., pop. 129, on US 70, 6 mi. SE of **Grandfield,** see Map 8). Platted in 1906 when the "Big Pasture" was opened to settlement by drawing (see **Grandfield**) and named for its first postmaster, J. F. DeVol. A railroad-siding community (M-K-T), it has never been large and, as if to fulfill the biblical injunction concerning the haves and the have-nots, a tornado in 1950 wiped out the small business district it did have. The businesses have not rebuilt.

To the town's credit, however, it is a pleasantly neat and clean residential community.

Dewar (Okmulgee Co., pop. 933, on US 266, 3 mi. NE of **Henryetta,** see Map 5). The decline of the coal industry halted the growth of this once-thriving community, established in 1909 and named for William P. Dewar, an official of the Kansas, Oklahoma and Gulf Railroad. Its residents are employed in manufacturing plants of nearby **Henryetta** and **Okmulgee.**

Dewey (Washington Co., pop. 3,958, on US 75, see Map 5). Founded in 1898 by the same Jake Bartles who started **Bartlesville,** Dewey was named for Admiral George Dewey, whose Manila Bay naval exploits were still fresh on the settlers' minds. Which may or may not help to explain the heroic way the town has managed to survive the recent loss of its largest industry. When it shut down in late 1963 the Dewey Portland Cement Co. plant employed 350 persons, had a production capacity of 2,250,000 barrels annually. The twin-stacked plant with its giant storage bins and sprawling production buildings is still an impressive monument to the past, beside US 75 on the north edge of town.

At the west end of the town's business district is the handsome old two-story Dewey Hotel. Bartles built the be-cupolaed walnut structure with its wide double galleries in 1899, as his home. He and his wife planted trees throughout the area and laid out the city park. They dug the first water well in town and placed in the front yard of their new home two millstones from their gristmill on the Caney River. The stones and the well are still preserved. The home was later converted to a forty-room hotel. In 1967 it became the property of the Washington County Historical Society, which is currently restoring it. (Open Tues.–Sat. 10–5, Sun. 12–5)

Across the street from the hotel is the Tom Mix Museum, containing personal collections, clothing, saddles, trophies, pictures, records and other mem-

Tom Mix Museum, in Dewey, contains collections and memorabilia relating to the popular Western star.

orabilia pertaining to the popular western movie star. It is operated by the Oklahoma Historical Society (Tues.–Fri. 9–5, Sat.–Sun. 2–5).

Dewey County (northwestern Oklahoma, see Map 3). Area, 977 sq. mi.; pop., 5,656; county seat, *Taloga.* Organized in 1892, when the Cheyenne and Arapaho Indian Reservation was opened to settlement, and named for Admiral George Dewey.

Dibble (McClain Co., pop. 184, on OK 39, 15 mi. W of *Purcell,* see Map 7). A scattered farm/ranch community settled as early as 1880, while still part of the Chickasaw Nation. John and James Dibble were local ranchers. It was for a time a half-way stop on the *Fort Sill* to Fort Smith Military Road, built in 1869 and used into the 1880's. There is considerable oil activity in the area.

Dickson (Carter Co., pop. 798, at junc. of US 70 & 177, see Map 7). A newly incorporated town formed of the scattered community homes and businesses built up in recent years around this important highway junction.

Dill City (Washita Co., pop. 578, on OK 42, 8 mi. W of *Cordell,* see Map 8). An agricultural community established in 1905 on the newly arrived Kansas City, Mexico and Orient Railway (now Santa Fe) and named for one D. S. Dill. The "City" was added, optimistically, in 1944.

Disney (Mayes Co., pop. 303, on OK 28, 16 mi. NW of *Jay,* see Map 5). Like *Langley,* at the west end of Pensacola Dam, Disney was established in 1938, on the east bank of *Grand River,* to serve as a construction camp for the 5,680-foot-long structure (see *Grand Lake of the Cherokees*). It was named for Wesley E. Disney, a member of Congress from Oklahoma. Like Langley, too, it serves today primarily as a sportsman's supply center for the sprawling Grand Lake playground. OK 82 south from Disney, through *Spavinaw* to *Salina,* is one of the most pleasantly scenic highways in Eastern Oklahoma.

Dramatic evidence that this is Cherokee country can be found on the side wall of a local drive-in. Hamburgers, hot dogs, and other items are listed in both English and Cherokee.

Doaksville (see *Fort Towson*).

Doby Springs (2 mi. N of US 64, 9 mi. W of *Buffalo*). Long a familiar rendezvous for Indians and early-day cowboys, this heavily wooded area with its generous artesian springs is today a pleasant county park (picnicking and camping). It was homesteaded in 1893 by C. C. Doby, and the little community that sprang up around the springs—which originally took the name of Bellaire—had hopes, for a time, of becoming the seat of *Harper County.* In 1907 the seat went to *Buffalo,* however, and the following year the settlement became Doby Springs. No trace of the town is visible today. Some of the springs supply water to *Buffalo.* Others have been dammed to create a small lake stocked with fish.

Dougherty (Murray Co., pop. 211, on OK 110, 12 mi. SE of *Davis,* see Map 7). An old settlement near the *Washita River* on the southeastern flank of the *Arbuckle Mountains.* It was named, in 1887, for William Dougherty, a Texas banker. On the main line of the Santa Fe Railroad, the town was long a busy shipping point for *Murray County* cattle. Today it is best known for two nearby crushed-limestone plants.

Dover (Kingfisher Co., pop. 390, on US 81, see Map 4). A small agricultural community with a diminutive, tree-shaded business district, Dover was known as Red Fork Station long before the opening of Old Oklahoma in 1889. Freighters hauling supplies to Indian agencies and military posts in Indian Territory followed the *Chisholm Trail.* But massive north-bound cattle herds often caused the freight wagons to detour. In time they finally beat out a trail of their own. Here at Red Fork Ranch a stockade was maintained where teamsters could change horses.

Just south of Dover the Rock Island Railroad crosses *Cimarron River.* Here on September 16, 1906, occurred one of Oklahoma's more spectacular railroad wrecks. A loaded passenger train plunged through a bridge that was weakened by a sudden flood, dumping all but two sleeping cars into the water. Miraculously, only four persons are known to have lost their lives. The locomotive is still buried in the quicksand beside the steel bridge that replaced the washed-out wooden span.

Near the river on April 4, 1895, five armed bandits held up another Rock Island train and made away with a box of gold containing the payroll for *Fort Sill.* The gold was never recovered, nor was anything ever learned definitely about the fifth member of the gang who apparently "stole" the hoard from the other four. The mystery has been sufficient to spark periodic treasure hunting expeditions over the years.

Dow (Pittsburg Co., pop. 300, on US 270, 11 mi. SE of *McAlester,* see Map 6). A once-thriving coal community, established in the 1890's and named for a local mine operator, one Andrew Dow. The town stirred to life in 1974 when the nation's critical energy needs prompted resumption of strip mining at site of the old Carbon No. 5 mine.

Drummond (Garfield Co., pop. 326, on OK 132, 15 mi. SW of *Enid,* see Map 4). A prosperous little agricultural community, established in 1901 and named for Harry Drummond, an official of the Blackwell, Enid and Southwestern Railway, now a part of the Frisco system. Flatlands west of the town fill with water during unusually rainy autumns, providing excellent duck hunting.

Drumright (Creek Co., pop. 2,931, at junc. of OK 33 & 99, see Map 4). Like *Oilton* and other nearby communities, Drumright was a rambunctious by-product of the rich *Cushing* Field, which opened in 1912. Known locally as Fulkerson, for the family owning the townsite, it was laid out the following year as Drumright, for another area landowner, Aaron Drumright.

For the next three years its tents, lean-tos, and ramshackle wooden buildings—set amid a forest of some 300 producing oil rigs—provided a haven for every human element known to the oil field boom towns, legal and extralegal, male and female. Not until 1916, when an aroused citizenry authorized chief of police "Fighting Jack" Ary to restore order, did the town begin to settle down to quiet growth.

Today Drumright's main street, running over steep Tiger Hill and said to be the state's longest up-and-down thoroughfare, bears little to remind one of the broad road, alternately ankle-deep in dust and hub-deep in mud, over which a colorful, cursing flood of mule-drawn wagons loaded with heavy equipment flowed back and forth between drilling operations. To even begin to appreciate those days one must visit the Oilfield Museum (Fri. & Sun. 1–5), located in the abandoned Santa Fe depot. As a further indication of the town's latter-day sedateness, its biggest annual events are an Arts and Crafts Festival and the Oil Patch Jamboree, both in the early fall.

Duke (Jackson Co., pop. 486, at junc. of US 62 and OK 34, see Map 8). Established in 1890 and named for F. B. Duke, a territorial judge, Duke never really stirred until 1964, when the big Republic Gypsum Company plant was built on the west edge of town. With 180 employees, it is now the county's largest private employer. Plant tours can be arranged.

At the northeast edge of Duke is the innovative new underground high school that doubles as community fallout and storm shelter. The so-called "Duke Plan" has prompted construction of similar underground school facilities in **Seiling, Blanchard, Comanche,** and other storm-shy communities.

Duke is served by the Hollis & Eastern Railroad Company, an independent operation that deserves at least footnote mention in any book on Oklahoma. When the M-K-T Railroad decided to abandon this branch in 1958, local interests took over the 33-mile stretch between **Altus** and **Hollis.** The highly informal line operates, profitably, with a minimum of fuss and bother—and, for that matter, equipment—and a maximum of fun and personalized service. The H&E is undoubtedly the only rail line in Oklahoma where the crew (of two men) can stop on the main line while they walk into town for a coffee break. Or tie a rope onto their engine and pull a truck from a trackside mudhole. (Alas, abandonment in 1975 of trackage beyond Duke in effect converted the Hollis & Eastern into the Altus & Western!)

Duncan (Stephens Co. seat, pop. 19,718, at junc. of US 81 and OK 7, see Map 7). A clean, progressive little city, born in 1892 with arrival of the Rock Island Railroad. William Duncan was a white man married to a Chickasaw Indian woman on whose allotment the townsite was laid out. By 1920 it was a pleasant county seat town of 3,000, dependent largely on agriculture.

Then in 1921 oil became an important factor in the Duncan area. By 1924 a local oilman, Erle P. Halliburton, perfected and began offering to others in the industry his now famous oil-well cementing service. In the half-century since then, Halliburton Services has spread around the world and Duncan, with more than a tenth of its citizens on the Halliburton payroll, has become something of a "company town," in the best sense of the word. Additional related payrolls in the area include refineries (see **Meridian**), drilling, and pipeline concerns, oilwell supply houses, and transport companies. Agricultural payrolls include a meat packer and several makers of horse trailers. Breaking the agriculture/petroleum pattern is a Haggar slacks manufacturing plant (tours available) opened in 1966.

Duncan has 80 acres of parks and playgrounds. Fuqua has a Kiddieland in addition to a regular complement of sport and recreation facilities. Memorial (also on US 81) has extensive flower beds, a notable fountain (colorful nighttime displays), and several interesting historical markers. One park notes the north/south passage through this area of the storied **Chisholm Trail,** over which hundreds of thousands of cattle were driven to railheads in Kansas in the 1870's and 1880's. Another memorializes the east/west Indian Base Line (see **Davis**), established in 1870 as the basis for almost all land surveys from Oklahoma north to South Dakota.

Duncan has active Art Guild and Little Theatre groups with regular programs. The Stephens County Historical Museum (196 Main Street; open Tues., Thurs., Sat. 2–5:30) features Indian artifacts, pioneer home furnishings, farm equipment, carriages, Civil War items. Interesting old oil field equipment is also displayed on the lawn in front of the Halliburton Research Center on US 81 at the south edge of the city.

Annual events, largely reflecting the area's agricultural heritage, include: Livestock Show (March), Championship All Girls Rodeo (early summer), County Fair (September), and Elks Invitational Golf Tournament (Labor Day). Water sports in the area center on four large lakes east and north of town (over 3,400 surface-acres in all). They include: Duncan (8 mi. E), and Humphreys, Chisholm Trail, and Fuqua (see **Marlow**). For further information on Duncan and **Stephens County** write or visit the Duncan Chamber of Commerce, 911 Walnut, Duncan, Ok. 73533.

Dunlap (Harper Co., on US 270, 5 mi. W of **Fort Supply,** see Map 3). A tiny rural community established in 1913 and named for homesite developer Homer H. Dunlap.

Durant (Bryan Co. seat, pop. 11,118, at junc. of US 69 & 75 with US 70, see Map 6). Booming today on the strength of agriculture, industry, education, and recreation, Durant began in 1882 with arrival of the M-K-T Railroad, which established Durant Station on land owned by the prominent Choctaw, Dickson Durant. The rich black soil of the **Washita** and **Red River** valleys early made the new town an important agricultural center. And today the marketing and processing of meat, peanuts, milk, feed grains, and other farm products help keep it prosperous. A 36-inch-long, foot-thick aluminum peanut on a granite monument in front of City Hall honors the county's peanut industry.

In recent years, however, industrial diversification has added significant payrolls in such fields as electronics, automotive equipment, women's wear, and construction machinery. A giant LeTourneau manufacturing facility is the city's latest.

Southeastern Oklahoma State University, which opened in 1909 as one of Oklahoma's six teachers' colleges, has expanded greatly in recent years. Its 58-acre campus on the north edge of the city now accommodates some 3,800 students. Along with the more traditional academic fields, Southeastern recognizes its rich Indian heritage by providing an important center of study for Choctaw and Chickasaw tribal history and culture. Oklahoma Presbyterian College, on the west edge of Durant, was long a preparatory school for girls. It closed as a college in 1966, is now owned by the Chickasaw Nation. The main building, now restored, accommodates the tribal headquarters and a small museum.

Durant calls itself the City of Magnolias. Its streets are lined with thousands of the fragrant trees, and they not only add beauty but also are appropriately complementary to the many white frame, galleried homes that dot the town and underscore its strong Old South charm.

Durant's sport and cultural activities center on the Southeastern campus. The city library, however, dedicated to former governor and Durant native Robert L. Williams, has a collection of his personal effects. Annual events include an arts festival (October), Little Dixie golf tournament (late June) and Bryan County Fair (mid-September). Rodeos, as throughout Oklahoma, are also scheduled regularly. Although the city has both municipal and college sport and recreation facilities, they are often overshadowed by the sprawling **Texoma Reservoir** a few minutes to the west.

Durham (Roger Mills Co., pop. 75, 2 mi. N of OK 33, see Map 3). A tiny trade center that serves an isolated farming/ranching area. Now reduced pretty much to a post office (established in 1902), a picturesque general store in the Early Americana style, a few churches, and a clutch of residences, its main street offers the best panoramic view available of the rugged **Antelope Hills** and **Canadian River** country to the north.

Southeast of the town (inquire locally) is the ranch home of Oklahoma's best-known primitive painter, the late Augusta Metcalfe. Her son, Howard Metcalfe, still operates the ranch and maintains a Pioneer Museum.

Dustin (Hughes Co., pop. 502, at junc. of OK 9 & OK 84, see Map 7). A small trade center for a large, rugged area between the **North** and **South Canadian** rivers. Shortly after the turn of the century it became a modest rail center with the crossing here of the Kansas, Oklahoma and Gulf and the Fort Smith and Western lines (see **Boley**). In 1904 the town changed its name from Spokogee in order to honor Henry C. Dustin, a FS&W official. The promotional ploy failed; the railroad was abandoned in 1939.

Dwight Mission (Sequoyah Co., 7 mi. NW of *Sallisaw*, see Map 5). The Presbyterian Mission Board established an Indian mission and school here in 1830 shortly after the Cherokees began arriving from their former homes in the southeastern states. They maintained the coeducational school, for Indians of many tribes, for over a century. It is now a church retreat grounds.

None of the original buildings still stand. However, logs contained in one of the earliest structures are incorporated into a replica cabin that serves as a small, informal museum. Visitors are welcome to the grounds. In the heart of the Cookson Hills, it is one of eastern Oklahoma's prettiest spots. The mission was named for Timothy Dwight, president of Yale University.

Eagletown (McCurtain Co., pop. 500, on US 70, see Map 6). One of the oldest and for many years one of the most important towns in Oklahoma. The community was first settled about 1820, when the area was still part of Arkansas Territory. Just south of the present village, Stockbridge Mission was established in 1837 by Rev. Cyrus Byington. Here the veteran missionary produced his monumental *Dictionary of the Choctaw Language.*

So-called "old" Eagle Town meanwhile—on the west side of *Mountain Fork River* and just north of present US 70—was the site of Bethabara Mission, established by the Presbyterians in 1832 as the first for the Choctaws. Missionary Loring S. Williams became the first postmaster when mail service was established in 1834. (Eagle Town post office was later moved to present Eagletown, which became the officially accepted spelling of the name in 1892.)

The mission grounds at Bethabara Crossing of the river also served as seat of Eagle County in the Choctaw Nation from 1850 to 1907. The log courthouse and pin oak "whipping tree" that once stood here have long since disappeared. Still standing, however, is the impressive two-story house built in 1884 by Choctaw chief Jefferson Gardner. Nearby is a cypress tree (100 feet tall, 45 feet in circumference) said to be one of the largest in the country. The 2,000-year-old giant served as a sentinel beside Bethabara Crossing to mark the end of the "Trail of Tears" for the Choctaws during their 1831–34 removal from Mississippi.

None of the historic old buildings in present Eagletown itself survive. But the history-minded visitor will be interested in the old cemetery just north of the town and the Howell burying ground nearby.

Eakly (Caddo Co., pop. 228, just NE of junc. of OK 58 and OK 152, see Map 8). A bustling cotton and peanut community in the fertile, well-irrigated valley of Cobb Creek. The post office, established in 1902, is a misspelling of Akly Montague, daughter of an early resident. Isolation from nearby larger towns enables the community to maintain a complete school system.

Along with "goobers," Eakly is known far and wide—farther and wider than a population of 228 would seem to justify—for "gobblers." Specifically, "gobblers" are members of the Eakly Gobbler Lodge, a light-hearted fun-and-games sort of social club, started back in 1928 by a retired medicine show operator. It has an ants-to-the-honeypot attraction for visiting politicians and hopeful traveling salesmen. Affiliate Gobbler Lodges have sprung up in various other places, but Eakly remains the club's national headquarters. And, presumably, should the need arise, its international headquarters as well.

Earlsboro (Pottawatomie Co., pop. 246, on OK 9-A at junc. with US 270 and OK 9, see Map 7). Although it dates back to the 1890's, Earlsboro (for James Earls, a popular local Negro barber, according to historian George H. Shirk) didn't come into its own until the 1920's, when the Greater *Seminole* Field was developed. Producing wells dot the area, but little other evidence remains of one of the state's most feverish oil booms.

Old North Tower, at Central State University in Edmond.

Edith (Woods Co., off US 64 NW of *Freedom,* see Map 3). A tiny community beside the *Cimarron River* that shares, with *Freedom,* a modest sub-industry in the marketing of salt from that river's extensive underground beds. The name honors the wife of townsite owner W. W. Vincent.

Edmond (Oklahoma Co., pop. 16,633, at junc. of US 77 and OK 66, see Map 4). A child of the "Run of '89" that opened Old Oklahoma to settlement—like *Oklahoma City, Norman,* and *Guthrie*—Edmond claims a number of Oklahoma Territory "firsts": church, newspaper (the *Edmond Sun*), public schools, and public library. However, in 1887, even before the opening, it was a watering and coaling station and cattle shipping point on the newly arrived Santa Fe Railroad.

Edmond is best known today as an educational center and a desirable suburban community on sprawling Oklahoma City's north side. Central State University opened its doors as a "Normal School" in 1891, the first institution of higher learning in Oklahoma Territory. The third largest today, with some 12,000 students, its landmark is Old North Tower. Completed in 1896, at a cost of $31,100, the handsome brownstone structure was completely restored in 1968, for continued academic use, at a cost of $308,898! Oklahoma Christian College moved to Edmond from *Bartlesville* in 1958. In the 1970's it comprised 20 modern buildings on a 200-acre campus. Operated by the Church of Christ, the college enrolled some 1,100 students in 40 major areas of study, but now has moved to *Oklahoma City.*

Sporting and cultural events tend to revolve around the two colleges. Central State has an annual Indian Heritage Week in October. But Edmond stages livestock and horse shows in March, a miniature rodeo in April, and an IRA-approved rodeo in early July. Seven municipal parks and the $1 million Kicking Bird Golf Course provide complete recreational facilities.

El Reno (Canadian Co. seat, pop. 14,510 on I 40 at junc. of US 66 & 270 and US 81, see Map 4). The "Reno" comes from Major General Jesse L. Reno, Union officer who died at Antietam. He was honored in the naming of *Fort Reno* in 1874. Reno City took its name from the fort when it sprang into being in early 1889, across the *North Canadian River* from present El Reno. But it was promptly abandoned when, following its refusal to share the townsite with the approaching Choctaw, Oklahoma and Gulf Railroad (now Rock Island), El Reno itself appeared. The railroad swung south into the more cooperative town. Most Reno Cityans soon followed, skidding their buildings—including one three-story hotel—across the shallow river to the new town. Until the Rock Island went bankrupt in 1980, El Reno was one of the state's largest railroad centers. Activity is greatly reduced today.

Opened as a result of the 1889 land rush into Old Oklahoma, El Reno itself hosted hordes of homeseekers in two subsequent openings: that of the Cheyenne and Arapaho reservation (by run) in 1892, and the giant Kiowa-Apache-Comanche reservation (by lottery) in 1901. With land figuring so prominently in its founding, the produce of the land—its growing, harvesting, storing, processing, and transporting—has pretty well determined its economic development. Its two large flour mills are presently shut down, but El Reno is still a large wheat storage point. Feed mills, fertilizer plants, implement dealers, cattle feeder and stock trailer manufacturers—all are important businesses.

One large, non-agricultural employer: the Fort Reno Federal Reformatory (for young, first-time offenders) on the west edge of town. It has 1,000 inmates, a staff of 275.

El Reno has some 800 acres in parks. Adams Park on the northwest contains a 3,000-seat coliseum, high school stadium, the Canadian County Fairgrounds, an 1876 log cabin from nearby Fort Reno, and a small zoo. A new 175-acre lake is the feature of El Reno Lake Park on the city's west side. It offers fishing, boating, extensive picnic and camping facilities.

Much of the area's colorful history is captured in the new Canadian County Historical Society Museum, housed in the still-handsome red brick Rock Island depot (10–5 Fri., 1:30–5 Sun.; special tours for groups of ten or more by calling 405-262-3550). Special Sunday afternoon feature: vintage silent movies in the "Popcorn Theater."

Proximity to **Concho** and the presence of many Indians living and working in the city assure El Reno a strong Indian atmosphere. This is most pronounced in mid-June, when the Inter-Tribal Indian Powwow is held.

Nearby points of interest: **Fort Reno, Concho, Darlington.**

Eldon (Cherokee Co., at junc. of US 62 and OK 51, 7 mi. E of **Tahlequah,** see Map 5). At the base of scenic Eldon Hill, the community of Eldon is pretty well reduced today to a lone, congenial country store.

To the west, US 62 climbs a heavily wooded ridge for a spectacular view of

Schoolroom in Old Town Museum, Elk City.

Barren Fork Creek and its fertile valley before dropping down into the valley of the **Illinois River,** which it crosses just east of **Tahlequah.** This is one of eastern Oklahoma's most beautiful stretches of highway, especially in April when the dogwood and redbud are in full bloom.

Eldorado (Jackson Co., pop. 737, at junc. of OK 34 & 44 and OK 5, see Map 8). An isolated farming/ranching community in the far southwestern corner of the county. It was founded in 1890 and probably got its name because of the rich native grasses that were so coveted by early-day cattlemen on both sides of **Red River.**

Elgin (Comanche Co., pop. 840, at junc. of US 277 and OK 17, see Map 8). Like **Fletcher,** an agricultural community established in 1902 with the coming of the Frisco Railroad. The name "honors" the Illinois city. (Though unlikely as a name, Ceegee—which lasted but a few months—would have been more likely as an "honor." C. G. Jones, for whom the town of **Jones** was named, was an important early-day **Oklahoma City** civic leader.) Also like **Fletcher,** the town sagged in the 1930's with the decline of King Cotton; has recently grown on the strength of the expansion of **Fort**

Room in Old Town Museum, Elk City.

Sill. Cattle raising has become increasingly important in both communities.

Elk City (Beckham Co., pop. 7,323, at junc. of I 40 and US 66 with OK 6 & 34, see Map 8). With **Clinton,** the principal trade center of west-central Oklahoma. It got its start in 1901 when the nearby settlement of Crowe moved here to the newly arrived Choctaw, Oklahoma and Gulf Railroad (now the Rock Island) and changed its name to Busch, to honor the St. Louis beer magnate. Fittingly enough, the name Elk City came in 1907, with statehood—and prohibition.

Although oil was found in this area as early as 1899, it was not until late 1947 that the important Elk City Field was opened—for a time the state's deepest. The economy remains basically agricultural, however, with cotton, beef cattle, and small grains leading the way. Just northwest of the city is the pioneering **Sandstone Creek** watershed project.

Elk City is also home of the famed Beutler Brothers ranch (off OK 34 just north of town). The Beutlers started promoting rodeos in 1927 and are today among the largest and most successful producers of rodeo stock and performers in the country. Visitors are welcomed to the ranch, as they are to Old Town Museum (on US 66 at west edge of the city). Housed in a restored Victorian home of the early 1900's, it features extensive pioneer and historical materials, along with the Beutler Brothers Rodeo Hall (Tues.–Sat. 10–5, Sun. 2–5). The special events calendar features a Quarter Horse Show in mid-May, Indian Powwow and Arts & Crafts Show in June, and the prestigious Rodeo of Champions (started in the 1930's) in early September.

Jess Willard was a mule team freighter in the Elk City area for a time before going into professional fighting and becoming world's heavyweight champion (1915–19).

Ellis County (northwestern Oklahoma, along the Texas border, see Map 3). Area, 1,222 sq. mi.; pop., 5,129; county seat, **Arnett.** Created at statehood in 1907, and including much of old Day County, it was named for Albert H. Ellis, vice president of state's Constitutional Convention.

Top travel lures: ghost town of **Grand,** bird hunting.

Elmer (Jackson Co., pop. 138, on OK 5, 11 mi. S of **Altus,** see Map 8). A dwindling agricultural community, established in 1902 with the building of the "Orient" line, the Kansas City, Mexico and Orient Railway (present Santa Fe) of which Elmer W. Slocum was an official.

Elmore City (Garvin Co., pop. 653, at junc. of OK 29 and OK 74, see Map 7). A community that dates back to 1890, owes much of its existence today to the relatively late development of nearby oil and gas fields. J. O. Elmore was an early-day resident. "City" was added to "Elmore" in 1911, with a seemingly limited salutary effect on the town's growth.

Elmwood (Beaver Co., pop. 15, at junc. of US 270 and OK 3 & 23, see Map 2). One of the county's oldest post offices. Established in 1888, Elmwood is now only a cluster of crossroads stores and homes.

Emet (Johnston Co., pop. 60, on OK 78, 11 mi. SE of *Tishomingo,* see Map 7). Although now only a store or two and a scattering of houses, Emet has been an important Chickasaw Indian settlement for well over a century. To the west, Pleasant Grove, a Methodist mission, was established in 1844. Site contains the grave of Chief (1852–56) Jackson Frazier.

On the northwest edge of Emet is the so-called "White House of the Chickasaw Nation." Built in 1895, the comfortable white frame home of Governor Douglas H. Johnston was the center of social and political life in the Nation from 1898, when he was first elected governor, until statehood in 1907. By Act of Congress, Johnston was then made lifetime governor of the Chickasaws.

The nine-room White House was familiar to two former governors of Oklahoma. The late William H. Murray was married (to a niece of Governor Johnston) in the mansion's front parlor. And Johnston Murray, his son and also a chief executive of the state (1951–55) was born in the west bedroom. Now the property of the Oklahoma Historical Society, the restored mansion, containing much of its original furnishings, is open to the public.

Enid (Garfield Co. seat, pop. 44,008, on US 60, 64, & 81, see Map 4). Enid was another of Oklahoma's famed "instant cities," a bustling tent city that emerged seemingly full-blown from the virgin prairie on September 16, 1893. At high noon that day the Cherokee Outlet was thrown open to settlement by "run," a run that attracted approximately 100,000 contestants for home and business sites in the city-to-be itself, as well as for quarter-sections of land in the surrounding countryside. In all, a 60 x 90-mile area was settled that day, some 6.5 million acres comprising all or part of eleven present-day Oklahoma counties.

Enid had been designated a government land office well in advance of the opening. The Rock Island Railroad was already serving the area. The city became at once the most important in northwestern Oklahoma and, growing steadily if unspectacularly over the years, it has never given up that position. As seat of **Garfield County,** it has of course gained immeasurably from the vast natural resources that surround it. The county is one of the nation's greatest wheat producers, and Enid has long been the state's most important center for the storing, processing, and marketing of the grain. (Its over 66 million bushels of storage is one of the largest in the country.) A leading cattlemen's magazine recently claimed that Garfield has more purebred cattle breeders than any other county. And Shell Oil Company has stated that the Schroeder Lease in the county's Garber Field has produced more oil in dollar value than any other quarter-section of land in the history of the oil industry.

Two additional "industries" support Enid's economy. Phillips University was founded in 1907. Today its 140-acre campus on the city's east side contains 19 buildings, accommodates some 1,500 students. The University, with its professional personnel and physical plant, plays a strong role in the city's social and cultural life.

Vance Air Force Base, an undergraduate pilot training base of the Air Training Command, was located south of Enid in 1941. Its $8 million annual payroll is now shared by over 2,000 military and civilian employees. Other Enid industries include a flour mill, two refineries, a manufacturer of portable drilling rigs, and other concerns generally related to some aspect of either agriculture or petroleum.

Sedate as the city is today, it was not always so. Enid waged one of the state's better known "townsite wars." The original site was present North Enid, and it was here the Rock Island built its depot. When a squabble erupted over land claims, however, the government ordered the townsite located 3 miles to the south, and it was here the land office, courthouse, and post office were located. But the Rock Island refused to recognize the government's ruling. It continued to run its trains through South Enid without stopping until July 13, 1894, when local partisans sawed through enough timber supports to weaken a bridge and derail a freight. In what is believed to be a unique action, a presidential proclamation finally validated the new site's claim and South Enid became Enid.

No such judicial determination has been made as to how the town received its name. Widely believed is the story that a Rock Island official, fond of Tennyson's "Idylls of the King," felt Geraint's wife deserved the honor of having Oklahoma's new city named for her. Others, however, claim it all started when a group of cattle drovers stopped at Government Springs—long a favorite watering hole on the Chisholm Trail—and one of the cowboys turned the DINE sign on the cook tent to make it read ENID. (There are even some who feel the name was simply devised by the fabricators of crossword puzzles to give them four easy letters to work with!)

Government Springs Park remains one of the city's favorite playgrounds to this day. It contains the Enid zoo, a small lake (boating), sunken garden, and picnic areas. The Museum of the Cherokee Strip, a university/city co-operative effort, moved into its handsome new building adjacent to the springs in 1975. It exhibits Indian artifacts as well as materials pertaining to the settlement of the Strip. (Hours: 9–12, 1–5 Mon.–Fri., 2–5 Sun.) The park is only a few blocks from downtown.

Meadowlake Park on the south edge of the city contains 235 acres, surrounds a 14-acre lake, offers a golf course, miniature train, other sport and recreation facilities. University Lake golf course (9 holes) is on the Phillips campus. Swimming is available at two pools: Owens and Champlin.

Of special interest at the new $500,000 Enid Public Library is the Marquis James Room, honoring the notable writer who grew up in the Short Grass Country of northwestern Oklahoma.

Among his best books is *The Cherokee Strip,* the appealing story of small-town boyhood in the strip. Also in the James Room are mementos of Clyde Cessna, one of Enid's best-known early citizens. An Enid automobile salesman, he designed and flew his own airplane in 1911, went on to become a well-known barnstormer in the heady early days of aviation, eventually led development of the world's largest manufacturers of corporate and private planes.

Enid is closely associated with two festive special events. The Tri-State Music Festival, inaugurated by Phillips University in 1932, is held on the campus three days each year in late April or early May. It attracts thousands of high school musicians from Kansas, Texas, and Oklahoma for vigorous competition in all phases of vocal and instrumental music. Not so venerable an event, but one rapidly attracting even wider attentions, is the annual November Grand National Quail Hunt. Headquartered in Enid but spreading northwest over private ranches to the **Great Salt Plains** near *Jet,* it is now a "prestige" event, invitation only, that draws prominent politicians, sport and entertainment personalities, and assorted celebrities from all over the country.

Enterprise (Haskell Co., pop. 100, at junc. of OK 9 & 71, see Map 6). Crossroads community, founded in 1890, it serves today as access to the 3,180-foot-long dam on the *Canadian River* that creates *Eufaula Reservoir,* Oklahoma's largest lake.

Eram (Okmulgee Co., pop. 45, just N of US 62, 11 mi. E of *Okmulgee,* see Map 5). An almost non-existent community that started life in 1913, thrived briefly with the development of nearby oil fields. Historian George H. Shirk is the authority for crediting its curious name to Ed Oates, a local Creek, who coined Eram from the first letter in the names of his four children: Eugene, Roderick, Anthony, and Marie.

Erick (Beckham Co., pop. 1,285, off I 40 at junc. of US 66 and OK 30, see Map 8). An agricultural community established in late 1901 by a townsite company (Beeks Erick was its president) working in advance of the Oklahoma Western Railroad (now Rock Island), then building westward toward the Texas Panhandle. The area was well known to cattlemen, however, many years earlier. Southwest of the present town at Salt Springs, cattle herds being driven north from Texas were frequently stopped to allow the animals to lick up needed salt. Evaporation of salt-laden waters for commercial salt (livestock, ice cream making, street de-icing) continues to this day in the area.

Largest "employer" in the Erick area, however, is Olin Wilhelm. The Wilhelm Bee Farm (1 mi. W, 1 mi. N) has some 500,000 workers producing honey in 500 hives. Visitors are welcome to tour the plant, observe the bees at work in special glass-sided hives, inspect the machinery used in preparing the honey for sale and in the making of beeswax candles.

Erin Springs (Garvin Co., pop. 100, off OK 76, 2 mi. S of *Lindsay,* see Map 7). One of the county's oldest communities, Erin Springs was settled in 1875 on an old wagon trail between *Pauls Valley* and *Fort Cobb.* It took its name from the homeland of its best-known citizen, Frank Murray.

A rancher who branched into many other frontier enterprises, Murray, before his death in 1892, had become one of the most influential men in this corner of the Chickasaw Nation. In 1879–80 he built the imposing three-story home that is today the town's sole claim to fame. (The recent rebuilding of a section of OK 76 seems to have put in limbo the namesake spring itself.)

After Murray's death the home was occupied by his son-in-law, Lewis Lindsay, for whom nearby *Lindsay* was named. Sold by the family to the Oklahoma Historical Society in 1967, the Murray-Lindsay Mansion has now been restored and opened to visitors (Tues.–Fri. 9–5, Sat.–Sun. 2–5).

Eucha Reservoir (on US 59, 6 mi. S of *Jay,* in Delaware County, see Map 5). A 3,190-acre reservoir owned by the

The Murray Mansion in Erin Springs.

City of Tulsa, that has long been a favorite of eastern Oklahoma fishermen. Facilities, most of them on the upper reaches of the lake, include picnic and camping areas, swimming pool and bathhouse, fishing piers, marina, and restaurant. The reservoir is on Spavinaw Creek, above a companion water supply pool, and was long known as Upper Spavinaw, before the name was changed to honor a one-time Cherokee principal chief. Address: Upper Spavinaw Recreation Area, Jay, OK 74347.

Eufaula (McIntosh Co. seat, pop. 2,355, at junc. of US 69 and OK 9, see Map 5). Named for an old Creek town in Alabama, Eufaula began in 1872 with the arrival of the Missouri-Kansas-Texas Railroad (the Katy), first to cross Indian Territory. Its roots go back somewhat farther, however. North Fork Town, at the crossing of the old Texas Road (see *Checotah*) with a branch of the California Road, had been settled by the Creeks shortly after their arrival from the Southeast in 1836. When the railroad bypassed it, the town simply moved to the new settlement.

The town has long been an Indian educational center. Influential in the cultural development of the Creeks

Dusk on an arm of Eufaula Reservoir, Oklahoma's largest lake, with 102,500 surface acres and 600 miles of shoreline.

from 1849 until it burned in 1889, was nearby Asbury Mission. Its successor, the Eufaula Boarding School, was opened by the Creek Nation in 1892. To this institution, built and maintained by Indians, the early-day village, lacking a school system of its own, for several years sent its boys and girls. It is an instance perhaps unique in the history of Oklahoma.

In Eufaula is published the *Indian Journal,* founded at **Muskogee** as a tribal organ in 1876. It is the state's oldest newspaper. A contributor to it for several years, before his premature death in 1908, was Alexander Posey, the Creek political and educational leader who is generally recognized as one of the finest of all Indian poets.

Travel and recreation have given the town an economic boost in recent years. When officially dedicated in 1964, *Eufaula Reservoir* was the nation's seventh largest man-made lake. Its octopus-like tentacles virtually surround the town.

On it are located two of the state's most complete resort facilities: *Fountainhead State Park* to the northwest and *Arrowhead State Park* to the south. The four-lane stretch of US 69 from **Checotah** south to **McAlester,** with sight of the sprawling lake all the way, is one of Oklahoma's most scenic highways.

Eufaula Reservoir (off I 40 and US 69 in McIntosh and Haskell Counties, see Maps 5 and 6). Oklahoma's largest lake (102,500 surface acres) was created in 1964 with a 114-foot-high dam on the *Canadian River* just below the junction of its north and south branches. A power/navigation/flood control affair, it sprawls octopus-like through a rolling, generally wooded area. Its primary resort areas are clustered around its two major state parks, but recreational development is expanding rapidly along 600 miles of shoreline.

Facilities: two deluxe lodges and related facilities at state parks, a score of public use areas maintained by the Corps of Engineers, and numerous visitor accommodations and services in the towns of the area and on or near the major highways serving it. Addresses: Arrowhead State Park, Canadian, OK 74425; Fountainhead State Park, Checotah, OK 74426; U.S. Corps of Engineers, Box 61, Tulsa, OK 74102; Lake Eufaula Ass'n., Box 759, McAlester, OK 74501.

Fairfax (Osage Co., pop. 1,889, Ok 18, see Map 4). Only a cluster of buildings housing perhaps a dozen families in 1902, Fairfax became a town when the Santa Fe Railroad located a station there rather than in nearby **Gray Horse**. Oil production in the 1920's added to the area's predominantly ranching economy. With addition of several small industries in recent years the town is now one of the county's most progressive.

At the southwest corner of Fairfax is the grave and statue of Chief Ne-Ka-Wa-She-Tun-Ka, the last Osage chieftain to receive the complete Osage burial ceremony. This included the killing of his favorite horse and the

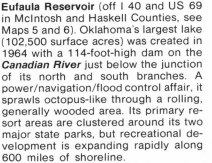

placing of a human scalp in the grave. Securing the necessary scalp, that of a Wichita chief in this case, understandably precipitated an intertribal incident that led the government to forbid all scalp-taking.

Fairland (Ottawa Co., pop. 814, on US 60, see Map 5). A pleasant little trading center on the Frisco Railroad that in recent years has benefitted greatly from recreational development in the Honey Creek and other nearby *Grand Lake* resort areas. But the area also prospers from cattle raising on the broad surrounding expanses of rich bluestem grass that gave the town its descriptive name in 1891 when it was established.

Fairview (Major Co. seat, pop. 2,894, on US 60 and OK 8, see Map 3). A prosperous farming and industrial community, established in 1894, that takes its name from its principal nearby scenic attraction, the *Glass Mountains*. It is located on a flat, fertile plain that early attracted agriculturally-inclined Mennonite farmers (see *Meno*) and their influence is strong in the area.

One such family, the brothers Henry and David Martens, maintains a noteworthy collection of antique tractors (just south of the Fairview airport). The Fairview museum is housed in the seventy-year-old, restored Frisco depot that once served nearby *Southard*.

An international flying group that originated in Oklahoma and has strong ties to Fairview is the International Flying Farmers. (David Martens is a past president.) IFF developed from the Oklahoma Flying Farmers, formed in 1944, largely through the efforts of the late Dr. Henry G. Bennett, then president of Oklahoma A.&M. College (now Oklahoma State University). The organization spread rapidly to Kansas, Nebraska, Iowa, and other Plains states where distances were relatively great and farmers relatively affluent. Three years later the national convention of state organizations drew 407 planes to Stillwater from four states and three foreign countries. A few years later Fairview held its first Fairview Fly-In, that draws heavily on flying farmers.

Held annually since then, the two-day meeting, starting with a fly-in breakfast, attracts over 200 planes and up to 700 persons.

Two industrial plant tours are free to visitors weekdays 9 to 5: Hallren Poultry and Creamery, one of the state's largest processors of turkeys; and Waldon, Inc., manufacturer of agricultural equipment and industrial tractors.

Fallis (Lincoln Co., pop. 39, on county road 6 mi. W of *Wellston*, see Map 4). A sleepy rural community that was a bustling railroad center for a time after the turn of the century when the Missouri, Kansas and Texas and the Fort Smith and Western lines crossed here. Settled as Mission in 1892, for nearby Mission Creek, it changed its name in 1894 to honor Postmaster William H. Fallis.

Fanshawe (LeFlore Co., pop. 199, on US 270, 10 mi. W of *Wister*, see Map 6). A railroad siding community dating from the early 1890's when the Choctaw Coal and Railway Company built westward through the Choctaw Nation.

Fargo (Ellis Co., pop. 262, on OK 15, see Map 3). A small agricultural community on the east-west main line of the Santa Fe Railroad. Although the town has had more name changes than most, none seems to have been too effective as a stimulant to growth. Whitehead, established in 1893 and named for E. E. Whitehead, an early-day druggist, became Oleta in 1901, for Oleta Ooley, daughter of an early settler. In 1905 Oleta gave way in turn to Fargo, presumably for the famed western express company, Wells Fargo.

Farris (Atoka Co., pop. 100, on OK 3 & 7, 18 mi. SE of *Atoka*, see Map 6). A scattered settlement dating from the turn of the century. The name honors John L. Farris, the first postmaster. Near the settlement is the unmarked grave of Captain Atoka, a Choctaw sub-chief who lived in this area and for whom the town and county of Atoka were named.

Near Farris, too, is the 5,190-acre

McLeod Honor Farm, a branch of the state's penal system. McLeod opened in 1962, now houses some 230 inmates without walls or security fences. Nearly a fourth of its acreage is under cultivation, the rest is in woodlands and cattle pasture. All contribute to the food needs of the other institutions.

Faxon (Comanche Co., pop. 121, on OK 36, 18 mi. SW of *Lawton*, see Map 8). An almost-vanished farming community established in 1902, once served by a now-abandoned Rock Island Railroad branch line. Ralph Faxon was the secretary of Senator Chester Long of Kansas.

Fay (Dewey Co., pop. 120, on OK 33, see Map 3). A small town near one of the relatively few bridged crossings of the *Canadian River*. It was named for Fay Fiscos, son of the first postmaster in 1894, two years after this Cheyenne and Arapaho reservation was opened to white settlement. Interestingly enough, the town's leading "industry," after agriculture, is a new craft shop that produces Indian ceremonial shawls and blankets and recordings of traditional Indian songs and music of most of the western Indian tribes. There is a showroom open to visitors.

Felt (Cimarron Co., pop. 100, on US 56 & 64, 20 mi. SW of *Boise City*, see Map 2). An isolated farming/ranching community that owes its establishment in 1925 to the Santa Fe Railroad, then building southwestward from *Boise City*. It was named for C. F. W. Felt, chief engineer of the line. Currumpa and Cienequillia Creeks, both of which head in New Mexico, join half a dozen miles northwest of Felt to form *Beaver River*, which, in turn, becomes the *North Canadian River* upon leaving the *Oklahoma Panhandle*. South and west of Felt are isolated sections of Rita Blanca National Grassland.

Discovery, in early 1974, of a Clovis Culture spear point indicates that Indians roamed this area as long as ten or eleven thousand years ago. Prehistoric pictographs and petroglyphs are not uncommon along the Currumpa.

Near the river, northwest of Felt, Juan Cruz Lujan established a crude ranch in 1879, the county's first permanent homesite.

Ferdinandina (Kay Co., 6 mi. E of *Newkirk*, see Map 4). Nothing to see today—although there is hope that there may be someday—Ferdinandina is something in the nature of a "ghost town." Here, where Deer Creek flows into the *Arkansas River*, French commercial interests established a trading post in the early eighteenth century that was almost surely Oklahoma's first white settlement. From 1740 to 1750 it may well have been at least a temporary home for as many as 300 traders, explorers, and Indians.

The site is on private property. Archeologists have done considerable research on the settlement, but much more remains to be done before visitors can be admitted. Thousands of relics from Ferdinandina are now in the possession of the Oklahoma Historical Society.

Feyodi Creek Recreation Area. See *Keystone Reservoir*.

Fillmore (Johnston Co., pop. 100, on OK 48-A, 14 mi. NE of *Tishomingo*, see Map 7). A sprawling, roadside community, established at the turn of the century and named for a local Chickasaw Indian, Elias Fillmore.

Finley (Pushmataha Co., pop. 50, on US 271 and OK 2, see Map 6). A scattered community on one of the state's most scenic roads. Big Cedar Falls is a mile south of town. Sulphur Springs nearby was the seat of old Cedar County in the Choctaw Nation and a rest station on the military road from Fort Smith to *Fort Towson*, marked out by Captain John Stuart in 1832. Sidney W. Finley was first postmaster of the town itself in 1903.

Fishing. Legends die hard. But Oklahoma today is a far cry indeed from the sere wasteland John Steinbeck pictured so dramatically in *Grapes of Wrath*. Over the state are more than a million acres of water backed up behind dams. Add to this total some 333,000 farm ponds, scores of city reservoirs, and half a dozen major river systems, and Oklahoma ends up with a greater acreage of impounded water than Minnesota!

Water, of course, means fish. And fishing. And thanks to a vigorous stocking program, Oklahoma has it in abundance, virtually year-round. Among the more popular sport fish species are black bass (largemouth and smallmouth), crappie, white bass, striped bass, several varieties of catfish, perch, walleye, and trout.

For complete information on seasons, license fees, and regulations write Department of Wildlife Conservation, 1801 N. Lincoln Blvd., Oklahoma City, OK 73105.

Fittstown (Pontotoc Co., pop. 200, on OK 99, 12 mi. S of *Ada*, see Map 7). A scattered community that, like *Harden City*, owes its short-lived boom to the development of the rich Fitts oil field in the mid-1930's. John Fitts, for whom the town and pool were named, was a petroleum geologist.

Three miles southwest of Fittstown is historic Byrd's Mill Spring, present source of *Ada*'s water supply. But the huge spring (up to 20 million gallons a day) was known to the Indians long before Europeans came to this area. The Choctaws and Chickasaws made it a popular camping site when they came west, and Chickasaw Frank Byrd established a water-powered grist mill here in the 1870's. This canyon-laced area of woods and clear-flowing streams has long been a popular recreation playground.

Fletcher (Comanche Co., pop. 950, on US 277, see Map 8). Agricultural community established on the Frisco Railroad in 1902 and named for Fletcher Dodge, an early resident. Booming into the 1930's on the strength of then-extensive cotton production in the area, the town came on hard times in the Dust Bowl days, has only recently begun to recover its losses, thanks in large measure to the mushrooming expansion of **Fort Sill** that began during World War II.

Flint (Delaware Co., just N of US 59, 5 mi. E of *Kansas*, see Map 5). An almost non-existent town today, Flint has known human activity for more than a century. The Beck, or Hildebrand, Mill was established here on Flint Creek well before the Civil War. In time, a sizeable little town grew up around it.

The site today is well worth the time of the unhurried motorist. Commercial activity is limited to a general store on the highway. To the north a gravel road beside Flint Creek leads to the picturesque ruins of the town's original business district, a few residences, and the still impressive old mill building, now on the National Register of Historic Places. At various times the town was also known as Beckwith and Hilderbrand (*sic*), for the owners of the mill.

Fonda (Dewey Co., 7 mi. E of *Seiling* see Map 3). Only a few houses now alongside an isolated county road, Fonda flourished briefly the first decade of the century. Missionaries worked among the Cheyennes and Arapahoes then, and many Indians still live here along the **North Canadian River**.

Foraker (Osage Co., pop. 52, on county road E of OK 18, see Map 4). A near-ghost town in the rolling Osage ranch country, what with abandonment of the historic Midland Valley Railroad in 1968 and the closing of its school. Post office was established here in 1903, and named for Ohio senator Joseph B. Foraker. Immediately north of the town is the vast K. S. Adams Ranch and Phillips Agricultural Demonstration Project.

Forgan (Beaver Co., pop. 496, on US 64 & 270 just W of junc. with OK 23, see Map 2). A small but attractive trade and schooling center for a rich farm and ranching area. It came into being in 1912, with completion of the Wichita Falls and Northwestern Railway (now M-K-T) to this point. The name honors James B. Forgan, a Chicago banker who helped finance the line.

For a number of years the town was

Fort Cobb Reservoir (photograph by Fred W. Marvel, courtesy of Oklahoma Tourism Department).

Restored stockade at Fort Gibson (photograph by Marcel Lefebvre).

something of a rail center. The co-operatively-built Beaver, Meade and Englewood railroad (see **Beaver City**) joined the Katy here and in 1930 pushed westward 105 miles to **Keyes**. The Katy, which took over the BM&E after World War I, finally abandoned the entire 333-mile-long route from **Altus** in 1973. Last relic: the Katy depot on the east side of Forgan, now restored as a museum/restaurant.

Fort Arbuckle. See **Davis**.

Fort Cobb (Caddo Co., pop. 722, on OK 9, see Map 8). As a farming community, Cobb was established in 1899 in the fertile valley of the **Washita River**. In 1902 it added the word "Fort" to honor the U.S. military post that during the Civil War years occupied a site a mile to the east. No trace of it remains today. Fort Cobb (for Howell Cobb, President Buchanan's secretary of the treasury) was established in 1859, garrisoned until the Union forces abandoned this part of Indian Territory. It was used but briefly after the war, and quickly fell into ruins.

Today the town is best known as the southern gateway to the sport and recreation facilities provided by **Fort Cobb Reservoir**. And for the vast flights of crows that inhabit the reservoir area, much to the chagrin of local peanut and feed-grain growers. Latest "secret" weapon in the continuing guerrilla war

on the crows is the propane "shotgun," a harmless noise maker, the effectiveness of which is waning in proportion to the exposure of the wily bird to its firing. Despite this problem the area produces enough peanuts to stage an annual Caddo County Peanut Festival in early September.

Fort Cobb Reservoir (off OK 9 N of town of **Fort Cobb**, in Caddo and Washita Counties, see Map 8). A Bureau of Reclamation facility created in 1959 with a 101-foot-high dam on Cobb Creek. The 4,100-acre lake serves irrigation, municipal water supply, flood control, and recreation needs in an otherwise relatively dry area. The state maintains a 3,500-acre public hunting area and a 4,495-acre recreation area adjoining the lake.

Fort Cobb area special feature: the common crow. Crow hunting in Oklahoma is a major sport, and most activity is centered here where some 6 million of the big black birds spend the winter months. They begin to arrive in October, reach their maximum⁻ population in-early February. The state park provides a refuge, but hunters may set up in business in most other nearby areas. The birds are voracious eaters, and farmers around the reservoir generally welcome hunters.

Facilities: picnic and camping areas, 3 concrete boat ramps and other accesses around the lake, covered boat stalls, enclosed fishing dock, marina and rental boats, 9-hole golf course and pro shop, small aircraft landing strip. Address: Fort Cobb Recreation Area, Fort Cobb, OK 73038.

Fort Gibson (Muskogee Co., pop. 1,418, at junc. US 62 and OK 80, 4 miles NE of *Muskogee*, see Map 5). As the state's first military post and then as a town, Fort Gibson, with the area immediately surrounding it—historic Three Forks—has been the cradle of Oklahoma history from 1824.

The name honored Colonel George Gibson, head of the Army Commissary. With only a brief interruption during the Civil War the fort itself served until 1890. Fort Gibson National Cemetery is just off US 62 half a mile east of the town. Among its more interesting graves are those of Diana Rogers, Cherokee wife of Sam Houston (who operated a trading post near here called Wigwam Neosho in the early 1830's); Captain Billy Bowlegs (see *Bowlegs*), the famous Seminole warrior; and the mysterious Vivia Thomas, a girl from the east who masqueraded as a man in order to join the army and thus be near a sweetheart who had rejected her.

Today's visitor has two distinct "forts" to inspect, both on the north edge of the little agricultural community. The original fort was built of logs, and in the 1930's the National Fort Stockade Commission and the Oklahoma Historical Society combined to reconstruct a four-sided square stockade and barracks. These, with some exhibits and artifacts, are open to the public (daily 9-7) without charge. The second fort was of stone. Many of its buildings, dating from the Civil War period, are still impressive ruins while several others have been restored. One, the former commandant's house, dates

Old commissary at Fort Reno.

from 1867 and is open by appointment. The one-time hospital, a two-story frame affair built in 1871, has been privately developed as the House of History (daily 10-5, fee). Historical markers throughout the area retell much of its important story.

Fort Gibson Reservoir (off OK 51 E of *Wagoner*, in Wagoner and Cherokee Counties, see Map 5). A 19,000-acre lake created in 1953 by the Corps of Engineers as a power/flood control project on *Grand* (Neosho) *River*. The ruggedly scenic area around the 110-foot-high dam is accessible from OK 80 north of the historic town of *Fort Gibson*.

Primary resort development is to be found at *Sequoyah State Park*, off OK 51. However, Oklahoma also maintains a 303-acre lakeside recreation area SE of Wagoner—off OK 16. And the Corps of Engineers has scattered more than a score of public use areas around the lake's 225 miles of mostly wooded shoreline. The state, in addition, provides the 19,025-acre Fort Gibson Refuge and Public Hunting Area.

Facilities: complete resort amenities at the state park, extensive picnic,

Guardhouse where Geronimo was held prisoner at Fort Sill (photograph courtesy Fort Sill Museum).

camping, sport and recreational advantages at the other public use areas. Addresses: Sequoyah State Park, Hulbert, OK 74441; U.S. Corps of Engineers, Box 61, Tulsa, OK 74102; Sequoyah Bay Recreation Area, Route 2, Wagoner, OK 74467.

Fort McCulloch. See *Kenefick*.

Fort Nichols. See *Camp Nichols*.

Fort Reno (Canadian Co., just N of I 40 W of *El Reno*, see Map 4). Established in 1874 to protect the *Darlington* Indian School on the opposite bank of the North Canadian River, Fort Reno remained an active military post until 1948. In its later years it was the U.S. Army's largest remount station.

The U.S. Department of Agriculture and Oklahoma A.&M. College (now Oklahoma State University) took over the facility in 1949, establishing the Fort Reno Livestock Research Station. One thousand acres of the 6,800-acre reservation is now under cultivation in connection with crop research. Many of the old buildings remain around the grassy parade ground. Of particular interest is the two-story red brick commissary, terminus of Oklahoma's first telephone line, strung between Fort Reno and *Fort Sill* in 1879.

Also of interest is the Military Cemetery on a cedar-dotted knoll just west of the old post. It contains the grave of Ben Clark, the famed Indian scout, and—in a special section—70 graves of German and Italian soldiers who died in the southwestern prisoner-of-war camps during World War II. Tours of the experiment station can be arranged by the superintendent.

Fort Sill (Comanche Co., at Lawton, see Map 8). General Philip H. Sheridan established Fort Sill as a cavalry post in Indian Territory on January 8, 1869. As the frontier passed and the Kiowa-Comanche-Apache lands were opened to settlement, the fort became the home of the U.S. Army Field Artillery. Today the 95,000-acre military reservation, embracing a ruggedly beautiful section of the *Wichita Mountains*, is headquarters of the U.S. Army Field Artillery Center and of the so-called "University of Artillery." At this Field Artillery School and on an adjoining firing range new generations of artillerymen are learning tube, missile, and aerial gunnery.

Though a bustling military installation, Fort Sill allows almost unrestricted access to visitors, daily 8–4:30. Maps and other helpful materials can be picked up at any of the gates. Guided tours for large groups can be arranged by writing to Director of Museums (Fort Sill, OK 73503) or going to the Museum office on Quanah Road. Now a register National Historic Landmark, Fort Sill is remarkable in that almost all of its original stone buildings still stand and are in daily use. The Old Post, just east of the Main Post with its modern structures and facilities, still retains much of its frontier appearance and atmosphere.

Outstanding points of interest include: Geronimo Guardhouse, the so-called "Geronimo Hotel" where the old war chief spent many years in one of its basement cells, now given over entirely to museum exhibits, including an animated display of Fort Sill in 1875;

View from McNair Hall, Headquarters U.S. Army Artillery and Missile Center, Fort Sill (photograph courtesy Fort Sill Museum).

Field Artillery Hall of Flags, original stone building now housing extensive displays of flags, uniforms, paintings, weapons, and equipment; Hamilton Hall, exhibits telling the fascinating story of the American Field Artillery from Colonial times to 1900; and Mc-Lain Hall, with exhibits depicting the eventful history, traditions, and development of the U.S. Field Artillery from 1900 to the present.

Also Cannon Walk, a notable outdoor display of U.S. and foreign weaponry from battlefields around the world; Old Post Corral, the stone stockade-type corral that dates from 1870 and, now restored, serves as a carriage museum, reception center, and gift shop; Old Post Headquarters, (1870–1911), handsome stone building on the old Post Quadrangle that serves as museum office; Old Post Chapel, dating from 1875 and believed to be the second oldest house of worship still in use in Oklahoma (see **Wheelock Church**); Sherman House, traditional residence of the Commanding Office from 1871 to the present, where Sherman himself narrowly escaped death at the hands of

Kiowa warriors during a front porch council on May 27, 1871.

These and a score of other historic buildings and sites on the reservation can be visited, including at least two cemeteries. The Post Cemetery, near the museum grounds, received its first military burial, a Private Jesse Bicheres, in 1869. Pierre Trudeau, one of Sheridan's scouts, was the first civilian burial, also in 1869. Kiowa Chief Satank, or Sitting Bear (killed by his guards while being taken to Texas for trial in 1871), was the first Indian burial. Many have followed him, and Chiefs Knoll now includes such notables as Comanche Quanah Parker and his white mother (see **Cache**); Kicking Bird, Satanta, Stumbling Bear, and Big Bow, all Kiowas; Arapahoes Yellow Bear and Spotted Wolf; and Black Beaver of the Delawares. Geronimo, the famed Apache chief, is buried under an unusual pyramid of stones in the Apache Prisoner-of-War Cemetery, located on the fort's East Range (follow the signs).

Throughout the year the U.S. Army Field Artillery School stages spectacular demonstrations of modern firepower, weapons, equipment, and battlefield

"Cannon Walk" at Fort Sill. Post Guardhouse in the background (photograph courtesy U.S. Artillery and Missile Center Museum).

Entrance to Fort Washita.

techniques for the benefit of student officers and men. These, although their scheduling is irregular, are always open to the public and provide an exciting attraction for thousands of visitors.

Fort Supply (Woodward Co., pop. 550, on US 183 & 270, see Map 3). A small community that developed from the nearby army post, *Camp Supply*, and continues to serve Western State Hospital, the sprawling state facility for the mentally ill that took over the old fort facilities. The town itself was started in 1902, as Fitzgerald, became Supply in 1903. It was not until 1943 that the name was officially changed to Fort Supply. (The fort, curiously enough, was always Camp Supply.)

When the army departed in 1893 the military reservation was given to the then Territory of Oklahoma, which established the mental hospital in 1903. Seven dormitory buildings and a hospital dominate the greatly expanded complex today. Of the 120 acres used by the hospital, 28 are in shaded lawns. A staff of some 400 persons is employed. A granite marker on the grounds commemorates the officers and troop units stationed at the old fort. The surviving military buildings are on the northeast corner of the hospital complex.

Fort Supply Reservoir (off US 270 just S of town of *Fort Supply*, Woodward County, see Map 3). A 1,800-acre empoundment on Wolf Creek just above its mouth in the *North Canadian River*. The flood control facility—created by an 85-foot-high dam and an 11,325-foot-long earthen embankment—was completed by the Corps of Engineers in 1942.

Facilities: picnic and camping area, boat ramps, swimming beach, marina and concessions. The state maintains a 4,805-acre public hunting area on the lake's eastern shore. Address: U.S. Corps of Engineers, Box 61, Tulsa, OK 74102.

Fort Towson (Choctaw Co., pop. 430, on US 70, see Map 6). Settlement in this area was first made in 1821 by the fur-trading Doaks brothers. In 1824, Fort Towson, the military post, was first established on *Red River* some five miles to the south. This crude camp was moved to its permanent location about two miles northeast of the present town in 1831. The settlement, then known as Doaksville, promptly began to grow, and until after the Civil War it was one of the most important towns in the Choctaw Nation.

The military post, which celebrated its 150th anniversary in 1974, had a rather checkered career. Abandoned in 1829, it was re-established four years later and used as a Choctaw Agency until the outbreak of the Civil War. It was then used as headquarters for Confederate General S. B. Maxey. Here, in June of 1865, two months after the official end of the war, Cherokee General Stand Watie became the last Confederate officer to surrender his forces. The old fort was then abandoned for good, and only a few stone walls stand today to mark it. The property is owned by the Oklahoma Historical Society and is open to visitors (Mon.–Fri. 9–5, Sat.–Sun. 2–5).

Doaksville, meanwhile, had also fallen on hard times. Before the war it had boasted two nearby girls' schools:

Goodwater (1837) and Pine Ridge (1845). But it faded in the post-war years. When the Frisco Railroad built through the area immediately to the south, the post office was moved to the present townsite, on the railroad, and the name changed to Fort Towson. "Thus," says historian George H. Shirk, "Fort Towson has the distinction of being the post office with the oldest name identical to that of its present name, yet it cannot say that it was in operation all that time under the same name." (For other post office "claims," see *Miller Court House* and *Eagletown*.)

Currently Fort Towson (the army post) and Doaksville (the ghost town reduced to a cemetery and a few crumbled stones) are being developed by the historical society as an interpretive exhibit of frontier military/civilian life. On Gates Creek just southeast of town is the 390-acre Lake Raymond Gary, a state-operated recreation area (hunting, camping facilities).

Fort Washita (Bryan Co., off OK 199, 20 mi. NW of *Durant*, see Map 6). One of Oklahoma's oldest and most important military posts for nearly twenty years, now being extensively restored by the Oklahoma Historical Society (Tues.-Fri. 9-5, Sat.-Sun. 2-5, free). Named for the nearby *Washita River*, the fort was established in 1843 by General (later President) Zachary Taylor. It was intended to protect the Choctaws and Chickasaws from border raids by the still hostile Plains Indian tribes on to the west.

When the Civil War broke out in 1861, U.S. troops were withdrawn. Confederate troops occupied the facility off and on throughout the war. Part of the time it served as headquarters for General Douglas H. Cooper, who lies buried in an unmarked grave in the post cemetery. Fort Washita was never reactivated after the war, but the nearby service town of Hatsboro lingered on for a number of years. The post office of Fort Washita existed from 1844 to 1880.

Camping and picnic facilities are available at the park.

Ruins at Fort Washita, established in 1843 by then General Zachary Taylor.

Foss (Washita Co., pop. 150, at junc. of I 40 & US 66 and OK 44, see Map 8). A dwindling farm community established at the turn of the century and named for J. M. Foss of *Cordell*. The town moved to its present location in 1902 after Turkey Creek engulfed a somewhat lower site nearby, killing nine persons. It is best known today for *Foss Reservoir* (off OK 44, 6 mi. N).

Foss Reservoir (off OK 44, in Custer County, 7 mi. N of I 40 at Foss, see Map 3). Western Oklahoma's largest lake, with 8,800 surface acres and 63 miles of shoreline. It was created in 1961 by the Bureau of Reclamation with a 134-foot-high dam on the *Washita River*. The state maintains a 6,970-acre recreation area on the lower end of the reservoir. Washita National Wildlife Refuge covers the lake's northern section. In late 1974 an electrodialysis desalination plant, the state's first, began supplying fresh water to the communities of *Cordell*, *Bessie*, *Clinton*, and *Hobart*.

Facilities: picnic and camping areas, swimming beaches and bathhouses, boat ramps and covered boat stalls, concessions. Address: Foss Recreation Area, Route #1 Box 68-C, Foss, OK 73647.

Picnic table overlooking Foss Reservoir (photograph courtesy Oklahoma Industrial Development and Park Department).

Fountainhead State Park (7 mi. S of I 40 from a point 7 mi. W of *Checotah*, see Map 5). The "best foot forward" of the Oklahoma state park system—a 3,401-acre recreation complex on *Eufaula Reservoir* centering on posh Fountainhead Lodge. With its 2,500-foot lighted air strip, eighteen-hole golf course, summer entertainment, and other resort features, it is a popular work/play convention facility and the state's most complete vacation resort.

Facilities: 180 lodge rooms and 22 cottages, extensive picnic and camping areas, trailer hookups, golf course and putting greens, tennis courts, swimming pool, beach and bathhouse, baseball diamonds, boat docks and ramps, ski school and archery range, lake excursion cruises. Address: Checotah, OK 74426.

Fox (Carter Co., pop. 350, at junc. of OK 53 & 76, 8 mi. N of *Healdton*, see Map 7). A scattered oil camp that dates back to 1894, when it was named for Chickasaw Frank M. Fox. But it owes its existence today to continuing exploitation of the vast *Healdton* oil field.

Intensive development can be seen from the highway all the way north to *Ratliff City* and *County Line*.

Foyil (Rogers Co., pop. 164, on US 66, 10 mi. NE of *Claremore*, see Map 5). A tiny community, dating from 1890, that is perhaps best known today for "the world's largest totem pole." The weird steel and concrete structure, the creation of a retired manual training teacher, N. E. Galloway, is 90 feet tall and contains his wood-working shop. Largest of its nine rooms is 10 x 12 feet (smallest is 5 x 5 feet) and the pyramid-like pole is adorned with more than 200 Indian symbols, birds, animals, and other designs. Statues of four Indian chiefs, each nine feet high, are at the top.

Francis (Pontotoc Co., pop. 283, on county road 12 mi. NE of *Ada*, see Map 7). Small farming/ranching community on the Frisco Railroad just south of the *Canadian River*. The settlement began in 1894 as Newton, changed its name in 1902 to honor David R. Francis, secretary of the interior under President William McKinley.

Frederick (Tillman Co. seat, pop. 6,132, at junc. of US 183 and OK 5, see Map 8). Born in 1901 with the opening of the Kiowa-Comanche lands to white settlement, Frederick (known as Gosnell its first year) has grown steadily into something of a prototype of the successful Western Oklahoma county seat. Though its roots are firmly in farming and ranching (elevators, gins, and cotton compresses dot the southwest part of town), it owes much of its prosperity to post-World War II industrialization centered on the Municipal Airport to the southeast. Principal payrolls include makers of leather goods, clothing, granite markers, and aircraft engines.

Perhaps the most celebrated event associated with Frederick and *Tillman County* was the six-day wolf hunt President Theodore Roosevelt made with Jack Abernathy, a young rancher of the area. The party left Frederick April 8, 1905. On the hunt Abernathy caught 16 coyotes ("wolves") with his bare hands,

Lodge and pool at Fountainhead State Park.

a feat Roosevelt later publicized in his writings. Abernathy afterward became a U.S. Marshal, oil field worker, minister, and coyote-catching stunt man for the movies.

In 1916 a local newspaper described Frederick as ". . . a city of the First Class . . . Miles of cement sidewalks and crossings . . . Has an Opera House . . . There are no saloons and no pool or billiard halls . . . Strict enforcement of the laws and a law abiding community." Such self-serving "puffs" were not unusual in their day. But a look at Frederick today—its neatly trimmed residential streets, solid business blocks, pleasant parks, and impressive public buildings—would indicate that perhaps the earlier writer merely recognized a good thing in the making when he saw it.

A downtown historical marker recognizes the original Tomlinson variety store. R. E. Tomlinson was the "T" in T. G. & Y. when that Oklahoma-based variety chain was formed (see **Cordell** and **Kingfisher**).

Freedom (Woods Co., pop. 292, on OK 50, 3 mi. S of US 64, see Map 3). Salt and the cowboy have played—and continue to play—important roles in the life of this little **Cimarron River** com-

munity. The town was established in 1901, five miles north of its present location. It moved here in 1919 when the Buffalo and Northwestern Railroad (now the Santa Fe) built here beside the river. Today, curiously enough, the bank and half a dozen other business establishments, either with new buildings or worked-over old ones, have restored much of the 1919 look with such features as sidewalk awnings, false fronts, and batten siding.

Much of the colorful and exciting early-day history of this area—and much of northwestern Oklahoma as well—can be read from a 9,000-pound granite monument erected in 1950 on the Freedom school grounds. Dedicated to "The Cimarron Cowboy" by the Cimarron Cowboys Association, it is an impressive affair, 10 feet long, 4 feet high, 14 inches thick. One side covers the period from 1883 to 1890. The big ranch spreads operating in the area are located on a large center map. The mural around it shows the arrival of the first cattle herds, the coming of the Santa Fe in 1886, and the killing blizzard that same year. The other side of the monument brings the history up to

Fountainhead Lodge, overlooking Lake Eufaula (photograph courtesy Oklahoma Industrial Development and Park Department).

107

date from the opening of the Cherokee Outlet in 1893. Included are names of cowhands and brands of the old spreads, and a tribute to the present-day rodeo, the only sport which had its beginning in an industry.

The nearby Little Salt Plain (also called the *Edith* Salt Plain for the little settlement northwest of Freedom) is some three miles wide, stretches for 12 miles along the Cimarron. Smaller than the *Great Salt Plains*, it is even more barren. Ninety-seven per cent pure, its salt is widely sold to ranchers for their stock and to cities and the state as a wintertime road de-icer.

The Blackmon salt plant northwest of Freedom welcomes visitors. Here water is pumped into huge brine pools, on the bottom of which evaporation deposits a thick layer of good, clean salt. With proper management 26.6 pounds of salt can be harvested from each 100 pounds of water. A one-acre brine pool produces an average of 1,000 tons of salt a year.

G **Gage** (Ellis Co., pop. 536, on OK 15, see Map 3). A small agricultural community established in 1895 and named for Lyman J. Gage, secretary of the treasury under President William McKinley. For its size, it is one of the best-known towns in the state.

In 1920, when long-distance air travel in the country was begun with the Post Office Department's opening of a transcontinental mail route between New York and San Francisco, seventeen radio stations were established at airfields along the way. One was at Gage. And today, with $2.5 million in electronic gear, the Gage Flight Service Station is part of a network spanning a good section of the globe, providing pilots with vital weather information and navigational guidance twenty-four hours a day.

Curiously, the personal interest of a Gage airport manager has given the installation something of the appearance of a transportation museum. On grounds dedicated primarily to serving the needs of high-speed, even supersonic, travel is a budding collection of vehicles more representative of the last century. Included in the display are

a painstakingly restored Studebaker farm wagon, a family buggy, a Pacific mountain spring wagon, an army escort wagon, and two army ambulances.

Gans (Sequoyah Co., pop. 238, on OK 141, 7 mi. SE of *Sallisaw*, see Map 5). A sleepy little community on the Kansas City Southern Railroad. Before 1899 its name was Gann, for the Cherokee family of that name, and the town, bypassed by the county's two federal highways, maintains a sleepy, old-fashioned appearance reminiscent of Indian Nation days. The 8-mile-long stretch of OK 141 from US 64 through Gans to US 59 south of *Sallisaw* is a pleasant byway that further strengthens this mood of an earlier, less harried age.

Gap. See *Limestone Gap*.

Garber (Garfield Co., pop. 1,011, on OK 15 & OK 74, 17 mi. E of *Enid*, see Map 4). Established in 1894, a year after the opening of the Cherokee Outlet, Garber is one of several towns to celebrate this September 16 land rush with an old settlers-type event. In a rich wheat-producing area, the settlement was strictly agriculture-oriented until discovery of the Hoy Well in 1916 led to development of the Garber Field, one of the state's more productive shallow oil fields.

Original site of the town was the Milton Garber homestead, a mile to the southeast. When the Enid and Tonkawa Railway (now the Rock Island) built through the area in 1899, Garber bought this site and moved the town to it. The family has been influential in the county down to the present.

Garfield County (north-central Oklahoma, see Map 4). Area, 1,054 sq. mi.; pop. 55,365; county seat, *Enid*. Established in 1893 when the Cherokee Outlet was opened to settlement. Named for President James A. Garfield.

Top travel lures: Government Springs Park and the Cherokee Strip Museum, both in *Enid*.

Garvin (McCurtain Co., pop. 117, on US 70, 8 mi. NW of *Idabel*, see Map 6). A small railroad-siding community laid out in the mid-1890's when the Frisco railroad was building through this region. Isaac Garvin was principal chief of the Choctaws 1878–80.

Garvin County (south-central Oklahoma, see Map 7). Area, 814 sq. mi.; pop. 24,874; county seat, *Pauls Valley*. Organized in 1907, when the Chickasaw Nation became a part of the State of Oklahoma. Large broomcorn production is the basis for its sometime claim: "We sweep the world." The name honors Samuel J. Garvin, a prominent early-day Chickasaw.

Top travel lures: Murray Mansion at *Erin Springs*.

Gate (Beaver Co., pop. 151, on US 64, see Map 2). At the northeastern "gateway" to the old Neutral Strip—later No Man's Land and now the *Oklahoma Panhandle*—this dwindling agricultural community dates back to the mid-1880's. It was known officially as Gate City until 1894.

Gateway to the Panhandle Museum, containing historical and pioneer items pertaining to the area, is housed in the restored M-K-T depot (see *Forgan*). Sporting its original 1912 colors—pea green with dark green trim—it also accommodates the town's library.

North of the town, and still used by area farmers and ranchers, are vestiges of an ancient irrigation system believed to have been used by prehistoric Indians. Many significant archeological sites have been identified in the Panhandle (see *Turpin, Optima, Kenton*).

Geary (Blaine Co., pop. 1,380, on US 270 & 281 and OK 8, see Map 3). Established in 1898, when the Rock Island Railroad reached this point in its push westward across the Cheyenne and Arapaho Reservation (opened to white settlement in 1892). The name is a corruption of that of Ed Guerrier, a well-known French-Canadian scout on the Southern Plains, who married an Indian woman. A bustling railroad junction in its early years, the town is today widely known for its annual high school Invitational Wrestling Tournament, one of the state's best. Prominent nearby landmarks are *Coyote Hill* on the east and the *Red Hills* to the northwest. Points of interest include *American Horse Lake*, 10 miles west of town, and the *Jesse Chisholm Grave* site at Left Hand Spring, 8 miles northeast of town.

Gene Autry (Carter Co., pop. 120, off OK 53, 14 mi. NE of *Ardmore*, see Map 7). From a lady known as Lou to a cowboy named Gene, that summarizes the four-name-change development of this tiny "Hereford Heaven" ranching community on the so-called Sunny Side of the *Arbuckle Mountains*. Lou Henderson was the wife of a local merchant in 1883. But her name for the town promptly gave way to Dresden, which lost out in turn to Berwyn in 1887. The present name came in 1942, after western movie star Gene Autry bought a ranch in the area.

Just north of the community, during World War II, the Ardmore Air Force Base was built. In 1959 the then surplus facility was turned over to the city of Ardmore for development of Ardmore Industrial Airpark. It now includes Ardmore Municipal Airport.

Geronimo (Comanche Co., pop. 587, on OK 8-A, 9 mi. S of *Lawton*, see Map 8). Small farming community that was established in 1903 with construction of a Rock Island branch line from *Lawton* to *Waurika*. The name honors the best-known of all Apache Indian chiefs, who is buried near *Lawton*. In recent years the town has grown considerably, largely as a result of continuing development of the *Fort Sill* Military Reservation.

Gerty (Hughes Co., pop. 139, 2 mi. W of US 75, 9 mi. S of *Calvin*, see Map 7). It takes longer to read the name changes—according to historian George H. Shirk—than it does to drive through this isolated little community. From Buzzard Flop it became Guertie in 1894, Raydon in 1907, and then Gerty in 1910—all honoring one Guertie Raydon, daughter of the postmaster. The changes were dictated, presumably, because postal authorities in this pre-zip code era feared the tiny hamlet might be confused with the capital city of Guthrie. Today its sole distinction, and almost only business, is Slim's General Store, a congenial half-century-old institution.

Gibson (Wagoner Co., pop. 125, on OK 16, 7 mi. S of *Wagoner*, see Map 5). Now little more than a railroad siding, the settlement began as Gibson Station with the coming of the M-K-T Railroad in 1872. It took its name, of course, from nearby *Fort Gibson*, Oklahoma's first military post, established half a century before.

Glass Mountains (alongside OK 15, W of *Orienta*, see Map 3). Name comes from millions of sparkling selenite crystals that cover the surface of these bold buttes south of the *Cimarron River* in *Major County*. Curiously, some old maps still indicate these as Gloss Mountains. One possible explanation: they were named and first described by an English engineer when the region was surveyed in 1880, and he thought they looked like "Glaws."

Rising abruptly and fancifully shaped, the "mountains" are part of the Blaine Escarpment, a great gypsum formation extending across much of western Oklahoma (see *Gyp Hills*). Most prominent is Cathedral Mountain, a 300-foot crystalline butte that stands out from the rest, its portals and towers suggesting a great church. From a distance its thick layer of gypsum often reflects varicolor light as from cathedral windows. The area is quite desert-like and picturesque. OK 15 cuts through the mountains east-west, connecting US 60 at *Orienta* with US 281 S of *Waynoka*.

Glencoe (Payne Co., pop. 421, on OK 108, 13 mi. SW of *Pawnee*, see Map 4). An agricultural community, dating from the turn of the century, with more-than-average small-town pride and spirit. In the vicinity one can still find a few abandoned shafts and other relics of an early-day copper mining boom.

Glenpool (Tulsa Co., pop. 770, at junc. of US 75 and OK 67, 15 mi. S of Tulsa, see Map 5). Like nearby *Kiefer*, Glenpool owes its existence to the spectacularly productive Glenn Pool—for Ida E. Glenn, the Creek Indian on whose land the original oil discovery was made December 1, 1905. When subsequent wells began to produce up to 2,500 barrels a day, oil men swarmed in to extend the development. (Today the entire field—which once had 1,022 wells that flowed and were pumped for more than 307 million barrels—produces a modest 5,400 barrels a day.)

Like *Kiefer*, too, Glennpool saw only the rough action, while *Tulsa* became headquarters for the companies and the men shaping that development and so reaped the real benefit therefrom. Today Glenpool is only a scattered community that looks for job opportunities to *Tulsa*, whose glittering skyline beckons symbolically from across the *Arkansas River* to the north.

Glover (McCurtain Co., pop. 200, off OK 3 & 7, 6 mi. E of *Wright City*, see Map 6). A scattered community on the beautiful *Glover River*. Established at the turn of the century, it owes its continuing existence to timber cutting and lumbering in nearby *Wright City* and *Broken Bow*.

Glover River. One of the state's last free-flowing streams, the Glover is a favorite of fishermen, floaters, and conservationists, who would preserve its "wild" nature by extending to it the Scenic River status now enjoyed by certain sections of the *Illinois* and *Mountain Fork Rivers*. It lies entirely in *McCurtain County*, flowing through a rugged, virtually uninhabited section of Oklahoma's southeastern corner. Its mouth is in *Little River*, southeast of *Wright City*.

Golden (McCurtain Co., pop. 90, off OK 3 & 7, 8 mi. W of *Broken Bow*, see Map 6). A lumbering community, established in 1911 and named for the first postmaster, James M. Golden. It straddles the Texas, Oklahoma and Eastern Railroad, which doesn't go to Texas, but rather to Arkansas, and serves the lumber industry in nearby *Wright City* and *Broken Bow*, to which residents owe their economic well-being.

110

Goltry (Alfalfa Co., pop. 262, OK 45, see Map 3). A small agricultural community on a branch line of the Frisco railroad. Started in 1894 as Karoma a mile to the southeast, its name was changed to Goltry—for Charles Goltry, a local businessman—in 1904.

Goodland (Choctaw Co., on OK 2A, 3 mi. SW of *Hugo*, see Map 6). Established by the Presbyterians in 1848 as a mission and school, Goodland Children's Home is said to be the nation's oldest Protestant Indian orphanage. It has operated continuously, although its functions have varied with changing conditions and needs. Its multi-million-dollar plant today embraces a dozen modern buildings and more than a section of fertile land, and few of its sixty "orphans" are that in fact. Rather, they are children from "problem" homes (alcohol, divorce, inadequate finances) who need "help and love."

Visitors are welcomed to the pleasant, tree-shaded campus. And especially to the Goodland Museum, housed in a 22 x 22-foot log house constructed with logs from the one-time home of Choctaw Governor Basil LeFlore, who lived just west of Goodland. Oldest building on the campus is the much-altered chapel. At least parts of the simple structure, and its pulpit, date back to the 1852 original.

Goodwell (Texas Co., pop. 1,467, on US 54, 10 mi. SW of *Guymon*, see Map 2). A small college town dating from the arrival of the Rock Island Railroad in 1902. A good well drilled there to serve the line also gave the rail siding its name.

The present Panhandle State College (which represents some 1,250 of the town's citizenry) was established in 1909 by the state legislature as a high school. In 1921 it was authorized to offer a two-year college course as Panhandle Agricultural and Mechanical College. In 1925 it became a four-year school. In addition to its tree-shaded campus at the south edge of Goodwell, the school operates over two thousand acres of experimental farmlands in the area.

Primary point of visitor interest in Goodwell is the excellent No Man's Land Museum (Mon.–Fri. and Sun 1–4). Most of its extensive historical, geological, archeological, and anthropological exhibits pertain to the Panhandle. One unusual item: the mummified body of an Indian child discovered in the so-called Mummy Cave southeast of *Kenton*. The museum also has an art gallery that features thirty-day and sixty-day exhibitions by regional artists.

Gore (Sequoyah Co., pop. 478, on US 64 at junc. of OK 10 and OK 100, see Map 5). One of the oldest settlements in Oklahoma, Gore first appeared on a map by French explorer Guillaume de Lille as Mentos, or Les Mentous, this in 1718. In 1888 it became Campbell (for Dr. W. W. Campbell, owner of the ferry at *Webbers Fall* across the *Arkansas River*), a stop on the Fort Smith-*Fort Gibson* stage line. The name was changed to Gore in 1909 to honor Oklahoma's U.S. Senator Thomas P. Gore.

The town is a convenient access point for two popular state parks, *Tenkiller* and *Greenleaf Lake*, and for the historic Three Forks area around *Fort Gibson*. OK 10 and OK 100 are two of eastern Oklahoma's most scenic byways.

Gotebo (Kiowa Co., pop. 376, at junc. of OK 9 and OK 54, see Map 8). A dwindling farming community established in 1902 on a Rock Island branch line and named for a Kiowa sub-chief. That same year a local man, Andrew Byars, while drilling for water struck oil—at 102 feet. Curiously, in 1974, not too many miles away, the No. 1 Bertha Rogers, after drilling to 31,441 feet, was declared the world's "deepest hole"—a record which will undoubtedly be broken before this appears in print!

Gould (Harmon Co., pop. 368, at junc. of US 62 and OK 5, 8 mi. E of *Hollis*, see Map 8). A farming/ranching community on the picturesque Hollis & Eastern Railroad (see *Duke*). Platted in 1908, it took its name from John A. Gould, the first postmaster.

A wooden tower over a concrete slab just northeast of the town recalls the wanderings of Oklahoma's western border (the Panhandle excluded). The 110th Meridian was first located, by the crude surveying instruments of the days, east of present **Fort Sill**, this in 1818. This error of some 80 miles was corrected, somewhat, by Captain George B. McClellan in 1853; he moved the boundary 40 miles farther west. Subsequent surveys in 1859, 1892, and 1902 located the Oklahoma-Texas line near its present location. But the final designation, for which this marker was one of the base marks used, was not made until 1927.

Gowen (Latimer Co., pop. 350, off US 270, 9 mi. W of **Wilburton**, see Map 6). Established in the early 1890's and named for a Philadelphia attorney, Francis I. Gowen. The town was once home to Lincoln Perry, the early-day Negro character actor who became known as Step'n Fetchit, for his most popular movie role.

Gracemont (Caddo Co., pop. 424, on US 281 and OK 8, 8 mi. N of **Anadarko**, see Map 8). A small agricultural community that began as Ison in 1902 when a Rock Island branch line was built north-south through the former Kiowa-Apache-Comanche lands, opened to white settlement the year before. The name Gracemont, apparently coined by the postmaster, was adopted in 1904. The rail line was abandoned in 1939. The fertile valley of Sugar Creek, which flows past the town, supports a strong, diversified farm economy.

Grady (Jefferson Co., pop. 25, on OK 32, 17 mi. E of **Ryan**, see Map 7). Established in 1890 and named for Henry W. Grady, this scattered community contains little more than a post office today. But a nearby site on **Red River** is among the first in present Oklahoma to be visited by a European.

In 1541 Cristobel de Oñate, an aide to the Spanish explorer Coronado, tells of visiting a large village of from 3,000 to 4,000 Indians living on both sides of the river in this area. Archeo-

logical research is still being carried on in connection with this so-called San Bernardo site. These were Tuscarora Indians, later known as Wichitas. In 1759 was fought here the last of several battles between the Spanish and the French, both sides using Indian allies. The defeated Spanish forces retreated to San Antonio and the river became the boundary line between the two colonies. The French maintained a flourishing trading post on the site for many years. In 1803 the Louisiana Purchase transferred the area north of the Red to the United States.

Grady County (central Oklahoma, see Map 7). Area, 1,092 sq. mi.; pop. 29,354; county seat, **Chickasha**. Part of the Chickasaw Nation until statehood in 1907, the county possesses both agricultural wealth (cotton and wheat) and rich underground reserves of oil and gas. Name honors Henry W. Grady, editor of the Atlanta Constitution.

Graham (Carter Co., pop. 200, on OK 53, 14 mi. SE of **County Line**, see Map 7). A scattered community, dating from 1891, that lies on the edge of the great **Healdton** oil field.

Grainola (Osage Co., pop. 66, on OK 18, see Map 4). Tiny trading center in the northwest corner of the sprawling Osage ranching country. It began in 1806 as Salt Creek, for a nearby **Arkansas River** tributary, adopted its present name in 1910. Just east of town is the vast K. S. Adams Ranch and Phillips Agricultural Demonstration Project.

Grand (about 2 miles off US 283, 13 miles S of **Arnett**, in **Ellis County**, see Map 3). Only the ruined vault of the old courthouse—and the spring that brought the settlement into existence—remain today to mark the river-bank site of one of Oklahoma's most celebrated ghost towns. Designated the seat of Day County, Oklahoma Territory, when the Cheyenne and Arapaho Indian Reservation was thrown open to white settlement in 1892, the settlement soon became a bustling little trade center for a wide area. Mail was brought down

Ruins at the site of Grand, in Ellis County.

daily from the railroad at **Shattuck**, sorted and sent on its way via a number of star routes. The town's name honored Grandville Alcorn, son of Robert Alcorn, the county judge.

The broad, treacherous **Canadian River** gave Grand a picturesque setting. But it was eventually to prove its undoing. Flooding, which constantly threatened the town, also isolated it from the southern part of Day County. Bridges were non-existent, and when fords were impassable official county business often came to a standstill for weeks at a time.

Statehood in 1907 changed all that. **Roger Mills County** was created south of the Canadian. The northern section became **Ellis County** with **Arnett** as its seat. Grand became semi-ghosted almost overnight, losing not only much of its population, but many of its buildings as well—including its pride and joy, the Woodsmen of the World lodge, the town's only two-story structure!

Grand River. See **Neosho River**.

Grandfield (Tillman Co., pop. 1,524, at junc. of US 70 and OK 36, see Map 8). Started in 1907 as Eschiti (for a Comanche medicine man), Grandfield changed its name in 1909 to honor assistant postmaster general Charles P. Grandfield. This is the heart of the "Big Pasture," a 480,000-acre preserve leased to Texas ranchers for cattle

grazing until August 16, 1906, when it was opened to settlement with a drawing—the state's last official land opening. An impressive granite marker on a landscaped downtown site details the "Big Pasture" story with map and text.

This is broad ranching country. Giant grain elevators mark the course of the M-K-T Railroad through the town—the state's wheat harvest traditionally begins in the Grandfield area—but flat grasslands stretch westward across the county unbroken but for isolated ranch houses. Although the "Big Pasture" has disappeared officially, it pretty well remains in fact. It will remain, too, in spirit, in the museum being planned as part of the town's public library, unusually complete as to books and services for such a small town.

Grand Lake of the Cherokees (off I 40 and US 59, 60, 66 & 69, in northeastern Oklahoma, see Map 5). One of Oklahoma's best-developed and most popular resort areas, this 46,500-acre lake sprawls octopus-like across three counties, backs up the waters of the **Grand** (or **Neosho**) **River** for 65 miles. Its 1,300 miles of shoreline are dotted with scores of fishing camps and resorts, most elaborate of which is Shangri-La on Monkey Island. A dozen recreation-minded small towns also serve the lake area.

US 60 crosses the upper (northern) end of the reservoir near where the Spring and **Neosho** rivers join, the so-called Twin Bridges area. US 59 crosses the middle section of the lake to serve the extremely well developed Grove/Honey Creek area. OK 28 and 82 serve the Pensacola Dam area around **Disney** and **Langley**.

Grand Lake is remarkable on a number of counts. For one thing, it was the first (1941) of a score of major eastern Oklahoma reservoirs that have helped to give the state a greater percentage of water surface than lake-famed Minnesota. For another, it is owned by the State of Oklahoma, along with its electric generating facility, which is paying off its construction costs. The idea of harnessing Grand River to generate power was first suggested in 1891.

113

Successive private efforts failed, however, and in 1935 the Oklahoma Legislature created the Grand River Dam Authority. Construction of the $22,750,000 Pensacola Dam began in 1938. When Completed in 1941, it was the longest (5,680 feet) multiple-arch dam in the world.

The lake area affords the widest possible range of accommodations and facilities for all types of sport and recreational activities. Special features would include lake excursion boats and the enclosed fishing dock. Now found in many areas, these modern docks originated on Grand Lake and are often air-conditioned for year-round comfort.

Addresses: Cherokee Recreation Area, Route 1, Fairland, OK 74343 (the state maintains half a dozen such areas on various parts of the lake); Grand Lake Association, Box 126, Grove, OK 74344.

Granite (Greer Co., pop. 1,808, at junc. of OK 6 and OK 9, see Map 8). There's an understandable air of permanence about this town, started in 1889 at the foot of Headquarters Mountain. (The year before old **Greer County**'s first public school was started near here, with funds appropriated by the State of Texas.) Other granite peaks rim the town, the most northwesterly outcropping of the much higher **Wichita Mountains** near **Lawton**. Quarrying has long been important in the area, and a local monument works (conducted tours available) dates from 1910. The beautiful red stone is used widely throughout the town for homes, business buildings—and Granite's biggest "industry," the Oklahoma State Reformatory.

The castle-like facility, constructed to house some 500 youthful offenders considered capable of rehabilitation, has 16-foot walls of granite. (They are painted white,however, to soften their suggestion of a bastille. Its fully accredited high school is thought to be the first of its kind within prison walls in the United States.

Interesting natural attractions in the area are Custer's Cave near Balanced Rock, Old Baldy, Devil's Slide, and Sulphur Springs. Ford's Museum (antique autos, pioneer equipment) is on Main Street. Annual events include Pioneer Day & Rodeo (late July) and the Greer County Fair (September).

Grant (Choctaw Co., pop. 273, on US 271, 5 mi. S of **Hugo**, see Map 6). An agricultural community established in 1889 when the Frisco Railroad was built through this rich **Red River** valley. The name honors President Ulysses S. Grant. Southwest of the town is horseshoe-shaped Roebuck Lake (hunting, fishing, camping). A cut-off Red River "oxbow," actually, its 145 surface acres makes Roebuck Oklahoma's largest natural lake.

Grant County (north-central Oklahoma along the Kansas border, see Map 4). Area, 999 sq. mi.; pop. 7,117; county seat, **Medford**. Established in 1893 when the Cherokee Outlet was opened to settlement and named for President Ulysses S. Grant.

Gray Horse (Osage Co., pop. 80, off OK 18, 4 mi. SE of **Fairfax**, see Map 4). An Osage community that dates back to 1890. It was named for the medicine man whose Osage name was Ko-Wah-Ho-Tsa. Ceremonials are still held in the area. Nearby is an interesting all-Indian cemetery.

Great Salt Plains (Alfalfa Co., see Map 3). The first white men to see this curious white desert along the **Salt Fork of the Arkansas River** are believed to have been those in the party of Major George C. Sibley, Indian agent from Fort Osage, Missouri, in 1811. Sibley called it the Grand Saline. Captain Nathan Boone, son of Daniel Boone, described the phenomenon as a "lake of white water" in 1843.

Great Salt Plains Reservoir was created in 1941. **Great Salt Plains State Park** has been developed near the dam. **Salt Plains National Wildlife Refuge** embraces 33,000 acres north and west of the reservoir.

Rock hounds know the Plains for the unequaled opportunity they present for the digging of selenite crystals. **Jet**, on the south, is the favorite take-off point for diggers as well as for waterfowl hunters. *Cherokee* offers easy access to the upper reaches of the Plains. Here, during World War II, air force bomber crews used the barren flats as a target range.

Geologists are still not in agreement on the origin of Great Salt Plains. Now being downgraded is the once popular theory that the wasteland represents the evaporated remains of a vast prehistoric salt sea. Another theory sees it as the result of constant weathering of a soil that does not support enough vegetation to prevent erosion. The soluble salts, laid down geologically perhaps fifty million years ago, were simply "sweated up" out of the ground or else crystallized around salt springs fed by water flowing through salt beds not far from the surface.

Around the edges of the reservoir the salt forms a thin, wafer-like crust on the flat surface. When it rains this salt crust dissolves and the clay and sand beneath the surface are extremely unstable. In the earliest days of settlement in Indian Territory wagonloads of salt were often hauled away from here by farmers and ranchers from as far away as Western Kansas and Texas.

Great Salt Plains Reservoir (off US 64 N of *Jet*, in Alfalfa County, see Map 3). This shallow, 8,890-acre lake was created in 1941 by the Corps of Engineers with construction of a 68-foot-high dam across the *Salt Fork of the Arkansas River*. It is noted primarily for its unusual setting (see *Great Salt Plains*) and its excellent waterfowl hunting. *Great Salt Plains State Park* is at the dam and 33,000-acre *Salt Plains National Wildlife Refuge* includes the upper part of the lake.

Facilities: picnic and camping areas, boat ramps and boat rentals, swimming beach, concessions. Address: Corps of Engineers, Box 61, Tulsa, OK 74102.

Great Salt Plains State Park (9 mi. NE of *Jet* via OK 38, see Map 3). Another exhibit in the "variety" claim made for the Oklahoma park system. This is the 840-acre developed area of *Great Salt Plains*, a sprawling, flatland expanse of gleaming white salt, the origin of which the experts are still disputing. There is no argument whatsoever that the area—including 9,300-acre *Great Salt Plains Reservoir*—offers excellent waterfowl hunting as well as fishing and other water sports, unexcelled digging for selenite crystals, as well as ample opportunity for hiking, riding, and the more traditional recreation activities.

Facilities: 6 cabins, picnic and camp areas, trailer hookups, playgrounds, swimming beach and bathhouse, stables. Address: Jet, OK 73749.

Greenleaf State Park (off OK 10, 3 mi. S of *Braggs*, see Map 5). A semi-rustic park of 565 heavily wooded acres tucked away beside the deep green waters of 930-acre Greenleaf Lake. The area is relatively quiet, secluded. Accommodations are simple, comfortable. Fishing, as at most Eastern Oklahoma state parks, is the primary activity.

Facilities: 13 rustic cottages, picnic, camp and trailer areas, swimming beach and bathhouse, docks, boat ramps and rentals, playgrounds and community building. Address: Braggs, OK 74423.

Greer County (extreme southwestern Oklahoma, see Map 8). Area, 637 sq. mi.; pop. 7,979, county seat, *Mangum*. Part of "Old Greer" County and the youngest part of Oklahoma. It was not until March 16, 1896, that the U.S. Supreme Court decided that Greer County between the 100th meridian and the North Fork of the *Red River* was not a part of the state of Texas, as claimed. The disputed territory became a part of Oklahoma Territory officially in May of that year. Part of the territory became *Jackson County* at statehood in 1907, and two years later another section was sliced off to form *Harmon County*. The name honors John A. Greer, a lieutenant governor of Texas.

Top travel lures: *Quartz Mountain State Park*.

Grimes (Roger Mills Co., pop. 25, off US 283 in the extreme southern part of the county, see Map 3). Founded in 1901, the tiny community honors William Grimes, territorial secretary of state.

Cooperative Publishing Company building in Guthrie, home of State Capital, *Oklahoma's first newspaper.*

Grove (Delaware Co., pop. 2,000, at junc. of US 59 and OK 10, see Map 5). An old town (its post office dates from 1888) in the extreme northern part of the Cherokee Nation, Grove was seat of **Delaware County** from statehood in 1907 to 1912 (see **Jay**). It struggled along as a trade town for the area's scattered farms, orchards, and berry patches until the building of **Grand Lake**. Since then it has become a bustling, increasingly prosperous resort center.

Three particularly well-developed recreation areas are served by Grove: Cowskin to the northeast, on the Elk River arm of the sprawling reservoir; Sailboat Bridge to the northwest; and Honey Creek to the south. The Grand Lake Association (Grove, OK 74344) serves as a clearing house for information on all the area resorts and visitor services and attractions.

One outstanding attraction is Har-Ber Village, 3 miles west of Grove. More than a score of old Tri-State Area buildings have been relocated on this pleasant lakeside site to reproduce an authentic pioneer village. The project represents, in the view of the founder, truck line executive Harvey Jones, an effort to preserve for future generations the way of life of "our forefathers who carved out of the wilderness this wonderful country we know today." There is no admission charge.

Heading the Grove area's special events calendar are the Miss Grand Lake Pageant in June, an Indian Arts & Crafts Festival in mid-June, the Green Corn Festival in August (see **Turkey Ford**), and Sailboat Regattas in October.

Guthrie (Logan Co. seat, pop. 9,575, at junc. of US 77 and OK 33, see Map 4). Capital of Oklahoma Territory and capital of the State of Oklahoma until June 11, 1910, Guthrie has grown up with disappointments. Its post office—named for John Guthrie, a director of the Santa Fe, principal railroad serving the city—was established April 4, 1889, more than two weeks before the April 22 "run" that opened Old Oklahoma to settlement. By sunset that first day Guthrie was a tent city of some 15,000 persons, a population figure it has shrunk from ever since.

Biggest blow came in 1910 when, according to an official historical marker, the capital was "stolen" by Oklahoma City. (However made, the transfer was legalized by a state-wide vote of the people.) This came after the constitutional convention of 1906–1907 had met in the old City Hall (304 W. Oklahoma Ave.) and the first state governor had been inaugurated on the steps of the Carnegie Library (402 E. Oklahoma Ave.). A new City Hall has replaced the old, but the original cornerstone, topped by the old bell, remains to memorialize the site. The one-time library, with a modern connecting building, is now the Oklahoma Territorial Museum.

Guthrie has yet another "capital" claim—that of "Fraternal Capital of the Southwest." In a ten-acre park near the eastern edge of the city is the Scottish Rite Temple (weekdays 8–5, Sun. 10–5), a $2.5 million affair of Greek Doric design that is the largest structure of its type in Oklahoma and believed to be the world's largest devoted exclusively to Masonic uses. Other fraternal buildings in Guthrie include the State Masonic Home for the Aged, State Masonic Home for Children, and the Grand Lodge Temple (Broad St. and Oklahoma Ave.).

Biggest annual affair in Guthrie is,

somewhat ironically, the '89ers Day Celebration, usually a three-day blow-out on or near the April 22 opening date. It regularly includes street dancing, rodeo, carnival, and an elaborate historical parade that draws upwards of 100,000 people. Interesting then, or anytime, are tours of the old business district, lined with ornate brick buildings, many of them dating to 1889 and the early 1890's, and equally rewarding loops through the tree-lined residential streets immediately to the northeast with their brick sidewalks and comfortable Victorian homes. (Much of Guthrie, as it existed in 1907, has been declared a Historic District by the National Park Service.)

Noteworthy downtown is the Cooperative Publishing Company, long-time home of the *State Capital*, Oklahoma's first daily newspaper. One of the more interesting old homes is that of Cassius M. Barnes, fourth Territorial governor.

Among the well-known figures to live in Guthrie at one time or another are Fred G. Bonfils, famed publisher of the *Denver Post* (his Foucart-designed store building still stands); Tom Mix, who once worked in a Territorial saloon here; Will Rogers; General J. B. Weaver, 1880 Presidential candidate on the Greenback ticket; and Cora V. Diehl, first woman to be elected to office in Oklahoma.

Largest employer in Guthrie is the Oklahoma Furniture Manufacturing Co. Established in 1901, it employs about 500 persons. Since Territorial days, too, the city has been a center for printing and publishing concerns. A federal Job Corps Center on the west side of Guthrie occupies the tree-shaded, 75-acre campus on which the Benedictines established Catholic College of Oklahoma in 1892, and operated Benedictine High School from 1955 to 1966.

A large section of downtown Guthrie, including many of the older historic homes in close-in residential areas, has been declared a Historic District and is being restored with National Park Service assistance to something resembling its turn-of-the-century appearance. An illustrated Green Line map/ folder, available from the Guthrie Chamber of Commerce, contains a helpful map and much background information on the state's first capital.

Guymon (Texas Co. seat, pop. 7,674, at junc. of US 54 & 64 and OK 3 & 136, see Map 2). The booming, progressive "capital" of the *Oklahoma Panhandle*, although it dates only from 1901, when the Rock Island Railroad began extending its main line southwestward from Liberal, Kansas. (E. T. Guymon of Liberal headed the townsite company.) In the decade of the 1960's its population increased by a third, making it the state's fortieth-largest city.

Permanent settlement of the area began in the early 1880's, however, when James K. Hitch built a two-room sod house for himself and his bride on Coldwater Creek, some 11 miles southeast of present Guymon. In the nearly ninety years that followed, four generations of the Hitch family have played an important role in developing the country's resources: land, water (extensive deep-well irrigation), petroleum and, most recently, cattle feeding and meat packing. The sod house gave way in 1892 to the rock home with two-foot-thick walls, in which his son, Henry Hitch, died in 1968. The greatly expanded Hitch Ranch headquarters today is a Panhandle landmark.

Oil and gas development in the county began in 1923, and Guymon is now the principal beneficiary of the rich Hugoton Gas Field (see *Hooker*), with Phillips Petroleum Co. one of the area's largest employers. Others are Adams Hard-Facing Co. (hard-facing of tillage tools; started in 1926, now employing 125) and Swift & Co. (employing 130 persons in a packing plant opened in 1967). Both offer tours. Swift's modern plant, along with the county's extensive, highly automated feed lots, which provide prime slaughter animals, and excellent highway and rail facilities, have made Guymon one of the nation's newest and biggest cattle markets.

Top special event is the annual Land Pioneer Day celebration (first weekend in May). It draws up to 50,000 visitors from a three-state area for parades, chuck-wagon feeds, street dancing, rodeos, and other activities. Recreation facilities cluster around twenty-three-acre Sunset Lake, the so-called "City Section" at the west end of 1st Street. They include nine-hole golf course, Olympic-size heated pool, miniature train, playground, picnic and camping areas. The park also includes the Panhandle Exposition Fairgrounds, Hitch Memorial Pioneer Stadium, and a game preserve featuring a prairie dog village. Write: Guymon Chamber of Commerce, Box 199, Guymon, OK 73942.

Gypsum Hills. A 100-mile-long string of rugged, colorfully eroded hills roughly paralleling, on the north, the southeasterly course of the **North Canadian River** through **Woodward**, **Dewey**, and **Blaine Counties**. Where erosion has worn away the thin top soil, bold, flat-topped knobs stand out, and ledges of chalky white gypsum (see **Southard**) appear etched on barren canyon walls.

The "Gyp Hills" are sparsely covered with cedar and scrub oak, with prickly pear cactus, and rattlesnakes (see **Okeene**). The few improved roads that penetrate the area are pleasantly scenic. The lodge at **Roman Nose State Park** gives the visitor an excellent panoramic view of the hills.

Gypsy (Creek Co., 10 mi. SW of **Bristow**, see Map 4). Now little more than a name on generous maps, Gypsy boomed briefly in the 1920's on the strength of oil discoveries in the area. Like **Barnsdall**, it was one of several Oklahoma towns to take the name of what was then its economic mainstay, in this case the Gypsy Oil Company.

Haileyville (Pittsburg Co., pop. 928, on US 270, see Map 6). Junior partner of the once-booming coal producing Twin Cities of Pittsburg County (see **Hartshorne**). Established with the arrival of the Choctaw Coal and Railway Company in 1890, and platted in 1902, it was named for Dr. David Morris Hailey, who came to Indian Territory from Louisiana after the Civil War. He assisted in opening the district's first coal mine.

Hallett (Pawnee Co., pop. 125, on OK 99, 10 mi. SW of **Cleveland,** see Map 4). Dating from just after the turn of the century, Hallett enjoyed but a modest—and brief—oil boom. Today only the post office and a single store prevent its lapsing into ghosthood.

Hammon (Roger Mills Co., pop. 677, on OK 33 at the county's eastern edge, see Map 3). A small trading community—its economy based largely on wheat, cotton, and cattle—that has long been an educational and cultural center for the Cheyennes and Arapahoes. The Red Moon sub-agency was established here in the 1880's. Red Moon Indian School was operated until 1925. One of the oldest communities in the county, it was named for Indian agent J. H. Hammon.

Hanna (McIntosh Co., pop. 181, on OK 52, 15 mi. S of **Henryetta,** see Map 5). An isolated rural community established about the turn of the century. The name presumably honors a local resident, Hanna Bullett.

Hanson (Sequoyah Co., pop. 50, just N of US 64, 6 mi. SE of **Sallisaw,** see Map 5). A rural community on the Missouri Pacific Railroad.

Harden City (Pontotoc Co., pop. 100, on OK 61-A, 14 mi. S of **Ada,** see Map 7). A scattered community that, like **Fittstown,** owes its brief boom to the oil play of the 1930's. Andrew Harden was a local resident.

Hardesty (Texas Co., pop. 223, on OK 3, 19 mi. E of **Guymon,** see Map 2). A relatively new agricultural community that moved to this highway/railroad site after the Rock Island built a second line through the county in 1928. Old Hardesty, interestingly enough, boasted one of the first post offices in Cimarron Territory (see **Oklahoma Panhandle**). The settlement was located in 1887 near the **North Canadian River,** some four miles northeast of present Hardesty. The site will be flooded when **Optima Reservoir** is filled.

Lake Schultz is 8 miles southeast of

Hardesty. The 120-acre state wildlife department empoundment offers fishing and general recreation.

Harmon (Ellis Co., pop. 20, on US 60 and OK 33, see Map 3). A small trading center established in 1906 and named for Judson C. Harmon, governor of Ohio and later United States secretary of state. Curiously, Judson Harmon fared much better with a second Oklahoma namesake, *Harmon County,* in the state's extreme southwestern corner.

Harmon County (in extreme southwestern Oklahoma, bordering Texas, see Map 8). Area, 532 sq. mi.; pop., 5,136; county seat, *Hollis.* The second youngest of the state's seventy-seven counties. It was created from the western section of *Greer County* by a special election on May 22, 1909. The name honors Judson C. Harmon, governor of Ohio and later United States secretary of state.

Harper County (the northwesternmost county in Oklahoma, excluding the Panhandle, bordering Kansas on the north, see Map 3). Area, 1,034 sq. mi.; pop., 5,151; county seat, *Buffalo.* Established in 1907 and named for Oscar G. Harper, clerk of the Constitutional Convention.
Top travel lures: *Doby Springs* park, game bird hunting.

Harrah (Oklahoma Co., pop. 1,931, at junc. of US 62 and 270, E of Oklahoma City, see Map 4). On the *North Canadian River,* Harrah is trading center for fertile farmlands lying between that stream and its Deep Fork tributary to the north. Started in 1894 and known successively as Pennington and Sweeney, it took its present name in 1898 to honor Frank Harrah, a local businessman. Older baseball fans will readily associate the town with Paul and Lloyd Waner, well known Pittsburgh Pirate stars of the 1930's. As Big and Little Poison (for the effect they had on opposition pitching staffs), they are one of the rare brother teams in baseball's Hall of Fame.

Just northwest of Harrah is Horseshoe Lake (fishing), which serves an Oklahoma Gas & Electric Co. steam generating plant.

Harris (McCurtain Co., pop. 100, on US 259, 16 mi. SE of *Idabel,* see Map 6). A scattered farming community in the fertile *Red River* valley. W. B. Harris moved his family to this area with the Choctaw migration of the 1830's, settling at Pecan Point (now shown on some maps as Harris Bend). At Pecan Point, in 1816, Methodists had held the state's first church service.
Henry Harris, for whom the town was named, was a son of W. B. Harris. For a time he operated a ferry on Red River at Pecan Point. His impressive home, four miles north of Harris (inquire locally), was built just after the Civil War. It has been restored by the Charles Harrises, filled with family furniture, documents, and artifacts dating to the American Revolution.

Hartshorne (Pittsburg Co., pop. 2,121, on US 270, see Map 6). Major twin of the rich coal-producing Twin Cities section of Pittsburg County. Both it and *Haileyville* were established in 1890 with arrival of the Choctaw Coal and Railway Company (now the Rock Island) and were platted in 1902. Until the decline of large-scale mining activity both, too, were bustling communities, grown together on either side of the connecting railroad and highway. Dr. Charles Hartshorne was a railroad official and early settler.
An electronics firm, established in 1964, has helped take up slack in the local economy caused by coal's fall from favor. A Russian Orthodox Church indicates the foreign-born origin of many of the county's early miners. Also of interest just northeast of Hartshorne is Jones Academy, well known Indian boys' school, established by the Choctaw Nation in 1891 as a companion to the *Tuskahoma* Female Academy. Now coeducational, it is operated by the federal government. Best-known native of Hartshorne is Warren Spahn, long the National League's star lefthanded

pitcher (Boston, Milwaukee), who lives on a nearby ranch.

Haskell (Muskogee Co., pop. 2,063, on US 64, see Map 5). A prosperous, progressive agricultural community in the fertile *Arkansas River* valley. It was founded shortly after the turn of the century and honors Charles N. Haskell, Oklahoma's first governor (1907–11).

Haskell County (eastern Oklahoma, see Map 6). Area, 614 sq. mi.; pop., 9,578; county seat, *Stigler.* A farming and strip coal mining area defined by the *Canadian* and *Arkansas* rivers on the north and the San Bois Mountains on the south. Created in 1908, the county was named for Charles N. Haskell, a member of the Constitutional Convention and the state's first governor.

Hastings (Jefferson Co., pop. 184, on OK 5, 10 mi. NW of *Waurika,* see Map 7). Little remains today of this town— established in 1902 on a branch line of the Enid & Anadarko railroad (present Rock Island) and named for a local resident—to remind one of its former importance. In 1904 it boasted 600 residents and Southwest Academy, later combined with a junior college in the northern part of the state to become present Oklahoma Baptist University at *Shawnee.* By 1908 it had a population of 1,000 and the usual complement of frontier businesses. Then it began gradually to lose out to *Waurika* and nearby *Temple.*

Haworth (McCurtain Co., pop. 293, on OK 3, 13 mi. SE of *Idabel,* see Map 6). A lumbering community on the Frisco Railroad in the heart of the *Ouachita National Forest.* Formerly known as Norwood, the town dates from the turn of the century.

Haywood (Pittsburg Co., pop. 150, on OK 31, 11 mi. SW of *McAlester,* see Map 6). Railroad-siding community (Rock Island) dating from the turn of the century. Bill Haywood was the famed socialist labor leader and founder of the Industrial Workers of the World.

Headrick (Jackson Co., pop. 139, off US 62, 11 mi. E of *Altus,* see Map 8). Townsite owner T. B. Headrick was honored in the naming, in 1902, of this now dwindling little farming community. Red granite hills pushing up from virtually level fields just to the north mark the southwestern edge of the *Wichita Mountains.*

Healdton (Carter Co., pop. 2,324, on OK 76, see Map 7). A town—born in 1883 and named for a local merchant, Charles H. Heald—that came of age in its thirtieth year. On August 4, 1913, the Franklin No. 1 was brought in, the first producing oil well in the billion-dollar Healdton Field. (The site is about two miles to the southwest, near the present near-ghost of *Wirt.*) The resulting oil boom spread eventually to much of western Carter County, virtually created such towns as *Wilson, County Line, Ratliff City, Tatums,* and *Fox,* and made a modern, progressive city of *Ardmore.* Still other camps spawned by the boom have, like Wirt, virtually disappeared.

Typical of oil patch folklore is the oft-told tale of how the Healdton discovery was made. How the wagon transporting the steam boiler that powered the cable tool rig broke down while crossing a stream and had to be off-loaded to complete the crossing. How next morning the drilling crew arrived and, assuming this was the designated site for the wildcat, started to make hole. And how the originally intended site, when finally tested, proved to be dry! Be that as it may, the extended field that developed from that 1913 discovery well was a major one. The visiting motorist wishing to get an idea of the scope of the field has only to drive OK 76 from US 70 on the south to County Line on the north. Bobbing pumper jacks dot the pleasant little city of Healdton itself. Oil well service and supply companies continue to provide the bulk of employment in the area. Plans are now being made to develop the Healdton Oil Museum, including, it is hoped, the original discovery site.

Heavener (LeFlore Co., pop. 2,566, at junc. of US 59 & 270, see Map 6). The

120

Ancient runic letters carved into rock at Heavener Runestone State Park.

town began in 1896, with arrival of the Kansas City Southern Railway. In 1910 it became a division point. And today, with some 300 employees in the area, the KCS remains its economic mainstay. In recent years, however, travel and recreation have become increasingly important. (Joseph Heavener was owner of the townsite.)

Nearby points of interest: *Heavener Runestone State Park* (2 miles east); *Cedar Lake* (11 miles southwest); and the Peter Conser House (see *Conser*).

Heavener Runestone State Park (Le-Flore Co., 2 mi. E of *Heavener,* see Map 6). In 1912, high on the side of Poteau Mountain, was discovered a large slab of Savannah sandstone (12 feet high, 10 feet wide, almost two feet thick) on which were deeply carved eight runic letters 6 to 9 inches tall. Age, origin, meaning—and authenticity—are still matters of some controversy. It is believed by many, however, that they record the visit to this area of a Viking party in 1017. Beyond question is the beauty of the natural setting, now preserved by the state as a picnic area.

Helena (Alfalfa Co., pop. 769, on OK 58, see Map 3). A pleasant little agricultural community, established in 1894, a year after the Cherokee Outlet was opened to settlement. The State Training School for Boys there occupies a score of buildings on a ten-acre campus. Enrollment hovers at about 175. All are boys fifteen to eighteen years of age who have come into conflict with the rules and regulations of organized society.

Hennepin (Garvin Co., pop. 350, on OK 7, see Map 7). A scattered community on the northwest flank of the *Arbuckle Mountains.* Settled in 1885, it was named for the famed Jesuit explorer, Father Louis Hennepin.

Hennessey (Kingfisher Co., pop. 2,181, on US 81, see Map 4). This agricultural community, now booming on the strength of recent extensive oil and gas discoveries, was laid out in 1889 with the opening of Old Oklahoma to settlement. It took its name from Pat Hennessey, a freighter on the *Chisholm Trail,* who figured in one of the county's few serious Indian encounters.

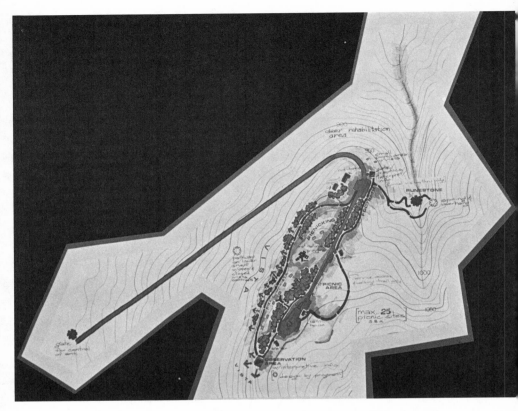

Park plan now being put into effect for Heavener Runestone State Park.

In 1874 the Plains tribes were on the warpath from Texas to the Dakotas. And on July 4, at what is now the northwest corner of the town, Hennessey's three-wagon outfit, on its way south with coffee and sugar for the Kiowa-Comanche Agency, was attacked. Hennessey and his three drivers were killed. It is presumed that Cheyennes were guilty of the attack, although no absolute proof has ever been established. Hennessey's grave and a rough-stone memorial feature a small memorial park near the site.

In a second park beside the highway, in the center of town, there is another impressive monument, this one to Roy Cashion. A trooper in the First U.S. Volunteer Cavalry (Rough Riders) in the Spanish-American War of 1898, and a native of Hennessey, Cashion was one of the first Oklahomans to die for his country on foreign soil. He was killed in the battle for San Juan Hill. Nearby an Oklahoma Historical Society marker notes establishment on this site in 1900 of the state's first rural mail route.

On the south edge of Hennessey another official marker calls attention to the site of Bull Foot Stage Station. The building was burned the day Hennessey was killed. Today the area is cluttered with oil well service and supply companies, symbols of the town's latter-day prosperity.

Henryetta (Okmulgee Co., pop. 6,430, on I 40 at junc. of US 62, 75, & 266, see Map 5). Founded in 1900 when the Frisco Railroad arrived and named its station for Creek Indian Hugh Henry and his wife Etta, this second largest town in Okmulgee County has always been Oklahoma's traditional labor capital. Its big Labor Day celebration, begun just after World War II, now draws upwards of 20,000 visitors and has long been the popular forum used by state politicians to announce their election plans.

As with most towns dependent on mining, however, Henryetta has had its economic ups and downs. The decline of coal mining was the first crippling blow. This was followed in the 1960's by the sag in lead and zinc activity in Oklahoma, which led to the closing of its smelter. But Henryetta has always managed to move into other areas and to thus take up the economic slack. Principal industries now include glass containers, iron castings, modular homes, game decoys, and fiber glass products.

Henryetta is the home of Jim Shoulders, winner of five World's Championship Cowboy titles, a fact proudly proclaimed on roadside billboards. The retired rodeo star now runs a 5,000-acre spread near town that sends bucking stock to rodeos from Texas to Canada. Since 1961 Shoulders has run one of the first schools in the country to teach bronc and bull riding. (Another school that specializes in instruction in bull-dogging is at nearby **Checotah.**)

Top close-in recreation facility is 550-acre Lake Henryetta to the east. User fees are collected.

Hess (Jackson Co., pop. 75, off US 283, 12 mi. S, 4 mi. E of **Altus,** see Map 8). Only a store and a handful of houses mark this old farming community, established in 1889 and named for Elvira P. Hess, the first postmaster. Far better known than the community itself was Doan's Crossing of **Red River** for the Western Cattle Trail.

Here, in the 1870's and 1880's, several million Texas longhorns swam or waded the river (relatively small here and formerly called the Prairie Dog Town Fork) to begin the long trek northward across Indian Territory to railheads in Kansas. Peak year was probably 1881, when over 300,000 cattle were herded up the trail. Doan's Store, from which the trail took its name, was on the Texas side of the river. The actual crossing point is some 8 miles south and east of Hess and virtually inaccessible by ordinary automobile.

Hester (Greer Co., pop. 22, off US 283, 9 mi. SE of **Mangum,** see Map 8). A dwindling farm community, established in 1910 with building of the Wichita Falls and Northwestern Railway between **Mangum** and **Altus.** As the M-K-T Railroad, later extended well into the Oklahoma Panhandle, it was only recently abandoned. Hester was the daughter of Sam Rude, an early-day cattleman in the area.

Hext (Beckham Co., off US 66, 7 mi. W of **Sayre,** see Map 8). Started in 1902 with arrival of the present Rock Island, this one-time railroad siding community never quite got off the ground. Mid-way between **Erick** and **Sayre,** it lost its post office before the year was out. It was, apparently, hexed—despite the fact it was named for local rancher William Hext.

Heyburn Reservoir (just N of I 44 at Heyburn exit, in Creek County, see Map 4). This 980-acre lake on Polecat Creek was created by the Corps of Engineers in 1950. The state maintains a 438-acre recreation area on its north shore, access to which is gained from OK 33 between **Sapulpa** and **Drumright.**

Facilities: camp and picnic areas, trailer hookups, swimming beach, boat ramps. Addresses: Heyburn Recreation Area, Kellyville, OK 74039; U.S. Corps of Engineers, Box 61, Tulsa, OK 74102.

Rock Mary, well-known landmark on the California Trail.

Hickory (Murray Co., pop. 62, off OK 12, 9 mi. E of *Sulphur,* see Map 7). A tiny ranching community, established in 1893 and named for a nearby grove of hickory trees.

Higgins (Latimer Co., on OK 1, 7 mi. SE of *Hartshorne,* see Map 6). A virtually non-existent community today, found on only the most charitable of maps, Higgins flourished briefly around the turn of the century. (R. W. Higgins was a territorial jurist.) A half-century before, from 1858 to 1861, this Gaines Creek valley echoed to the rattling of Butterfield Overland stages.

The site of Pusley's Station, about two miles southwest of Higgins, is now isolated on a private ranch. But the history-minded motorist will swing north from OK 1 (in town, inquire locally) and loop up onto wooded Blue Mountain to the site of Mountain Station. An official Butterfield route marker is there beside the road, although this was not an official stage stop. In 1867, after the Civil War, the Choctaw Council granted tollroad privileges to one Olasechubi. His home was in the woods on the west side of the road. On the east is one of Oklahoma's most picturesquely located old cemeteries.

Hinton (Caddo Co., pop. 889, at junc. of US 281 & OK 8 and OK 37, see Map 8). A prosperous farming community that began in 1902, a year after the area was opened to white settlement, when the present Rock Island ran a rail line south through these one-time Kiowa-Apache-Comanche lands. The branch was abandoned in 1939, but discovery of vast underground water reservoirs since then has made widespread well irrigation feasible. To wheat, cotton and livestock raising has now been added peanuts, and this section of *Caddo County,* with an average yield of 2,500 pounds per acre, presently contributes almost half of Oklahoma's total peanut production.

Near Hinton are several highly scenic areas of deeply eroded red rock canyons and dense woods where one can find nearly half the 140 species of trees that grow in Oklahoma. **Red Rock Canyon State Park** is one of these. It was first developed in 1930 by the Hinton Kiwanis Club. In the colorful canyon, in 1931, was staged the initial Hinton Kiwanis Rodeo. Still held annually (three days, including July 4), though now in Hinton, it is the state's oldest in continuous operation.

Fully as beautiful is Devil's Canyon (off OK 37, 7 mi. SE), a 560-acre preserve that includes 14 flowing natural springs and, like Red Rock, appropriate legends of outlaw gangs that used these natural rock corrals to hide stolen horses and cattle. Purchased by Oklahoma Methodists in 1954, the area has been extensively developed as a church campground and assembly center—under the more discreet name of Methodist Canyon.

Four miles west of Hinton is Rock Mary (private, inquire locally), a prominent landmark on the *California Trail* first visited and named by a party under the escort of Captain R. B. Marcy. Rock Mary is the farthest east of a series of flat-top red rock mounds that can best be seen from I 40 near *Hydro.*

Hitchcock (Blaine Co., pop. 160, on OK 8, 10 mi. NE of *Watonga,* see Map 3). Established in 1901 with the arrival of the present Rock Island Railroad, it was named for Ethan A. Hitchcock, then secretary of the interior. Though the center of a rich farming area (wheat, primarily), its business life has pretty well shrunk now to a single, towering concrete grain elevator and an attractive, locally popular restaurant.

Hitchita (McIntosh Co., pop. 160, off US 266, 15 mi. NW of *Checotah,* see Map 5). Small rural community established in 1910 and named for a small Muskhogean Indian band now absorbed into the Creek tribe.

Hobart (Kiowa Co. seat, pop. 4,638, on OK 9 just west of its junc. with US 183, see Map 8). A rather typical Western Oklahoma county seat, in history, development, and present-day appearance. The town sprang to life full grown, after a fashion, on August 6, 1901, the day the sprawling Kiowa-Comanche lands were thrown open to settlement. Some 150,000 persons registered for the land lottery and 13,000 reserved allotments in the area.

The townsite company had opened a number of businesses in tents and "Ragtown" was said to have had 2,000 tents before the first building was thrown up. Its more formal name honors Vice President (under McKinley) Garrett A. Hobart.

Despite a series of devastating fires— and the *Babbs Switch* tragedy in 1924— Hobart developed steadily into a progressive community with just enough oil development and generally farmbased industry to maintain a strong diversified economy. (A local feed milling company and a spray foam insulation manufacturer offer plant tours.) Wheat and cattle dominate the farm scene, although cotton still plays a role. Industrial development centers around the crossing of the Rock Island and Frisco railroads at the southeast edge of town. A traditional courthouse square anchors the solid business section. An attractive school plant straddles Main Street three blocks to the north.

Hunter Park with its small lake, on the city's northwest corner, provides recreational facilities, supplemented by sprawling Hobart Lake near *Rocky.* The

annual special events calendar features the traditional spring junior livestock show, an Arts & Crafts Festival in late April, and the Kiowa Little Britches Rodeo in mid-July. An interesting area site is the historic Elk Creek Indian Cemetery (4 mi. S). Among the many interesting stones is that marking the grave of Lone Wolf, the respected Kiowa chief for whom the town of *Lone Wolf* was named.

Hodgen (LeFlore Co., pop. 175, on US 59-270, 4 mi. S of *Heavener,* see Map 6). Texas hero Sam Houston lost out in 1910 to Kansas City Southern Railway timber buyer J. W. Hodgens when this little community, established in 1896, changed its name. Ironically, it managed to "honor" its presumed benefactor by simultaneously misspelling his name! Which could—but probably doesn't—explain its somewhat startling lack of growth, especially when one considers its highly scenic location on the north edge of *Quachita National Forest* and the *Kiamichi Mountains.* It also lies at the eastern terminus of the beautiful Holson Valley Road (see *Summerfield*). Since 1971 Hodgen has been best known for the nearby Quachita Vocational and Technical Camp, a rehabilitation center operated as a branch of the state penal system.

Hoffman (Okmulgee Co., pop. 262, off US 266, 9 mi. NE of *Henryetta,* see Map 5). A small rural community on the Kansas, Oklahoma and Gulf Railroad, named in 1905 for Oklahoma City attorney Roy Hoffman. With the nearby communities of *Dewar, Schulter,* and *Wildcat,* it has suffered from the sharp decline of coal mining.

Holdenville (Hughes Co. seat, pop. 5,101, on OK 48 just S of junc. with US 270, see Map 7). After two site and three name changes, this town came into being officially in 1895 at the crossing of the Choctaw, Oklahoma and Gulf (now the Rock Island) and the Frisco railroads. The name honored the CO&G's general manager, J. F. Holden. Its greatest period of growth came in the 1920's with development of the Greater

Seminole oil field to the west. In more recent years the manufacture of women's clothing, fishing gear, and modular homes, among other products, has helped take up the economic slack.

Although nothing remains to be seen there today, the area south of Holdenville, where Little River flows into the *South Canadian,* is historically important. Here in 1834 the U.S. Dragoons established Fort Holmes. Nearby, the trading firm of Edwards and Shelton subsequently established a store. As Edwards Store, or Fort Edwards, it was a stop on the busy *California Trail.* In its later years it was run by the well known Jesse Chisholm, who married Edwards' daughter. Then it was a popular trading point for Plains Indians to the west, particularly the Comanches.

Hollis (Harmon Co. seat, pop. 3,150, at junc. of US 62 and OK 30, see Map 8). Settlement by ranchers in this corner of old *Greer County* began as early as 1880. However, the town of Hollis—for townsite owner George W. Hollis—was not established until 1901, with opening of the Kiowa-Comanche-Apache lands to white settlement. It is still primarily a farming/ranching area. Largest employer is a cotton oil mill, which manufactures animal feeds for the export market. Biggest annual event is the Riding Club Rodeo in late July. Legion Park provides swimming, picnic facilities. Hall Lake (off OK 30, 10 mi. N) is a 50-acre fishing empoundment managed by the Oklahoma Department of Wildlife Conservation. Until 1975 Hollis was western terminus of the curiously individualistic Hollis & Eastern Railroad (see *Duke*).

Hollister (Tillman Co., pop. 105, on OK 54, 11 mi. SE of *Frederick,* see Map 8). A dwindling railroad siding community (M-K-T) that came into being in 1909, taking the name of *Frederick* station agent Harry L. Hollister.

Homestead (Blaine Co., pop. 65, off OK 51, 4 mi. NW of *Okeene,* see Map 3). A rail's-end "elevator town" that has served a dwindling number of homesteaders since 1893.

Hominy (Osage Co., pop. 2,274, at junc. of OK 20 and OK 99, see Map 4). A modern, predominantly Indian town in the southern part of the county near the upper reaches of *Keystone Reservoir,* Hominy's prosperity is based solidly on oil and the richness of its surrounding grasslands. Indeed, much of the area's history and economic development is readily apparent in these lush, rolling pastures with their grazing cattle, pumping oil wells, and large, solidly built farm homes, vintage the 1920's, when the oil boom was at its peak. Two-story affairs, often with wide porches, porte-cocheres, large detached garages, and other signs of affluence, many of these homes are now empty. But they still reflect the scope of the oil boom of fifty years ago as in few other sections of the state.

Hominy began as a sub-agency for the Osages in 1874, shortly after their arrival from Kansas and Missouri. It acquired a post office in 1891, a railroad (the M-K-T) in 1903. In 1904 it built the first permanent public school building in the county, a stone affair that still stands. Oil was first discovered in the area in 1916. Recently the town's economy has been buttressed by several small industries, one of the largest of which is a garment plant.

The name Hominy has long been the subject of some speculation. Historian George Shirk believes it is a corruption of Harmony, from Harmony Mission in Missouri. But local sources credit it to the Osage leader Ho Moie, meaning He-Who-Walks-in-the-Dark. All are agreed that it does not refer to the Indian corn food, hominy.

Two annual events underscore Hominy's strong Osage heritage. Ceremonial (War) Dances are held at the Indian Village the last week in June. The last week in September Osages celebrate their removal to Oklahoma. Both events are open to the public and draw large crowds. Three city lakes near Hominy provide hunting, fishing, camping and picnic areas.

Honey Creek Recreation Area. See *Grand Lake of the Cherokees.*

Honobia (LeFlore Co., pop. 25, on OK 144, 15 mi. SE of *Talihina,* see Map 6). A scattered forest community on flood-prone *Little River* is one of the most isolated—and highly scenic—areas of Oklahoma. The name is that of an early-day Choctaw settler. From Honobia a series of graded and graveled roads fan out to serve similarly isolated settlements in *Pushmataha* and *McCurtain* counties. OK 144 runs west through Fewell, Nolia, and *Nashoba* to a junction with US 271—southeast through *Bethel* to US 259. Unnumbered graded roads twist eastward through Ludlow and Octavia to US 259 and south through Pickens and *Alikchi* to OK 3. The so-called Indian Road climbs northwest over the *Kiamichi Mountains* to *Talihina.*

Hooker (Texas Co., pop. 1,615, at junc. of US 54 & 56 and OK 94, see Map 2). Prosperous farming/ranching community that sprang into being in 1901 when the Rock Island started laying track across the *Oklahoma Panhandle.* Joseph Hooker was a local cattleman. Tall concrete elevators, feed mills, implement houses, and farm supply stores mark the slashing parallel course of highway and rail line across the southeast edge of the town. A compact business section and tree-shaded residential area lie to the west and north.

Another element of Hooker's prosperity is apparent just to the southwest of town. The sprawling Dorchester Corp. plant and a Natural Gas Pipeline Co. facility attest to the vast petroleum wealth that underlies much of the Panhandle. The Hugoton (Kansas) Gas Field—which begins half a dozen miles east of Hooker and extends westward for some 50 miles—is perhaps the world's largest single gas field. Oil and gas development in the county began in 1923.

Hopeton (Woods Co., pop. 75, on US 281, 7 mi. S of *Alva,* see Map 3). A tiny trade center with a population just big enough to staff its bank—a bank with deposits more than big enough to reflect the general prosperity of this rolling farming/ranching region.

Howe (LeFlore Co., pop. 403, on US 59, 5 mi. N of *Heavener,* see Map 6). A community that grew up at the turn of the century around the crossing point of the Kansas City Southern and Rock Island railroads. Dr. Herbert M. Howe was an early KCS director.

Hoyt (Haskell Co., pop. 140, off OK 9, 8 mi. W of *Whitefield,* see Map 6). Rural community in rugged country near the *Canadian River.* Started in 1890, it was named for an early ferryboat operator, Babe Hoyt.

Hughes County (east-central Oklahoma, see Map 7). Area, 810 sq. mi.; pop., 13,228; county seat, *Holdenville.* An oil rich county created at statehood and named for a member of the Constitutional Convention, W. C. Hughes.

Hugo (Choctaw Co. seat, pop. 6,585, at junc. of US 70 & 271, see Map 6). Founded in 1901 and named for the famed French novelist, Hugo enjoyed a brief boom with the coming of the Arkansas and Choctaw Railroad (now the Frisco). It is still an important rail division point. With World War II, however, there was the loss of population common to agriculturally oriented communities all across Oklahoma. It was then the town launched its successful industrialization drive. Payrolls today include plants turning out gloves, modular homes, processed food, furniture, and other wood products.

Unique in Oklahoma is Hugo's "Circus Town" status. For years the town has provided winter quarters for the Carson & Barnes Circus (the former Al G. Kelly & Miller Bros. Circus) and, at various times, other smaller outfits. Their grounds (which feature some 25 elephants) are usually open to visitors from October to April. Interesting any time is the Showmen's Rest section of Mount Olivet Cemetery, the only burial area in the Southwest exclusively for

127

show people. Impressive marker at the entrance is a granite shaft picturing a performing elephant and a giant circus tent. The inscription: IN TRIBUTE TO ALL SHOWMEN UNDER GOD'S BIG TOP. The special cemetery was opened in 1960 following the death of Kelly Miller.

Indian influence remains strong in and around Hugo. Dedicated in 1972 and covering an entire block is the quarter-million-dollar Choctaw Cultural Center. It provides a handsome forum for all aspects of Choctaw arts and culture. Traditional annual event is a Memorial weekend rodeo.

Of special visitor interest in the Hugo area: *Goodland* Children's Home, *Rose Hill, Fort Towson,* and the Chief's House at *Swink.*

Hugo Reservoir (off US 70 at *Sawyer,* 8 mi. E of *Hugo,* see Map 6). A 13,250-acre empoundment on the *Kiamichi River,* approximately 18 miles upstream from its mouth at *Red River.* The rolled earthfill dam is 10,200 feet long, stands 101 feet above the streambed. When fully developed the reservoir's public use areas—six of them around the lake, one below the dam—will include camping, picnicking, and swimming facilities, boat ramps. Address: U.S. Corps of Engineers, Box 61, Tulsa, OK 74102.

Hulah (Osage Co., on OK 10, see Map 4). A tiny community platted in 1918 and best known today for nearby *Hulah Reservoir* on Caney River. The Osage word *hulah* means "eagle." The once-sprawling Cross Bell Ranch, owned and operated by three generations of the E. C. Mullendore family, is now headquartered on 1,000 acres of Osage grassland near Hulah. Until 1972 it ran cattle on 445,000 acres of land, owned and leased, in four separate ranches in Oklahoma and Kansas.

Hulah Reservoir (off OK 10, 22 mi. NE of *Pawhuska,* in Osage County, see Map 4). A 3,600-acre lake on Caney River, created by the Corps of Engineers in 1951. There is a waterfowl refuge on

the north shore, a 3,535-acre public hunting area maintained by the state on the south shore.

Facilities: many picnic and camping areas, swimming beaches, boat ramps, and concessions. Address: U.S. Corps of Engineers, Box 61, Tulsa OK 74102.

Hulbert (Cherokee Co., pop. 505, on OK 51, 11 mi. W of *Tahlequah,* see Map 5). A small trading center named in 1903 for Ben H. Hulbert, a prominent Cherokee. Its economy has been stimulated in recent years by the recreational activity surrounding *Fort Gibson Reservoir* and *Sequoyah State Park.*

Hunter (Garfield Co., pop. 274, off OK 74 in the NE corner of the county, see Map 4). Another "elevator town" on a Frisco branch line in a rich wheat-producing region. It was established in 1901 and named for the townsite owner, Charles Hunter.

Hunting. Oklahoma can no longer boast a border-to-border carpeting of buffalo, of course. In several other categories, however, the state can probably boast hunting opportunities as good as, if not indeed better than, those in the so-called good old days. After years of propogation and management many once-plentiful game birds and animals are being brought back, and most of Oklahoma's seventy-seven counties can now offer one or more legal targets for the sportsman throughout the year.

Deer herds are increasing steadily in almost all sections of the state. Wild turkey have grown rapidly in numbers since 1948, now afford spring and fall shooting in a majority of the counties. The Oklahoma quail kill is one of the nation's highest. In recent years pheasant can be taken in the *Oklahoma Panhandle.* Prairie chickens are hunted legally in both the northwestern and northeastern sections of the state. Waterfowl hunting is generally excellent on Oklahoma lakes in the fall. One Sooner State extra: crow hunting (see *Fort Cobb Reservoir*).

For complete information on seasons, license fees, and regulations write Department of Wildlife Conservation, 1801 N. Lincoln Blvd., Oklahoma City, OK 73105.

Hydro (Caddo Co., pop. 805, at junc. of I 40 & US 66 and OK 58, see Map 8). Settlement began here in 1898, when the Rock Island was laying tracks westward across Oklahoma. Elevators, feed mills, and a large peanut buying station indicate the town's strong agricultural base. South of the town and the highway are the striking Hydro Mounds, a series of isolated, flat-topped mesas that have caught the eye of travelers since the California Trail days of 1849 (see **Hinton**). The red cap rock on the mounds, cut into building stones, is used widely in this area. Hydro is yet another tornado-conscious Oklahoma town (see **Seiling**) to build a storm-proof underground school.

Idabel (McCurtain Co. seat, pop. 5,946, at junc. of US 70 & 259, see Map 6). Settled in 1903 with arrival of the Choctaw and Arkansas Railroad (present Frisco) and named for the two daughters (Ida and Belle Purnell) of a C&A official, Idabel today is the bustling heart of Oklahoma's expanding lumber industry. It is headquarters town for giant Weyerhaeuser Company's Dierks Division, and while it lacks the big lumber mills and factories that sustain **Broken Bow**, **Wright City**, and **Valliant**, it does possess half a dozen smaller timber-related facilities. Also sustaining the town's economy—along with agriculture—are factories producing such things as men's wear, mobile homes, and modular homes.

Illinois River. Oklahoma's favorite river in many ways. It enters the northeastern corner of the state from Arkansas, flows south-southwestward 109 miles to enter the **Arkansas River** near **Gore**. From Lake Francis on the Arkansas line to **Tenkiller Reservoir** near its mouth it is a free-flowing and highly scenic stream. Since 1970 the Illinois, with its Flint Creek and Barren Fork Creek tributaries, has been protected

Canoeing on the Illinois River, popular stream for float trips.

as a Scenic River, its present form unalterable without express permission of the state legislature.

The Illinois is perhaps the state's best single fishing stream. Nearly every game fish found in Oklahoma can be taken from its waters. It is the only stream in the state that can accommodate float trips of up to several days in length. They are available at a dozen privately owned camps dotting the river above **Tahlequah** and accessible from OK 10. Threading a narrow, heavily wooded course between the river on the east and picturesquely overhanging bluffs on the west, the road is one of the most eye pleasing in Oklahoma. Along it, too, are a number of state-maintained public access areas.

The river, according to historian George H. Shirk, was named for the

Illinois Indians, once an important Algonquin tribe. The name was probably brought to this area by the Osages, their traditional allies.

For details on Illinois River recreation, write Department of Wildlife Conservation, 1801 N. Lincoln Blvd., Oklahoma City, OK 73105.

Indiahoma (Comanche Co., pop. 434, off US 62, 21 mi. W of *Lawton*, see Map 8). Small trading center, established in 1902, that has always been closely associated with the Comanche Indians and their best known chief, Quanah Parker (see *Cache*). On the northwest edge of town is the modern Post Oak Mennonite Brethren Church and nearby cemetery. The Mennonites were the first missionaries to be allowed by Parker to work among the Comanches. The original mission, established in 1894, was located 2 miles east and 3 miles north of here. The site was abandoned in 1957 to make way for expansion of the *Fort Sill* firing range. At that time the graves of Parker and his mother, Cynthia Ann, were moved to *Fort Sill*. The other graves, Indian and white, including those of Rev. and Mrs. A. J. Becker, who served at the mission from 1901 to 1953, were moved here. The Post Oak parochial school near by is now closed. A paved road north from Indiahoma leads to the *Wichita Mountain Wildlife Refuge* headquarters.

Indianola (Pittsburg Co., pop. 205, on OK 113, 8 mi. W of *Canadian*, see Map 6). Tiny community on the south shore of *Eufaula Reservoir*. It was settled in the early 1890's.

Ingalls (Payne Co., pop. 50, off OK 51, 10 mi. E of *Stillwater*, see Map 4). A near-ghost today—established in 1890 and named for Senator John J. Ingalls of Kansas—this once-lively little frontier community is best known for the September 1, 1893, shoot-out that cost the lives of three U.S. marshals and an innocent bystander, a fracas that led, eventually to the break-up of the notorious outlaw gangs of Bill Doolin and Bill Dalton.

This section of Indian Territory had been used from time to time by the outlaws as a refuge. It was to this place they retreated after the disastrous attempt to raid two Coffeyville (Kansas) banks simultaneously. And it was here the federal officers found and attacked them.

The furious battle left more than 225 bullet holes in the walls of the Ransom-Murray Saloon, where the outlaws were playing cards when the officers attacked. Understandably weakened, the walls have long-since disappeared. But the site is suitably marked, as is that of the O. K. Hotel, where Arkansas Tom was captured; the H. F. Pierce Livery, where one of the marshals was killed; and other now-vanished structures. The restored log cabin is authentic, but was moved to its present site from several miles to the west. Biggest event in the town is the annual Ingalls Homecoming, a reunion of oldtimers held in early September.

Ingersoll (Alfalfa Co., pop. 17, on US 64, 5 mi. NW of *Cherokee*, see Map 3). Now a tiny community on a lightly-used Rock Island branch line, Ingersoll was established in 1901 and for a time was a bustling little railroad center. The name honors C. E. Ingersoll, Philadelphia railroad official.

Inola (Rogers Co., pop. 948, near the junc. of OK 33 and OK 88, 12 mi. SE of *Claremore*, see Map 5). A bustling little agricultural community near the *Verdigris River* that began in 1890, takes its name from the Cherokee word for "black fox." This is one of the few areas in the state where the horse-drawn wagons and buggies of conservative Mennonite farmers can still be seen. And it is near Inola, ironically enough, that the Public Service Company of Oklahoma began building the state's first nuclear power station. The $800 million facility would have had a generating capacity of 1,100,000 kilowatts. Public opposition to nuclear power caused the company to cancel the project.

Isabella (Major Co., just W of OK 8, 8 mi. N of *Okeene*, see Map 3). A tiny farming community, dating from 1894, that owes its name to a local landowner's wife, Belle Isbell.

J

Jackson County (in extreme southwestern Oklahoma on the *Red River*, see Map 8). Area, 780 sq. mi.; pop. 30,902; county seat, *Altus*. Created at statehood in 1907 from the southern section of old *Greer County* and named for Confederate General Thomas J. "Stonewall" Jackson.

Top travel lures: *Altus Reservoir*, Museum of the Western Prairie in *Altus*.

Jay (Delaware Co. seat, pop. 1,594, at junc. of US 59, OK 10, and OK 20, see Map 5). A relative newcomer among towns in this area, Jay did not get its post office until 1909, two years after statehood. But three years later, on January 3, 1912, by proclamation of the governor, it took over the seat of county government, from *Grove*. The name honors Jay Washburn, nephew of Stand Watie, the Cherokee Indian who became a general in the Confederate army during the Civil War (see *Big Cabin*). Watie is buried in Polson Cemetery, some 14 miles northeast of Jay.

Today Jay is a supply center for the growing recreation industry. Heavily wooded hills surround the town, and three of Oklahoma's best-known fishing lakes (*Grand*, *Spavinaw*, and *Upper Spavinaw*) are only minutes away. Cherokee Indian culture is still strong in the area, however. The Bull Hollow Arts & Crafts Center, on the Kenwood Indian Reserve Area south of Jay, is open daily to US 59 motorists. And at least two Indian churches—Hillside, off OK 28 northwest of Jay, and Piney, on OK 20 east of town—still hold regular services in the Cherokee language to which visitors are always welcome.

Jefferson (Grant Co., pop. 128, on US 81, 7 mi. SW of *Medford*, see Map 4). Now a dwindling farm community in a fine wheat growing area (it had its own flour mill until quite recently), Jefferson boasts a good bit of exciting early-day history. Tall elms and cottonwoods just south of town mark the site of Rock Island Park, once planned as a townsite,

then later used as a park. Though weed-grown and neglected, the plot contains the still impressive monument to Sewell's Stockade, built in the early 1870's for protection from Indian raiding parties. At nearby Round Pond are some of the most clearly visible signs that remain of the historic *Chisholm Trail*, along which Sewell's was a popular stopping place. Plans are currently under way by the Grant County Historical Society (see *Medford*) to rehabilitate the historic park and dramatize its role in the development of the area.

Jefferson began as Pond, had a post office by that name from 1879 to 1887, well before this area—the Cherokee Outlet—was opened to settlement in 1893. The following year Jefferson proper was established after present *Pond Creek* abandoned this site for a new one three miles to the south. However, major floods on Osage and Pond creeks have plagued the town since 1944. Those in 1970, 1973, and 1974 finally succeeded in driving all business activity away except for that of a single grain elevator. But for the homes of its loyal residents and two churches, Jefferson is now a picturesque, and historic, ghost.

Jefferson County (south-central Oklahoma along the *Red River*, see Map 7). Area, 755 sq. mi.; pop. 7,125; county seat, *Waurika*. Created at statehood in 1907 from parts of *Comanche County*, Oklahoma Territory, on the west and the Chickasaw Nation, Indian Trritory, on the east.

Jenks (Tulsa Co., pop. 1,997, off US 75 at S edge of *Tulsa*, see Map 5). Now a pleasant little Tulsa suburb on the west bank of the *Arkansas River*, Jenks came into being in 1905, largely on the strength of a rapidly spreading oil play in the area. However, like nearby *Kiefer*, *Glenpool*, and *Red Fork*, it had the action, but saw the growth and significant development go to the self-styled "Oil Capital." Elmer E. Jenks was a long-time area resident.

Jennings (Pawnee Co., pop. 338, on OK 99, see Map 4). A small rural com-

Grave of Jesse Chisholm, famed trader for whom the Chisholm Trail was named.

munity dating from the opening of the Cherokee Outlet in 1893. The name honors George Jennings, allottee of the land. The roughly eroded, mostly wooded area stretching east from Jennings to where the **Cimarron** and **Arkansas** Rivers join was long a favorite haven of such notorious outlaws as the Daltons, the Doolins, Matt Kimes, and Wilbur Underhill.

Jenson (LeFlore Co., on the Oklahoma-Arkansas border, 17 mi. NE of **Poteau**, see Map 6). A rail-siding community distinguished primarily for its possession of the state's only railroad tunnel. The 1,180-foot bore, completed in 1886 by the Fort Smith and Southern Railway (present Frisco), penetrates Backbone Mountain, on the state line, and was originally called Backbone Tunnel.

Jesse Chisholm Grave (site is 8 mi. NE of **Geary** on US 270 & 281, see Map 4). A sod mound and marker overlook Left Hand Spring and a cutoff section of the **North Canadian River**. Here, on March 4, 1868, the Indian trader Jesse Chisholm—for whom the famed **Chisholm Trail** was named—died while visiting his friend Left Hand, the Arapaho chief, who was camped at the spring (then known as Raven Spring). Left Hand later took the area around the spring as his allotment. His now-abandoned home, built in the 1880's and one of the first substantial houses erected in western Oklahoma, stands nearby. The spring and the grave site are maintained by the Oklahoma Historical Society.

Jet (Alfalfa Co., pop. 317, on US 64, see Map 3). Though small, Jet is one of the oldest towns in the county. It was established in 1894, a year after the Cherokee Outlet was opened to settlement, and named for W. M. Jett, miller and first postmaster. Thanks to its fortuitous location on the south edge of the **Great Salt Plains**—and no little amount of commercial aggressiveness—it is also one of the best known towns in northwestern Oklahoma.

With its 32,000 acres of national wildlife refuge, the Plains area is home to turkey and deer, and to vast numbers of waterfowl. As many as 200,000 mallards have wintered here at a time, and over 20,000 Canadian geese. Jet serves as an informal headquarters for the hunters. Area farmers rent blinds, local women clean and dress the game brought in. The town also hosts an annual Catfish Derby in May.

Jet has yet another hand in the sport and recreation game. It is a favorite take-off point for those who dig for selenite crystals in the gypsum flats to the north. **Great Salt Plains** is believed to be the world's only source of these crystallized forms of gypsum. They form here just below the salt-encrusted surface, usually no deeper than two feet. Digging is permitted 8 to 5 on Saturdays, Sundays, and holidays, from April 1 to October 15. Diggers are permitted to take away up to ten pounds of the unusual crystals for their personal use only.

Johnston County (south-central Oklahoma, see Map 7). Area, 636 sq. mi.; pop. 7,870; county seat, **Tishomingo**. Long the center of Chickasaw Indian political life and, until 1907, possessing the Chickasaw National Capital—the town of **Tishomingo**. The county was named for the Nation's last chief, Douglas H. Johnston.

Top travel lures: the Chickasaw Nation's first, and last, Capitol, both in **Tishomingo**, the so-called White House of the Chickasaws at **Emet**, **Devils Den Park**, **Tishomingo National Fish Hatchery**, fishing and hunting on **Blue River** and **Lake Texoma**.

Jones (Oklahoma Co., pop. 1,666, between US 62 and US 66 at NE edge of **Oklahoma City**, see Map 4). A pleasantly prosperous small town on a lazy meander of the **North Canadian River** in the shadow of the state's largest city. It began as Glaze in 1896, changed its name in 1898 with arrival of the Frisco Railroad. C. G. Jones (see **Elgin**) was one of Oklahoma City's leading businessmen and railroad promoters of that period—and the "groom" in the symbolic 1907 wedding ceremony (see

Guthrie) uniting Oklahoma and Indian territories to create Oklahoma.

Historic Nine Mile Flat lies in the flood plain of the Canadian just northwest of Jones. Here in 1832 occurred the famed "Ringing the Wild Horse" incident, celebrated by Washington Irving in his *Tour on the Prairies*. Surprisingly enough, considering its proximity to a major metropolitan area, the flat remains essentially unchanged. Remove a fence or two, conjure up appropriate herds of buffalo and wild horses—and stir in a cadre of mounted, over-eager eastern greenhorns—and the entire scene could be replayed from bumbling start to frenzied finish.

Jumbo (Pushmataha Co., pop. 40, county road 14 mi. N of OK 3 & 7, see Map 6). This tiny community in the rugged woods along the county's western border—isn't. Nor, presumably, was its naming an exercise in frontier boosterism. When established in 1906 the post office "honored" the Jumbo Asphalt Company.

K

Kansas (Delaware Co., pop. 317, on OK 33, 1 mi. W of US 59, see Map 5). A tiny trading center that dates back before the turn of the century. Older and historically more interesting is the nearby settlement of **Oaks**.

Kaw City (Kay Co., pop. 283, on OK 119, 16 mi. E of US 77, see Map 4). For at least a few more years the "old" and the "new" will vie for visitor attention as workmen put finishing touches on the $116 million Kaw Dam and Reservoir on the Arkansas River east of **Ponca City**.

The original town was established on the south bank of the river in 1902 when a Santa Fe branch line was laid through here. It took its name from the Kaw Indians, whose agency was at **Washunga** on the opposite bank. With discovery of oil in the Osage country to the east it became a bustling little supply town. For many years it was best known for the Clubb Hotel and its Laura A. Clubb Collection of paintings, now at the Philbrook Museum in **Tulsa**. Mrs. Clubb was the wife of a local cattleman

made wealthy by an oil strike in 1922.

The hotel has now been demolished. Most of the hillside town's other buildings have been torn down or moved uphill to the west to "new" Kaw City. The Santa Fe depot, no longer needed in the rail-less town, now houses a historical museum. The backed-up waters of **Kaw Reservoir** have not yet reached the deserted town, but the transition from old to new is virtually complete. And the new settlement will offer the sportsman the nearest possible access to **Kaw Reservoir** sport and recreation facilities.

Kaw Reservoir (off US 60, 8 mi. E of **Ponca City**, see Map 4). Part of the $1.2 billion main control plan for the **Arkansas River** in Oklahoma and Arkansas, this 17,000-acre reservoir was authorized in 1962. Construction on the $116 million project began in 1966 and is scheduled for completion in 1977. The 11,000-foot-long earthfill embankment and spillway will rise 121 feet above the streambed, create a 38-mile-long lake with 168 miles of shoreline.

Facilities (in eight public-use sites on the lake and one site below the dam) are still under development. They will include boat ramps, picnic tables, fireplaces, sanitation facilities and water supply, parking areas and walkways. Address: U.S. Corps of Engineers, Box 61, Tulsa, OK 74102.

Kay County (north-central Oklahoma bordering Kansas, see Map 4). Area, 944 sq. mi.; pop. 48,791; county seat, **Newkirk**. Oklahoma's richest county in agricultural production and also boasting extensive petroleum wealth underground. Created at statehood, it took its name from the original "K" County of **Oklahoma County**, whose boundaries it roughly followed.

Top travel lures: **Chilocco** Indian School, **101 Ranch**, Pioneer Woman Statue & Museum and Ponca City Cultural Center & Indian Museum, both in **Ponca City**.

Keefeton (Muskogee Co., pop. 70, on US 64, 12 mi. S of **Muskogee**, see Map 5). A tiny community struggling for survival after a devastating tornado destroyed half its remaining buildings in 1973. Established in 1905, the town was named for Santa Fe Railroad official J. H. Keefe.

Kellyville (Creek Co., pop. 685, on US 66, 8 mi. SW of *Sapulpa*, see Map 4). Founded in 1893 and named for a local businessman, Kellyville is perhaps best known today for two disparate events. On Sept. 28, 1917, two Frisco trains collided head-on just west of town, killing twenty-three persons and injuring eighty others. It was Oklahoma's worst train disaster. And in 1971, a mile north of town, work began on the state's first (and only) ski area, to be served by artificial snow-making machines. The scheme was stillborn.

Kemp (Bryan Co., pop. 153, off OK 78, 18 mi. S of *Durant*, see Map 6). A small trade center in a bend of *Red River*. Its post office was established in 1890 and honors Jackson Kemp, a prominent Choctaw.

Kendrick (Lincoln Co., pop. 126, on OK 140, 5 mi. N of *Davenport*, see Map 4). A railroad-siding community that began as Avondale in 1902, changed its name in 1903 to honor J. W. Kendrick, a Santa Fe vice president.

Kenefick (Bryan Co., pop. 153, near junc. of OK 22 & 48, 6 mi. W of *Caddo*, see Map 6). A dwindling community on the Kansas, Oklahoma & Gulf Railway. It began in 1888 as Nail (see below), changed its name in 1910 to honor William Kenefick, a rail official. Long before tracks or white men arrived, however, the area was an important Choctaw Nation transportation point. Three miles to the southwest was Nail's Crossing of *Blue River*. It served the Texas Road (from *Fort Gibson* to Colbert's Ferry on *Red River*, see *Colbert*) and, from 1858 to 1861, the Butterfield Overland Mail. Just east of the ford was the home of Joel H. Nail, whose home became the stage stand. The old Nail home was destroyed by fire in the 1930's, but the interesting family cemetery is nearby. On the west

bank of the Blue is the now almost indistinguishable site of *Fort McCulloch*. The post was established in 1862 by General Albert Pike and named for Brigadier General McCulloch, who commanded the Confederate forces in Indian Territory the first year of the Civil War. It existed only briefly and consisted for the most part of earthen bastions and redoubts. The site is now on the National Register of Historic Sites and the Oklahoma Historical Society hopes to make it accessible eventually to visitors.

Kenton (Cimarron Co., pop. 30, on a paved county road 36 mi. NW of *Boise City*, see Map 2). Now a store, a post office, a pair of churches, and a clutch of private homes, Kenton was once a rambunctious saloon town known as the Cowboy Capital. First called Carrizo (in 1886, for the nearby creek of that name, the Spanish word for a marsh grass common to the area), it became Kenton in 1891 (apparently a somewhat less than literate spelling of Ohio's Canton), and was finally platted as a townsite the following year by a nephew of P. T. Barnum.

The town lies in the shadow of hulking *Black Mesa*, the state's highest point, and in the center of a rugged, isolated, extremely colorful ranching country. Nearby points of interest include *Black Mesa State Park*; a now abandoned Dinosaur Quarry (9 mi. E); the three-state boundary marker (Oklahoma, Colorado and New Mexico, 8 mi. N); site of the annual Kenton Easter Pageant (just east of town); and such isolated spots (inquire locally) as Robbers Roost, Mummy Cave, the Devil's Tombstone, Hallock Park (Indian pictographs and petroglyphs), Natural Arch, Old Maid Rock and other curious erosion formations.

The Dinosaur Quarry is marked by a concrete replica of the femur of a Brontosaurus, excavated in the early 1930's. The reassembled skeleton—65 feet in length and 85 per cent complete—is on display at the University of Oklahoma's Stovall Museum in *Norman*. The leg bone represented here is six feet in length, 24 inches across the base, and 21 inches across the upper end. Weighing 425 pounds, it was one of the prize finds of fossilized bones in the southwest. More than 18 tons of fossilized dinosaur bones have been taken from **Cimarron County** quarries.

Keota (Haskell Co., pop. 685, on OK 9, see Map 6). A small coal mining town, settled around the turn of the century on the old Midland Valley (now Texas & Pacific) railroad. Today it is making a modest comeback, with the eastern Oklahoma coal industry (see **McCurtain**), on the strength of low **Arkansas River Navigation System** barge tariffs. **Robert S. Kerr Reservoir** extends to the town limits.

The name is a Choctaw word translated roughly as "fire gone out." According to historian George H. Shirk. it refers to a tribal tragedy in which 175 newly-arrived Choctaws died from pneumonia, wiping out an entire clan.

Ketchum (Craig Co., pop. 238, on OK 85, 15 mi. SE of **Vinita**, see Map 5). Neat, progressive, and growing little gateway village to resorts and recreation areas on the west shore of **Grand Lake**. The town was started in 1899 and, despite what passing fishermen may think, the name was not inspired by the chamber of commerce. Instead, it honors a long-time area resident, James Ketchum.

Keyes (Cimarron Co., pop. 569, on US 56, 17 mi. NE of **Boise City**, see Map 2). Like **Boise City** and **Felt**, a community that owes much of its development to the building of the Santa Fe Railroad through this part of the Panhandle in 1925. Henry Keyes was president of the line. Six years later the Beaver, Meade and Englewood Railroad (later the M-K-T and now abandoned) built westward from **Forgan** to this point.

Latest economic stimulus to the town was construction in 1959 of the $12.5 million U.S. Bureau of Mines helium plant three miles to the northeast. Employing sixty persons, it was the biggest of five such federal installations that extract helium from natural gas for a variety of uses ranging from arc welding

to the operation of Telstar. That plant was shut down in 1982, but towering grain elevators are evidence of the area's continuing dependence on farming and ranching.

Keystone Reservoir (off US 64, 15 mi. W of **Tulsa**, in northeastern Oklahoma, see Map 5). The Corps of Engineers created this giant V-shaped lake in 1964 with construction of a 121-foot-high dam on the **Arkansas River** just below the mouth of the **Cimarron**. Its 26,300 surface acres spread back to the northwest and southwest to cover parts of **Creek**, **Payne**, and **Osage** counties. In addition to **Keystone** and **Walnut Creek** state parks, its 240 miles of shoreline are also served by the state-maintained **Feyodi Creek Recreation Area** (Cleveland, OK 74020), 2 miles south of **Cleveland**, a number of small private enterprises, and several nearby small towns.

Facilities: picnic and camping areas, boat ramps, swimming beaches, concessions. Address: U.S. Corps of Engineers, Box 61, Tulsa, OK 74102.

Keystone State Park (just N of OK 51 from a point 16 mi. W of **Tulsa**, see Map 5). This 715-acre recreation area has been developed near the south end of the **Arkansas River** dam forming 26,500-acre **Keystone Reservoir**.

Facilities: picnic and camp areas, trailer hookups, marina with boating supplies and repairs, 2 boat ramps. Address: Mannford, OK 74044.

Kiamichi (Pushmataha Co., on US 271, 6 mi. E of **Tuskahoma**, see Map 6). A scattered community dating from 1887 when the Frisco Railroad built through here. Many of the residents are descendants of one-time Negro slaves of Choctaw Indians, set free after the Civil War and located on 40 acres of Choctaw Nation land in this area. The name (pronounced Ki-a-MISH-ee) is from the nearby **Kiamichi River**, one of the state's better fishing streams.

Kiamichi Mountains. See **Ouachita Mountains.**

Kiamichi River. A justly famed fishing stream that enters southeastern Oklahoma from Arkansas, makes a lazy counter-clockwise loop to cut off a three-county chunk of the state before flowing into **Red River**. The ruggedly scenic **Kiamichi Mountains** lie to the north. Newly built **Hugo Reservoir** sprawls just above its mouth.

Cutting a 169-mile course through the old Choctaw Nation, the Kiamichi offers the history buff such once-important sites as **Tuskahoma** and **Fort Towson**. It was mentioned as early as 1805, when Dr. John Sibley, the explorer, reported a Red River tributary "which is called by the Indians *Kiomitchie*." The name, according to George H. Shirk, is derived from the French *kamichi*, meaning "horned screamer," probably a shrike.

Kiefer (Creek Co., pop. 803, on US 75 Alt., 6 mi. S of **Sapulpa**, see Map 4). Another of Oklahoma's legendary oil boom towns—and admittedly one of the toughest— Kiefer (for Smith Kiefer, a long-time resident) was born with the spectacular Glenn Pool discovery well December 1, 1905. The town profited initially from a Frisco railroad connection with **Tulsa**. But this link proved to be a two-edged sword. The budding young "Oil Capital of the World" was quick to capitalize on the Glenn Pool wealth. A daily commuter train was soon in operation, and hundreds of workers in the Kiefer area were able to live in more comfortable (and far safer) Tulsa. The town boomed mightily while drilling progressed, but the wealth— and permanent development—drifted northward to Tulsa. A few pumper jacks remain today in the area, to recall its heyday, along with a maze of above-ground pipelines, rusty gauges, and oil-smeared tanks.

Kildare (Kay Co., pop. 79, off US 77, 8 mi. N of **Ponca City**, see Map 4). A once-bustling trade center that sprang up with the opening of the Cherokee Outlet in 1893. Now reduced to a post office, grain elevator, and a scattering of houses, it bases its chance for survival on the relocation of eastern Kay

Restored Seay House, in Kingfisher.

County residents caused by the construction of **Kaw Reservoir** and the flooding of such towns as **Kaw City** and **Uncas**.

Kingfisher (Kingfisher Co. seat, pop. 4,042, at junc. US 81 and OK 33, see Map 4). This area was well known long before Old Oklahoma was opened to settlement in 1889. Kingfisher was laid out on the land of a cattleman named King Fisher, who had also operated a stage line and maintained a stage station. The **Chisholm Trail** ran east of the town, and eroded ruts can still be found in the vicinity.

In the early days of Oklahoma Territory, Kingfisher was one of the most important towns in northwestern Oklahoma. It boasted Kingfisher College for a number of years. And for a time it even had hopes of wresting the state capital from Guthrie. In 1892 the Oklahoma Territory Press Association was organized here. That same year, Judge Abraham J. Seay, whose jurisdiction extended as far northwest as the **Oklahoma Panhandle**, was appointed the Territory's second governor.

Governor Seay's handsome three-story mansion (at least it was a mansion for the frontier) has been restored to its comfortable 1892 elegance. At 11th & Overstreet, it is now open to the public daily 9–7 (9–5 November through April). Across the street is the Chisholm

Trail Museum (also state-operated, open same hours as the Seay House), with relics and artifacts of cattle trail days and pioneer life. Adjacent to it is a "Pioneer Town" of representative structures moved to the site and restored to recreate an early-day community. Already relocated: the original Bank of Kingfisher and the old Gant School from northwest of Kingfisher.

Well-known figures who once lived in or near Kingfisher include Don Blanding, the poet; W. C. Coleman, who started here with the improved gasoline lamp that grew eventually into The Coleman Company of Wichita, Kansas; and the Daltons.

Parents of the notorious Dalton Boys lived on a farm some 15 miles northeast of Kingfisher. Their 15- x 17-foot, hand-hewn log house has now been moved to the Chisholm Trail Museum, where it has been restored to its original condition.

Career of the Daltons ended October 5, 1892, at Coffeyville, Kansas, in one of the west's best-known shoot-outs. Robert and Gratton Dalton and two other members of the gang were killed, Emmett Dalton seriously wounded and captured, while staging a daring raid on two banks simultaneously. Robert Dalton had been a deputy U.S. marshal in Indian Territory in 1888. This once led Governor John Anderson Jr. of Kansas to chide a group of visiting Oklahomans: "The Daltons were peace officers in Oklahoma. Then they came up to Kansas and discovered for the first time it's against the law to rob a bank."

Other Oklahoma Park facilities include nine-hole golf course, swimming pool, tennis courts, picnic areas.

A downtown historical plaque notes the original Young Store. R. A. Young was the "Y" in T. G. & Y. when that Oklahoma-born variety chain was formed (see *Cordell, Frederick*).

Kingfisher County (central Oklahoma, see Map 4). Area, 894 sq. mi.; pop., 12,857; county seat, *Kingfisher*. An agriculturally rich county, organized with the opening of Old Oklahoma in 1889. It was named for King Fisher,

operator of a stage station on the *Chisholm Trail*, which cut through this section from north to south.

Top travel lures: Seay House and Chisholm Trail Museum at *Kingfisher*.

Kingston (Marshall Co., pop. 710, at junc. of US 70 and OK 32, see Map 7). Another long-time agricultural community, established in 1894 and named for a local resident, Jeff King. It exists today primarily to serve the sport and recreation needs of nearby *Texoma Reservoir*. *Texoma State Park* is five miles to the east. OK 70-A and 70-B fan out to the south and east to serve another score of lakeside resorts, fishing camps, and recreation areas.

Kinta (Haskell Co., pop. 247, at junc. of OK 2 & 31, see Map 6). A sagging community established in 1902 as the Fort Smith & Western Railroad (see *Boley*) was building westward. Four miles east of Kinta (Indian for "beaver") is the San Bois community, now marked only by a cemetery in which are buried many members of the illustrious McCurtain family (see *McCurtain*).

Kiowa (Pittsburg Co., pop. 754, on US 69, see Map 6). Founded in 1872 when the M-K-T railroad reached this point on its way southward. Kiowa Hill is near by. Pine Mountains, to the east, provide dependable fall deer hunting.

Kiowa County (southwestern Oklahoma, see Map 8). Area, 1,032 sq. mi.; pop. 12,532; county seat, *Hobart*. An agriculturally rich county (cotton, wheat, cattle), organized in 1901 when this area was opened to settlement by lottery. One of fifteen Oklahoma counties named for an Indian tribe.

Top travel lure: *Quartz Mountain State Park*.

Knowles (Beaver Co., pop. 52, on US 64, see Map 2). A tiny agricultural community on the recently abandoned Beaver, Meade and Englewood Railroad. Started in 1907, its name honors a local teacher, F. E. Knowles.

Konawa (Seminole Co., pop. 1,719, at junc. of OK 9A & 39, see Map 7). A prosperous farming community that also benefits from nearby oil fields. It was established in 1904. The name is of Seminole origin and means "string of beads."

Largest and best-known annual event in Konawa is the mid-August All Night Singing in Veterans Memorial Park. Dozens of musical groups from a wide area fill the thirteen-hour program, attract up to 25,000 persons to the park's large natural amphitheater. The event is thought to be the country's largest all-night gospel sing.

Lake Konawa, just northeast of the city, is a 1,350-acre empoundment constructed by Oklahoma Gas & Electric Co. to serve its new $100 million Seminole generating plant. Water is pumped to it from the **South Canadian River** 2 miles to the south. It has been stocked with game fish and sportsmen are welcomed. Facilities include boat ramp, picnic grounds, and a special swimming area.

Krebs (Pittsburg Co., pop. 1,515, off US 270, 3 mi. E of **McAlester**, see Map 6). A century-old town that long lived on the mining of coal, but is best known today for a pair of Italian restaurants. Settled in 1871 when the M-K-T railroad first reached the area's rich coal veins—and named for Judge Edmond F. Krebs, a Choctaw—it reached its peak around the turn of the century. For a time its population approached 7,000, and an even dozen mines produced sufficient wealth to maintain two opera houses.

One of the state's worst mine disasters occurred here January 7, 1892. An explosion caused by blackdamp killed nearly 100 miners.

Krebs and nearby **McAlester** often join in staging an Italian Festival.

Kremlin (Garfield Co., pop. 200, just E of US 81, 8 mi. N of **Enid**, see Map 4). Established in November, 1893, just after the "run" that opened the Cherokee Outlet to settlement, Kremlin has a number of points of interest out of all proportion to its size. Thanks to the productivity of the surrounding wheat fields, its location on the main north-south line of the Rock Island—and business acumen—the bustling country store of Floren Zaloudek is one of the largest tractor headquarters in the state. It is also believed to be the biggest Case dealership in the world.

Rail service and an abundance of natural gas nearby also helped to locate a large Great Lake Carbon plant just south of Kremlin. Here small mountains of coke are burned in a giant kiln at temperatures in excess of 2,300 degrees Fahrenheit to produce the carbon that goes into flashlight batteries, electrodes, and anodes, and helps to make aluminum and steel.

But fully as interesting—if not as important economically—is the way Kremlin received its name. Oddly enough, it did not spring from the nostalgia of early settlers for the old country. It came rather from the spur-of-the-minute subjective response of a young girl to the sight of some ponies standing near the well of the still-unnamed Santa Fe depot. The daughter of a railroad official, she had just returned from a trip to Russia. "I'm reminded of ponies just like those, gathered next to a well near the Kremlin. "Why, then," her father said, "we'll just call this place The Kremlin." And so it was. Or so they say.

Lacey (Kingfisher Co., on OK 51, 10 mi. W of **Hennessey**, see Map 4). Now reduced to a store and a few houses, Lacey was a busy little farming community in the first two decades that followed its founding in 1890. The name honors John F. Lacey, one-time Iowa Congressman.

Lahoma (Garfield Co., pop. 299, on US 60, 10 mi. W of **Enid,** see Map 4). Little is left but an elevator to mark this agricultural community, established in 1894. The name would seem to be Oklahoma without the OK, an explanation with which fortune has apparently concurred.

Lake Murray State Park (7 mi. S of **Ardmore** on US 77, 2 mi. E on OK 77-S, see Map 7). Oklahoma's largest (18,224 acres, including 6,500-acre Lake Murray itself) and one of its most complete

L

and most popular resort parks. The first to have a deluxe vacation lodge, Murray has become widely known throughout the Southwest.

Some of its more unusual features include a motorcycle trail, 36 miles of riding trails, field trial grounds for bird dogs, kennels, scuba diving (with rental equipment), ski school, and a Geological Museum. The latter is housed in Tucker Tower, perched atop a rocky crag jutting out from the southern end of the lake. Built in the 1930's as a summer home for Oklahoma governors, it was never used for that purpose.

Facilities: 54-room Lake Murray Lodge, 86 cottages, 4 Youth Camps, abundant picnic, camp, and trailer areas, 9-hole golf course, enclosed fishing dock, 2,500-foot air strip, facilities and rental equipment for almost all water and land-based sport and recreational activities. Address: Ardmore, OK 74044.

Lake Wister State Park (off US 270, 2 mi. S of *Wister,* see Map 6). Good fishing and water sports of all kinds feature this 3,040-acre wooded preserve, set alongside 4,000-acre *Wister Reservoir* between the scenic San Bois and *Winding Stair Mountains.* Buffalo, longhorn cattle, and deer are found in the park.

Facilities: 15 cottages, picnic and camp and trailer areas, swimming beach and ski dock, boat ramps and rentals. Address: Wister, OK 74966.

Lamar (Hughes Co., pop. 153, on OK 84, 16 mi. E of *Holdenville,* see Map 7). A scattered community, established in 1907 in the isolated *South Canadian River* brakes of the county's east-central section.

Lamont (Grant Co., pop. 478, on US 60, see Map 4). Established in 1893, within months of the opening of the Cherokee Outlet to settlement. The name honors Daniel Lamont, U.S. secretary of war from 1893 to 1897. It is the trade center for a rich area of farms and ranches along the *Salt Fork of the Arkansas River,* which follows an undulating west-to-east course just south of town. For many years Lamont was widely known for the quality of its watermelons.

Langley (Mayes Co., pop. 48, at junc. of OK 28 and OK 82, 12 mi. E of *Adair,* see Map 5). A small recreation-minded community at the west end of Pensacola Dam, established in 1938 when construction began on that structure (see *Grand Lake of the Cherokees*). It was named for J. Howard Langley, chairman of the state-created Grand River Dam Authority that built the $22,750,000 hydroelectric facility. Private resorts on both sides of the dam (see *Disney*) combine with state recreation areas to create one of Oklahoma's most popular playgrounds.

Langston (Logan Co., pop. 486, on OK 33, 11 mi. NE of *Guthrie,* see Map 4). An all-Negro town founded in 1890 by E. P. McCabe and named for Virginia's John M. Langston, a black educator and member of Congress. McCabe had been state auditor of Kansas. As Oklahoma Territory was primarily southern in its racial attitudes, he saw Langston as a natural mecca for Negroes. And for a time it attracted as many as two thousand residents. In the long run, however, the promotion failed because of the lack of job opportunities, the same weakness that afflicts the town today, despite its school and the fact that there is no longer legalized segregation in the state.

The Territorial legislature authorized Langston University in 1897. Physical and academic growth over years has been slow, but consistent. Enrollment today is around 1,200. Though desegregation of all schools was ordered by the U.S. Supreme Court in 1954, the coeducational student body is still overwhelmingly black.

Recently, following a trend started by *Taft* and *Boley,* Langston named entertainer Sammy Davis Jr. honorary police chief.

Latimer County (southeastern Oklahoma, see Map 6). Area, 737 sq. mi.; pop., 8,601; county seat, *Wilburton.* A rough, wooded area cut by the scenic Fourche Maline Creek. Established in 1902, it was named for James S. Latimer, a member of the state Constitutional Convention.

Museum of the Great Plains, at Lawton (photograph courtesy Museum of the Great Plains).

Top travel lures: **Robbers Cave State Park,** scenic back roads in the Jack Fork and San Bois Mountains, traces of the old Butterfield Stage Route near **Red Oak.**

Laverne (Harper Co., pop. 1,373, on US 283, see Map 3). In the productive valley of the Beaver *(North Canadian)* River, this tree-shaded, obviously prosperous little community often surprises travelers as something of an oasis on the generally treeless short-grass plains of northwest Oklahoma. Wheat, alfalfa, broomcorn, sorghum crops, and native hay, along with herds of registered cattle, provide its economic backbone. In recent years an active oil play has added a rich frosting to the cake. As in other areas farther west, an abundant underground water supply has greatly increased irrigation. Laverne is the home of Joe A. Dooley, a widely acclaimed wood sculptor whose carvings are exhibited in the Pioneer Museum in nearby **Woodward.**

Lawrence (Pontotoc Co., pop. 30, off OK 1, 6 mi. SW of **Ada,** see Map 7). Settlement began here in 1906 with opening of a limestone quarry to serve the needs of the Ideal Cement Com-

pany in nearby **Ada.** Originally it was called Oolite, the name of the local limestone. This was changed in 1907 to the more prosaic Lawrence, for a local resident. Of interest to the visitor is the informal museum of stone quarrying equipment, preserved by the company and displayed on a concrete apron near the maintenance shop. Included are a wheeler, a western dump wagon (1907), a railroad track maintenance cart, and an electric Woodford hauler (1918).

Lawton (Comanche Co. seat, pop. 74,470, at junc. of H. E. Bailey Turnpike, US 62, 277 & 281, and OK 7 & 36, see Map 8). Oklahoma's third-largest city came into being August 6, 1901, when a giant lottery threw open the two-million-plus-acre Kiowa-Comanche-Apache reservation to white settlement. As an understandable nod in the direction of nearby **Fort Sill,** already thirty-two years old, the new town was named to honor Major General Henry W. Lawton, who had been killed two years earlier in the Philippines.

Although a typical service town in many ways—and certainly the military is responsible for much of its growth

141

and prosperity over the years—Lawton has developed a modest industrial base (a men's slacks maker is the largest "civilian" payroll) and supports one of the state's more important research-minded museums. The Museum of the Great Plains (Elmer Thomas Park, Mon.–Sat. 10–5, Sun. 2–5) contains exhibits pertaining to the fur trader, cowboy, settler, buffalo hunter, and the Plains Indian, prehistoric and historic.

Nearby McMahon Auditorium, with seating capacity of 1,500, accommodates the Philharmonic Orchestra, Civic Ballet, Community Theatre, and other city cultural events. For recreational facilities Lawton maintains forty-nine parks with a total of 400 acres, to supplement the extensive resources provided by the *Wichita Mountains Wildlife Refuge* at its doorstep. Indian dances and powwows representing half a dozen Plains tribes are also open to visitors in the area. In Lawton are the historic Fort Sill Indian School (closed in 1980) and Cameron University (some 6,000 students).

Leach (Delaware Co., pop. 35, on OK 33, 8 mi. W of *Kansas,* see Map 5). A tiny crossroads community that dates back well before the turn of the century. First called Ulm, it took the name of Postmaster John R. Leach in 1897.

Leedey (Dewey Co., pop. 465, on OK 34, see Map 3). A small farming-ranch community best known to most Oklahomans for having been hit on May 31, 1947, by a particularly destructive tornado. It was named in 1900 for Amos Leedey, its first postmaster.

LeFlore (LeFlore Co., pop. 175, off US 270 SW of *Fanshawe,* see Map 6). An isolated, scattered community dating from the 1880's. Like the county, it honors one of the most distinguished of all Choctaw Indian family names.

LeFlore County (eastern Oklahoma bordering on Arkansas, see Map 6). Area, 1,515 sq. mi.; pop., 32,137; county seat, *Poteau.* An historically rich, highly scenic county, organized in 1907 with statehood and named for a prominent Choctaw Indian family. Indian Mounds near *Spiro* represent one of the country's most significant archaeological discoveries.

Top travel lures: *Talimena Trail, Ouachita National Forest, Cedar Lake, Heavener Runestone State Park, Lake Wister State Park,* Peter Conser House at *Conser,* Kerr Museum near *Poteau,* glass blowers around *Spiro.*

Lehigh (Coal Co., pop. 296, on OK 3, 5 mi. S of *Coalgate,* see Map 7). Coal was first mined here in 1880, the settlement taking its name from the Pennsylvania coal-mining city. However, it remained little more than a company town until 1887, when a disaster at *Savanna* caused the removal to this area of coal-mining equipment and some 135 houses. By 1907 the town was prosperous enough to be named seat of Coal County, but lost the office to *Coalgate* the next year. A mining disaster of its own in 1912 and the gradual decline of coal combined to reduce the town to its present status.

In 1883, in a farmhouse near Lehigh that is no longer standing, was born Patrick J. Hurley, secretary of war (1929–33) and ambassador to China (1944–45). A major general in World War II, Hurley was the only Oklahoman ever to attain cabinet rank. He and his father both worked in district mines.

Lenapah (Nowata Co., pop. 325, at junc. of US 169 and OK 10, see Map 5). A sagging community that acknowledges, with its name, that this area was originally settled by the Delaware Indians, who used tribal funds in 1867 to purchase equal rights with the Cherokees in the Cherokee Nation. The town was established in 1890. Lenapah is an adaptation of the original word for the Delaware tribe.

Biggest annual event is the traditional Fred Lowery Memorial Rodeo, an RCA-approved affair scheduled for the Fourth of July holidays.

Leon (Love Co., pop. 112, on OK 76, see Map 7). A scattered farming community near **Red River.** Its post office, dating from 1883, took for its name the Spanish word for "lion."

Leonard (Tulsa Co., pop. 100, on US 64, 7 mi. E of **Bixby,** see Map 5). A dwindling farm community established in 1908 following construction of the Midland Valley Railroad (now Missouri Pacific) between **Muskogee** and **Tulsa.** Only scattered stones northwest of the village mark the site of once-important Wealaka Mission, established by the Creek Nation in 1881.

Lequire (Haskell Co., pop. 150, at junc. of OK 31 & 82, 12 mi. S of **Stigler,** see Map 6). A scattered community, established in 1906 and named for the operator of a local sawmill, P. H. Lequire.

Lexington (Cleveland Co., pop. 1,516, at junc. of US 77 and OK 39, see Map 7). Though its population continues to grow modestly—no mean feat for a small agricultural community—Lexington's most exciting days are in the past. At Camp Mason (now but a field about 4 miles NE of town) a giant council, involving some 5,000 Indians from the Five Civilized Tribes and several Plains tribes, assembled in 1835 to agree to peace terms that lasted until the Civil War. That same year the Chouteau family (see **Salina**) established a nearby trading post in the area, one of the first this far west into Indian Territory.

All evidence of both were gone, however, when Old Oklahoma was opened to settlement in 1889. Lexington proper began then—with the Sand Bar Saloon, built on stilts near the **Canadian River** to be as convenient as possible for citizens of "dry" Indian Territory across the way (see **Purcell**). The settlement acquired a post office the next year (with a familiar Kentucky name) and was on its way. Biggest employer today is the Regional Community Treatment Center (on OK 39, 7 mi. E), a state corrections department facility that trains inmates in working skills. It occupies a one-time World War II Navy base.

Lexington Public Hunting Area, northeast of the city, is an 8,613-acre pre-serve around 80-acre Lake Dahlgren. The state wildlife facility also provides fishing, camping, and general recreation.

Lima (Seminole Co., pop. 238, off US 270, 6 mi. W of **Wewoka,** see Map 7). A tiny railroad-siding community on the Rock Island that dates from 1907. Nearby is **New Lima.**

Limestone Gap (Atoka Co., on US 69, 9 mi. S of **Kiowa,** see Map 6). Although now virtually deserted, this scenic notch in one of the many limestone ridges that characterize northern **Atoka** and southern **Pittsburg** counties has been settled for more than a century. The Texas Road passed the gap, followed in 1872 by the Missouri-Kansas-Texas (Katy) Railroad. For a time nearby Buck Creek was spanned by a toll bridge operated by Captain Charles LeFlore, member of the prominent Choctaw family. Beside the highway just north of the gap his once-pretentious two-story frame house still stands. Nearby is the LeFlore family cemetery.

The town of Limestone Gap had a post office from 1875 until 1922. Briefly it was known as Limestone. If noted on the map at all today it is merely as Gap. Scenic as it undeniably is, the Gap itself was dreaded by railroad trainmen in the nineteenth century because it was a favorite ambush point for outlaw gangs.

Lincoln County (central Oklahoma, see Map 4). Area, 973 sq. mi.; pop., 19,482; county seat, **Chandler.** Oil rich, pecan growing county organized in 1891 and named for President Lincoln.

Lindsay (Garvin Co., pop. 3,705, at junc. of OK 19 and OK 76, see Map 7). Like **Maysville,** Lindsay has successfully negotiated the transition from agriculture to small industry. Fertile **Washita River** farmlands have long established **Garvin** and neighboring **Grady County** one–two in broomcorn production in the state. Over the years the world market for the crop has often been determined by the harvest-time price set in the of-

Dune buggy rides are a popular feature at Little Sahara State Recreation Area (photograph courtesy Oklahoma Industrial Development and Park Department).

fices of Lindsay buyers.

Recently, however, interest in broomcorn has waned and the town has actively competed with **Pauls Valley** for the lead in developing the rich Golden Trend oil discovery. The town now boasts half a dozen small industries to take up the slack in farm employment. A broom factory and a ladies-wear plant both offer tours to visitors. Also of prime interest: the Murray Mansion in nearby **Erin Springs.**

Lindsay was established in 1902. Lewis Lindsay was owner of the townsite. Annual events, still reflecting the town's strong agricultural heritage, include a Junior Livestock Show (mid-March) and the Lindsay District Fair (mid-September).

Little Axe (Cleveland Co., off OK 9, 15 mi. E of **Norman,** see Map 7). A once important settlement now memorialized by a recreation facility on the east shore of Lake Thunderbird (see **Little River State Park**). Some Shawnee Indians still live in this area, but the Friend's Mission established here in 1897 has long since closed.

Little City (Marshall Co., pop. 80, on OK 199, 9 mi. E of **Madill,** see Map 7). A "little" community that sprang up with discovery of oil near **Cumberland,** but named for **Madill** attorney and oilman Ruel Little, rather than for its size. Nearby Cumberland Cut diverted **Washita River** water, thus permitting development of the field, located during the building of Denison Dam (see **Texoma Reservoir).**

Little River. In extreme southeastern Oklahoma, a 140-mile-long stream that drains extensive sections of mountains and woodlands in **LeFlore, Pushmataha,** and **McCurtain** counties. The Little vies with the **Mountain Fork** and **Kiamichi** rivers for the favor of sportsmen. Newly completed near its middle course is **Pine Creek Reservoir.** (Note: this is not the small Central Oklahoma stream on which **Little River State Park** is located.)

Little River State Park (12 mi. E of **Norman** on old OK 9, see Map 7). **Thunderbird Reservoir** on Little River is one of Oklahoma's newest man-made reservoirs and this 1,834-acre preserve is being developed on its west shore. Although it does not yet have overnight accommodations, it offers an increasing range of land and water sport opportunities. Nearby is a 1,280-acre public hunting area.

Facilities: 6 individual camping areas, trailer hookups, picnic areas, boat ramps and rentals, swimming beach, ski dock, 2 fishing piers, 10 miles of bicycle trails, 8 miles of hiking trails. Address: Route 4, Norman, OK 73069.

Little Sahara State Recreation Area (off US 281, 3 mi. S of **Waynoka,** in Woods County, see Map 3). One of northwestern Oklahoma's most unusual, and most popular, playgrounds. Over the years predominantly southwestern winds have driven white quaternary sand deposits from the nearby **Cimarron River** into towering dunes. Nearly devoid of vegetation here, they are still active sand dunes, constantly changing with the wind.

A small zoo (Japanese Fan Tail and native deer, Australian Fainting goats) is maintained at the entrance. Camels and longhorn cattle are also found in the 335-acre park. Special feature: dune buggy rides over the dunes.

Facilities: picnic and camp areas, playground, Youth Camp for up to 80 people. Address: Waynoka, OK 73860.

Lloyd Vincent Lake (Ellis Co., off OK 46 some 14 mi. SW of *Arnett,* see Map 3). A 165-acre reservoir that, with 3,771 land acres surrounding it, makes up the Ellis County Public Hunting Area, maintained by the state wildlife department. Fishing, hunting; no facilities.

Loco (Stephens Co., pop. 193, on OK 53, 18 mi. ESE of *Comanche,* see Map 7). Little more than a school and post office remain to mark this town, established in the 1890's and apparently named—despite denials by some latter-day Locoites—for the infamous loco-weed. A member of the pea family, the plant is not uncommon on native grasslands and is usually poisonous to livestock.

Locust Grove (Mayes Co., pop. 1,090, junc. of OK 33 and OK 82, see Map 5). An old Cherokee Nation town established in 1872 and named for a nearby grove of locust trees. A Civil War engagement was fought on the site July 3, 1862. In recent years it has prospered with construction of the dam that created *Markham Ferry Reservoir* and resulting recreational development. It is perhaps best known as the home of famed Cherokee sculptor Willard Stone, whose striking wood figures are featured in the Restaurant of the Cherokees near *Tahlequah* and in museums and private collection throughout the United States.

Logan County (north-central Oklahoma, see Map 4). Area, 747 sq. mi.; pop., 19,645; county seat, *Guthrie.* Organized in 1890, a year after it was opened to settlement by run, the county was named for Senator John A. Logan of Illinois.

Top travel lures: the $2.5 million Scottish Rite Cathedral, the old Carnegie Library (now a museum), the Co-operative Publishing Co. building, and other historic structures in *Guthrie,* the old Territorial capital. Also the annual '89er Celebration, commemorating the opening of Oklahoma Territory on April 22, 1889.

Lone Wolf (Kiowa Co., pop. 584, at junc. of OK 9 and OK 44, see Map 8). A quiet agricultural community, established with the opening of the one-time Kiowa lands to white settlement in 1901 and named for one of that tribe's best-known chiefs. Lone Wolf himself is buried in the historic Elk Creek Indian Cemetery three miles south of *Hobart.*

Long (Sequoyah Co., on OK 64-B, 7 mi. N of *Muldrow,* see Map 5). A "long gone" community (its post office, established in 1894, was lost in 1937) that exists today primarily so that one-time residents of *Nicut*—itself having disappeared from all but the most charitable maps—can locate their almost non-existent community as being "halfway between Long and *Short.*" Peter Long, whom the town honored, was a Cherokee leader.

Longdale (Blaine Co., pop. 331, on OK 58, 6 mi. N of *Canton,* see Map 3). A small trading center that now serves primarily the recreation-seekers at nearby *Canton Lake.* It was established in 1903 on land donated by Lucious Walter (Luke) Long and his wife, who had homesteaded it before her marriage. The original name of Longview was abandoned to avoid confusion with nearby *Fairview.*

Lookeba (Caddo Co., pop. 165, on OK 281 & OK 8, 4 mi. N of *Binger,* see Map 8). Yet another little agricultural community that owes its start to the arrival of a Rock Island branch line in 1902, a year after the Kiowa-Apache-Comanche Indian Reservation was thrown open to white settlement. The name, according to place-name expert George H. Shirk, was coined from those of the townsite developers, Messrs. Lowe, Kelly, and Baker. Which may help to explain why, despite the spelling, the pronounciation is Lo-KEE-bah.

145

Lookout (Woods Co., pop. 5, off OK 34, see Map 3). The county's northmost community, established in 1901 and serving an isolated farming and ranching area.

Lotsee (Tulsa Co., pop. 5, on OK 51, 7 mi. W of *Sand Springs,* see Map 5). One of Oklahoma's smallest incorporated (in 1965) towns, Lotsee deserves at least footnote status for its independent spirit. Actually a 60-acre section of a 1,400-acre ranch, it maintains its "sovereignty" by refusing on principle to accept any money potentially due it from any county, state, or federal source. Possibly significant: Lotsee is a Comanche Indian word meaning "bright child."

Love County (south-central Oklahoma along the *Red River,* see Map 7). Area, 488 sq. mi.; pop., 5,637; county seat, *Marietta.* Love County was organized in 1907 with statehood. Name honors a well-known Chickasaw family.
Top travel lure: *Lake Murray State Park.*

Loyal (Kingfisher Co., pop. 107, 11 mi. W of Dover, see Map 4). A tiny inland community that began life in 1894 as Kiel, for the mother country of many of its first settlers. In 1918, when anti-German feelings stirred up by World War I were at their height, the name was changed to Loyal.

Lucien (Noble Co., pop. 100, on US 64, 10 mi. W of *Perry,* see Map 4). An "elevator" town on the Frisco, established in 1903.

Lugert (Kiowa Co. on OK 44, 7 mi. SW of *Lone Wolf,* see Map 8). Only an elevator on a rail siding remains of this settlement, established in 1908 with arrival of the Kansas City, Mexico and Orient Railway (now Santa Fe). Frank Lugert was an early-day merchant. Several tornados have buffeted the town over the years, but the final indignity came in the 1940's when backed up waters from *Altus Reservoir* flooded much of what was left of the settlement. (In periods of drouth wrecked buildings

still emerge ghost-like from the sagging surface of the lake.)

There are two points of interest in the area. In 1902 what is thought to be the first paved road in Oklahoma was constructed south of here to get travelers through a stretch of ground made virtually impassable by a spring in the mountainside. And just southeast of *Quartz Mountain State Park* is Devil's Canyon, a rugged pass through the mountains that has figured in history and legend since Coronado's trek across the Southern Plains in 1541. Father Juan de Salas is supposed to have established a mission at an Indian village in the canyon in the early 1600's. Spanish miners are also thought to have dug the rocky slopes for gold in the mid-seventeenth century. The site (privately owned, not open to visitors) is on the National Register of Historic Places.

Most significant event associated with Devil's Canyon was the peace conference that was held near its mouth in July, 1834, between Plains Indians and a U.S. Dragoon Regiment under the command of Colonel Henry Dodge. The ill-fated expedition lost almost half its men—including General Henry Leavenworth, who led the party out of *Fort Gibson*—to disease, exposure, and accidents. It is best known to history because of the artistic accomplishments of its official chronicler, the famed George Catlin.

Lugert Lake. See *Altus Reservoir.*

Luther (Oklahoma Co., pop. 836, off US 66, 8 mi. W of Wellston, see Map 4). Small agricultural community established in 1898 with arrival of the Frisco Railroad. Luther was the businessman son of C. G. Jones (see *Jones, Elgin*), prominent capital city industrialist and railroad promoter of the day.

Macomb (Pottawatomie Co., pop. 41, off US 177, 14 mi. S of *Shawnee,* see Map 7). A crossroads community established in 1903 when the Santa Fe Railroad (see *Shawnee*) was building through this area. The line (on which

Macomb was an engineer) was abandoned in 1963.

Madill (Marshall Co. seat, pop. 2,875, at junc. of US 70 and OK 99 & 199, see Map 7). Established in 1901 when the Frisco Railroad built through this section of "Little Dixie" and named for George A. Madill, an attorney for the line. Located in a fertile area between the *Red* and *Washita* rivers, the town has long depended on farming and ranching. Stock trailer manufacturing is an important local industry and a fall Pecan & Peanut Show is an annual fall event.

Over the years, however, there has been considerable diversification. The Cumberland Oil Field was discovered in 1939, and pumping oil wells, some standing in shallow, backed-up waters of *Texoma Reservoir* (off OK 199 east of Madill), are a familiar sight. The town also has a large men's clothing factory. But the most significant changes in Madill have come with development of the sprawling Lake Texoma playground.

Until recently this was best appreciated each June when for a week the National Sand Bass Festival turned Courthouse Square—and indeed the entire area—into a giant carnival ground. Billed as "the world's largest free fish fry" (as many as 25,000 people fed), it featured fishing contests and boat races, a full complement of land-based fair/carnival activities. A victim of its own success, so to speak, the Festival is being restructured as a cooperative venture of the whole Lake Texoma area.

Major County (northwestern Oklahoma, see Map 3). Area, 945 sq. mi.; pop., 7,529; county seat, *Fairview.* A rich farming section cut by the *Cimarron River.* The "fair view" hailed in the name of its seat is that of the *Glass Mountains,* the county's outstanding scenic attraction. Organized with statehood in 1907, it was named for J. C. Major, a member of the state's Constitutional Convention.

Top travel lure: the *Glass Mountains.*

Manchester (Grant Co., pop. 165, on OK 132, see Map 4). A tiny trade center just south of the Kansas line in a broadly rolling area of grasslands and wheat fields, broken only here and there by an isolated, tree-marked farmhouse. The settlement started in 1897, taking its name from the English city of that name.

Mangum (Greer Co. seat, pop. 4,066, at junc. of US 283 and OK 9 & 34, see Map 8). Settlement began here in 1881 —in what was then Greer County, Texas—when the state gave land to Civil War veterans for their service to the Confederacy. Captain A. S. Mangum located on the old Mobeetie (Texas) Trail, and on his land in 1883 Henry C. Sweet platted the Mangum townsite. A post office was established in 1886, and two years later the *Mangum Star* first appeared. The town was well on its way, although it was not until 1896 that the U.S. Supreme Court finally determined that the area was part of Oklahoma and not Texas. In the meantime, however, the federal government had recognized the titles of the Texas veterans to their land.

Mangum is a prosperous farming/ ranching community with the businesses and special events to prove it. Principal payrolls are those of a brickyard (dating from 1909), processing plants for dairy and meat products, manufacturers of livestock feed, feeding equipment, and trailers, of cotton gin machinery and equipment. The town also has a large livestock commission house with sales of over $3 million a year.

Annual events include a traditional Pioneer Reunion & Rodeo (July 4), the Greer County Fair (mid-September)— and that old Oklahoma specialty (although strictly non-agricultural), the Mangum Rattlesnake Derby (see also *Okeene, Waynoka,* and *Waurika.*) The three-day event in early April regularly draws some 200 snake hunters and as many as 6,000 spectators who sample rattlesnake meat, observe the weighing-in and measuring ceremonies that determine the various winners, and take part in the general fair/carnival

147

festivities.

A granite monument on the courthouse lawn calls attention to the curious two-state history of Old Greer County. New in downtown Mangum: the Old Greer County Museum, sponsored by the Greer County Pioneer Association.

Manitou (Tillman Co., pop. 308, at junc. of US 183 and OK 5-C, see Map 8). A dwindling railroad siding community, established in 1902, a year after arrival of the Frisco Railroad. The Indian word means Great Spirit.

Mannsville (Johnston Co., pop. 364, on US 70, see Map 7). A recreation-minded trading center on the edge of the sprawling *Texoma Reservoir* playground. Established in 1888, the town honors Wallace A. Mann, its first postmaster.

Marble City (Sequoyah Co., pop. 299, on paved county road 8 mi. N of *Sallisaw,* see Map 5). An isolated rural community with a history that goes back to the first years of the Cherokees in Indian Territory. A post office with the name of Kidron (for the Biblical stream) existed here from 1835 to 1858, when it was moved, its name changed to Marble Salt Works.

Kidron reappeared, however, the following year, became Kedron in 1886, Marble in 1895, and—apparently determined to come up with a winning combination—Marble City in 1906. None of the names helped too much, if success is to be measured in numbers. However, the settlement has continued to exist. And the Cookson Hills country that surrounds it is some of Oklahoma's most beautiful.

Marietta (Love Co. seat, pop. 2,013, at junc. of I 35, US 77, and OK 32, see Map 7). An agricultural community that, since World War II, has successfully met the challenge of mechanized farming by attracting several small industries. A cookie making company, employing 150 persons and now marketing nationwide, was the first. A men's slacks manufacturer, with some 400 workers, is the town's largest employer.

The town grew up around the Santa Fe depot when that line laid rails through Love County in 1887. Much of this area was then owned or leased by two of the largest ranchers in the Chickasaw Nation, brothers Jerry and Bill Washington. The former's wife was named Marietta and the Santa Fe honored her in naming the new town. Bill Washington, a man as colorful as he was powerful, ran his empire from a handsome Victorian home (private) that still stands four miles southwest of Marietta. It is now listed in the National Register of Historic Places.

The town's biggest annual event is a two-day Frontier Days celebration in early June that features such traditional attractions as Indian dances, gun fights, tractor-pulling contests, arts and craft displays and, now and then, a rattlesnake handling act. Sport and recreation tend to center on *Lake Murray State Park.* Hickory Creek Public Hunting Area, northeast of Marietta, is a 6,417-acre, state-owned preserve that also includes 926 acres of fishing waters.

Markham Ferry Reservoir (off OK 20 in eastern Mayes County, see Map 5). This 10,900-acre lake was constructed in 1964 by the Grand River Dam Authority (an agency of the State of Oklahoma) to augment the hydroelectrical generating capacity of *Grand Lake of the Cherokees.* The Corps of Engineers, however, directs its flood control capacity. Most of its limited recreational development to date is maintained by the state, off OK 20 on either side of the lake.

Facilities: Salina Recreation Area near the historic town of *Salina* offers picnic and camping, and a playground; Snowdale Recreation Area, 2 mi. W of *Salina,* provides a picnic area, 12 trailer hookups, a floating dock. Addresses: U.S. Corps of Engineers, Box 61, Tulsa, OK 74102; State Parks Division, 500 Will Rogers Building, Oklahoma City, OK 73105.

Marland (Noble Co., pop. 236, on OK 156, see Map 4). A small ranching community in the lush, rolling grasslands south of the **Salt Fork of the Arkansas River.** The town was established in 1898 as Bliss, for secretary of the interior Cornelius N. Bliss. It changed its name to Marland in 1922, when the fantastically successful oil wildcatter, E. W. Marland (see **Ponca City**), was developing field after field in the area.

It was as Bliss that the town received its greatest publicity. In this area George W. Miller established his famed **101 Ranch** in the 1870's. Here in 1905 the ranch played host to the annual convention of the National Editorial Association and entertained thousands of newspapermen and visitors from all over the country with an exhibition of riding, roping, and other western skills. From that extravaganza was born the Miller Brothers' 101 Ranch Wild West Show, that toured the United States under various names until 1931.

Marlow (Stephens Co., pop. 3,995, at junc. of US 81 and OK 29, see Map 7). A clean, prosperous town—ablaze in spring with blooming redbud and wisteria trees—Marlow has come a long way from its tent-city origins in 1892 when the Rock Island laid track through the county. For two decades before that the **Chisholm Trail** had poured hundreds of thousands of cattle north through this area. And extensive pens and loading chutes were among the first facilities built in the new town. Cattle also figured prominently in the town's naming.

Although details vary, and facts at this late date are somewhat difficult to tie down, it is known that the town took its name from Dr. Williamson Marlow, who in 1880 settled his wife, daughter, and five sons in a cave on the east bank of Wildhorse Creek in what is now Redbud Park. It is around the activities of the five Marlow brothers that much of the controversy centers. Some sources say they worked for a large cattle outfit in the area, in their spare time gathered up for themselves stray cattle left behind by **Chisholm Trail** drovers. Others consider their daytime work minimal, accuse them of raiding the trail herds by night, running off into the timber a

few head at a time. After two or three days they would then drive the cattle back to the herd, claim they had found them straying—or in the possession of rustlers—and claim a sizeable reward. Lending credence to this account is the fact that the Marlows departed for Texas in 1883. And 'G. T. T.' (for "Gone to Texas") was long the traditional code word for leaving an area voluntarily to spare local lawmen the bother of precipitating such action involuntarily.

This shadowy past probably has nothing at all to do with the erection of a Monument to all Oklahoma Peace Officers at the junction of Marlow's two highways. The pear-shaped monument of pink **Wichita Mountains** granite was inspired by the killing near this spot in 1930 of Sheriff W. A. Williams.

In recent years development of several small industries here and in nearby **Rush Springs** has expanded Marlow's already strong farming/ranching economic base. The Wildhorse Creek Watershed project to the southeast not only conserves county soil and water, but also provides extensive opportunities for hunting, fishing (especially for bass), and other sports at Lakes Humphreys, Clear Creek, and Fuqua. Also open to visitors: an 18-hole golf course.

Marshall (Logan Co., pop. 420, on OK 74-E, 3 mi. N of OK 51, see Map 4). A pleasant little agricultural community established shortly after the 1889 "run" into Old Oklahoma. Its name, like that of **Marshall County,** honors the mother of an Oklahoma Constitutional Convention member. Biggest annual event is the Prairie City Days celebration in April. It was inspired by the book, "Prairie City," written by the town's best-known citizen, historian Angie Debo. Festivities usually range from the old (cake walks, square dancing, patriotic presentations) to the new (rodeos, queen contests).

Marshall County (south-central Oklahoma, see Map 7). Area, 360 sq. mi.; pop., 7,682; county seat, **Madill.** The smallest of Oklahoma's 77 counties, Marshall was organized in 1907 with statehood. It honors the maiden name of the mother of Oklahoma Constitutional Convention member George A. Henshaw of Madill.

Top travel lures: sprawling *Lake Texoma,* one of the world's largest man-made lakes, and *Texoma State Park.*

Martha (Jackson Co., pop. 268, off US 283, 6 mi. NW of *Altus,* see Map 8). A dwindling farming community on a recently abandoned M-K-T Railroad branch line across western Oklahoma. Established in 1889, it was named for Martha Medlin, daughter of an early-day preacher.

Mason (Okfuskee Co., pop. 40, off OK 48, 15 mi. N of *Okemah,* see Map 4). Rural community dating from 1910 and named for Postmaster Daniel S. Mason.

Maud (Seminole Co., pop. 1,143, on OK 59, 11 mi. SW of *Seminole,* see Map 7). Like *Seminole* and many other towns in the county, Maud is an old settlement (founded in the 1890's) that mushroomed in size with development of the Greater Seminole Field in the 1920's and has since slipped back into a quieter way of life. Most of the brick business buildings, many of them empty, are of that vintage. Extensive oil activity, though on a greatly diminished scale, is apparent all around the town.

May (Harper Co., pop. 91, on US 270, 11 miles W of *Fort Supply,* see Map 3). An old town—established in 1896 and named for May Innis, daughter of the townsite developer—May is but one of many rail-siding "elevator towns" (the railroad itself is now gone) that dot this relatively flat northwestern corner of Oklahoma. And although no one has developed it as such, it might well claim to possess a museum of pioneer home architecture.

The *Sod House* north of *Cleo Springs* is now owned by the Oklahoma Historical Society and open to visitors. But another of these once-common houses on the virtually treeless plains, can be found on the northwest corner of May. Still owned by the family that built it in 1896, it is plastered inside and out for protection. Still standing examples of two other characteristic home-build-

ing styles on the Plains can also be found by the interested traveler. One is a native rock house (just west of May) built in 1901. The other is a picket house (8 mi. NW of May), constructed of logs set vertically, the cracks chinked with crushed gypsum-rock mortar.

Mayes County (southeastern Oklahoma, see Map 5). Area, 676 sq. mi.; pop., 23,302; county seat, *Pryor.* A booming county in which recreation and industry have now replaced agriculture as principal economic mainstay. In it are both the state's oldest permanent settlement, *Salina,* and its first big multi-purpose dam, at *Pensacola.* Created at statehood, the county honors Samuel H. Mayes, a Cherokee chief.

Top travel lures: *Upper Spavinaw Reservoir, Grand Lake, Markham Ferry Reservoir.*

Maysville (Garvin Co., pop. 1,380, at junc. of OK 19 and OK 74, see Map 7). Like nearby *Lindsay,* Maysville seems to have succeeded—where many other Oklahoma small towns have not—in making the traditional transition from agriculture to small industry. The rich *Washita River* bottomlands have long made this the state's principal broom-corn-producing area. In recent years, however, this cash crop, though still important, has been pushed aside by petroleum. Maysville likes to consider itself the "Heart of the Golden Trend," after one of Oklahoma's more significant latter-day oil discoveries. A Warren refinery is the town's biggest employer.

Settlement here began in 1878, making Maysville one of the county's older communities. David and John Mayes were local ranchers. Best known native son, however, is Wiley Post, the pioneer airman who was killed with Will Rogers in a plane crash in Alaska in 1935 (see *Claremore*). Maysville stages an annual Wiley Post Day tribute to him (late November), as well as a traditional Fourth of July celebration.

Mazie (Mayes Co., pop. 160, on US 69, 15 mi. S of Pryor, see Map 5). A small community on the M-K-T railroad. In a rich farming area, it was established in 1905 and named for a friend of the townsite developer. From Mazie south to *Wagoner* numerous side roads serve the resorts and recreation areas on the west shore of *Fort Gibson Reservoir.*

McAlester (Pittsburg Co. seat, pop. 18,802, at junc. of US 69 & 270, see Map 6). A century-old town, best known, perhaps, for coal the first half of its existence, for the Oklahoma State Penitentiary ("Big Mac") the second half. It was born in 1870 as a tent store operated by James J. McAlester where the California Trail crossed the heavily traveled Texas Trail (in present North McAlester). Arrival two years later of the Missouri-Kansas-Texas Railroad, which paralleled the latter trail, assured success of the settlement. McAlester (he became Oklahoma's lieutenant governor 1911–15) is also credited with the discovery of coal in the county. Pre-eminence of the industry was virtually guaranteed in 1890 when the Choctaw Coal and Railway Company gave McAlester access to the east and west.

The city grew up around the crossing point of its two rail lines, two blocks south of the present junction of its two federal highways. Its modern business district has developed astride Grand Avenue, now Carl Albert Parkway in honor of the Speaker of the U.S. House of Representatives (1971–77), highest elective office ever held by an Oklahoman.

Downtown buildings of note include the massive, block-long McAlester Consistory of Scottish Rite Masonry and the Rainbow Temple. The $1.5 million Consistory (conducted tours available daily, free) is crowned by a great copper sphere, rising 170 feet above the street. Containing 168 multicolored lenses, this "light of Masonry" can be seen at night for miles around. The temple is headquarters of the International Order of Rainbow for Girls, which began here in 1922 and now embraces 3,330 assemblies around the world.

North McAlester points of interest include the modest frame building which served as Tobucksy County Courthouse from 1876 until the Choctaw Nation was dissolved with statehood in 1907 (on Smith Street); the recently restored mansion of Founder J. J. Mcalester; and, at the Frisco depot, a 5,000-pound block of coal—believed to be largest ever mined—which was cut from the old Homer mine near *Krebs* in 1921. On the northwest edge of McAlester, is the brooding, turreted Oklahoma State Penitentiary. Important economically to the community, "Big Mac" hardly qualifies as a tourist attraction—although it did attract considerable attention in the summer of 1973 when most of its buildings were destroyed or extensively damaged in a savage riot.

More important economically is the 72-square-mile Naval Ammunition Depot southwest of McAlester. Established in 1942, its payroll has been reduced from a wartime high of 8,000 to around 2,000 employees. Leading private employers in the area include makers of women's clothing, sporting goods, electronics gear, animal feeds, automotive parts, and baked goods.

McAlester's best-known annual event is the traditional Prison Rodeo. Temporarily cancelled after the prison riot in 1973, it was resumed in 1976. Two other rodeos also are staged annually. Lake McAlester, northwest of the city, offers complete water sports facilities, has twice hosted world championship outboard motorboat races. Sprawling *Eufaula Reservoir* backs its vast waters to within a few miles of the city limits.

McClain County (central Oklahoma, see Map 7). Area, 559 sq. mi.; pop., 14,157; county seat, *Purcell.* A largely agricultural area lying south of the *Canadian River.* It was organized as a county in 1908 and named for Charles M. McClain, member of the state's Constitutional Convention.

McCurtain (Haskell Co., pop. 515, on OK 31, see Map 6). An old town with an illustrious name from the past and what is believed to be, today, the nation's deepest coal mining operation. Settled originally in 1890 as Panther, the town changed its name in 1902 to honor Green McCurtain, last elected

151

chief of the Choctaw Nation (and one of several McCurtains to serve the tribe in that capacity). The Kerr-McGee mine has created a modest economic boom in the area. McCurtain is western terminus of the 21-mile-long Fort Smith and Van Buren Railroad, all that remains of the rambunctious Fort Smith & Western Railroad (see *Boley*) that once stretched all the way to *Guthrie.* Despite its new name, curiously enough, it does not get out of Oklahoma.

McCurtain County (extreme southeastern Oklahoma, bordering both Texas and Arkansas, see Map 6). Area, 1,854 sq. mi.; pop., 28,642; county seat, *Idabel.* The state's third largest, most mountainous and most heavily forested county, McCurtain is best known for its extensive commercial timber operations and its virtually unlimited recreational opportunities. Created at statehood in 1907, it honors a well-known Choctaw family, of which a father and three of his sons became chiefs.

Top travel lures: *Beavers Bend State Park, Broken Bow Reservoir,* Wheelock Academy and Wheelock Church near *Millerton, Pine Creek Reservoir, Glover River*, McCurtain County Wilderness Area.

McCurtain County State Game Refuge, see *Sherwood.*

McIntosh County (east-central Oklahoma, see Map 5). Area, 715 sq. mi.; pop., 12,472; county seat, *Eufaula.* Long a relatively poor agricultural county, cut by the two main branches of the *Canadian River* and several of their tributaries, McIntosh is now the center of a booming vacation playground. It was established at statehood in 1907 and named for an important Creek family, several of whose members served as chiefs.

Top travel lures: *Arrowhead State Park* and *Fountainhead State Park,* both on *Eufaula Reservoir.*

McLoud (Pottawatomie Co., pop. 2,159, on US 270 & OK 3, see Map 7). A prosperous farming community beside the *North Canadian River.* The town, long associated with the production of blackberries, was established in 1895, when the Choctaw, Oklahoma and Gulf Railroad (present Rock Island) reached this point. John W. McLoud was an attorney for the line.

This area, part of the Kickapoo Indian Reservation, was not opened to white settlement until 1895. And a sizeable number of the tribe, conservative and clinging fiercely to traditional ways, live near the river just northeast of town. A Society of Friends mission here, established in 1883, is still active.

Mead (Bryan Co., pop. 140, off US 70, 7 mi. W of *Durant,* see Map 6). A scattered community on the Frisco Railroad, established in 1894 and named for Minor Mead, a Chickasaw.

Medford (Grant Co. seat, pop. 1,304, at junc. US 81 and OK 11, see Map 4). Established with the opening of the Cherokee Outlet in 1893, Medford (for the Massachusetts town of the same name) was designated the county seat in 1908, a year after statehood. At the north edge of Oklahoma's most productive wheat-growing region, its economy has long been geared to agriculture. Grain elevators and feed mills dominate its "skyline" and small local industries produce such related products as rotary hoes, bale loaders, and stock trailers. Oil and gas have become increasingly important in recent years.

From Medford came two brothers—Apollo and Zeus Soucek—who played notable roles in the early years of aviation. As pre-teenagers they experimented with a homemade glider. As a Navy flyer in 1930, Apollo established what was then an American altitude record of 43,165 feet. Zeus, also a Navy pilot, designed some of the equipment used in his flights. The Grant County Historical Society maintains a small pioneer museum on Main Street. Much of its material pertains to the Cherokee Strip and to the Chisholm Trail, which sliced directly through Grant County. Up this trail from 1867 to 1889 some 10 million head of Texas cattle were driven to railheads in Kansas.

The largest known blackjack oak

(American Forestry Association's Register of Big Trees) stands on the Loyd Martin farm, off Ok 11 some 17 miles west of Medford. Circumference of its trunk is 11.5 feet. It stands 47 feet high and has a spread of 76 feet.

Medicine Park (Comanche Co., pop. 600, on OK 49, 11 mi. NW of *Lawton,* see Map 8). One of Oklahoma's first and, through the 1920's and 1930's, most popular summer playgrounds. Laid out beside Medicine Creek in 1908, the community was boosted in 1909 by construction of Lake Lawtonka (Lawton's water supply) just upstream from the town. A long-since defunct railroad company promoted it as a resort spa. The late Senator Elmer Thomas built a cobblestone house there in 1910 (it still stands), to help make the town a summer home area. Dr. Baird's health baths were offered visitors in 1922. A three-story cobblestone hotel was built, and for a time the popular playground boasted a population of over 2,000.

World War II, however, hurt the resort. As have, since then, changing recreation patterns and expansions of the *Fort Sill* Military Reservation. All of its beauty remains today, and many of its recreational facilities, but little of its once fashionable popularity.

Meeker (Lincoln Co., pop. 683, at junc. of US 62 & OK 18, see Map 4). Started as Clifton in 1892, this small farming community took its present name in 1903 to honor townsite owner Julian L. Meeker. It is best known in Oklahoma as the hometown of one-time New York Giant pitching star Carl Hubbell.

Meers (Comanche Co., pop. 5, off Ok 49, 10 mi. NW of *Medicine Park,* see Map 8). One of Oklahoma's smallest "towns"—and one of its most interesting—Meers was born in 1902 when gold fever was sweeping the *Wichita Mountains* area. Frank Meers was an early-day miner. In 1903, at the height of the rush, the town boasted up to 3,000 people. Now it is pretty well reduced to a small store/branch post office just north of the Meers entrance

to the *Wichita Mountains Wildlife Refuge.* The original townsite is at the foot of Mount Sheridan just inside the refuge. Near a cedar grove is a restored arrastra, or ore grinder, believed to have been used by Spanish miners in this area well before the turn of the century.

Meno (Major Co., pop. 119, on US 60, see Map 3). Trade and cultural center for the state's largest community of Mennonites. Predominantly farmers, they claimed land here in 1893 when the Cherokee Strip was opened to settlement, and the area still has a strongly characteristic stamp of neatly kept farmyards and well-cared-for land.

The sect was founded in Europe by Menno Simons (1492–1559), a Dutch priest who left the Roman Catholic church to join the Anabaptist movement in the early years of the Reformation. He gave his name to the group and probably to the town, despite the changed spelling. (An alternate version is that it resulted from the faulty English of an early settler, one of many in the area who came from Germany by way of Russia. "Me know," he said in a meeting where the new town's name was being discussed, "let's call it Little Moscow." He was over-ruled, but "Meno" stuck.) A large Mennonite church and the group's parochial high school, Oklahoma Bible Academy, dominate the community.

Mennoville (Canadian Co., on US 81, 8 mi. N of *El Reno,* see Map 4). Only a plain white church remains of what was once a thriving community of German Mennonite farmers, who took up rich North Canadian River farms here following the opening of Old Oklahoma in 1889. Mennonite mission work among the Arapahoes began in 1880 at nearby *Darlington,* where the Indian school was located. The church itself was built in 1893, and the churchyard contains many early graves.

Meridian (Stephens Co., pop. 104, E of US 81, 2 mi. N of *Comanche,* see Map 7). A "company town" also known as Sunray Village for the Sunray-DX refinery that brought it into existence in 1947. Guided tours of the sprawling facility, one of the country's largest with its soaring towers, cat cracker and coking units—some taller than twenty-story buildings—can be arranged.

Miami (Ottawa Co. seat, pop. 13,880, on US 69, see Map 5). Yet another northeastern Oklahoma town (see *Wyandotte, Quapaw,* and *Peoria*) named for a small Indian tribe living on the site in the nineteenth century. It got its post office in 1891. Before that, however, the area of present North Miami was served by a trading post known locally as Jimtown, for four nearby farmers with Jim for a first name. One, Jim Palmer, established the post office and named it in honor of his wife, who possessed Miami blood.

The town profited immensely from the Tri-State mining boom (see *Picher*) and soon became the financial hub of this corner of Oklahoma. Establishment in 1919 of the Miami School of Mines, now Northeastern Oklahoma A. & M., made it an educational center as well. Building of the giant Goodrich Plant (1,500 employees) after World War II has added industrial strength to the town's economy. A $2 million downtown beautification program has recently given Miami's Main Street a new look. A modified mall—limited auto travel is permitted—it features tree-studded concrete islands, roof-covered benches, play areas for children, shrubs and other landscaping.

Near downtown is the new Dobson Memorial Center. Featuring landscaped and lighted gardens, it includes the Solomon Bedford Dobson home (he came to the newly established town as a merchant in 1892) and the Ottawa County Historical Museum. Charles Banks Wilson is one of Miami's best-known sons. A lithographer and painter, his most seen works are the giant historical murals and heroic size portraits of Sequoyah, Will Rogers, Robert S. Kerr, and Jim Thorpe that hang in the State Capitol rotunda. Miami annual events include the Green Country Rodeo in late May, the Quapaw Pow-wow June 4 (in nearby Quapaw), and a late August fair that features horse racing.

Midwest City (Oklahoma Co., pop. 48,114, on I 40 and OK 3, see Map 4). Tinker Air Force Base was activated on March 1, 1942, as Midwest Air Depot. A year later, on March 11, 1943, Midwest City was incorporated by W. P. Bill Atkinson, to serve it. Today Tinker (for Major General Clarence Tinker, an Oklahoman of Osage Indian extraction), with its Oklahoma City Air Material Area Depot, is the state's largest single industry (some 26,500 civilian employees). And Midwest City—having long since out-lived its brief, unpaved "Mudwest City" infancy—has grown to become Oklahoma's fifth-largest.

Oscar Rose Junior College, opened in September, 1970, now has an enrollment of over 6,000 students. The city also has large new municipal buildings, health facilities, and modern secondary education plant. In recent years there has been a concerted effort to attract more small industries and thereby lessen the city's dependence on Tinker, which employs over 5,000 of its residents. Several score small-to-medium-sized plants now process and manufacture a variety of products, including one that turns out some 8,000 pairs of blue dungarees a day. (Guy H. James Industries, it offers plant tours.)

Midwest City maintains 400 acres in parks and recreational areas, but depends heavily on nearby *Oklahoma City* and *Norman* for its spectator sports, cultural events, and museum fare.

Milburn (Johnston Co., pop. 275, on OK 78, 8 mi. E of *Tishomingo,* see Map 7). A small trading center, established at the turn of the century and named for a well-known resident of the area, W. J. Milburn.

Milfay (Creek Co., pop. 110, just off US 66, 5 mi. E of Stroud, see Map 4). A tiny railroad-siding community that coined its name from two Frisco officials, Charles Mills and Edward Fay.

Mill Creek (Johnston Co., pop. 234, at junc. of OK 7 & 12, see Map 7). Cyrus

Harris, whose first of many terms as governor of the Chickasaw Nation began in 1858, lived two miles west of here on Mill Creek, so named for the gristmill he once operated. When the settlement acquired a post office, in 1879, it was given the name of the creek.

Today Mill Creek, on the Frisco Railroad, is one of the state's relatively few "mining towns." Biggest employer is Silica Sand Corp., at north edge of town. Seven miles south is the Delta Mining Corp., producing dolomite (magnesium carbonate), an important factor in plant and livestock growth. One-hour plant tours are available (Mon.–Tues. 10–4). Near Mill Creek, too, are several of the dozen or more granite quarries in the state (see *Snyder*).

Millerton (McCurtain Co., pop. 250, on US 70, see Map 6). One of the oldest communities in the Choctaw Nation, dating from about 1832. In 1844 nearby *Wheelock Seminary* was established and a post office by that name existed from 1845 to 1895. In 1902 an office called Parsons served this area, and six years later its name was changed to Millerton to honor townsite owner Benedict Miller.

Minco (Grady Co., pop. 1,640, at junc. of US 61 and OK 37, see Map 7). Settlement started here in 1889, was given a boost the following year when the Rock Island arrived. In 1890, too, the county's first school, started at *Silver City* by Mrs. Meta C. Sager, was moved here. It was later called El Meta Bond College, a name the town's name now preserves. Elevators and feed mills beside the railroad remind the visitor this is still a pleasant little agriculturally-oriented community. Minco is an Indian word meaning "chief."

Moffett (Sequoyah Co., pop. 312, on US 64 at the Arkansas line, see Map 5). A small "border town" that suffers most of the trials and tribulations common to such communities, especially when the area across the border—Fort Smith, Arkansas, in this case—forbids or restricts certain activities that can, as a result, be indulged in more conveniently, and safely, in a smaller community unable or unwilling to enforce such restrictions.

Moffett began in 1908, its name honoring the family of the wife of Dr. Samuel H. Payne, a local planter. Which is altogether fitting for the flat, fertile fields of black soil surrounding the town are more characteristic of plantation areas to the south and east than they are of the rest of Oklahoma stretching away to the west.

Monroe (LeFlore Co., pop. 200, on OK 83, 9 mi. E of *Howe,* see Map 6). A Rock Island railroad-siding community, established in 1881 and named for its first postmaster, Simon Monroe Griffith.

Moodys (Cherokee Co., pop. 40, off OK 10, 8 mi. N of *Tahlequah,* see Map 5). A tiny rural community that takes its name from the nearby Moody's Springs, for an early settler, William Moody.

Moon (McCurtain Co., pop. 100, off OK 3, 18 mi. SE of *Idabel,* see Map 6). With Bokhoma, another scattered community in the *Ouachita National Forest,* which provides most of the jobs in the area.

Moore (Cleveland Co., pop. 18,761, at junc. of I 35 & US 77 and OK 37, see Map 7). Established in 1889, with the opening of Old Oklahoma to settlement—and named for Al Moore, a Santa Fe Railway conductor—Moore spent its first seven decades of community existence slowly accumulating 1,783 residents. Then in the 1960's, capitalizing on its fortuitous location between fast-growing *Oklahoma City* on the north and *Norman* on the south, its population mushroomed an official 952.2 per cent, making it one of the nation's fastest growing cities. Virtually without industry, it is in fact a commuter community.

Mooreland (Woodward Co., pop. 1,196, at junc. of OK 15 and OK 50, see Map 3). An extremely progressive, prosperous little farming/ranching community. Several petroleum industry installations and a large generating plant help provide jobs for the community. Employing over 70 people and serving a wide area, the Mooreland Community Hospital is one of the finest small-town medical facilities in the state.

The town was established in 1902 and originally as Dail City. Curiously, its present name is a mistake. According to historian George H. Shirk, the treeless nature of the surrounding terrain was suggestive of moors and the name Moorland was turned in to the Post Office Department. Through oversight, however, an 'e' was added and Mooreland resulted. The weekly *Mooreland Leader,* established in 1903, is the county's oldest newspaper.

Morris (Okmulgee Co., pop. 1,119, at junc. of US 62 & OK 52, see Map 5). A small agricultural community founded in 1903 with the arrival of the Frisco Railroad and named for an official of that line.

Morrison (Noble Co., pop. 421, on US 64, see Map 4). An agricultural community that began as Autry in late 1893, just after the Cherokee Outlet was opened to settlement. The name was changed to Morrison in early 1894 to honor James H. Morrison, owner of the townsite. The surrounding Black Bear Creek farmlands are rich, but proximity to *Perry,* on the west, and *Pawnee,* on the east, has adversely affected the town's business life.

Mounds (Creek Co., pop. 766, on US 75 Alt., 11 mi. S of *Sapulpa,* see Map 4). A now relatively quiet agricultural community, laid out beside the Frisco tracks before the turn of the century, that boomed for a time with development of the famed Glenn Pool (see *Kiefer*). The name comes from prominent natural formations west of the town.

Mountain Fork River. A sportsman's river, this mountain stream cuts through the most rugged section of *McCurtain County,* in Oklahoma's southeastern corner. *Broken Bow Reservoir* now

covers much of its lower course. But the free-flowing condition of its upper reaches are protected, like those of the *Illinois River,* by a state law passed in 1970.

Mountain Park (Kiowa Co., pop. 458, on US 183, 3 mi. N of *Snyder,* see Map 8). A farming/ranching community that started in 1901 as Burford, changed its name the following year in deference to the nearby *Wichita Mountains.* A few miles northwest of the town, in 1859, Major Earl Van Dorn established the short-lived Camp Radziminski.

Nearby Mount Radziminski also memorializes one of the state's better-known free enterprise tales. In 1915 one Anton Soukup (or Sarekup), a native of Bohemia, brought a herd of goats to this area, started buying up land around the granite jumble, presumably to sustain the goats and thereby provide a living for his consumptive wife. When "the crazy Bohemian" had acquired much of the mountain, he sent for his wife and daughter (both in apparently excellent health), and a fellow countryman, one Frank Svoboda, a skilled stone finisher. Extensive development of the granite followed, and at one time as many as 500 cutters and finishers were employed in the area. Today, however, much of the granite industry is centered on *Snyder* and the name Svoboda can be found only on the most generous maps.

Mountain Park Reservoir (see *Tom Steed Reservoir*).

Mountain View (Kiowa Co., pop. 1,110, at junc. of OK 9 and OK 115, see Map 8). A pleasant farming/ranching community that has had three locations, two names, and an apparently well-deserved reputation for toughness. It has also survived a serious fire (in 1901) and flood (from the *Washita River,* in 1903). The town began life as Oakdale, moved to this location when the Rock Island laid rails through here in 1900. The name change recognizes a fine panorama of the *Wichita Mountains* some 20 miles to the south.

Yet another name is associated with

this Mountain View area. The story is told of a cattleman, one Bill Wilbourn, who ran cattle here in the late 1880's—and who reputedly cut his stock losses by adopting a new brand, thereby reminding would-be rustlers of the ultimate penalty of their wrongdoing with HELL seared in large letters on the flanks of all his cows and horses!

Muldrow (Sequoyah Co., pop. 1,680, on US 64, 10 mi. E of **Sallisaw,** see Map 5). A small town that has bucked the trend of non-county-seat towns in Oklahoma. Proximity to I 40, as well as to expanding job markets provided both by Fort Smith, Arkansas, on the east and **Sallisaw** to the west, enabled it to enjoy a 50 per cent growth in population between 1960 and 1970.

The town got its post office in 1887. The name honors Henry L. Muldrow, a Member of Congress from Mississippi.

Mulhall (Logan Co., pop. 250, on US 77, see Map 4). Like the Miller Brothers (see **Marland**) and "Pawnee Bill" Lillie (see **Pawnee**), Colonel Zack Mulhall—for whom the town was named—was both a rancher and a showman. He came to this area in 1889 and headquartered a large ranch that extended north into the **Cherokee Outlet**. Like them, too, he entertained lavishly, staging "wild west shows" for visitors that were the forerunners of today's rodeos. It was in 1900, at a show put on for his friend Theodore Roosevelt, that Lucille Mulhall, his 16-year-old daughter—later to be billed as the world's first "cowgirl" —made her debut. Another gift of the Mulhall shows to the entertainment world: Will Rogers. The old Mulhall ranch has long since been sold, the fourteen-room ranch house torn down.

Murray County (south-central Oklahoma, see Map 7). Area, 428 sq. mi.; pop., 10,669; county seat, **Sulphur.** Third smallest of Oklahoma's seventy-seven counties, Murray contains its best-known national park facility and mineral spa. Organized in 1907 at statehood, it was named for William H. Murray, president of the state's Constitutional Convention and later governor of

Union Agency.

Oklahoma, and the only person honored in the naming of two counties (see **Alfalfa County**).

Top travel lures: the rugged, geologically interesting **Arbuckle Mountains, Turner Falls Park, Platt National Park, Lake of the Arbuckles,** mineral bathing at **Sulphur.**

Muse (LeFlore Co., pop. 100, on OK 63, 7 mi. W of **Big Cedar,** see Map 6). A scattered ranching community in the **Kiamichi River Valley.** The name honors the Rev. Joseph Muse, a Baptist preacher.

Muskogee (Muskogee Co. seat, pop. 37,331, at junc. of US 62, 64, & 69, see Map 5). The Three Forks region of Oklahoma—where the **Verdigris, Grand** (Neosho), and **Arkansas** rivers meet—is the cradle of Oklahoma history. **Fort Gibson** was established in 1824. Muskogee itself was not started until the M-K-T Railroad built across Indian Territory in 1872. But it soon became the territory's leading city and, with the exception of **Tulsa,** is Eastern Oklahoma's main cultural and commercial center to this day.

The city's name honors the Muskogee (Creek) Indians who began their forced emigration into this area from Alabama in 1829. The original Creek agency was located a few miles northwest of the present city. With establishment in 1874 of the Union Agency of the Five Civilized Tribes, Muskogee's pre-eminence was assured, although it was not incorporated until 1898 (under Arkansas statues) and did not grow appreciably until 1904, with the opening of nearby oil and gas fields. Oil development brought three new railroads and, in time, improved highways. Industry was stimulated and the city today is an important manufacturing, wholesale, and distributing point. Opening of the *Arkansas River Navigation System* has further solidified its economic position.

Although the independent Indian Nations ceased to exist in 1907, Indian influence is strong. Handsomely restored, the stone Union Agency building (atop Agency Hill just west of the business district) is now the Five Civilized Tribes Museum (weekdays 10–5, Sundays 1–5). Opened in 1966 as both a museum and art gallery, it carries on an active educational program designed to preserve and promote Indian arts and crafts. Also strengthening the Indian influence is the venerable Bacone Indian College, at the northeast edge of Muskogee. Established in 1879 and moved here in 1885, the Baptist-supported junior college draws Indians of many tribes. Along with academics it stresses the importance of preserving ancient Indian arts. On campus is the Ataloa Lodge Indian Museum (Mon.–Fri. 8–5) with exhibits of Indian artifacts and handcrafts.

Other points of interest include the Thomas-Foreman House, 1419 W. Okmulgee St. (Tues.–Fri. 9–5, Sat.–Sun. 2–5), long-time home of the late Grant and Carolyn Foreman, well known state historians; Horseless Carriages Unlimited, 2215 W. Shawnee (daily 10–5, fee), a million-dollar collection of sixty rare vintage automobiles; the USS Batfish, a World War II submarine now permanently berthed at the Port of Muskogee and open to visitors; and Honor Heights Park, on the west side of Agency Hill.

Recognized as one of the top ten municipal parks in the country, Honor Heights annually draws thousands of visitors to its mid-April Azalea Festival,

when its 22,000 plants are at their best. One of thirty-two parks in the city, it features blooming flowers, shrubs and trees throughout much of the year, while offering a full roster of regular recreational facilities. Other important annual events include a Science Fair in March and the Muskogee State Fair in mid-September.

Muskogee County (east-central Oklahoma, see Map 5). Area, 820 sq. mi.; pop., 59,542; county seat, *Muskogee.* Long the commercial center of eastern Oklahoma and the cradle of Indian Territory history. The county was created at statehood in 1907 and named for the Muskogee, or Creek, Indians.

Top travel lures: *Fort Gibson* Stockade, *Greenleaf State Park,* Bacone College museum and Union Agency museum and art gallery, both in *Muskogee,* Honey Springs Battlefield at *Rentiesville.*

Mustang (Canadian Co., pop. 2,637, on OK 152, SW of *Oklahoma City,* see Map 4). A fast-growing "bedroom community" on the southwestern corner of the state capital. Founded in 1895 and named for a nearby creek, it remained a small agricultural community until the 1960's. Its population in 1960: 198.

Mutual (Woodward Co., pop. 94, just W of US 270, SE of *Woodward,* see Map 3). A tiny community in the southern part of the county established in 1895.

Nardin (Kay Co., pop. 135, off OK 11 W of *Blackwell,* see Map 4). A tiny "elevator" town on a Santa Fe branch line in a rich wheat-producing area. It was laid out in 1898 and named for George F. Nardin, townsite owner.

Nash (Grant Co., pop. 294, on US 64, see Map 4). Another of the rich wheat belt's "elevator towns" beside a Santa Fe branch line. Established as Nashville in 1894, a year after the Cherokee Outlet was opened to settlement, it did not become Nash until 1911. In neither case was the Tennessee city honored, but the town's first postmaster, Clark L. Nash.

N

Navajoe (Jackson Co., 10 mi. E and 4 mi. N of *Altus*, 1 mi. W and 4 mi. N of *Headrick*, see Map 8). Today only a cemetery marks the site of this historic town in old Greer County, Texas. Established in 1886, it took its name from nearby Navajoe Mountain, itself so named because of the Comanche tradition that a battle had once been fought there with the Navahos. The town is best known for *Buckskin Joe's Emigrant Guide*, published there in 1887. The settlement persisted into the nineteenth century and its name is now preserved in the new Navajoe School (4 mi. W, 2 mi. N), a consolidation of separate schools in the nearby Friendship and *Warren* communities.

Nelagoney (Osage Co., pop. 100, on a county road 7 mi. SE of *Pawhuska*, see Map 4). A tiny Indian community that takes its name from the Osage word meaning "spring" or "good water."

Nelson (Choctaw Co., on county road 7 mi. N of *Soper*, see Map 6). Now a virtual ghost, this Choctaw community was settled in 1881, named for Cole Nelson, a prominent pre-Civil War Choctaw leader whose home was nearby. Here in 1883 Spencerville Academy was re-established (see *Spencerville*). The school closed in 1896, when its major building burned to the ground.

Neosho River. Entering Oklahoma from Kansas north and west of *Miami*, the Neosho (generally known as the Grand in the Sooner State) meanders southward for 164 miles before joining the *Arkansas River* at *Muskogee*. Also flowing into the Arkansas here—the historically important Three Forks area of Indian Territory (see *Fort Gibson*)—is the *Verdigris River*. Neosho waters are dammed at three locations to form *Grand*, *Wash Hudson*, and *Fort Gibson* reservoirs.

Principal tributaries are the Spring, Elk, Honey, Spavinaw, Big Cabin, and Pryor creeks. All provide generally dependable fishing along much of their length. Neosho is Osage for "clear water."

New Alluwe (Nowata Co., pop. 117, on OK 28, 8 mi. NW of *Chelsea*, see Map 5). Little settlement near the east bank of *Oologah Reservoir*. The original town of that name is one of the oldest in this area. It started in 1872 as Lightning Creek, for a nearby *Verdigris River* tributary, took the name Alluwe in 1883. The Delaware Indian word means "superior" or "better quality."

New Lima (Seminole Co., pop. 150, on US 270, 5 mi. W of *Wewoka*, see Map 7). A highway trading center with a large consolidated school. Its post office was established in 1929. Nearby is the older town of *Lima*.

New Mannford (Creek Co., pop. 892, on OK 51, see Map 4). A relatively new town near *Keystone Reservoir*, whose backed-up waters in the early 1960's forced abandonment of "old" Mannford some 4 miles to the northwest. The original townsite, now in part a lakeside recreation area, was settled in 1903, taking its name from Tom Mann, who once owned the land and established a *Cimarron River* ford there.

New Prue (Osage Co., pop. 202, on county road 10 mi. SE of *Hominy*, see Map 4). A tiny community established in 1905, "old" Prue, and recently relocated with construction of *Keystone Reservoir*. It now serves as a supply point for the nearby *Walnut Creek State Park*.

Newcastle (McClain Co., pop. 1,271, on US 62 & 277, 17 mi. SW of *Oklahoma City*, see Map 7). A newly incorporated town that dates back to 1894 but has only recently developed into a "bedroom" community of Greater *Oklahoma City*, thanks to its proximity to Will Rogers World Airport and nearby F. A. A. Center. Named for Newcastle, Texas, it was previously best known for the 2,296-foot-long Newcastle Bridge, a pioneer affair over the treacherous *South Canadian River*. The span was opened to traffic in 1923, the first project of any kind built in Oklahoma with federal aid. Its primary function taken over by twin concrete structures in 1962, the old steel truss bridge, though barricaded to cars, still serves as a river crossing for gas and telephone lines.

Newkirk (Kay Co. seat, pop. 2,173, on US 77, see Map 4). Newkirk is something of an oddity in Oklahoma, the county seat that has grown and prospered modestly over the years, yet remains but the third largest city in the county . . . after **Ponca City** and **Blackwell**.

The town came into existence with the opening of the Cherokee Outlet in 1893. Originally called Santa Fe—it is on the railway's north-south main line—it acquired its present name the following year. The "New" apparently was to distinguish it from a nearby stop on the Santa Fe called Kirk. Oil development began in this area in 1919 and continues to the present, but the town depends primarily on its rich surrounding farmlands.

In a special six-acre plot just east of the town cemetery is the grave of Washunga, last hereditary chief of the Kaw Indians, who died in 1911. With some 600 others, his grave was moved here in 1972 from nearby **Washunga**, when that old Kaw Agency town was threatened by the backed-up waters of **Kaw Reservoir**.

Nichols Hills (Oklahoma Co., pop. 4,478, off OK 74 on N edge of **Oklahoma City**, see Map 4). The capital city's first exclusive, and still most fashionable, residential suburb. Incorporated in 1929, it was developed by civic leader G. A. Nichols. For the most part, it occupies the mile square between North Western and Pennsylvania Avenues and Northwest 63rd Street and West Wilshire Blvd.

Nicoma Park (Oklahoma Co., pop. 2,560, on US 62 & 270 at E edge of **Oklahoma City**, see Map 4). A relatively new suburban community established in 1929 by Oklahoma City developer G. A. Nichols (see **Nichols Hills**). The name combines that of founder and state.

Nicut (Sequoyah Co., on OK 101, 19 mi. NE of **Sallisaw**, see Map 5). Name changes have apparently failed to help this now virtually non-existent rural community. The old Cherokee settlement took the name of Swimmer in 1890, changed that to Vrona in 1912, and adopted its present in 1925, apparently because it was on the "nigh cut" (short cut) road to **Muldrow**. It is also known locally as the town "halfway between **Long** and **Short**."

Two miles west of Nicut is the salt spring given to Sequoyah (see **Sequoyah's Home**) by the Cherokee Treaty of 1828 as partial payment for his having invented the Cherokee alphabet. He operated a salt works here until he left for Mexico in 1842. He died there the following year.

Niles (Canadian Co. just N of OK 37, about 10 miles SE of **Hinton**, see Map 4). Once a bustling little trading center in the heavily timbered red canyon country south of the **Canadian River**. It had a post office for over a quarter of a century after its founding in 1902, but is now reduced to a scattering of houses and a few empty store buildings.

In dry weather —and provided one is in possession of a detailed county map—the rough area around Niles extending north and east to the river offers adventurous motorists some of western Oklahoma's finest off-trail sightseeing.

Ninnekah (Grady Co., pop. 30, off US 81, 6 mi. S of **Chickasha**, see Map 7). Yet another farming community established along the Rock Island in the early 1890's. The word derives from the Choctaw term for "night" or "darkness."

Noble (Cleveland Co., pop. 2,241, on US 77, 6 mi. SE of **Norman**, see Map 7). Like nearby **Lexington**, a small trading center that has bucked the current trend and continued to grow modestly. It began in 1889 with the opening of Old Oklahoma to settlement. John W. Noble was secretary of the interior at the time, under President Benjamin Harrison.

Proximity to **Norman**, long a damper

to its growth, now seems ironically to be acting as a stimulant. The fast-growing college town, the state's fourth-largest today and itself a popular Oklahoma City bedroom community, has sprawled sufficiently to give Noble a certain suburb-within-a-suburb status of its own.

Noble County (north-central Oklahoma, see Map 4). Area, 744 sq. mi.; pop., 10,043; county seat, **Perry**. A rich agricultural county created in 1893 when the Cherokee Outlet was opened to settlement. It was named for John W. Noble, Secretary of the Interior under President Benjamin Harrison.

Top travel lures: Cherokee Strip Museum and the annual Cherokee Strip. Celebration (September 16) in **Perry**.

Norman (Cleveland Co. seat, pop. 52,117, off I 35 at junc. of US 77 and OK 9 & 74, see Map 7). One Abner Norman, a Santa Fe Railroad surveyor, pitched camp on this site in 1886. Camp Norman served as construction headquarters when track-laying crews appeared the following year, with a boxcar on a siding serving as "Norman Switch." The town appeared on April 22, 1889, the day Old Oklahoma was opened to settlement with a run. It had 150 citizens by nightfall and has been jogging ahead steadily ever since. Today it is the state's fourth-largest city.

From the beginning Norman seems to have pegged its development to the human mind—to improving it, when well; to healing it, when ill. The University of Oklahoma opened its doors in 1892, on the south edge of the village. The following year saw opening of the Oklahoma Sanitarium, which in 1915 became the state-owned Central State (mental) Hospital, on the town's east side. Little that has happened in the town since is unrelated to at least one of them.

(Indeed, so important has been the role of these two institutions in Norman's development that it has become the butt of one of the state's hoariest stories. The main difference between them, the late Professor—and U.S. Senator—Josh Lee always insisted,

Bizzell Memorial Library, University of Oklahoma, Norman (photograph by Gil Jain, Media Information, University of Oklahoma).

was that one had to show improvement to get out of the east-side institution.)

The Central State Griffin Memorial Hospital complex has evolved into the state's principal mental health facility, employing more than 1,200 persons. It is now active in such areas as training and research, war veterans' care, medical-surgical work, community mental health, vocational-rehabilitation training, and children's mental health. Also in Norman is the Oklahoma Cerebral Palsy Center, a therapy and training facility. It, too, serves the entire state.

The University has also grown in size and complexity. A faculty of some 1,400 now serves more than 20,000 students in 130 fields of study on a 3,000-acre campus. If at times the foot-

161

Rupel J. Jones Theater, University of Oklahoma, Norman (photograph by Gil Jain, Media Information, University of Oklahoma).

ball Sooners seem to command a disproportionate share of the publicity, it should not be allowed to overshadow the scope and importance of the university's research and development facilities and services. Many privately produced goods and services in Norman today grew out of university projects, often in cooperation with the University of Oklahoma Research Institute. And the Oklahoma Center for Continuing Education, established in 1962 in cooperation with the Kellogg Foundation, extends this "mind" influence on the entire state into the field of adult and extension education.

The University has two major museums. Stovall Museum (Mon.-Fri. 9-5, Sat.-Sun. 1-5) contains nearly 2,500,000 scientific and historical items valued at over $6 million. The Museum of Art (Tues.-Fri. 10-4, Sat. 10-1, Sun. 1-4) has permanent collections of European and Oriental as well as American works, with a changing schedule of exhibits in all media. Of special interest at the Bizzell Memorial Library are the Phillips, Western History, and Bizzell Bible Collections. University and visiting ar-

tists in all fields perform at Holmberg Hall, a fortress-like Collegiate Gothic structure that is one of the first on the original North Oval, and nearby Rupel J. Jones Theater, a strikingly modern building. (For information on all aspects of the university, its facilities, services, and special events, write: Bureau of Public Relations, University of Oklahoma, Norman, OK 73019.)

Norman the town, as opposed to Norman of the two institutions, has developed pretty much as the *Norman Transcript* predicted it would in 1893. "It is not claimed for this city that she will ever be a great metropolis, but it is a city of homes, and one of the most desirable places of residence of which the mind can conceive." In 1940 the population had climbed only to 11,433. **Then came World War II and three** military bases. The pace of growth quickened as several small industries developed in the post-war years. More recently the development of improved highways has made "university town living" both appealing and feasible to a steadily increasing number of commuters working in *Oklahoma City* and *Midwest City*.

The city's facilities for sports and recreation are among the most complete in the state. (For more information write: Chamber of Commerce, Box 370, Norman, OK 73070.) As is, thanks to the University, the special events calendar—from sporting events (an RCA Rodeo in early June) to concerts and recitals, drama and art festivals, lectures and seminars. As a college town, Norman also offers a larger than usual selection of accommodations, eating places, and specialty shops. Most of these are strung out along the two principal I 35 access roads to the campus—Main and Lindsey streets— and around the campus itself.

North Canadian River. Principal tributary of the (South) *Canadian River* and the state's longest stream—758 miles. It heads in extreme northwestern New Mexico (as the Currumpa), flows the length of the *Oklahoma Panhandle* as Beaver River. Earliest maps show the North Fork of the Canadian formed by

162

the confluence of Beaver and Wolf creeks near **Fort Supply**. Some early maps also called it the Río Nutrio. It joins the main Canadian near **Eufaula**.

North Fork of Red River. The 148-mile-long tributary of **Red River** that formed "Old" **Greer County**, the southwestern corner—and "newest" section—of Oklahoma. It was not until 1896 that the U.S. Supreme Court officially decided that the main stream of Red River was not the North Fork, but rather the Prairie Dog Town Fork. This moved the southern border of the state to its present position, adding present **Greer**, **Harmon**, and **Jackson** counties to Oklahoma.

Nowata (Nowata Co. seat, pop. 3,679, at junc. of US 60 and US 169, see Map 5). A neat, progressive town that developed from a trading post established on the site shortly after the Delaware Indians, in 1867, bought land from the Cherokees and moved here from Kansas. For a time it was known locally as California Station. In 1887 it became Metz, for Postmaster Fred Metzner. Two years later, with arrival of the present Missouri Pacific railroad, the name was changed to that of the Delaware word meaning "We welcome you to come."

The town has an unusual number of substantial public buildings and business blocks, for a town its size, and comfortable, tree-shaded residential streets lined with homes sporting the turrets, towers, and gingerbread ornamentation typical of turn-of-the-century architecture. In general, it reflects an affluence that stems in large part from some 20,000 producing wells in what is said to be one of the world's largest shallow oil fields.

Biggest annual event is the Pioneer Days Rodeo the last weekend in May.

Nowata County (northeastern Oklahoma bordering on Kansas, see Map 5). Area, 577 sq. mi.; pop. 9,773; county seat, **Nowata**. An oil rich area that was the home of the Delaware Indians until statehood in 1907. Just east of the town of Nowata is what is believed to be the world's largest shallow oil field—more

than 20,000 wells. This field is also one of the first in the world to demonstrate the effectiveness of "water flooding" as a conservation technique. The field is first "unitized," then a single operator is authorized to manage it to secure maximum recovery of the petroleum remaining in the individual wells. Nowata is derived from the Delaware word "no-we-ata," meaning "welcome."

Nuyaka (Okmulgee Co., pop. 40, off OK 56, 14 mi. W of **Okmulgee**, see Map 5). A tiny agricultural community that is best known for nearby **Nuyaka Mission**, established in 1882. Today its brick and native stone business houses stand mostly vacant. However, in the early 1880's the town was the center of insurrectionist activity connected with the so-called "Green Peach War." The name is an Indian corruption of New Yorker Town, a Creek settlement in Alabama.

Nuyaka Mission (Okmulgee Co., off OK 56, 16 mi. W of **Okmulgee**, see Map 5). Only one original building remains of this once important Creek Indian school established in 1882 by Alice Robertson, who later became Oklahoma's first congresswoman. A handsomely plain two-story frame affair, it is now a private home.

Oakland (Marshall Co., pop. 317, on OK 199, 2 mi. NW of **Madill**, see Map 7). Established in 1881 as the seat of Pickens County in the old Chickasaw Nation. Today it serves as something of a residential "suburb" of nearby **Madill**.

Oaks (Delaware Co., pop. 219, on OK 33-C, 5 mi. SW of **Kansas**, see Map 5). Settlement in this area began in 1842 when Moravian missionaries to the Cherokees erected a combination log schoolhouse and church. New Springplace Mission, named for its location at a ford on Spring Creek used by a branch of the old military road from **Fort Gibson** to St. Louis, flourished—but for the troubled Civil War years—until 1898. Only a stone chimney and foundation sills remain to mark the site.

Oakwood (Dewey Co., pop. 129, on US 270-281, see Map 3). A tiny railroad-siding community that lives up to its name in part by serving several nearby orchards (peaches primarily) and berry patches. Largest and best known is the one operated by Roy "Blackberry" Johnson, established by his father soon after the turn of the century.

Ochelata (Washington Co., pop. 330, 2 mi. W of US 75, 11 mi. S of Bartlesville, see Map 5). A small community that sprang up beside the Santa Fe Railroad when it built through the county in 1898. The name is the Indian name of Charles Thompson, principal chief of the Cherokees 1875–79. Lying in the fertile valleys of Caney River and Double Creek, the town is surrounded by many fine ranches.

Oilton (Creek Co., pop. 1,087, at junc. of OK 51 & 99, see Map 4). A now relatively sedate monument to one of Oklahoma's famed oil booms (see *Cushing*). The townsite was a cornfield in 1915 when it was platted as the oil development was reaching its crest. Lots sold at first for $500. Within a week a hundred houses had been thrown up. Owners of Main Street lots were soon asking $4,000 and, when would-be merchants rebelled, the present business district was developed a block to the north. The state's first river-bed oil well was drilled in the *Cimarron* near Oilton.

Okarche (Kingfisher/Canadian Cos., pop. 826, on US 81, see Map 4). Laid out in 1890, a year after Old Oklahoma was thrown open to settlement, this prosperous little agricultural community straddles the Kingfisher/Canadian county line and manages to combine the first syllables of OK(lahoma), AR(apaho) and CHE(yenne) to create its unique name.

German-speaking Catholics, Lutherans, Evangelicals, and Mennonites first settled on the rich farmlands in this area. The town once had its own German language newspaper and other institutions, and remains for the most part a close-knit German community to this day. Aside from towering wheat-country elevators, Okarche's principal structures are church-owned: impressive churches, Catholic and Lutheran schools, a Catholic hospital.

An Okarche extra: the Schwarz winery, Oklahoma's first commercial winery. It is located on the Pete Schwarz farm two miles southeast of Okarche.

Okay (Wagoner Co., pop. 419, on OK 16, 9 mi. S of *Wagoner,* see Map 5). Few towns in Oklahoma are older than Okay—or have suffered more vicissitudes. A trading post was set up here on the *Verdigris River* shortly after the turn of the nineteenth century. This is the historic Three Forks area, where the *Verdigris* and the *Grand* (Neosho) rivers join the *Arkansas,* and the town, though plagued by fires, was long a bustling shipping point. It was known then by various names, including Falls City, Verdigris Falls, Verdigris Landing, Three Forks, Creek Agency, and Sleepyville.

Devastated by the Civil War, the town was rebuilt a short distance to the north in 1871 when the M-K-T Railroad arrived. It was then known successively as Coretta Switch, North Muskogee, and Rex. The name Okay came in 1919 with the OK Truck Manufacturing Co., one of several local industries (stoves, plows, airplanes) that subsequently failed. Ironically, the town's most impressive building is the ruined truck plant near the highway bridge over the *Verdigris.* A tornado (1911), flood (1927) and another bad fire (1936) combined to further batter the old settlement, which now lives largely as a supply center for recreation seekers at nearby *Fort Gibson Reservoir.*

Okeene (Blaine Co., pop. 1,421, at junc. of St. 8 and St. 51, see Map 3). A prosperous farming community (wheat, cattle) with a predominantly German flavor. Its flour mill is one of the very few established in pioneer days still operating in Oklahoma. Okeene's notable contribution to the state's special-events calendar is the annual spring Rattlesnake Roundup in the *Gyp Hills* west of town. The weekend event draws hundreds of hunters (supplied with gunny sacks and forked sticks) who compete for a variety of "biggest," "longest," and other prizes. And thousands of spectators who take part in the crowning of the Rattlesnake Queen, oversee the milking of venom for laboratory use, and eat—or at least buy—rattlesnake meat. Success of the event has resulted in similar hunts at **Waynoka, Waurika,** and **Mangum,** but Okeene remains headquarters of the International Association of Rattlesnake Hunters.

Okemah (Okfuskee Co. seat, pop. 2,913, off I 40 at junc. of US 62 and OK 56, see Map 4). Petroleum, a men's work clothes factory, and agricultural products (notably pecans) keep this town bustling and prosperous. Yet it is perhaps best known today for a not-always-appreciated native son—and a nice sense of humor.

A few years ago, faced with the problem of what to do with side-by-side water towers on a hill overlooking I 40, city officials came up with an inspired solution: paint them black and gold in the school colors, mark the smaller one HOT, the larger COLD. When a third tower was subsequently added, the passage of time had erased much of the town's resentment over alleged youthful communist leanings, and HOME OF WOODY GUTHRIE was painted on it.

The famed folk singer, who died in 1967 at the age of 55, was born in Okemah in 1912, lived there until he "lit out" at 15 to become the best-known balladeer of the Depression/Dust Bowl Days. His boyhood home was recently demolished after plans to restore it fell through.

Okemah—a Creek name for "big chief"—was established in 1902 with the building of the long-since-abandoned Fort Smith & Western Railroad. The Five Star Ranch west of town is one of several large producers and sellers of pecans in this area. Nearby, on OK 48 at the I 40 exit, is the Indian Territory Town Museum (Apr.–Sept. daily 9–9, fee), a collection of false-fronted buildings containing Indian and western materials. Okemah City Lake, 171 acres, is five miles north of town.

A specimen caught in the annual rattlesnake hunt at Okeene.

It is one of nearly a dozen fishing and recreation lakes in the area.

Okesa (Osage Co., pop. 200, off US 60, 8 mi. W of **Bartlesville,** see Map 4). A tiny community that began shortly after the turn of the century, was given the Osage word for "halfway" because it lay midway between **Pawhuska,** the Osage capital, and the Cherokee Nation on the east.

Okfuskee County (east-central Oklahoma, see Map 4). Area, 638 sq. mi.;

Oil wells in a hay field—a frequent sight in central Oklahoma.

1887. Oklahoma Territory emerged in 1889 and then, in 1907, the State of Oklahoma.

The forty-sixth in age, Oklahoma ranks seventeenth in size, its 69,919 square miles making it larger than any state east of the Mississippi. It is bordered by six states: Colorado and Kansas on the north, Missouri and Arkansas on the east, Texas and New Mexico on the south and west.

Oklahoma tilts generally from northwest to southeast—from the 4,973-foot high point on **Black Mesa** to the 324-foot level where **Red River** leaves the tip of **McCurtain County.** The range in rainfall is just as remarkable—from under 18 inches to more than 56 inches —as are the resulting differences in flora and fauna.

Short grasses are the native cover for much of western Oklahoma (part of the much larger, so-called Short Grass Country). They include wire grass, grama, and buffalo grass. Over all, however, a fourth of the state is forest covered, representing 133 varieties of native trees.

pop., 10,683; county seat, **Okemah.** An oil-rich agricultural area that was part of the Creek Nation until 1907. Organized at statehood, the county took the name of a Creek town in Cleburne County, Alabama. It refers to the origin of a Creek clan. The area is also a heavy producer of cotton and pecans.

Oklahoma. A Choctaw phrase meaning "Red People," the word "Oklahoma" goes back, at least linguistically, to the Treaty of Dancing Rabbit Creek in Mississippi in 1830. Then it referred specifically to the Choctaws.

In 1866 Chief Allen Wright (see **Boggy Depot**) suggested "Oklahoma" as the name for the proposed Indian Territory. Soon it became fairly common, although its first official use did not come until 1881 when the present **Whitefield** was born as Oklahoma. The name change to Whitefield came at the request of the Post Office Department in order to avoid confusion with Oklahoma Station (present **Oklahoma City**) established by the Santa Fe Railway in

Oklahoma City (Oklahoma Co. seat, pop. 366,481, at junc. of I 35, 40 & 44,

Robert S. Kerr Park at night, downtown Oklahoma City (photograph courtesy Kerr-McGee Corporation).

Robert S. Kerr Park, downtown Oklahoma City (photograph courtesy Kerr-McGee Corporation).

tion was determined by arrival of the railroad, the Santa Fe's boxcar depot, Oklahoma Station, in 1887. It had a brief pioneer period of lawlessness—its first provisional mayor, William L. Couch, was killed in a land dispute. And a controversy between rival townsite companies lingers on today in the peculiar jog of north-south streets at Sheridan in the downtown area.

After statehood and acquisition of the capitol, however, growth was steady and relatively rapid. Successive stimulants were World War I, the establishment of Packingtown (the city is still an important livestock market and processing center), removal of the railroads from the center of town (making room for the impressive Civic Center complex of public buildings, parks, and some notable statuary), opening in 1928 of the rich Oklahoma City Oil Field (hundreds of producing wells scattered over the eastern half of the city, including the Capitol grounds, many of them still producing), and World War II with establishment of Tinker Air Force Base (see **Midwest City**) and subsequent industrial expansion that continues to the present.

Like **Tulsa,** Oklahoma City maintains

US 62, 66, 77 & 270, and OK 3, 4 & 77-H, see Map 4). Born almost literally on the run—the Run of April 22, 1889, that opened Old Oklahoma to settlement—Oklahoma's largest city has been forging ahead ever since. From a first-day sundown population of some 10,000 it has acquired a Metropolitan Area count of over 650,000 today. And a sprawling geographical configuration that stretches into five counties, making it the country's second largest.

Still, the capital city (since 1910, when it spirited that plum away from **Guthrie**) has much about it representative of the state as a whole. It stands in almost the exact geographical center of Oklahoma—where the rolling woodlands of the southeast meet the grassy plains of the northwest, where the drab sandstones of the east suddenly give way to the Permian redbeds of the west, where northern wheat lands meet the cotton fields of the south.

Like many Oklahoma towns, its loca-

Civic Center Music Hall, downtown Oklahoma City (photograph courtesy OKC Tourism Center).

167

The Oklahoma State Capitol has oil wells on the lawn.

quarters of the Oklahoma Historical Society), Oklahoma Science and Arts Foundation (at Fairgrounds Park and including the Kirkpatrick Planetarium), Oklahoma Art Center (also at Fairgrounds Park, itself an interesting complex), Oklahoma Heritage House (one of the city's early mansions, now restored and containing the Oklahoma Hall of Fame gallery), the Oklahoma Museum of Arts (now housed in the **Nichols Hills** mansion of early-day oilman Frank Buttram), the Black Liberated Arts Center (Black visual arts, drama, dance, literature, music, and history) and the Overholser Mansion, carefully restored by the Oklahoma Historical Society and now on the National Register of Historic Places. Indian arts are

an active and efficient Convention and Tourism Center (3 Santa Fe Plaza, Oklahoma City 73102). A letter or telephone call (405/232-2211) will bring abundant material on things to see and do in the capital city, as well as help in trip planning (limited conducted tours are available) and answers to specific questions.

Museum and gallery lovers can choose between such top attractions as the National Cowboy Hall of Fame and Western Heritage Center (outstanding western art), Wiley Post Building (head-

National Cowboy Hall of Fame and Western Heritage Center (photograph by Mike Shelton, State of Oklahoma).

Oklahoma Heritage Center, The Hefner Mansion in Oklahoma City.

featured in almost all of the city's museums and galleries and sold in many shops and private galleries.

Scattered over the city are numerous other galleries, public and private. And smaller, more specialized museums and/or halls of fame recognizing the state's firefighters and the nation's softball players (both in Lincoln Park), stagecoaches (at Fairgrounds Park), vintage autos (Heritage Hall), and the petroleum industry (still developing on the Oklahoma Historical Society grounds). Oklahoma's domeless State

Center pool and fountains, National Cowboy Hall of Fame and Western Heritage Center, Oklahoma City (photograph courtesy National Cowboy Hall of Fame and Western Heritage Center).

Fidelity Plaza Building, with the city's most exciting mobile outdoor fountain. Still under development are the Myriad Gardens, a three-square-block Tivoli-type park/amusement center; a four-square-block Retail Galleria; and another major office tower.

Sport and recreational facilities in the capital city are also ample. And varied. The Oklahoma City Zoo in Lincoln Park is widely hailed as one of the better zoos in the country. Frontier City USA is a family amusement park featuring shops, museums, train and

Capitol also offers conducted tours— and a graphic exhibit to show the envious visitor how oil is "whipstocked" from under the building itself to help finance state government.

Whether for sightseeing, shopping, or conventioneering, downtown Oklahoma City is an exciting place—albeit one that seemingly has hung out a permanent "Under Construction" sign. Competing for skyline attention are the thirty-six-story Liberty Tower, completed in 1971, and two slightly smaller structures, the First National Bank and the Kerr-McGee Tower. Each of these anchors a block-square complex. Robert S. Kerr Memorial Park, in the latter complex, features an outdoor amphitheater.

Other interesting downtown features: the Myriad Convention Center ($23 million, 15,000-seat facility that sprawls over four square blocks); Santa Fe Plaza, an office and parking structure handling 1,550 cars; the Metro Concourse, and "underground" pedestrian system, lined with restaurants and shops, connecting 16 downtown structures; the Oklahoma Theater Center, a $3 million, controversially-designed theater for the performing arts; and the

The original of James Earle Fraser's famous statue "End of the Trail," carefully restored in the National Cowboy Hall of Fame and Western Heritage Center (photograph courtesy OKC Tourism Center).

National Softball Hall of Fame, Oklahoma City.

Firefighters Museum, Oklahoma City (photograph courtesy OKC Tourism Center).

All-College Basketball Tournament at the Myriad Convention Center, Oklahoma City.

stage rides, and other attractions. The city maintains an all-year recreational program in a baker's dozen community centers, all under supervision of trained leaders. There are nine public golf courses in the area. Professional sports include the '89ers (American Association baseball) and the Blazers (Central Hockey League).

For a comparatively young city, Oklahoma City supports an impressive number of performing arts groups, too. They include the Oklahoma City Symphony Orchestra and the Junior Symphony, Oklahoma City Opera and Ballet Societies, Oklahoma Theatre Center, Lyric and Jewel Box Theaters, Canterbury Choral Society, and others. Many of the groups perform at Kirkpatrick Fine Arts Auditorium on the campus of Oklahoma City University, which supports a year-round program of cultural and entertainment features of its own.

Highlights of the special events calendar each year include 4-H and FFA livestock shows (Mid-March), a week-long Festival of the Arts in Civic Center (Mid-April), International Arabian Horse Show (late August), State Fair of Oklahoma (late September), and World Championship Paint Horse Show (late October).

Oklahoma County (central Oklahoma, see Map 4). Area, 709 sq. mi.; pop., 526,805; county seat, *Oklahoma City.* Once a rich agricultural area that is now almost entirely covered by a sprawling city and its suburbs, including the lakes that provide it with drinking water and recreation. Part of Old Oklahoma and theoretically free of white settlers until opened by run on April 22, 1889, the county contained a "city" of 10,000 by nightfall. Its name, first suggested by the noted Choctaw Indian leader, Allen Wright, means "home of the red people."

Top travel lures: the domeless Capitol surrounded by oil wells, Fair Park with its museums and galleries, Lincoln Park, Oklahoma Historical Society Museum, Hefner and Overholser Lakes, all in *Oklahoma City.*

Oklahoma Panhandle. The three northwestern counties of Oklahoma (see Map 2), a 5,738-square-mile rectangle (roughly 168 miles east-west, 34 miles north-south) that fancies itself so iso-

Administration building at Oklahoma City University (photograph courtesy OKC Tourism Center).

171

Petroglyphs and "The Wedding Party" rock formation in No Man's Land, the Oklahoma Panhandle.

lated and neglected that it likes to boast of being bordered by five states: Kansas and Colorado on the north, New Mexico on the west, Texas on the South, and Oklahoma on the east—the Panhandle can claim a long and colorful history. Coronado was the first non-Indian to see it. And he was amazed at such a "level, smooth country," saying in his report that "one can see the sky between the legs of the buffalo, and if a man lay down on his back, he lost sight of the ground."

The flags of five nations have flown over the Panhandle: France until 1803, Spain until 1821, Mexico until 1836, Texas until 1846, and then the United States. Admission of Texas as a slaveholding state forced return to the United States of that part of Texas lying north of Latitude 36 degrees, 30 minutes, the western extension of the Mason-Dixon Line. This so-called Neutral Strip became a true No Man's Land, an official part of no other state or territory.

After the buffalo hunters had removed the buffalo, cattlemen drifted into the area with their herds, followed in time by homesteaders claiming squatter's rights to 160-acre tracts. It was the natural friction resulting from cowman/nester competition for limited grass and water that led to vigilante

action and the organization in 1887, in **Beaver City,** of "Cimarron Territory." It was never recognized by the federal government, however, and with passage of the Organic Act of 1890, it was automatically dissolved, becoming Beaver County within Oklahoma Territory. Upon statehood in 1907 it was divided into the three counties of **Beaver, Texas,** and **Cimarron.**

If the Panhandle's past has been checkered, it has also been hard. It lay at the heart of the Dust Bowl in the "dirty thirties." Before that it had known killing blizzards and searing heat many times. And almost always too little rainfall. (Today, however, some 270,000 acres are being irrigated, mostly from deep wells, more than in the rest of the state combined.) One wry verse of a song popular with the pioneers sums up the harshness of Panhandle life in the early days:

Pickin' up bones to keep from starving,
Pickin' up chips to keep from freezing,
Pickin' up courage to keep from leaving,
Way Out West in No Man's Land.

"Bones" and "chips" were relics of the vast herds of buffalo that once roamed the treeless Panhandle. Between 1872 and 1874 wagon trains criss-crossed this area carrying out 6,750,000 pounds of buffalo meat to

Old Creek Council House at Okmulgee (photograph by Paul E. Lefebvre).

railheads in Texas and Kansas. What was left behind served the homesteaders in yet other ways, as the song memorializes.

Even today the pioneer spirit lingers on. At **Beaver City** the past is playfully recalled with a Cow Chip Throwing Contest. And as recently as 1974 **Beaver County** was one of the few in the United States that saw no official need for a food stamp program, figuring it could on its own better meet its limited welfare obligations. Beaver is twelfth among Oklahoma's seventy-seven counties in per capita income; Texas is sixth, Cimarron third. The Panhandle's population is sparse, the 1970 census figure of 26,779 (or something over four people per square mile) representing a loss of some 10,000 people since statehood in 1907.

Oklahoma State Parks. Though forty-sixth in age among the fifty states, Oklahoma ranks near the top in state park systems. Some thirteen million visitors a year now have the run of twenty-two regular parks, a score or more special recreation areas, a dozen monuments, shrines, and memorials. In all, these facilities create a 1,500-square-mile playground, with features ranging from airy mountains to bat-filled caves, from sparkling lakes to colorful canyons, from famous homes to once-important forts, from posh resorts to simple camp sites.

Development varies from park to park, of course. As do rules, regulations, and statistical details. In general, though, there is no admission charge, and no camping fee unless trailer hookups are used. For more information one should write Oklahoma Parks, 500 Will Rogers Building, Oklahoma City, OK 73105. Lodging reservations should be requested of the individual park superintendent.

Okmulgee (Okmulgee Co. seat, pop. 15,180, at junc. of US 62 & 75, see Map 5). A bustling trade and manufacturing town that has been the political and cultural center of the state's Creek Indians for more than a century. Okmulgee is Creek for "bubbling water." The tribe, following its removal from the Alabama-Georgia region to Indian Territory, 1829–36, established its capital at High Springs, some twenty miles southeast of here. In 1868 Okmulgee became the capital of the Creek Nation, and in 1876 the tribal government was moved into the handsome, stone, two-story-with-cupola Creek Council House in the center of Okmulgee that is still the city's most striking and significant landmark.

When tribal government was dissolved in 1907 the structure became the Okmulgee County courthouse. In recent years it has been restored to house a free museum of Indian murals and paintings, artifacts, and pioneer materials (Mon.–Sat. 9–5, Sun. 1–5). It also contains the Chieftain Art Gallery (Tues.–Sun. 1–4), and the Creek Council still holds quarterly meetings in the historic building.

As a modern city Okmulgee's history began in 1899 when Creek tribal lands were broken up into individual allotments, bringing an influx of white settlers. The first bank appeared in 1900, as did railroad service. The first significant oil discovery in the area came in 1907, and the city's "golden decade" had begun. The opening of extensive coal deposits between Okmulgee and **Henryetta** kept the boom going through the 1920's. By 1930 the city's population had reached 17,907. Since then, however, it has varied little, as oil and coal have both declined sharply in economic importance in the county. Two glass plants and a refinery are the town's largest employers today. Ball Brothers (glass containers) and the refinery offer weekday tours, with advance notice.

Establishment of a World War II army hospital on the east edge of Okmulgee was to give the city a significant post-war change in direction. With the hospital no longer needed, its 164-acre campus and about a hundred permanent buildings became Oklahoma State Technical School. At that time it had no strict academic requirements, but offered learn-by-doing instruction in two score different fields. One of only two such institutions west of the Mississippi when established, Okmulgee, now considerably expanded, is the nation's largest residential vocational-technical school, with an annual enrollment of some 4,400 full-time students.

Indian powwows and art shows dominate the special events calendar. Recreation centers around 720-acre Okmulgee Lake, 7 miles west on OK 56. The city's water supply, it provides fishing, camping and picnic facilities, along with a 5,360-acre public shooting area.

Okmulgee County (east-central Oklahoma, see Map 5). Area, 700 sq. mi.; pop., 35,358; county seat, **Okmulgee.** A moderately industrialized area that was part of the Creek Nation until statehood in 1907. The name is that of a Creek town in Alabama. "Oki mulgi" in Creek, it means "boiling waters."

Top travel lures: the old Creek National Capitol in Okmulgee, **Okmulgee Reservoir.**

Okmulgee Lake Recreation Area (on OK 56, 5 mi. W of **Okmulgee,** in eastern Oklahoma, see Map 5). A 535-acre

state-maintained facility beside a 643-acre lake (the municipal water supply of the city of **Okmulgee**). Nearby is a 5,360-acre public hunting area (quail, squirrels, furbearers, waterfowl). Public facilities include picnic and camping areas, lighted boat ramps. Swimming is not permitted. Address: Route 3, Okmulgee, OK 74447.

Oktaha (Muskogee Co., pop. 193, on US 69, 14 mi. S of **Muskogee,** see Map 5). A small farming community that began with the building of the M-K-T Railroad through here in 1872. It was named for Oktarharsars Harjo, a prominent Creek leader. A few miles to the south was fought the important Civil War Battle of Honey Springs (see **Rentiesville**).

Olustee (Jackson Co., pop. 819, on OK 44, 11 mi. SW of **Altus,** see Map 8). A farming/ranching community on the Frisco Railway near the Salt Fork of Red River. Established in 1895, its name—from the Seminole Indian word for "pond"—recalls the Battle of Olustee in the Seminole Wars in Florida.

Since 1965 it is perhaps best known in other parts of Oklahoma for the Eagle-Picher strip mine a few miles to the southwest that gives the state its only copper production. The round-the-clock stripping operation employs nearly a hundred persons. In pleasant contrast to previous operations in eastern Oklahoma, a full-scale restoration of the scarred land has proceeded apace with the mining itself. However, in 1975 a depressed market for new copper caused what residents hope will be a temporary shutdown of operations.

Omega (Kingfisher Co., pop. 25, off OK 33, 15 mi. W of **Kingfisher,** see Map 4). This tiny rural community is all that's left of a curious two-town tandem established in 1892. Alpha, for the first letter of the Greek alphabet, was laid out 5 miles to the east. It has long since disappeared. As for Omega, the last Greek letter, it has managed to cling to its post office. But its school has been merged with that of nearby Loyal —to become Lomega—and its last busi-

174

ness of any size is, ironically, one that manufactures burial vaults!

101 Ranch, see *Marland.*

Oologah (Rogers Co., pop. 458, at junc. of US 169 and OK 88, see Map 5). The tiny farming/ranching community made famous by Will Rogers, who was born a few miles to the northeast (see *Will Rogers State Park*). A tiny replica of the Clem Rogers ranch house, along with a bust of Will, stands beside the highway near the railway station. The town began in 1887 when the present Missouri Pacific line built through here. The Indian name is that of a Cherokee chief, Dark Cloud.

Oologah Reservoir (off OK 88, 10 mi. N of *Claremore,* in Rogers County, see Map 5). A 5,850-acre lake created in 1963 by the Corps of Engineers with a 129-foot-high dam across the *Verdigris River.* The Oologah Public Hunting Area contains 16,310 acres around the northern half of the reservoir. Most of the recreational development is on either side of the dam. Special feature of the area: *Will Rogers State Park,* which contains the famed humorist's restored birthplace.

Facilities: picnic and camp area, boat ramps, swimming beaches. Address: Corps of Engineers, Box 61, Tulsa, OK 74102.

Optima (Texas Co., pop. 103, on US 54 & 64, 9 mi. NE of *Guymon,* see Map 2). A dwindling agricultural community on the main line of the Rock Island that, ironically, boasts one of the county's oldest post offices (1886) and certainly its most distinguished name (Latin for "best" or "greatest"). Even before that, Optima was site of a prehistoric Indian village and several archaeologically significant ruins are to be found in the area.

Optima Reservoir (5 mi. NE of *Hardesty,* in Texas County, see Map 2). A 6,000-acre reservoir newly completed by the Corps of Engineers on the *North Canadian River* just below the mouth of Coldwater Creek. Its earthen embankment is 85 feet high, 16,875 feet long. When filled to capacity the flood control empoundment will have 31 miles of shoreline extending some 7 miles up both streams.

The $34.1 million project had been talked of for nearly fifty years, has appeared on maps (though up the Canadian about 20 miles to near *Optima,* hence its name) for half that time. It received its first appropriation in 1936, but was delayed by the Great Depression and by two wars. The reservoir floods the site of historic Old Hardesty (see *Hardesty*). Facilities are still being developed. Address: Corps of Engineers, Box 61, Tulsa, OK 74102.

Orienta (Major Co., pop. 15, at junc. of US 60 and OK 15, see Map 3). A tiny community on the south bank of the *Cimarron River.* It was established in 1901, taking its name from the ambitiously-named Kansas City, Mexico and Orient Railway (now part of the Santa Fe). To the west lie the picturesque *Glass Mountains.*

Orion (Major Co., on US 60, 18 mi. W of *Fairview,* see Map 3). A rather high-flown name (from either Greek mythology or the constellation) for a town that time has reduced to the proverbial "wide place in the road." Its country store, however, is well worth visiting. Founded in 1896 by W. H. Painton and owned now by his son, the internationally recognized painter Ivan Painton, it .is one of the last of a rapidly dying breed in rural America. Painton is a leading exponent of "rock art" and operates a rock shop in addition to the filling station/grocery. His paintings, mostly in oil, are displayed in a nearby studio.

Orlando (Logan Co., pop. 202, on US 77, see Map 4). A somnolent village today, Orlando began with the Oklahoma land rush of April 22, 1889, and boasted a somewhat restless population of 60,000 on the night of September 15, 1893. This unusual atmosphere was occasioned by the opening of the vast Cherokee Outlet, immediately to the north. Next morning the crowd was gone, and the town returned gradually to normal. Equally ineffective as a growth stimulant was the brief gold rush of 1896, triggered by swindlers who "salted" a farm southwest of Orlando.

Osage County (extreme north-central Oklahoma bordering on Kansas, see Map 4). Area, 2,293 sq. mi.; pop., 29,750; county seat, *Pawhuska.* The largest of Oklahoma's seventy-seven counties and the home until statehood of one of its most colorful—and richest —Indian tribes. Dotted with the "walking beams" of pumping oil wells, it is also one of the state's best-known "pastures" for fine cattle and quarterhorses. The name is a corruption by the French of the Osage "Wah-Sha-She," a tribal name the exact meaning of which is not known.

Top travel lures: *Osage Hills State Park,* Agency Hill (Osage Agency, tribal museum) and Osage County Historical Museum, both in *Pawhuska, Hulah Reservoir,* idle sightseeing along secondary roads through rolling, oil well-dotted ranching country.

Osage Hills State Park (2 mi. S of US 60 from a point 12 mi. W of *Bartlesville,* see Map 4). The isolated, wooded retreat of Oklahoma's park system, 1,217-acre Osage Hills features winding roads, a deep forested canyon, a small (18-acre) lake for fishing, and a handful of comfortable rock cottages. Hiking through the woods is perhaps the favorite activity of most visitors. There are several pleasant bridle paths and hiking trails. One leads to an old stone water tower atop Osage Lookout and an excellent panoramic view of the entire park.

Facilities: 8 cottages, picnic and camp areas, trailer hookups, swimming pool and bathhouse, boat dock and rentals. Address: Pawhuska, OK 74056.

Oscar (Jefferson Co., pop. 50, off OK 32, 12 mi. E of *Ryan,* see Map 7). A scattered agricultural community near *Red River.* Established in 1892, it took the name of a local cattleman, Oscar W. Seay.

Otoe Indian Agency (Noble Co., just W of US 177, 15 mi. S of *Ponca City,* see Map 4). A rusted water tower broods over the cluster of empty and partly ruined buildings that was once a bustling agency and school. The still solid stone building, east across the lane from the now padlocked brick school buildings, was erected soon after the agency was established in 1881.

Ottawa County (extreme northeastern Oklahoma bordering on both Kansas and Missouri, see Map 5). Area, 461 sq. mi.; pop., 29,800; county seat, *Miami.* Once the heart of the rich Tri-State mining area (lead and zinc, of which it was the nation's leading producer for many years), Ottawa county now looks to manufacturing (tires) and water-oriented recreation to sustain its booming economy. Created at statehood in 1907, it is one of fifteen in the state named for Indian tribes. An Algonquian term "adawe," it means "to buy and sell."

Top travel lures: Indian ceremonials, fishing on *Grand Lake of the Cherokees.*

Ouachita Mountains. Oklahoma's most extensive range of hills and mountains, the Ouachitas extend westward from Arkansas to cover large parts of *Le-Flore, Pushmataha,* and *McCurtain* counties. The system includes a number of separate ranges or ridges best known by their own picturesque names —names like Winding Stair, Jackfork, and Kiamichi.

Rich Mountain, on the Oklahoma-Arkansas border, is the highest elevation in Oklahoma—in relation to the surrounding lowlands. It stands 2,900-feet above sea level, some 2,000 feet higher than the valley of the *Kiamichi River,* which flows at its base.

The name Winding Stair originally applied to a single ridge of the Ouachitas astride the Fort Smith-to-*Fort Towson* military road, which looped back and forth in making the ascent of its steep sides. Ouachita itself (as in WASH-i-ta) is the French spelling of the two Choctaw words for the river, *owa* and *chito,* meaning "big hunt."

On the Talimena Trail in the Kiamichi Mountains, part of the Ouachita Mountain range.

Individual ranges within the Ouachitas run generally east-west in direction, though tending to arc southward as they reach farther into the state. They were formed by the faulting of thick layers of sandstone. Many of their valleys are narrow, rugged, and cut by spring-fed creeks. These join to create such excellent fishing streams as the **Mountain Fork, Kiamichi, Little** and **Glover** rivers. In this extreme southeastern corner of the state, too, are Oklahoma's best pine and hardwood forests (see **Wright City, Broken Bow,** and **Valliant**).

Ouachita National Forest (LeFlore and McCurtain Counties, see Map 6). Some 237,850 acres of this forest (most of which lies in Arkansas to the east) is in Oklahoma, administered through district ranger offices in **Heavener, Tali-**

hina, and **Idabel.** The lands are open to the public for fishing, hunting, and general recreation. More than seventy-five streams course through the forest, which provides seven developed recreation areas. Visitors are welcome to climb any of the forest's seven lookout towers, ranging from Blue Mountain (1,800 feet) to Rich Mountain (2,950 feet). More information can be supplied by the District Ranger in any of the three district offices.

Overbrook (Love Co., pop. 50, on US 77, on I 35 and US 77, 9 mi. N of **Marietta,** see Map 7). A town laid out on the Santa Fe Railroad when that line built through here in 1887. It was named for the Pennsylvania city of that name. Overbrook provides convenient access to the scenic rim road, US 77-S, that serves **Lake Murray State Park.**

Owasso (Tulsa Co., pop. 3,491, on US 75 & 169, see Map 5). The Osage word for "the end," according to historian George H. Shirk, Owasso came into being in 1900 as "the end" (temporarily) of a Santa Fe Railroad into Indian Territory from Kansas. Long a bustling farm trading center, it is today pretty much a suburban residential community on *Tulsa*'s northeast side.

Paden (Okfuskee Co., pop. 442, on US 62, 7 mi. E of *Prague*, see Map 4). This once-bustling agricultural community that began just after the turn of the century was hurt, with many other towns in this area, by the 1939 abandonment of the Fort Smith & Western Railroad (see *Boley*). It was named for a U.S. deputy marshal, Paden Tolbert.

Panama (LeFlore Co., pop. 1,121, on US 59 & 271, see Map 6). A one-time coal-mining center that came into being in the mid-1890's as the Kansas City Southern Railroad built south through this area. It took its name from the canal then under construction. Farming and ranching now supplement the reviving coal industry to sustain the community. West of Panama on a graded road (inquire locally) is an abandoned stone jail dating back to early Choctaw Nation days. Scullyville County (in the Choctaw Nation) was established in 1850, but the courthouse that once stood here has long since been razed.

Panola (Latimer Co., pop. 100, on US 270, 6 mi. E of *Wilburton*, see Map 6). A scattered railroad/highway community. The name is Choctaw for cotton.

Paoli (Garvin Co., pop. 480, at junc. of US 77 and OK 145, see Map 7). An agricultural community established on the Santa Fe in 1888, a year after that road built its main north-south line across the state. The name apparently "honors" Paoli, Pennsylvania.

Park Hill (Cherokee Co., pop. 170, off US 62, 3 mi. S of *Tahlequah*, see Map 5). One of Oklahoma's oldest and historically most important settlements, Park Hill owes its birth to the establish-

ment by the Presbyterians of Park Hill Mission in 1836. Rev. Samuel Austin Worcester moved his printing press here from Union Mission, and the settlement soon became both a religious and education center. In 1846 the Cherokee national council established the Cherokee Female Seminary at Park Hill, and the town flourished until the tragic Civil War years.

The seminary was destroyed by fire in 1887. Nearby *Tahlequah*, meanwhile, was flourishing as the political capital of the Cherokee Nation. When the decision to rebuild was made, a *Tahlequah* site was chosen, and Park Hill's fate was sealed. Three brick columns of the old seminary remained, however, and these are incorporated today into the Cherokee National Museum and Archives, final step of the ambitious development plan of the Cherokee National Historical Society.

Already completed at the Cherokee tribal center called Tsa-La-Gi is the Cherokee Village, which recreates tribal life as it was in the 1700's. From early May through Labor Day, young Cherokees conduct visitors through the reconstructed village as still other tribal members demonstrate the various aspects of the community life of that period. Open daily except Mondays, 10-5.

Also a completed part of the Cherokee Cultural Center is the Tsa-La-Gi Theater, a handsome 1,800-seat amphitheatre of striking design claiming to be "the world's only artificially cooled outdoor theatre." Staged at 8:15 nightly (except Sundays) from late June to late August, the "Trail of Tears" dramatizes the tribe's tragically difficult early years in Indian Territory, from arrival in their new homeland through the destructive Civil War ordeal. For more complete information on the entire Cherokee Cultural Center write Tsa-La-Gi, Box 515, Tahlequah, OK 74464.

Other points of historical interest in the immediate Park Hill area include the Worcester Mission Cemetery (both Samuel and Ann Worcester are buried here), the Ross Family Cemetery (with the grave of John Ross, highly respected leader of the Union faction of Chero-

Tribal crafts demonstration at Tsa-La-Gi, Cherokee village in the Park Hill area.

kees), and the Murrell Mansion. Built in 1844 by George Murrell, a prominent merchant and friend of John Ross, it is one of the few fine private homes of the pre-Civil War era still standing in Oklahoma. Owned and restored by the state, it is open daily 9–5 CST, 9–7 CDT. There is no charge.

Pauls Valley (Garvin Co. seat, pop. 5,769, at junc. of US 77 and OK 19, see Map 7). Settlement here in the fertile *Washita River* valley began in 1847 with the arrival of Smith Paul, a white man who came west with the Chickasaw Indians to find "a section where the bottom land was rich and blue stem grass so high that a man on horseback was almost hidden in its foliage." He built a double log cabin on what is now Walnut Street and from it he farmed and ranched thousands of acres of "Smith Paul's Valley."

The town itself developed slowly. A post office was established in 1871. The following year Paul built a stone house on Jackson Hill that still stands. The Santa Fe Railroad arrived in 1887, but a townsite was not laid out until 1892. Not until 1897 was the town finally incorporated as Pauls Valley.

For 500 years, from A.D. 1100 to 1600, this area was inhabited by a people believed to be ancestors of the present Wichita Indians. Apparently nomads, they turned to farming, developed certain artistic skills. Considerable archeological and anthropological research in the area has produced the tools, weapons and other artifacts that feature the extensive Indian exhibits in the newly established Washita Valley Museum in Wacker Park (open by appointment Thurs.–Sun. 1–4). Also included: collections of guns, fossils, paintings. Elsewhere in the park is a restored log cabin (brought here from the *Elmore City* area and believed to be county's oldest house), an old Santa Fe steam locomotive, extensive recreation facilities. Of strong visitor interest, too, is the recently restored Old Cemetery, where many of the city's pioneers are buried. Its earliest marked grave is dated 1868. The last known burial was in 1901. The Smith Paul stone is marked "May 27, 1809—Aug. 18, 1893."

Though petroleum has become increasingly important in *Garvin County* in recent years, agriculture continues to be an economic mainstay. This is the heart of a rich native pecan area (over 2,500,000 pounds a year) and two companies produce pecan pies and other delicacies. Field's Pie Kitchen, which began in 1925 as a home-kitchen adjunct to the still-popular Field's Restaurant, has grown over the years into a million-dollar operation with more than thirty employees. The firm started producing frozen pecan pies in 1964, now distributes them nationally from an expanded new plant capable of turning out 2,000 pies an hour.

Principal annual events are agriculture-related. They include a Junior Livestock Show (mid-March), the Garvin County Fair (September), and the

Pawnee Bill Museum, former home of Major Gordon W. Lillie, in Pawnee.

World Championship Watermelon Seed Spitting Contest (July). The current record: 47 feet, 7½ inches! Pauls Valley Lake, a 750-acre municipal empoundment 2 miles northeast of town, offers hunting and fishing, camping facilities.

Pawhuska (Osage Co. seat, pop. 4,238, at junc. of US 60, OK 11, and OK 99, see Map 4). Often as not, a person in north-central Oklahoma intending to make a trip to Pawhuska is likely to say he's "going up to the Osage." The colloquialism is not lacking in historic justification. The boundaries of *Osage County* are the same as those of the old Osage Indian Nation. The largest of Oklahoma's seventy-seven counties, it possesses a certain geographic charisma. And "going up to the Osage" unconsciously reflects this conviction that the county is still just a bit different—and perhaps better—than most. As county seat and Osage Agency town, Pawhuska shares this charisma.

The name honors the famous Osage chief, Paw-Hu-Scah, or White Hair. Where the Triangle Building now stands, downtown at Ki-he-kah Avenue and Main Street, funds were first distributed to the Osages after their removal to this tract of almost 1.5 million acres they had purchased in 1872 from the Cherokee Nation. Since they had been paid $9 million by the federal government for their Kansas land and lived on the interest from their money, they were known as the wealthiest Indians in the country. The claim was substantially strengthened after oil was discovered in the Nation in 1897. As field after field was developed, the Osages' wealth continued to grow until, by 1926, the peak year, each full headright was worth $15,000.

All Osage business is still transacted at the Osage Agency, a 104-acre tract on Agency Hill immediately north of the business district. Immediately to the north of the Agency itself is the so-called "Million Dollar Elm" where open-air oil lease auctions were held in the boom years. On Agency Hill, too, is the Osage Tribal Museum (costumes, beadwork, historic treaties, other Osage materials). It is free, open daily 8–12, 1–5. The Osage County Historical Society Museum, beside US 60 on the east edge of town, is housed in the old Santa Fe depot. With exhibits tracing the history and development of the area, it is also free, open 9–5 in summer, 9–4 in winter.

Annual events include the Ben Johnson Memorial Steer Roping Contest in late June, the International Roundup Cavalcade in late July. Osage War Dances are held at Pawhuska on three weekends each June. Visitors are welcome to these and other special ceremonials held on holidays and special occasions throughout the year.

A granite marker in Pawhuska lists the nineteen charter members of what is believed to have been the first Boy Scout Troop in America, organized by Rev. John Mitchell in May 1909. Also of interest is a stained-glass window in the Church of the Immaculate Conception that pictures Christ talking to a group of children. In this Osage capital it is only fitting that the children should also be Osages. Lake Bluestem, six miles west of Pawhuska, is an 800-acre

Old stagecoach in the Pawnee Bill Museum in Pawnee.

municipal empoundment (user fees) that offers fishing, camping, general recreation.

Pawnee (seat of Pawnee Co., pop. 2,443, at junc. of US 64 and OK 18, see Map 4). The town began as a trading post in 1876, when an Indian agency was established on the site to serve the Pawnees, then moving to a new reservation from their old homeland in Nebraska. Organization of the town itself came in 1893, when the Indians accepted individual allotments and the Cherokee Outlet was opened to settlement.

Pawnee has remained pretty much an "Indian town" ever since, in appearance as well as in spirit. This is particularly apparent east of Bear Creek. The Pawnee Indian boarding school is now closed, but most of its picturesque stone buildings remain, as does the Pawnee Indian Hospital, the original Pawnee Agency (a one-story stone building now used by the hospital), and the one-time Superintendent's House (still used as a residence).

Pawnee's best-known annual event, and one of the state's primary Indian ceremonials, began in 1946 as a modest powwow, older Indians simply wanting to honor and welcome home their World War II servicemen. (Pawnees have had an important role in U.S. Army life since the day General George A. Custer first recruited some of them to serve as scouts in one of his campaigns.) The Pawnee Indian Homecoming, the first weekend in July, has expanded since then until it is billed as the world's largest free Indian powwow. As many as three hundred lavishly costumed dancers, representing more than two dozen tribes, compete each evening. Roping, cutting, and other horsemanship events can be witnessed almost every night during the summer at the fairgrounds just north of Pawnee. The town also stages a big one-day Music Festival each year in early April.

Year-round Pawnee's prime attraction for visitors is the Pawnee Bill Museum, a state-owned park that embraces the rambling fourteen-room home of the town's best-known native son. (Another well-known son: Dick Tracy-creator Chester Gould.) Major Gordon W. Lillie came to Indian Territory in 1882 and went into the cattle business. An Indian interpreter and frontier scout, he originated the Pawnee Bill's Wild West Circus, which he showed successfully in both America and Europe. In 1910 he and his wife built this comfortable brick home to house their paintings and tapestries, Indian artifacts, frontier relics, gifts of celebrities, and other personal memorabilia. They occupied it until they died, he in 1936, she in 1942.

The park includes the home, atop Blue Hawk Peak, the new Pawnee Bill Museum, the Lillies' first cabin (built of native logs by Pawnee Bill himself), and other ranch buildings. Buffalo are also kept on the ranch to remind visitors of Pawnee Bill's effort to preserve the breed. The park, with its picnic facilities and museums, is free (daily 9–7 CDT, 9–5 CST).

New in Pawnee, but a long-time state favorite, is the annual Steam Threshing Bee, a three-day nostalgia binge staged by the Oklahoma Steam Threshers Association. The group was organized in **Waukomis** in 1954. Members get together in late July and operate the steam-powered farm equipment they have lovingly preserved, restored, or at times built from scratch as authentically scaled replicas.

The first steam traction engine for farm use was built in the 1880's. Peak period of use was from 1890 to 1915, after which the gasoline-powered tractor began to appear. Members bring in a variety of equipment for the annual Bee, operating it for their own nostalgic pleasure and for the wonderment (and edification?) of their children. Along with displays of antique farm machinery there are often different types of stationary steam engines, running such things as a grist mill to grind corn into meal and a sawmill to turn cedar logs into shingles.

The event is staged each summer after today's highly mechanized farm equipment has the harvest safely in the bins for another year. Then, for at least a few hours, the "good old days" of the pioneer settlers seem little farther back than the day before yesterday.

Pawnee County (north-central Oklahoma south of the Arkansas River, see Map 4). Area, 591 sq. mi.; pop. 11,338; county seat, **Pawnee**. One of fifteen counties in Oklahoma named for an Indian tribe, Pawnee still has a heavy Indian population. And the county seat still houses the Pawnee Agency and Indian hospital. The county was organized in 1907 with statehood.

Top travel lure: Pawnee Bill Museum on Blue Hawk Peak near **Pawnee**.

Payne County (north-central Oklahoma, see Map 4). Area, 592 sq. mi.; pop. 50,654; county seat, **Stillwater**. An oil-rich agricultural section of Old Oklahoma, organized in 1890, a year after it was opened to settlement. Name honors the man most responsible for that opening, David L. Payne, the Boomer.

Top travel lures: Oklahoma State University museums and galleries in Stillwater, **Carl Blackwell Reservoir**.

Peckham (Kay Co., pop. 65, 7 mi. W of **Newkirk**, see Map 4). A small trading center on the Frisco in a rich wheat-producing area. Post office, established in 1899, honors Ed L. Peckham, railroad developer.

Peggs (Cherokee Co., pop. 82, on OK 82, 16 mi. NW of **Tahlequah**, see Map 5). A tiny community that took its name from Thomas Pegg, who served as acting chief of the Cherokee Nation during the Civil War period.

182

Pensacola (Mayes Co., pop. 56, on OK 28, 8 mi. E of *Adair*, see Map 5). A town, probably named for the Florida city, that is best known today for the impressive dam that created the state-owned *Grand Lake of the Cherokees*. Since completion of the 5,680-foot-long structure in 1941, the town has declined steadily.

Peoria (Ottawa Co., pop. 179, off OK 10, 13 mi. E of *Miami*, see Map 5). An almost-deserted settlement that commemorates another of the small Indian tribes settled in the extreme northeast corner of Indian Territory in the nineteenth century. The Peoria word means "carrying a pack on his back."

Perkins (Payne Co., pop. 1,029, near the junc. of US 177 and OK 33, see Map 4). Established at the opening of Old Oklahoma in 1889, the town was named for Sen. B. W. Perkins of Kansas. Homesteader in that April 22 "run" for land, and Perkins' best-known citizen until he died in 1958 at the age of ninety-seven, was Frank "Pistol Pete" Eaton, a U.S. deputy marshal out of the frontier court of Isaac "Hanging Judge" Parker of Fort Smith. He was a peace officer in one capacity or another for more than sixty years.

South of Perkins, across the *Cimarron River*, is the 665-acre I-O-A (for Individual, Opportunity, Achievement) Youth Ranch, a Lions-supported "Home-School in Family Living" for boys in trouble with the courts. The project began in 1952 when G. W. Main, a Stillwater businessman, donated the family farm to the project (see *Vinco*). More than three hundred Oklahoma boys have "graduated" from the ranch since its founding.

Pernell (Garvin Co. pop. 150, on OK 76, 10 mi. SW of *Elmore City*, see Map 7). A scattered community, established in 1922 and named for a long-time resident, Thomas Pernell. There is considerable oil and gas production in the area. West of the community lies Wildhorse Creek Watershed, one of many significant water and soil conservation projects being developed in the state by local Soil Conservation districts in cooperation with the U.S. Department of Agriculture.

Perry (Noble Co. seat, pop. 5,341, 2 mi. E of I 35 at junc. of US 64 & US 77, see Map 4). Another of Oklahoma's famed "instant cities" (see *Guthrie*), Perry boasted 25,000 residents by sundown September 16, 1893. (An official land office, it was named for J. A. Perry, a member of the Cherokee Strip Commission during the administration of President Grover Cleveland.) At noon on September 16 some 5,700,000 acres of land had been thrown open to settlement with the firing of guns. As many as 100,000 men, women and children are believed to have taken part in the "run" that followed, for 160-acre farms and town lots.

The Cherokee Outlet (popularly called the Strip) was about 57 miles wide north/south, extended east/west along the Kansas border for approximately 200 miles. It made up all or part of eleven of Oklahoma's present seventy-seven counties and comprised roughly one-fifth of the state's total area. The Strip's dramatic opening was one of the great moments in Oklahoma history, an event still celebrated at annual get-togethers in many Outlet towns and cities, commemorated in museums, libraries, and schools, recalled in the names of historical societies, cattlemen's associations, and business incorporations. As the centennial of the event nears, the mystique of the Cherokee Strip seems steadily to intensify, almost as if an increasingly urbanized and sophisticated people were seeking consciously to maintain their cultural and spiritual heritage.

Pioneer spirit was strong in Perry from the start. One of the more enterprising of the run-makers was Jack Tearney. From the south boundary of the Strip he made it to Perry in thirty-one minutes. By 4 p.m. he had his Blue Bell Saloon in operation. That dusty, thirsty first day, beer sold at $1.00 a bottle, due only in part to the fact that water was scarce. At any rate, it is said that 38,000 glasses of beer were sold on the day of the run. "Hell's Half Acre" sprang up just east of the present town square, and as many as a hundred saloons and gambling houses were reported to have operated there for a time.

But the town soon settled down to a solidly respectable blending of business and agriculture. With the addition of several sizeable manufacturing concerns and extensive oil development, this is still the economic mix that keeps the community prosperous. Charles Machine Works, one of the world's largest makers of ditch-digging machines, is Perry's biggest employer. The "Ditch Witch" plant, just off I 35 west of the city, is open for one-hour tours weekdays 8–5.

Perry keeps its pioneer heritage alive in at least three ways. The Triton Insurance Group, the town's second-largest private employer, maintains home offices on the town square in several old buildings that it has handsomely restored to their Victorian elegance. The state-owned Cherokee Strip Museum on West Fir Avenue (Tues.-Sat. 9–5, Sun. 1–5) preserves the history of the Strip during the period of the run and the development years immediately following it. Also included is the library and recreated office of Henry S. Johnston, one of Perry's first lawyers and later (1927–29) governor of Oklahoma. The city's biggest annual event is the Cherokee Strip Celebration in September.

Two municipally managed lakes— CCC Lake southeast of town, and Perry Lake to the southwest—offer camping and picnic facilities, hunting, fishing, and general recreation.

Pershing (Osage Co., pop. 35, on OK 11, 8 mi. SE of *Pawhuska*, see Map 4). A declining oil camp, established in 1919 and named for General John J. Pershing.

Pharoah (Okfuskee Co., pop. 150, off I 40, 10 mi. E of Okemah, see Map 4). A local rancher, O. J. Pharoah, rather than some far-wanderer from the Nile, gave his name to this scattered community in 1921.

Phroso (Major Co., 8 mi. NE of *Chester*, see Map 3). Now only a dot on the map, this one-time trading community (it had a post office from 1900 to 1937) took its unusual name from a novel by Anthony Hope. (The "h" is silent and it is pronounced "Prossoe.")

The town was founded in 1895 by James Case, who had been appointed Land Commissioner for the district. The last business closed in the early 1940's, the school in 1948. But what the Phroso community has lacked in numbers it has always made up for in spirit. The Phroso Old Settlers reunion began in 1952, has been held each year (the second Sunday in August) ever since.

Picher (Ottawa Co., pop. 2,363, on US 69, 7 mi. N of *Miami*, see Map 5). Motorcyclists now race up and down the enormous chat piles that pock this corner of Ottawa County, including that of the old Premier Mine, beside US 66 in downtown Picher. And thereby lies the rather sad story of a half-century of boom and bust in what was once one of the country's most important lead and zinc producing regions.

Mining began in earnest shortly after the turn of the century, boomed during both World War I and World War II. For a time the Tri-State district was the world's largest producer of zinc. Some five thousand men were employed in the early 1940's. By the end of the decade, however, the number had dropped to two thousand. By the mid-1960's, employment in the Picher area was down to around three hundred men in a score of mines. Gradually this has dwindled to the vanishing point.

Signs of past glory are not so easily erased, however. Tri-State mining is of the shaft type, but not the customary narrow, twisting shafts of most mining districts. So rich were the Tri-State ore veins that huge subterranean caverns (some large enough for a football field) have been scooped out of the earth. This activity built up the characteristic mountains of waste aboveground. And, as the support pillars of the underground chambers deteriorate, the earth begins to settle and add to the eerie air of impermanence so apparent in Picher.

184

One four-block area in the center of town is scored by enormous cracks and dotted with the ruins of abandoned buildings. A high fence protects the area, now converted into a bird sanctuary. Adding to the transitory atmosphere is the helter-skelter arrangement of business houses and largely unpainted houses scattered over the area to utilize ground not already claimed for mine shafts, railroad yards, and chat piles.

Closing of the mines and the Eagle-Picher mill at nearby *Cardin* has given Picher the air of a picturesque semi-ghost. The town was established in 1916 and named for W. S. Picher of the Eagle-Picher company that long dominated the region.

A Tri-State extra for the visit is a trip down into an abandoned lead and zinc mine. One or more mines near Picher offer such conducted tours of underground shafts, where the temperature holds to about 65 degrees the year around.

Piedmont (Canadian Co., pop. 269, on OK 4, 13 m. N of *Yukon*, see Map 4). A fast-growing "bedroom community" on the extreme northwestern corner of Oklahoma City. The town was founded about the turn of the century, started growing only in recent years.

Pine Creek Reservoir (off OK 98, W of *Wright City* in extreme southeastern Oklahoma, see Map 6). This 3,750-acre lake was created on *Little River* in 1969 by the U.S. Corps of Engineers, largely as a flood control project. Recreational development, near the dam and off OK 3 near the upper end of the reservoir, is still relatively light.

Facilities: boat ramps at four locations, picnic and camping areas. Address: U.S. Corps of Engineers, Box 61, Tulsa, OK 74102.

Pink (Pottawatomie Co., pop. 30, on OK 9, 10 mi. W of *Tecumseh*, see Map 7). A crossroads trading center dating from before the turn of the century.

Pittsburg (Pittsburg Co., pop. 282, on OK 63, 3 mi. E of *Kiowa*, see Map 6). One-time coal mining center, first de-

Bear Falls on Travertine Creek, Platt National Park, now part of Chickasaw National Recreation Area (photograph courtesy National Park Service, U.S. Department of the Interior).

veloped in 1903 as Edwards, for coal operator J. R. Edwards. It took the county name in 1909, two years after statehood. Today it is a largely residential community clustered around its high school, looking to nearby *Kiowa* for its other needs.

Pittsburg County (east-central Oklahoma, see Map 6). Area, 1,359 sq. mi.; pop. 37,521; county seat, *McAlester*. The heart of Oklahoma's coal producing region since before statehood, now depending more and more on Eastern Oklahoma's lake-oriented recreation boom. Created in 1907, the county took its name from a more famous coal producer, Pittsburgh, Pennsylvania.

Top travel lures: *Eufaula Reservoir*, *Arrowhead State Park*, Scottish Rite Temple and headquarters for the International Order of Rainbow in *McAlester*.

Platt National Park (Murray Co., at junc. of US 177 and OK 7, in *Sulphur*, see Map 7). Though its 912 acres makes

A quiet pool in Platt National Park, now part of Chickasaw National Recreation Area (photograph courtesy Oklahoma Land Development and Park Department).

Platt our smallest national park, the heavily wooded, spring-filled nature preserve is also one of the most visited. With nearby Arbuckle Recreation Area, surrounding 2,350-acre **Arbuckle Reservoir**, it creates a sprawling woods-and-water playground that attracts more than a million people annually.

In the 1890's Sulphur Springs was a popular Chickasaw Nation resort. When the government bought this area from the Chickasaws in 1902 (see **Sulphur**), it became Sulphur Springs Reservation. In 1906 the park was renamed to honor Connecticut Senator Orville Hitchcock Platt, a long-time friend of the Indians.

Platt is considered "an oasis of woodlands in the prairie," containing geological and geographical features of both the eastern oak-hickory forestlands and the cactus and sagebrush-dotted western prairies. This unique transitional feature is underscored for the visitor at the Travertine Nature Center, along an extensive network of nature trails, and from the Bromide Hill Overlook. The new Center—a handsome sandstone structure that blends unobtrusively with the tree trunks and rocky canyon walls crowding in from both sides—is remarkable in its own right. Spanning Travertine Creek on concrete pilings, it is said to be the first National Park Service facility of its kind in the west.

The park offers both roads and trails for leisurely sightseeing, mineral and freshwater springs, modest waterfalls, bass-filled streams, buffalo and deer preserves, and extensive picnic and camping facilities. Address: Superintendent, Platt National Park, Sulphur, OK 73986.

In 1976 Platt was designated to become a part of the newly created **Chickasaw National Recreation Area**.

Platter (Bryan Co., pop. 200, off US 69 & 75, 7 mi. SW of **Calera**, see Map 6). A scattered community, established on a Frisco Railway branch line in 1901 and now serving primarily as a supply point for area farmers and recreation seekers on nearby **Texoma Reservoir**. A. F. Platter was a Denison (Texas) businessman.

Plunkettville (McCurtain Co., pop. 50, S of OK 4, 10 mi. SE of **Smithville**, see Map 6). Scattered community near the Arkansas Line. Name is that of its first postmaster, Robert C. Plunkett.

Pocasset (Grady Co., pop. 200, on US 81, 10 mi. N of **Chickasha**, see Map 7). A tiny farming community established shortly after the Rock Island Railroad built its north-south line through the county in 1890. The name is that of an Indian village in Massachusetts and means "where the strait widens out." (Straits are few and far between in this often-a-bit-too-dry section of Oklahoma, but at least highway and rail line both follow a straight course through the town and the flat landscape widens to east and west as far as the eye can reach.

Pocasset is best known perhaps for being the site of a bungled train robbery attempt by one of Oklahoma's better-known pioneer characters. Al Jennings, who attempted only to open the safe and succeeded in blowing up the entire express car, was at one time or another in his long and checkered career a lawyer, train robber, evangelist, convict, author—and candidate for governor.

Ponca City (Kay Co., pop. 25,940, at junc. of US 60, 77 & 177, see Map 4). Ponca City, they used to say, was "built on oil, soil, and toil." And so it has been. But oil is the most obvious prime mover. From 1920 to 1930 the petroleum industry in all its aspects more than doubled the city's population, firmly established its economic base, created the personal fortunes that have shaped many of its social and cultural patterns down to the present.

Ponca City was born in the afternoon hours of September 16, 1893, when the 6 million plus acres of the Cherokee Outlet were thrown open to settlement. The "Big Spring," near the present intersection of Fourteenth Street and South Avenue, determined its location. By nightfall the city-to-be had some three thousand residents. It was chartered a village in 1895, incorporated as a city four years later. But growth, though steady, was unspectacular until E. W. Marland arrived on the scene. A Pennsylvanian with a "nose for oil and the luck of the devil," he became a fantastically successful wildcatter. Neither Ponca City nor Oklahoma was ever quite the same after that.

Marland's luck ran out on him eventually. His Marland Oil Company became the Continental Oil Company, no longer under his control. But he had given the city at least three of its best-known landmarks (see below). In the 1930's he shifted his emphasis to politics and was elected governor of Oklahoma. Meanwhile another successful oil man, Lew Wentz, was leaving his mark on the city, too.

Though usually standing around tenth in size among Oklahoma's cities, Ponca consistently ranks third and fourth in such significant economic criteria as manufacturing, business volume, per household income, per capita consumer purchases. This relative affluence is reflected in other ways, too. Municipal buildings are not only impressive, but follow a striking Mediterranean style unique in Oklahoma.

Pioneer Woman Monument near Ponca City.

Museums include the Ponca City Cultural Center (at 1000 East Grand in a former Marland Home) with its excellent Indian and pioneer items, and the Pioneer Woman Statue State park.

The massive (17-foot, 6-ton) bronze of a sunbonneted pioneer woman and her son is one of Oklahoma's best-known symbols. It has been chosen as the official emblem of the four-state Ozark Frontier Trail. An international competition for the design was financed by Marland. After a nation-wide tour of the twelve models entered, Bryant

187

E. W. Marland Mansion, now a municipally owned museum in Ponca City.

Baker's was chosen by popular vote. The statue was dedicated in 1930. The other models are only part of the free pioneer museum operated in connection with the statue. There is also a rose garden. The park is at the southwest corner of what was at the time the baronial Marland estate, now mostly broken up into housing units. But his magnificent, walled villa remains. It is now owned by the city and open to the public.

Ponca City's parks (thirteen of them) and recreational facilities are equally impressive. Lake Ponca, three miles east of the city, offers boating, water skiing, fishing, sailboating. Lake Ponca Park offers camping, an eighteen-hole golf course. Lew Wentz' primary benefaction is the Wentz Educational Camp, on the north end of the lake. An elaborate facility, it boasts the state's most beautiful pool.

Among Ponca City's best-known annual events are the Rose Show in May, Indian Powwow and the 101 Ranch Rodeo, both in August. The city also has concert and play seasons each winter. Those especially interested in industrial matters can arrange for tours of the sprawling Continental refinery (the city's largest employer, Continental has some 3,600 employees in all phases of its area operations), the Coca Cola Bottling plant, and the city's municipally-owned water and light plant.

Pond Creek (Grant Co., pop. 903, at junc. of US 60 and US 81, 11 mi. SW of *Medford*, see Map 4). A pleasant little agricultural community in the fertile valley of the *Salt Fork of the Arkansas River*, Pond Creek started in 1879 as Pond, three miles to the north, a site now occupied by *Jefferson*. When it was established here, in 1893 with the opening of the Cherokee Outlet, it was called Round Pond, for the natural lake that existed at this site in the trail-herding days of the Chisholm Trail. Pond Creek Stage Station once stood near the lake.

Pond Creek was the southern terminus of the Rock Island in 1889 when Old Oklahoma was thrown open to settlement, some 40 miles to the south. Its population that April 22 "run" day has probably never been equaled since. It was named seat of *Grant County* with statehood in 1907, but lost out to *Medford* the following year.

Pontotoc (Johnston Co., pop. 150, on OK 99, 17 mi. N of *Tishomingo*, see Map 7). One of the oldest towns in the county, this once prosperous trading center for a rich ranching area was established in 1852. *Pontotoc County* originated as a sub-division of the old Chickasaw Nation. The present county of that name, however, lies a few miles to the north of Pontotoc the town.

Pontotoc County (south-central Oklahoma, see Map 7). Area, 719 sq. mi.; pop., 27,867; county seat, *Ada*. An area rich in oil and nutritious native grasses. As "Hereford Heaven" it is widely recognized as one of the nation's leading production centers for purebred Hereford cattle. Previous to statehood in 1907, Pontotoc was a county in the Chickasaw Nation. The name in both cases came from that of a Chickasaw settlement in northern Mississippi. The word means "cattails growing on the prairie."

Robert S. Kerr Museum, atop Cavanal Mountain near Poteau.

Pooleville (Carter Co., pop. 75, on OK 74, 8 mi. SE of *Ratliff City*, see Map 7). An isolated ranching community on the west slope of the *Arbuckle Mountains*. Known as Elk in 1890, a year after formation of Indian Territory, it changed its name in 1907, statehood year, to honor Ardmore banker E. S. Poole.

Porter (Wagoner Co., pop. 624, on OK 51-B, 13 mi. NW of Muskogee, see Map 5). A progressive little town that honors famed Creek chief, Pleasant Porter. Best known today for its peaches, the town was established in 1903, first commercial peach orchard in 1913.

Peaches have been grown in the fertile Choska Bottoms (see **Choska**) since 1890, and Wagoner County orchards account for a fourth of the state's total production. The season lasts from the end of May to mid-September, and Porter stages a Peach Pageant in mid-June and a Peach Festival in early August.

Porum (Muskogee Co., pop. 658, on OK 2, 11 mi. S of *Warner*, see Map 5). An old agricultural community near the OK 2, 11 mi. S of *Warner*, see Map 5). An old agricultural community near the *Canadian River*. It is perhaps best known as the one-time home of Tom Starr, one of whose sons, Sam, became the husband of notorious woman outlaw Belle Star. A half-blood Cherokee, Tom was a leading figure in the tragic internecine warfare that for years wracked

the tribe because of the signing of the Removal Treaty with the United States. Curiously, he eventually signed a treaty, as an individual, with the Cherokee Nation government, moved to the nearby *Briartown* area, and became a respected community leader.

Sam, however, married the one-time Missouri-born Confederate spy, Myra Belle Shirley, whose first husband, Jim Reed, was a Quantrill raider. Their farm near *Eufaula* soon became an outlaw rendezvous. Both met violent deaths, Belle from ambush on February 3, 1889, two days before her forty-first birthday. Her badly vandalized stone crypt and once elaborate tombstone are in a briar-guarded field near *Eufaula Reservoir* southwest of Porum.

Poteau (LeFlore Co. seat, pop. 5,500, on US 59 & 271, see Map 6). A Choctaw Nation Record Town that dates back to 1887. Its name (the French word for "post") was taken from the nearby Poteau River, Oklahoma's only north-flowing major stream. Major impetus for growth came with arrival of the Frisco Railroad in 1888 and the Kansas City Southern a few years later. Coal was the first important industry to supplement agriculture. Later lumbering grew in importance, and now manufacturing (industrial controls, ladies wear, carpets) has made the town one of eastern Oklahoma's most prosperous.

189

Though built in a broad river valley, Poteau is surrounded by some of the highest mountains in eastern Oklahoma. On the west is Cavanal (2,369 feet above sea level), with a road leading to a small city park on its crest. The name probably comes from the French *caverneaux*, meaning "cavernous, containing caves." (Since the British classify hills as being under 2,000 feet and Cavanal rises 1,999 feet above Poteau, local boosters refer to it as "the world's highest hill.") On the east is Sugar Loaf (2,600 feet), one of the highest in the Ouachita region. It was called Point de Sucre by the early French.

Prime point of interest to visitors is the Kerr Museum (daily 1–5, modest fee). Housed in the palatial mountainside mansion of the late Robert S. Kerr, off US 59 6 miles south of Poteau, it is now headquarters for the Eastern Oklahoma Historical Society and the agricultural division of the Kerr foundation. One large room is a painstaking reconstruction of the Senator's Washington office. Other exhibits include runestones found in the area, Spiro Mounds materials (see **Spiro**), Indian and pioneer artifacts, and geological displays. The native stone structure stretches for 365 feet across a mountainside overlooking the picturesque Poteau River valley. It was completed in 1960, only two years before Kerr's death. The mansion-turned-museum is headquarters for an annual Dogwood Art Festival in April. Spring dogwood tours in late April and early May are common through **LeFlore County**, as are fall foliage tours in late October.

Rail buffs consider the Poteau City Hall one of the most interesting in the state—or have since 1974, when the town moved its municipal offices into the old Frisco Railroad depot following a complete renovation. In Poteau, too, is Carl Albert Junior College, with an enrollment of over 400 students.

Pottawatomie County (central Oklahoma, see Map 7). Area, 797 sq. mi.; pop., 43,134; county seat, **Shawnee**. Established at statehood in 1907 and named for the Pottawatomie Indians. The name itself, however, is a Chippewa term meaning "people of the place of the fire."

Prague (Lincoln Co., pop. 1,802, at junc. of US 62 & OK 99, see Map 4). Named in 1902 for the capital of Czechoslovakia, homeland of many of its early settlers, Prague is a clean, prosperous looking town, now thoroughly Americanized. But it still clings to two evidences of its cultural heritage. In May each year thousands of visitors join homefolks for the music making, street dancing, queen crowning, and fruit-roll eating that go to make up the annual Kolache Festival.

More significant, at least for Catholics, is the Infant Jesus of Prague, 19-inch-tall symbol of a 350-year-old devotion, in St. Wenceslaus Church. The original Infant disappeared from its shrine in Czechoslovakia after World War II when the Communists took control of the country. The replica was installed in 1949 and declared a national shrine by Pope Pius XII in 1955. It is seen each year by thousands of visitors. Special services honor the Infant during Christmas week.

Preston (Okmulgee Co., pop. 250, off US 75, 8 mi. N of **Okmulgee**, see Map 5). A rural community that came into being in 1909 in the wake of development of the fabulously productive Glenn Pool oil field (see **Kiefer**). It was named for oilman Harry Preston.

Price's Falls (Murray Co., 3 mi. E of US 77 from point 4 mi. S of **Davis**, see Map 7). On Price's Creek, in the eastern section of the **Arbuckle Mountains**. Both creek and falls were named for Wilson N. Price, prominent early-day rancher. Long a popular resort area—other points of interest are Seven Sisters Falls, Burning Mountain, White Mound, and Oil Springs—it is perhaps best known today as the well-developed retreat grounds of Oklahoma Baptists.

Proctor (Adair Co., pop. 65, on US 62, 14 mi. NE of **Tahlequah**, see Map 5). A small community in the rolling Cherokee Hills. It was named for Ezekiel Proctor, a principal figure in the area's best-known historic event, the so-called Goingsnake Massacre.

Proctor was being tried in tribal court for the murder of Polly Chesterton at Hildebrand's Mill (see *Flint*). He had surrendered to the sheriff of the Goingsnake District, and the trial was under way at the Goingsnake Schoolhouse, just south of Proctor, when federal officers from Fort Smith arrived. They had come in response to charges brought by Polly Chesterton's husband, who was dissatisfied with the apparent slowness of the Cherokee judicial system processes. In the pitched battle that followed, seven officers were killed, along with the court clerk. The prisoner and the judge were wounded.

All indictments and charges were eventually dropped, however, and after recovering from his wounds, Proctor led a law-abiding life. He was eventually elected Flint District sheriff and a member of the Cherokee National Council.

Pryor (Mayes Co. seat, pop. 7,057, at junc. of US 69 and OK 20, see Map 5). One of northeastern Oklahoma's most progressive little cities, Pryor began as Pryor Creek in 1887. For five years before that it was known as Coo-Y-Yah, Cherokee for "mulberry grove." In 1909 it officially dropped the "Creek" to become just Pryor, for Nathaniel Pryor, a scout with the Lewis and Clark expedition, Battle of New Orleans veteran, and later, after establishing a nearby trading post, Osage Indian agent.

Today the city is a prosperous and growing symbol of Oklahoma's drive for greater industrialization. An agricultural community before the building of *Grand Lake*, it has capitalized fully on the abundance of nearby electrical power, water, and natural gas. World War II brought development of the Pryor Ordnance Works (now the Mid-America Industrial District) southeast of Pryor, a multi-million-dollar complex of mills and plants for the production of paper, cement, fertilizer, and other products.

Pryor has impressive public facilities, including Whitaker Park on the southeast edge of town and Graham Memorial Auditorium. Whitaker State Orphans Home, first established in 1879 for the orphans of Indian Territory, is a modern facility on the south edge of town.

Pumpkin Center (Okmulgee Co., 17 mi. NE of *Okmulgee*, see Map 5). A rural community that existed—presumably—to give the University of Oklahoma's late Professor Kenneth C. Kaufman, scholarly linguist and columnist, the opportunity to point out to his students that the only Oklahomans who pronounced "pumpkin" other than "punkin" were either new to the state or hopelessly affected.

Purcell (McClain Co. seat, pop. 4,076, at junc. of I 35 & US 77 and OK 19, see Map 7). A strategic location on the border between the Chickasaw Nation and Old Oklahoma, at a crossable point on the *South Canadian River*, assured Purcell a certain significance. It was settled in 1887 when the Santa Fe arrived (taking its name from E. B. Purcell, a director of the railroad), and has been an important division point ever since, with extensive switching yards under the bluff on which the business district has developed.

Even before the Santa Fe, however, this area was well known to travelers. A branch of the California Road crossed the river north of present Purcell, as did a branch of the Chisholm Cattle Trail. Still other roads and trails passed just to the south (see *Wayne*). And the area near present *Lexington*, across the river from Purcell, was well known to whites a full half-century before Old Oklahoma was opened to settlement.

That opening came on April 22, 1889, and Purcell, thanks to its location on the Santa Fe, was one of the four main "jump-off" points for prospective settlers. Some 100,000 persons are believed to have crossed the Canadian here in the dash for land.

But for those fortunate enough to get aboard one of the special trains, all this horde crossed the sometimes treacherous river in wagons, on horseback, or afoot. It was not until 1910 that the first non-railroad bridge worthy of the name was built here. A toll affair, it charged $10 a crossing for a time, a toll that had been progressively lowered to $1 by 1931, when the operating company's charter expired and the state refused to renew it. (The present US 77 bridge, which replaced it, was built in 1938.)

The river, with its extensive sand beds, also figures prominently in some colorful pre-statehood history, when slaking the thirst of "dry" Indian Territory was one of the more important and lucrative, business enterprises of "wet" Oklahoma Territory. The Sand Bar Saloon, on stilts in the middle of the river and served by crude wooden footbridges, drew its stock from a Lexington distillery, its customers via a succession of crude wooden footbridges—from Purcell. It was an area institution for many years.

Despite its seamier moments, Purcell matured quickly into its county seat role. For its place and time it soon acquired the reputation of being something of a cultural center. An area Catholic school was founded in 1888. The town also had an opera house. And when a devastating fire in 1895 virtually wiped out the jerry-built business section, it was soon restored in much more permanent brick and stone. Today, residential streets on the steep red bluff overlooking the river are generously shaded with fine mistletoe-draped elms and maples, and the town boasts an almost smug appearance of prosperous complacency.

Several small industries (women's wear, metal framing) bolster an essentially agriculture-oriented economy. Livestock shows in the spring, a Territorial Rodeo (late June), and McClain County Fair (mid-September) dominate the annual special events calendar.

Pushmataha County (southeastern Oklahoma, see Map 6). Area, 1,423 sq. mi.; pop., 9,385; county seat, *Antlers*. A rugged mountainous area that offers some of the state's finest fishing and deer hunting. This was the heart of the Choctaw Nation until statehood and still contains the tribally owned National Capitol at Tuskahoma. Organized in 1908, the county honors a well-known Choctaw chief and statesman.

Top travel lures: the rough *Kiamichi*

Mountains and headwaters of the *Kiamichi* and *Little* rivers, *Clayton Recreation Area*, *Tuskahoma*, unexcelled fishing and hunting.

Putnam (Dewey Co., pop. 84, on US 183, see Map 3). A small trading center on the high ridge between the *Canadian River* on the north and the *Washita River* on the south. The name honors Revolutionary War hero General Israel Putnam.

Putnam City, see *Warr Acres*.

Quapaw (Ottawa Co., pop. 967, on US 66, 4 miles S of the Kansas border, see Map 5). The town began in 1897 on land once owned by the Quapaw Indians, who moved to Indian Territory in 1833. Surrounded by lush grasslands, it was important primarily for cattle raising until lead and zinc mining began in the Tri-State district around the turn of the century (see *Picher*). In recent years most of the mines have shut down, and the town's business district reflects the economic shift.

Indian dances dominate the Ottawa County special events calendar. The Seneca-Cayuga Green Corn Feast and Dances are held near Quapaw each August. One of the county's oldest events is the Quapaw Indian Powwow, traditionally held over July 4. It dates back to the tribe's early years in Oklahoma. Whites are always welcomed.

Quartz Mountain State Park (off OK 44, 7 mi. S of *Lone Wolf,* see Map 8). A colorful southwestern Oklahoma playground that combines 4,284 land acres with 6,770-acre *Lugert Reservoir.* Red granite hills, varying from 600 to 800 feet in height, rim the park on the west, their slopes covered with house-size, lichen-crusted boulders. Cedar, mesquite, and several kinds of oak cover the hillsides, providing shelter for a variety of birds and small game. The park offers a wide range of accommodations and recreational opportunities.

Facilities: 20-room lodge and 14 cottages, picnic, camp and trailer areas, pool and bathhouse, swimming beaches, boat ramps, enclosed fishing docks, boat houses and rental boats, 9-hole golf course and pro shop. Address: Lone Wolf, OK 74056.

Quay (Pawnee and Payne Cos., pop. 41, on county road 5 mi. N of *Yale,* see Map 4). A community that first saw light in 1894, as Lawson, "sprawls" today over two counties and still can count but twoscore souls and one. The name change in 1903, to honor Pennsylvania's U.S. senator M. S. Quay, was apparently to no avail.

Quinlin (Woodward Co., pop. 81, just off OK 15 some 16 miles E of *Woodward,* see Map 3). A small trading center on the main line of the Santa Fe Railroad in rolling, isolated, picturesquely beautiful ranching country. Named in 1901 for the three Quinlan brothers, well-known area cattlemen.

Quinton (Pittsburg Co., pop. 1,262, at junc. of OK 31 & 71, see Map 6). Settled about the turn of the century and named for a prominent area Choctaw, Martha E. Quinton. Impressive concrete ruins east of town are all that remain of the large zinc smelter whose payroll of 400 employees once sustained this area. It closed with abandonment of the Fort Smith and Western Railroad in 1939, and the town has never fully recovered. The once active mines were north and west of Quinton.

R

Ralston (Pawnee Co., pop. 443, on OK 18, see Map 4). A small farming community platted in 1894 beside the *Arkansas River* (its original name was Riverside) and named for the town developer J. H. Ralston.

Ramona (Washington Co., pop. 600, on US 75, 15 mi. S of *Bartlesville,* see Map 5). A ranching community that grew from a Santa Fe Railroad depot built here in 1900. The name is that of the heroine of the Helen Hunt Jackson novel about Indians in California. Three older trading posts in the vicinity—Old Rinber, Austin, and Hillside Mission—later merged with the new town.

Randlett (Cotton Co., pop. 384, at junc. of US 70 and US 271 & 281, see Map 8). Platted in 1906 when the "Big Pasture" was opened to settlement (see *Grandfield*) and named for James F. Randlett, a Kiowa-Comanche Indian agent. The town prospered sufficiently to compete with both *Walters* and *Temple* for the seat of newly declared *Cotton County* in 1912. Since losing out, it has declined steadily. Completion of the H. E. Bailey Turnpike three miles to the west has drawn much of the traffic from the town's three federal highways, and it is now largely a residential community. Southwest of Randlett is Cotton County's only highway crossing of *Red River* into Texas. The Burkburnett Bridge was the only one to be replaced of the three washed away by floods in 1937.

Ratliff City (Carter Co., pop. 250, at junc. of OK 7 & 76, see Map 7). A scattered oil camp that has grown up in recent years around the junction of the two state highways serving the highly developed fields of western Carter County (see *Healdton*). When it finally acquired a post office of its own in 1953, it took the name of Ollie Ratliff, a local businessman.

Rattan (Pushmataha Co., pop. 250, at junc. of OK 3 & 7, and OK 93, see Map 6). A scattered community in the timber country of southern Pushmataha County. The name, given its post office in 1910, is that of a Texas town.

Ravia (Johnston Co., pop. 373, at junc. of OK 12 & 22, 4 mi. W of *Tishomingo,* see Map 7). A small trading center on the Frisco Railroad, established in 1894 and named for an early resident, Joseph Ravia.

Raymond Gary Recreation Area (off US 70, 16 mi. E of *Hugo,* in southeastern Oklahoma, see Map 6). A 60-acre state-maintained facility on 390-acre Lake Raymond Gary, named for a former Oklahoma governor. It provides picnic and camping areas, with electrical hookups for trailers, a play-

The Edwards home near Red Oak was once a stop for Butterfield Overland stage passengers.

ground, two boat ramps. Address: Route 2, Fort Towson, OK 74735.

Raymond Gary Reservoir (see *Fort Towson*).

Red Bird (Wagoner Co., pop. 230, on OK 51, 5 mi. S of *Coweta*, see Map 5). A tiny agricultural community in the rich valley of the *Arkansas River.* It was established in 1902.

Red Fork (Tulsa Co., in SW *Tulsa,* see Map 5). Now a heavily industrialized section of southwestern *Tulsa,* Red Fork—for the Red Fork of the Arkansas, the *Cimarron River*—dates from the 1880's. Here on June 25, 1901, the state's first commercially important oil well was brought in. A few years later, development spread south to the *Glenpool* area, and *Tulsa* soon became the self-proclaimed Oil Capital of the World. Red Fork was absorbed into Metropolitan Tulsa in the late 1920's.

Red Oak (Latimer Co., pop. 609, on US 270, see Map 6). One of the state's older towns, and one of its most interesting. Established in 1868, it was named for a large red oak tree that stood in the center of the town and was used as a whipping post under Choctaw

Nation law when district court was held here. The last execution under tribal law (see *Alikchi*) was carried out in Red Oak on November 5, 1894.

From Red Oak an unnumbered graveled road (inquire locally) runs northeast to *Shadypoint,* much of it along the 1858–61 route of the Butterfield Overland stages. Scenic highlight is The Narrows (2 mi. NE), a picturesque notch first used in 1838 by Chickasaws on the way to their new homelands near *Boggy Depot.* A double log house (5 mi. beyond The Narrows), built by Thomas Edwards in the 1850's and used to serve meals to stage passengers, is the only remaining physical structure pertaining to the Butterfield operation in Oklahoma. It is still lived in by Edwards family descendants. Two regular stations—Holloway's, near the Narrows, and Trahern's, near Brazil Creek—are also on the route. Their sites are marked.

Red River. A major stream that forms the 517-mile-long southern border of the state (but for the *Oklahoma Panhandle*) from the 100th Meridian on the west to Arkansas on the east. It was used to define the boundaries established by the Adams-Onís Treaty of 1819 (setting limits to Spanish and American territories), although it was not until March 16, 1896, that its Prairie Dog Town Fork, rather than the *North Fork,* was officially determined by the U.S. Supreme Court to be the principal one.

The Red is dammed but once in the state—southwest of *Durant* to form sprawling *Texoma Reservoir.* Its other principal Oklahoma tributaries are the *Washita, Blue,* and *Kiamichi* rivers.

Redland (Sequoyah Co., on the *Arkansas River* 20 mi. SE of *Sallisaw,* see Map 5). An isolated Kansas City Southern Railroad siding on the north bank of the Arkansas. Dating back to the 1880's, the community is best known today for the KCS bridge across that river. The Redland span, the world's longest welded, high-level railroad bridge, was required by the *Arkansas River Navigation System.* More than

2,300 feet long, it has a channel clearance of 330 feet.

Red Rock (Noble Co., pop. 233, on OK 15, see Map 4). An "elevator" town on the Santa Fe main line in a rich wheat producing area. The name recognizes the red sandstone outcroppings that dot this region.

Red Rock Canyon State Park (off US 281, 1 mi. S of *Hinton,* see Map 8). One of the deepest and most colorful of the many sheer-walled canyons that cut this west-central section of Oklahoma. Traces of the *California Trail* can be found carved into one of its red cliffs. Many stories exist of outlaws using this and nearby box canyons as a refuge from lawmen or a convenient corral in which to hide stolen cattle. Widely used the year around, the park is especially beautiful in the fall when its great variety of trees begin to color. The 211-acre preserve includes a small lake.

Facilities: abundant camp and picnic areas, modern trailer spaces, swimming pool and bathhouse, playgrounds and hiking trails. Address: Hinton, OK 73047.

Reed (Greer Co., pop. 40, on OK 9, 12 mi. W of *Mangum,* see Map 8). A scattered community, first settled in the early 1890's, in the brakes rimming the north bank of the Salt Fork of *Red River.* Near Reed (inquire locally) is Cave Creek, along the banks of which are many tunnels and grottoes. Some of these so-called Bat Caves, for the thousands of bats that inhabit them during daylight hours, are large enough to permit careful probing by curious spelunkers.

Four miles north of Reed, at the crossing of the Elm Creek Fork of *Red River* is "Jaybuckle Springs," an old landmark. It was the ranch headquarters for the Haney-Handy-Powers-Murphy cattle company in 1880 when old *Greer County* was part of Texas.

Renfrow (Grant Co., pop. 39, on US 81, see Map 4). A tiny "elevator town" on the main line of the Rock Island. Established in 1894, a year after the Cherokee Outlet was opened to settlement,

it is notable today primarily for the man it honors: W. C. Renfrow, the third governor of Oklahoma Territory.

Rentiesville (McIntosh Co., pop. 96, just E of US 69, 4 mi. N of *Checotah,* see Map 5). A tiny, predominantly Negro settlement that dates from 1904 and was named for the townsite developer, William Rentie. Its best-known "hometown boy who made good" is Dr. John Hope Franklin, one-time chairman of the history department at the University of Chicago and a 1972 Distinguished Service Citation winner from the University of Oklahoma.

Immediately north of Rentiesville is the important Honey Springs Battlefield. Fought in the summer of 1863, the battle was a distinct Union victory and proved a turning point in the Civil War so far as Indian Territory was concerned. Also significant: Honey Springs gave the Union's Negro troops, for the first time, an opportunity to prove their worth as combat soldiers. The battle area, owned for the most part by the Oklahoma Historical Society, is currently being developed as an important Civil War memorial.

Reydon (Roger Mills Co., pop. 215, at junc. of OK 30 and OK 47, see Map 3). A small trading community near the Texas line. Limited recreation facilities are available at nearby *Skipout Lake.* The town was founded in 1929 when the Santa Fe Railroad built west from *Cheyenne* into the Texas Panhandle.

Richards Spur (Comanche Co., pop. 50, on US 62, 277 & 281, 11 mi. N of *Lawton,* see Map 8). A Rock Island Railroad loading area for a large limestone crushing plant that has been chewing away at an exposed *Wichita Mountains* limestone ledge here for over half a century. A town of Richards existed briefly several miles to the north, founded in 1901 and named for William A. Richards, a General Land Office commissioner at the opening that year of the Kiowa-Comanche Indian lands.

Ringling (Jefferson Co., pop. 1,206, at junc. of US 70 and OK 89, see Map 7).

Robber's Cave State Park, near Wilburton.

A struggling, one-time oil boom town with a name that appropriately, and honestly, reflects the circus world. Several years before the town was started, in 1914, flamboyant Ardmore oilman Jake L. Hamon and circus man John Ringling (of Ringling Brother-Barnum and Bailey Circus) had shared lucrative business ventures in southern Oklahoma. When Hamon struck oil in this area, he persuaded Ringling to finance a railroad west from **Ardmore** to serve the field.

On August 4, 1913, the first spike of the so-called Ringling Railroad (now Santa Fe) was driven in **Ardmore,** with Hamon and Governor Lee Cruce taking part in the ceremonies. On that same day, curiously enough, the Franklin No. 1 discovery well came in near Healdton leading to development of the incredibly rich Healdton field that boomed and still largely sustains this entire area west of **Ardmore.** The 20-mile branch line spawned **Wilson** on its way westward, led to the founding of Ringling in 1914, with Hamon and Ringling as townsite owners.

Ringwood (Major Co., pop. 241, at junc. of US 60 and OK 58, see Map 3). A small agricultural community best known for its watermelons. It stages an annual Watermelon Festival each September, complete with Watermelon Queen and free watermelon to all comers. Although the surrounding land was homesteaded in 1895, the townsite was not platted and lots sold until 1901. It takes its name from the "ring of woods" encircling the town. The area was one of the first significant oil and gas producers in northwestern Oklahoma.

Ripley (Payne Co., pop. 307, on OK 108, 8 mi. W of **Cushing,** see Map 4). An agricultural community laid out at the turn of the century in a bend of the **Cimarron River.** It was named for William P. Ripley, president of the Santa Fe Railroad, which in recent years abandoned its branch line through the town.

Robber's Cave State Park (off OK 2, 6 mi. N of **Wilburton,** see Map 6). This rugged playground, half-hidden in southeastern Oklahoma's mountains, features an outlaw hideout (real or fancied). A handful of small lakes make up 189 of its 8,435 acres. The park is known for its wide variety of native trees, shrubs, vines, and wildflowers. The cave itself, reached by steps carved in the sandstone, is a hundred feet up the side of an imposing cliff.

Like most caves in the region, this one is said to have been used as a hiding place by the James brothers and other assorted outlaws. One colorful tale has it that "Fiddlin' Jim," a swain of the notorious Belle Starr, was slain here by a jealous rival—as he sat playing his fiddle at the entrance to the cave. Needless to say, old—and imaginative—natives can still be found who have heard (or know someone who once heard), when the harvest moon was shining just right, Fiddlin' Jim's last weird song.

Facilities: 23 cabins, 2 Youth Camps, abundant picnic, camp, and trailer areas, 2 youth camps, swimming beach, pool and bathhouse, boat docks and rentals, miniature golf course. A 4,000-acre section of the park is now open to hunters. Address: Wilburton, OK 74578.

Rugged country overlooking Robbers Cave State Park.

Robert S. Kerr Reservoir (off I 40, 2 mi. S of *Sallisaw,* in extreme eastern Oklahoma, see Map 6). One of Oklahoma's newest, this 42,000-acre lake was created in 1970 by the U.S. Corps of Engineers as an integral part of the *Arkansas River Navigation Project.* Although its dam is only 75 feet high, it backs up 494,000 acre-feet of *Arkansas River* water that is also used to generate power. As yet recreational development is still relatively light.

Facilities: camp and picnic areas at half a dozen public use areas, 13 boat launching ramps. Address: U.S. Corps of Engineers, Box 61, Tulsa, OK 74102.

Rock Island (LeFlore Co., pop. 150, at junc. of OK 112 & 120, 15 mi. NE of *Poteau,* see Map 6). A scattered community dating from the turn of the century and probably named for the Illinois

city on the Mississippi River. Oddly enough, it is on the Frisco Railroad rather than the nearby Rock Island.

Rocky (Washita Co., pop. 260, on US 183 near junc. with OK 55, see Map 8). A trim, but dwindling, agricultural community on the Frisco Railroad. Established in 1898, it took its name from the rock store building of Merchant W. F. Schultz.

Hobart Lake (just NW of Rocky) is one of southwestern Oklahoma's better fishing spots. The 450-acre empoundment, constructed by *Hobart* in 1933 as a municipal water supply, also offers camping and general recreation in an 800-acre park.

Roff (Pontotoc Co., pop. 632, on OK 1, 15 mi. SW of *Ada,* see Map 7). Somewhat unusual for Oklahoma, Roff is a

Entrance to Roman Nose State Park.

"mining" town. Begun in 1890 and named for an area rancher, Joseph T. Roff, it owes much of its prosperity to the mining and processing of silica, which started here in 1913. It is served by the Frisco Railroad.

Roger Mills County (in extreme west-central Oklahoma bordering on Texas, see Map 3). Area, 1,124 sq. mi.; pop., 4,452; county seat, *Cheyenne.* A rolling, grassy ranch country with its topography and history shaped largely by two rivers. The *Canadian* forms the county's northern boundary, curving around the picturesque *Antelope Hills* that give western Oklahoma its best-known physical landmark. The *Washita River* meanders through the county from west to east, draining much of its best farming and ranch areas. Highly significant in controlling its periodic floods is the widely acclaimed *Sandstone Creek Project.* Beside the Washita in 1868, near the present town of *Cheyenne,* was fought the famed *Battle of the Washita.* The county, which received its present boundaries in 1907, honors Roger Q. Mills, a Texas Congressman who advocated statehood for Oklahoma.

Rogers County (northeastern Oklahoma, see Map 5). Area, 713 sq. mi.; pop.,

28,425; county seat, *Claremore.* A farming/ranching county in which tourism has in recent years come to play an increasingly important role. A part of the Cherokee Nation until statehood in 1907, it was named for Clem Vann Rogers, member of the Constitutional Convention and father of one of the state's best-known sons, Will Rogers.

Top travel lures: *Will Rogers State Park, Oologah Reservoir,* the Will Rogers Memorial, Davis Gun Collection, Lynn Riggs Memorial, and Long's Historical Museum, all in *Claremore.*

Roland (Sequoyah Co., pop. 827, 1 mi. N of US 64, 5 mi. E of *Muldrow,* see Map 5). A tiny trading center near the Arkansas line. Started in 1902 as Garrison—for nearby Garrison Creek, on the "garrison road" to Fort Smith—it took its present name two years later.

Roll (Roger Mills Co., pop. 30, at junc. of US 283 and OK 33, see Map 3). A tiny crossroads community serving the needs of isolated farmers and ranchers, travelers, and recreation seekers at nearby *Dead Indian Lake.* A roadside marker notes the crossing here of the *California Trail,* first traveled by California-bound gold-seekers in early 1849 under the military escort of Captain Randolph B. Marcy. Five miles to the north is the Packsaddle Bridge over the *Canadian River,* one of the first to span (permanently) that treacherous stream.

Roman Nose State Park (3 mi. off OK 8, from a point 4 mi. N of *Watonga,* see Map 3). A colorful 540-acre canyon area in the heart of the *Gypsum Hills.* The park was named for the last warrior-chief of the Cheyenne Indians, Henry Roman Nose, who used this rugged, spring-fed canyon as a winter encampment for his band. When the area was opened to settlement in 1892, he claimed it for his homestead. Near the site of the Roman Nose dugout the "Spring of Everlasting Water" still gushes from the cliff, filling the park swimming pool, 18-acre Boecher Lake, and 55-acre Lake Watonga. Both are regularly stocked.

Facilities: 20-room Roman Nose Lodge, 14 cabins, 5 picnic and camping areas, trailer hookups, 2 youth camps, pool and bathhouse, boat rentals, 9-hole golf course and pro shop, stable. Address: Watonga, OK 73772.

Roosevelt (Kiowa Co., pop. 353, at junc. of US 183 and OK 19, see Map 8). A struggling agricultural community, established in 1903 with arrival of the Blackwell, Enid and Southwestern Railroad (the so-called "Bess Line," now Frisco). A former Rough Rider, Charley Hunter, named the town for his one-time commander. In 1905, when President Theodore Roosevelt came to Oklahoma for his celebrated wolf hunt (see **Frederick, Grandfield**), he left his train here, went the rest of the way on horseback with his host, John Abernathy.

Just east of US 183 about six miles south of Roosevelt is the Wildman gold mining area (inquire locally). Although significant amounts of gold were never taken from the **Wichita Mountains,** the frenzied search for it established several booming camps. Wildman probably boasted several thousand people for a time, and on a nearby hillside are the still impressive stone piers of an old mill. This winding road through the hills, coming out on OK 19 between **Roosevelt** and **Cooperton,** is one of southwestern Oklahoma's most pleasant byways.

Rose (Mayes Co., pop. 50, on OK 33, 9 mi. E of **Locust Grove,** see Map 5). A tiny community whose name, adopted for its post office in 1891, is a corruption of nearby Rowe's Prairie, which had been named for an early-day resident, David Rowe. Half a mile south of OK 33 just east of Rose is Saline Court House, the only one of nine original district courthouses in the Cherokee Nation that still stands.

Erected in 1871 on the Siloam Springs-Tahlequah Road, the two-story frame structure is now owned and maintained as a state park and open to visitors. (Tues.–Sun. 9–5, closed Mon.) The main courtroom and judge's office remain much as they were nearly a century ago. On the grounds are a springhouse that once doubled as a jail, an execution tree, a number of interesting gravestones, and the foundations of a long-since-vanished general store, blacksmith shop, and barn.

Rose Hill (Choctaw Co., on graded county road, 3 mi. SE of **Hugo,** see Map 6). One-time mansion of the half-blood Choctaw planter, Robert M. Jones, who came to present Oklahoma in the early 1830's. He established a store here and at **Scullyville,** developed at least half a dozen plantations (see **Shawneetown**) operated by as many as 500 slaves. The handsome two-story house burned in 1912, but the rock-walled Rose Hill Cemetery, now owned by the Oklahoma Historical Society, is one of the more interesting in the state. Also buried here, with Jones and other members of his family, is Joseph T. Thoburn (1866–1941), one of Oklahoma's best-known historians.

Rosston (Harper Co., pop. 56, on US 64-283, see Map 3). A tiny "elevator town," typical of many rail-siding farming communities in western Oklahoma and the Panhandle. Established in 1914, it was named for two residents: R. H. Ross and A. R. Rallston.

A "Mystery Grave" stands in the highway right-of-way two miles west of Rosston where US 283 swings north for Kansas. The inscription reads: "MARY wife of EDWARD KENDRICK 1863–1919 Her memory shall ever be A guiding star in heaven." The grave was uncovered in 1952 when the highway was being widened. The legend was put on a new stone and the angle of the curve was changed so as to miss the restored grave. But to date no one has been able to identify Mary Kendrick.

Row (Delaware Co., pop. 50, 1 mi. N of OK 116, 4 mi. E of OK 10, see Map 5). A tiny settlement that got its post office in 1905, lost it in 1930 when it was moved a mile south to become **Colcord.** Explanation could be found in the story, perhaps apocryphal, that Postmaster James R. Wilson gave his office its original name because of the area's penchant for "drunken brawls and killings."

Rubottom (Love Co., pop. 50, on OK 32, 19 mi. W of **Marietta,** see Map 7). A dwindling farm-ranching community near **Red River,** named for William P. Rubottom, a prominent area landowner at the turn of the century. It provides the county's extreme western section with its only postal service, having survived such nearby offices as Courtney (1886), Watkins (1883), and Jefferson County's Petersburg (1891).

Rush Springs (Grady Co., pop. 1,381, at junc. of US 81 and OK 17, see Map 7). Several fine springs, one of them in the center of what is now Municipal Park, formed the source of Rush Creek and provided a pleasant camping place for drovers on the **Chisholm Trail.** When the Rock Island laid tracks across the county in 1892, a townsite was laid out, given the logical name of Rush Springs. In 1883 the town of Parr had been established some six miles to the east, but it moved to the new railhead in 1893 and ceased to exist. Near the Parr site, in 1858, was fought the tragic Battle of the Wichita Village—tragic because it was largely due to a misunderstanding that some seventy Comanche warriors were killed by a cavalry force under Captain Earl Van Dorn.

Rush Springs today has succeeded in bolstering its heretofore farm-based economy with industrialization. But even here it hasn't strayed too far from the soil. It has a dog food manufacturer. But its biggest employer—over 200 workers—makes implements and trailers. And its biggest annual event (since 1940) is an August Watermelon Festival. Drawing up to 10,000 visitors, who eat some twenty tons of the ripe, juicy fruit (a full boxcar load), the three-day affair usually includes street dancing, a rodeo, grandstand shows, queen crowning, and other traditional features. Watermelons in the Rush Springs area bring in a quarter of a million dollars annually.

Ryan (Jefferson Co., pop. 1,011, at junc. of US 81 and OK 32, see Map 7). Settle-ment began in this area as early as 1881, when the Baldwin post office was established. The name Ryan, for an early settler, appeared in 1890. In 1894, two years after arrival of the Rock Island, the town obtained a Federal Court and an impressive stone courthouse. The town is unusual in that it was surveyed on the pattern of the Spanish land survey, on 45-degree angles.

Ryan, as Record Town for District No. 20, Indian Territory, became temporary seat of Jefferson County with statehood. But in 1912, after several contested elections, it lost a bitter, three-way struggle for the seat with **Sugden** and, the eventual winner, **Waurika.** The town has never recovered from the loss.

S

Sacred Heart (Pottawatomie Co., off OK 39, 8 mi. E of **Asher,** see Map 7). The impressive Sacred Heart Church, with its adjoining cemetery, stands today as a monument to the so-called "Cradle of Oklahoma Catholicism." The Benedictines established a mission here in 1876, and for sixty-seven years it was the center of their work among the Indians. At one time the abbey had a three-story, fifty-room monastery. The last remaining relics of this era, aside from the church itself, are the old stone bakery and a two-story log cabin dating from the 1880's. They were restored in the 1960's.

Best-known of the boys attending the boarding school: Sac and Fox Indian athlete, Jim Thorpe (see **Yale**), and the statesman and ambassador, Patrick J. Hurley (see **Lehigh**). St. Mary's Academy, a convent school for Indian girls, also operated here from 1884 to 1943.

Sacred Heart can lay claim, too, to being a "Cradle of Oklahoma Culture." Best-known Benedictine associated with the educational program here is Father Gregory Gerrer. A young painter, he came to Sacred Heart in 1891, received wide acclaim when his canvas of Pope Pius X was selected in 1904 to hang in the Vatican. His works were long a feature of the Gerrer Museum at St. Gregory's College in **Shawnee.** (One of the state's first prep schools, St.

Gregory's opened in 1915 as an outgrowth of the Sacred Heart effort.) Father Gerrer, a member of the Oklahoma Hall of Fame, died in 1946.

St. Louis (Pottawatomie Co., pop. 207, on OK 59, 7 mi. SW of *Maud*, see Map 7). Another product of the Greater *Seminole* Field. The town began in 1928. It is still surrounded by producing wells and all the other grease-spattered paraphernalia of a well-developed oil field, but the center of activity has long since moved elsewhere.

Salina (Mayes Co., pop. 1,024, at junc. of OK 20 and OK 82, 10 mi. E of *Pryor*, see Map 5). The town of *Chouteau*, a few miles to the southwest, has the name, but Salina is recognized as the first permanent white settlement in what is now Oklahoma. Its founding has been called the "opening chapter of Oklahoma's story," and on October 10 each year, on the birthday of Major Jean Pierre Chouteau, the town celebrates Oklahoma Historical Day.

Major Chouteau, with a party of French traders and trappers, first visited this area in the Spring of 1796. A trading post was established here on the bank of *Grand River* in the early 1800's. August Pierre, the founder's son, took over the Chouteau trading operations in 1817. His pretentious home here, visited by Washington Irving in 1832, was described as a large, two-story log structure with valuable furnishings and surrounded by trees, shrubbery, and flowers. Chouteau died in 1838, and the family holdings were dispersed, but the settlement, known then as Grand Saline, soon became an important point on one of the California trails. It obtained a post office in 1849.

John Ross, chief of the Cherokees, and his brother Lewis acquired many of the Chouteau holdings. The Ross home was a brick mansion on the site now occupied by the Salina High School gymnasium, just south of the town's main street at the east edge of the business district. In a corner of the schoolyard stands a stone Blockhouse, built by Ross, that encloses one of the springs used since the founding of Chouteau Trading Post. Nearby, on OK 20, is the handsome new Chouteau Memorial (Tues.–Sat. 9–5, Sun. 1–5, free), housing family and area memorabilia. (On the west edge of the business district, near the bridge and protected by a wire fence, is a Tree of Paradise, planted by the Chouteaus in the early 1800's.)

The Ross home and surrounding lands were bought by the Cherokee Nation in 1872 for use as the Cherokee Orphan Asylum. A post office of that name existed until 1884, when the name Salina was accepted. The name is a variant of Saline, one of the districts of the Cherokee Nation. Salt Works existed here throughout much of the nineteenth century and an old iron vat used in salt making still stands near the blockhouse.

Construction of **Markham Ferry Reservoir** has backed water to the western edge of the Salina business district and given the town a progressive, recreation-oriented appearance. Oklahoma Historical Day on October 10 is its biggest annual event. Often in attendance are Colonel C. E. Chouteau, great-great-grandson of Major Jean Pierre, and his daughter, ballerina Yvonne Chouteau. The founder's great-great-great-granddaughter, now of Oklahoma City, was inducted into the Oklahoma Hall of Fame in 1947 at the age of eighteen.

Salina Recreation Area. See *Markham Ferry Reservoir*.

Sallisaw (Sequoyah Co. seat, pop. 4,868, at junc. of US 59 and US 64, see Map 5). East-central Oklahoma's fastest growing industry-minded city, thanks to two railroads (Missouri Pacific and Kansas City Southern), I 40, the *Arkansas River Navigation System,* and Blue Ribbon Downs. Agriculture continues to be economically important, too, as does the strip mining of coal in the area, which has increased with the availability of barge transportation.

Sallisaw began as a trading post and a camping site on the Fort Smith-*Fort Gibson* road. Its first post office was known as Childer's Station (for the prominent Cherokee, John Childers)

Home of Sequoyah, inventor of the Cherokee alphabet, near Sallisaw (photograph courtesy Oklahoma Industrial Development and Park Department).

from 1878 to 1888, when it became Sallisaw. First recorded use of the word was in 1819 when English naturalist Thomas A. Nuttall noted: "We passed the mouth of a rivulet or brook called by the French 'Salliseau' from hunters having killed a quantity of bison and salted the beef for traffic." Salliseau was soon corrupted into Sallisaw. The stream is a major county tributary of the **Arkansas River**.

The Cherokee and Cookson Hills to the north and the river bottoms to the south offer visitors excellent hunting and fishing, as well as noteworthy sightseeing. The Sallisaw Chamber of Commerce organizes dogwood tours in the spring. The area also has much of interest for the history lover. This was one of the first sections of Indian Territory to be settled by the Cherokees, and visitors will be rewarded with a visit to the state-owned **Sequoyah Cabin** (7 mi. NE), once the home of the famed inventor of the Cherokee alphabet, **Dwight Mission** (8 mi. NW), and the Red Bird Smith stomp grounds (18 mi. NW) to which the public is welcomed. The

site of Tahlonteeskee, first capital of the Western Cherokees, (17 mi. NW) is known, but not now marked.

A log cabin built by Judge Franklin Faulkner in the late 1830's a few miles northeast of Sallisaw is believed to be one of the oldest buildings in Oklahoma. Moved into town in 1957 and carefully restored, it serves in summer as a tourist information center. It can offer information on tours at the Southwestern Wood Preserving Company plant west of Sallisaw (Tues.–Thurs. 9–12 and 2–4:30), provide maps of Sequoyah County and the Robert S. Kerr Lock and Dam facility on the Arkansas south of the city.

Salt Fork of Arkansas River. Like the major stream of which it is a branch, the Salt Fork enters Oklahoma from Kansas at a point some 20 miles northwest of **Alva**. Principal feature of its meandering, 160-mile, generally easterly course through **Woods**, **Alfalfa**, **Grant**, and **Kay** counties, are the **Great Salt Plains** east of **Cherokee**.

Salt Plains National Wildlife Refuge (Alfalfa Co., off OK 11, 10 mi. E of **Cherokee**, see Map 3). A 33,000-acre section of the geologically curious **Great Salt Plains** along the **Salt Fork of the Arkansas River**. Most of the preserve lies on the north and west sides of **Great Salt Plains Reservoir**. Headquarters area has the new mile-and-a-quarter Eagle Roost Nature Trail. Bald eagles are generally seen here from October through April. The more common waterfowl inhabit the refuge year-round. Address: Bureau of Sports Fisheries and Wildlife, Cherokee, OK 73728.

Sand Springs (Tulsa Co., pop. 11,519, at junc. of US 64 and OK 51 & 97, see Map 5). A hard-working, shirtsleeve industrial community that is a living memorial to one of Oklahoma's first oil-rich humanitarians. Wisconsin-born Charles Page came to Indian Territory in 1903, soon struck oil in the **Sapulpa** and **Glenpool** areas. In 1908 he established Sand Springs Home for widows and parentless children (he strongly disliked the word "orphan"). Almost singlehandedly he built Sand Springs to support the Home.

Successively, Page laid out the city, set up a natural gas system (drawing on his own wells), constructed an electric power plant, organized a water company (utilizing the nearby springs that gave the town its name), set aside Sand Springs Park, established a bank, ran a rail line out from *Tulsa* to serve an industrial park in which he built a cotton mill (the largest textile mill west of the Mississippi for many years) and a steel mill. Over the years this park has attracted some sixty industries (fruit jars, electrical fixtures, fiberglass pipe, paints and varnishes, dog food, many other products).

Additional monuments to the philanthropist, who died in 1926, are the Page Memorial Library, a $100,000 downtown memorial built by Mrs. Page; the Lorado Taft bronze of Page, across the street in Triangle Park (with its fringe of children and the inscription: "Inasmuch as ye have done it unto the least of these, My brethren, ye have done it unto Me"); and Sand Springs Home (1 mi. N of town), the greatly expanded and modernized facility for women and children that started Sand Springs.

For all its newness as a town, the Sand Springs area has long been occupied. A Creek Indian settlement was located on the present business district in 1833. It was called Adams Springs, for a prominent Creek family. The year before, Washington Irving first saw the nearby *Cimarron River* (his "Red Fork of the Arkansas River") from a bluff just to the north.

If the Sand Springs Home was humanitarian and innovative in its day, so was the Hissom Memorial Center a little more than half a century later. The $7 million, 24-building community for the mentally retarded opened on an 85-acre site just south of the Arkansas River in 1964.

So far as recreational and cultural facilities are concerned, Sand Springs enjoys the best of two worlds. Metropolitan *Tulsa* crowds in on the small city from the east, while the vast watery playground created by *Keystone Reservoir* beckons just to the west.

Sandstone Creek Project (Roger Mills Co., see Map 3). A dramatic demonstration of a new upstream approach to flood control and soil conservation. The idea—as simple as it is effective—is to make many small dams do the work of one big one. Sandstone Creek, a tributary of the *Washita River*, has a watershed 15 miles long and 6 miles wide, an area of 65,000 acres. On it the federal government constructed twenty-four small dams to impound runoff water where it falls. With approved soil conservation practices the project has virtually eliminated flood damage on this section of a river notorious over the years for its flooding. The Sandstone approach to flood control is now being widely used elsewhere.

Santa Fe Trail, see *Camp Nichols*.

Sapulpa (Creek Co. seat, pop. 15,159, at junc. of I 44, US 66, and OK 33, see Map 4). A bustling industrial city that dates back to the middle of the nineteenth century when Jim Sapulpa, a newly arrived Creek Indian farmer opened a store in his home. (Fittingly enough, his name means "sweet potato" in the Creek language.) A rail terminus, briefly, when the Frisco arrived in 1886, Sapulpa boomed mightily in 1905–1906 with development of the spectacular Glenn Pool (see *Kiefer*) a few miles to the south.

Steel products and heavy equipment, much of it used by the oil industry, are manufactured in the city. The largest single employer, however, is the Liberty Glass Company. And the best-known manufacturer, because its colorful, western-oriented wares are sold throughout the world, is the Frankhoma Pottery Plant (tours weekdays 9–3). Started on a shoestring in *Norman* in 1933 (John Frank, who died in 1973, was then a young ceramics instructor at the University of Oklahoma), the company moved to Sapulpa in 1938. Still essentially a family operation, it has 125 employees today, turns out 2 million pieces a year in some 350 patterns.

Sapulpa's special events range from annual livestock shows (late March) and flower and garden shows (May) to July rodeos and Indian dances.

Sardis (Pushmataha Co., pop. 253, off US 271, 6 mi. NW of **Clayton**, see Map 6). A community near the rugged Jack Fork Mountains, established shortly after the turn of the century and named for a nearby Indian mission.

Sasakwa (Seminole Co., pop. 321, on OK 56, see Map 7). An old Seminole Indian settlement that developed near the rambling two-story frame house of Chief John F. Brown. The house has recently been torn down, but an old Indian church and a large camp-meeting grounds are in the area. The town itself won a post office in 1880. The name is the Creek word for "goose."

The Sasawka area rates a footnote in history as locale for the so-called Green Corn Rebellion of 1917. It was a short-lived syndicalist movement involving some 500 armed whites, Indians, and Negroes opposed to the World War I draft. They formed a Working Class Union, staged an attempt of sorts to take over the government. The try was made in the season the nearby Shawnee Indians held their green-corn dance, hence the name of the rebellion.

Savanna (Pittsburg Co., pop. 948, on US 69, 9 mi. S of **McAlester**, see Map 6). Old coal mining town that dates back to 1872 and the arrival of the M-K-T railroad. The name was that of the private car of the road's general manager, Robert Stevens. The area was a thriving coal producer until 1887, when an explosion killed eighteen miners and caused many of the operators to close their mines and move to other locations. Scars from later surface strip mining operations are evident around the town.

Sawyer (Choctaw Co., pop. 175, on US 70, 8 mi. E of **Hugo**, see Map 6). Established at the turn of the century when the Arkansas and Choctaw Railroad (present Frisco) built through this area. Charles H. Sawyer was a Dawes Commission attorney. The dwindling settlement is on the east bank of the **Kiamichi River**, just downstream from **Hugo Reservoir**.

Sayre (Beckham Co. seat, pop. 2,712, off I 40 at junc. of US 66 & 283 and OK 152, see Map 8). Established in 1902 with arrival of the present Rock Island—and named for Robert H. Sayre, an official of the line—Sayre became the seat of Beckham County with statehood in 1907. Long the center of a good farming-ranching area, it now calls itself the "Cradle of the Quarter Horse," with some twoscore horse breeders within a 50-mile radius. Area horses appear regularly on racing cards at tracks in New Mexico, Arkansas, Louisiana, California, and elsewhere.

The town is still a division point on the Rock Island. Sayre Junior College, founded in 1938, serves a wide area of west-central Oklahoma.

Schulter (Okmulgee Co., pop. 300, on US 75, 6 mi. S of **Okmulgee**, see Map 5). Established in 1903, the town boomed for a time on the strength of nearby coal mines. There is now little mining activity in the area. The name honors Matt Schulter, a St. Louis jurist.

Scipio (Pittsburg Co., pop. 75, on county road 12 mi. NW of **McAlester**, see Map 6). Isolated rural community dating from 1890. The name of the distinguished Roman general who defeated Hannibal was first assigned to nearby Scipio Creek, a **South Canadian River** tributary.

Scullyville (LeFlore Co., pop. 125, off US 271, 2 mi. NE of **Spiro**, see Map 6). This now scattered settlement, formerly known as Skullyville, in the Choctaw Nation, is one of the oldest in present Oklahoma. For a time it was one of the most important as well. It began in 1832, when the Choctaw Indians were being removed from the Southeast and the government established its agency here as a center for payment of promised annuities. (Scullyville, or Skullyville, is derived from the Choctaw word "iskuli," meaning money.) Two years later Fort Coffee was established on the **Arkansas River** six miles to the north. Immediately to the east of Scullyville was New Hope Seminary, set up in 1842.

When Choctaw Agency was moved to

Fort Washita in 1858, Governor Tandy Walker took over the building for his home. It also served as "Walker's Station" from 1858–61, the first west of Fort Smith on the famed Butterfield Overland Mail Route. Fire finally destroyed it only a few years ago. Today only historic Ainsworth Spring, still flowing 22,000 gallons of pure water a day, marks the agency site.

In 1871 the settlement's post office name was changed from Choctaw Agency (officially, Scullyville was used but briefly) to Oak Lodge. In 1917 the office itself was closed. But the town still boasts a cluster of homes, a few empty store buildings and, behind the abandoned Oak Lodge school, one of the state's most historic cemeteries. Here under towering trees are the graves of scores of Choctaw Nation leaders over the years.

Seiling (Dewey Co., pop. 1,033, on US 60 & 270 & 281 and OK 3 & 51, see Map 3). A bustling agricultural community strung out along the main (highway) street. It was established in 1894 and named for the townsite owner, Louis A. Seiling. Many Cheyennes and Arapahoes live in and around the town, but two of the best-known names associated with its early history were non-Indians.

Amos Chapman, the famed army scout in the last few decades of the nineteenth century, lived his retirement years east of Seiling and is buried in the family cemetery there. Chapman was the hero of the Buffalo Wallow fight (in the Texas Panhandle) when he lost a leg attempting to save a soldier. Colonel Richard I. Dodge of General W. T. Sherman's staff called him "one of the best and bravest scouts . . . I have ever known."

Seiling was also the home in the early 1900's of Carry A. Nation, the hatchet-wielding prohibitionist. Her two-story log house just west of town is no longer standing. In 1967 Seiling became the state's second city (see **Duke**) to pay its respects to Oklahoma's spring tornado season by constructing an underground school building.

Selman (Harper Co., pop. 75, 8 mi. SE of **Buffalo**, see Map 3). A small farm/

Skullyville Cemetery, where many leaders of the Choctaw Nation are buried.

ranch trading center, established in 1901 as Charleston. Present name was given to the post office in 1923.

Seminole (Seminole Co., pop. 7,878, off US 270 at junc. of OK 9 & 99, see Map 7). Named for the Indians on whose allotted lands it was located, Seminole was strongly Indian in background and appearance until July 1926, when the explosive development of the Greater Seminole Field made the word virtually synonymous with oil booms and the frenzied activity and uninhibited lawlessness accompanying them.

Mekasukey Academy (now completely vanished) was built just southwest of present-day Seminole in 1890. Joe Tidmore was the contractor and freight shipments were billed simply to "Mr. Tidmore." And the community went by that name until 1907. It still boasted less than 800 inhabitants when one of the greatest oil pools in history was discovered on its doorstep.

The year was 1926, the day July 16— a date still celebrated. At 3 p.m. the Fixico No. 1 blew in about a mile and a half due east of present downtown. Seminole has never been the same. Within a year it had swollen to a hard-driving, hard-living population of 35,000.

One W. A. Bishop, a quiet attorney, sought to alleviate the critical housing situation by platting a north-side addition of small houses and "cribs." It was promptly taken over by those operators, male and female, who made their money, not from drilling for oil, but from

Western Hills Lodge at Sequoyah State Park.

pumping wealth from those who did. "Bishop's Alley" soon boasted the "Palace," the "Bic C," the "49er's Dance Hall," and a wide assortment of similar establishments. The killing of a state peace officer, however, brought reaction, and the town gradually settled down to a more ordered existence.

Petroleum in the area is still important (though oil production is a far cry indeed from the 527,000-barrels-a-day peak of the '20's). But employment provided by two refineries and numerous oil field service and supply companies is now augmented by that of makers of such things as sporting goods, sewer pipe, and men's clothing. And boom days are recalled primarily in connection with annual rodeos and golf tournaments.

However, a replica of the famed Fixico No. 1 stands in Municipal Park, along with other pieces of oil drilling equipment. Current plan is to develop the site into an Oil Drilling Museum.

Seminole County (central Oklahoma, see Map 7). Area, 629 sq. mi.; pop., 25,144; county seat, *Wewoka*. An oil rich county whose name has become virtually synonymous with the rough, roaring, ramshackle "oil patch" boom town of which there were scores scattered throughout Oklahoma in the first third of the twentieth century. The heart

of the Seminole Nation until statehood in 1907, the county carries on the name of this fifth of the so-called Five Civilized Tribes that once owned almost all of Oklahoma.

Sentinel (Washita Co., pop. 984, at junc. of OK 44 and OK 55, see Map 8). An attractive farming community on a Santa Fe Railroad branch line. The power of the press is indicated in its naming. Established in 1899 as Barton, the community changed its name shortly after the turn of the century to honor the *Herald Sentinel,* a newspaper published in the one-time county seat of *Cloud Chief.*

Sentinel is in the center of the Elk Creek Watershed Development Project, which provides lake fishing and recreational facilities as well as flood protection for some of the county's most productive bottomlands. Cotton, wheat, and alfalfa are all important in the area.

Sequoyah Bay Recreation Area. See *Fort Gibson Reservoir.*

Sequoyah County (in extreme eastern Oklahoma, north of the *Arkansas River* and bordering on Arkansas, see Map 5). Area, 703 sq. mi.; pop. 23,370; county seat, *Sallisaw.* A rolling, wooded section that was part of the Cherokee Nation until statehood in 1907. The name honors the famed Cherokee Sequoyah, inventor of the Cherokee alphabet. It means shut in or shut away.

Top travel lures: *Sequoyah's Home, Tenkiller State Park.*

Sequoyah State Park (off OK 5, 9 mi. E of *Wagoner*, see Map 5). A spectacularly set, 2,875-acre playground developed over a rocky spit of land projecting from the north shore of *Fort Gibson Reservoir.* Cottages flank the central lodge, with its convention facilities. All accommodations are within a few feet of the lake, around which center most of the park's sport and recreational activities. Land-based features include stagecoach rides, eighteen-hole golf course, summer theater.

Facilities: 102-room deluxe lodge, 62 cottages, abundant picnic, camp and trailer areas, swimming pool and bathhouse, lake excursion cruises, ski tow and rental skis, hiking and bridle trails, stable, putting green and practice range, and a 3,000-foot paved, lighted, radio-equipped air strip. Address: Hulbert, OK 74441. For lodge reservations: Box 276, Wagoner, OK 74467.

Sequoyah's Home (Sequoyah Co., on OK 101, 11 mi. NE of *Sallisaw*, see Map 5). Sequoyah was born in the 1760's in the area where Tennessee, Georgia, and North Carolina meet. The son of a Cherokee woman and a white man named Guist, he was in his forties—married and the father of two or three children, a skilled blacksmith, but illiterate so far as the English language was concerned—when he became intrigued with the thought that white men could convey messages by writing to each other.

Although accused of being a dreamer and a ne'er-do-well, he toyed with the idea of producing an alphabet for his own native Cherokee. Eventually he devised a syllabary of eighty-four characters, so simple and easy to use that he and his daughter Ahyoka, his first pupil, were teaching their fellow Cherokees to write within a week or so. The tribe became the first to have a written language of its own.

Sequoyah came to Oklahoma in 1829, built the crude one-room log cabin now preserved inside a stone museum building. Owned by the Oklahoma Historical Society, it is open Tues.–Friday 9–5, Sat.–Sun. 2–5, admission free.

Seward (Logan Co., pop. 49, on county road 6 mi. SW of *Guthrie*, see Map 4). An inland community founded with the opening of Old Oklahoma in 1889 and named for President Lincoln's secretary of state, William H. Seward.

Shadypoint (LeFlore Co., pop. 300, on US 59 & 271, see Map 6). A town dating back, officially, to the early 1890's. Before that, however, an early Choctaw settlement flourished nearby. And to the west was the once well-known Brazil Station on the Butterfield stage route and the military road from Fort

Golfing at Sequoyah State Park.

Smith to **Fort Towson**. This rugged area—rolling, wooded, and lightly populated—offers the adventurous motorist one of the state's most interesting byways. A meandering county road, mostly unpaved (inquire locally), stretches southwesterly from Shadypoint to **Red Oak**, much of it along the old Butterfield route. It is both richly historic and highly scenic.

Shamrock (Creek Co., pop. 204, on OK 99, 5 mi. S of *Drumright*, see Map 4). The legendary luck of the Irish failed with this oil boom camp, despite street names like Cork, Dublin, Kilarney, and Tipperary. And even an official "blarney stone," hauled in by wagon from the nearby blackjack-covered hills. Shamrock's boom began in 1912 with development of the fantastically rich *Cushing* Field. It peaked in 1917 when the town boasted 10,000 people. Its lusty St. Patrick's Day celebration that year featured a giant parade—and a fresh coat of green paint on every storefront!

Interesting, if not necessarily significant, is the fact that Shamrock was the birthplace (in 1913) of Thomas Michael Sullivan, designer of some of the nation's greatest airports and now director of the recently opened Dallas-Fort Worth terminal, the world's largest.

Sharon (Woodward Co., pop. 155, on OK 15, 12 mi. W of *Woodward*, see Map 3). A tiny trade center on the main line of the Santa Fe Railroad. It was formerly known as Hackberry.

Shattuck (Ellis Co., pop. 1,546, at junc. of US 283 and OK 15, see Map 3). A prosperous farming/ranching community that reflects both the hard-working frugality of its early settlers and its latter-day importance as a regional health center. A post office was established here in 1893 and named for George O. Shattuck, a Santa Fe Railroad director (this on the road's east-west main line). But it was just after the turn of the century that the bulk of its settlers arrived, descendants of hardy German-Russians who had first come to the United States in the 1870's.

Originally German, these people had lived for a century in Russia, enjoying freedom from taxation and military service. When these favors were cancelled, they emigrated to America. Farming was and remains the area's major industry, with emphasis laid increasingly in recent years on registered cattle. Ellis annually is among the two or three top counties in the state in the production of broomcorn.

In its early years, Shattuck gained mightily from the precipitous demise of nearby *Grand*, seat of old Day County. With statehood in 1907, Day was divided into *Roger Mills*, south of the *Canadian River*, and Ellis, to the north, with *Arnett* its seat. The rush from Grand was on, and among those moving to Shattuck was Dr. O. C. Newman. Expanded greatly over the years, the Newman Memorial Hospital and Clinic is today one of northwestern Oklahoma's best known and most highly respected medical institutions, serving a broad three-state area.

Shawnee (Pottawatomie Co. seat, pop. 25,075, at the junc. of US 177 & 270 and OK 3 & 18, see Map 7). An educational center today—following successive periods of "center" status in such divergent areas as the Indian trade, railroad building, and oil development—modern, progressive Shawnee has had something of a Horatio Alger career. Curiously enough, it also stands near the geographic center of Oklahoma. And this has led one writer to describe it as a "Sooner State miniature, so far as racial background, early-day history, preliminary accomplishments, shattering vicissitudes, and heroic mid-twentieth-century strivings are concerned. In each of these categories the Shawnee story reflects to a varying degree that of Oklahoma as a whole."

Shawnee began as a trading post in 1872, near the West Shawnee Cattle Trail from Texas north to Kansas. It was located on the south bank of the *North Canadian River* (just southwest of the present city) and from 1876 to 1892 it was known officially as Shawneetown. (Unofficially it was "Old Shawneetown," to distinguish it from the better known *Shawneetown*, Choctaw Nation, in present *McCurtain County*.) Shawneetown was, and this south-of-the-river area still is, the center for Shawnee Indian affairs. Here is located the Shawnee Indian Agency and the Shawnee Indian Sanatorium. Nearby is the Shawnee Mission Church, established in 1872 by the Society of Friends (see *McCloud*) and now preserved as a museum by the Pottawatomie County Historical Society.

Present Shawnee began with opening of the Shawnee Indian lands to white settlement in 1892. The townsite was laid out the following spring. In 1895 the Choctaw, Oklahoma and Gulf (present Rock Island) arrived, followed by the Santa Fe in 1902, the Oklahoma City-Ada-Atoka in 1904. The first two lines located shops here (they are now gone), and for a time the railroads employed close to a thousand persons.

Meanwhile, however, Shawnee had lost to *Oklahoma City* a three-way contest with *Guthrie* for the state capital. Not until 1930 was it able to win, permanently, the county seat from *Tecumseh*. And the 1920's brought two additional blows: a devastating tornado (1924) and a destructive flood (1928).

Then came oil! Shawnee was the principal beneficiary of the spectacular Greater *Seminole* Field boom. And the town soon had half a dozen nearby fields of its own, a temporary population of 35,000 and a well deserved reputation for mud-caked violence and lawlessness. But stability returned with passing of the oil "frontier," and Shawnee was left with the size and spirit needed to develop still other latent resources.

Oklahoma Baptist University, at the northwest corner of the city, opened in 1911, now has an enrollment of some 1,600 students. Most notable campus structure: handsomely classic John Wesley Raley Chapel, with its 200-foot tower. "The Chapel," dedicated in 1962, contains two auditoriums, the Mabee Fine Arts Center, other school facilities.

St. Gregory's Junior College, with some 500 students, moved here in 1915 from *Sacred Heart*. Its landmark building (completed that same year) is a massive six-story Tudor Gothic affair of red brick and white stone with turrets atop the corners of its square tower. The school's famed Gerrer collection of art (62 American works, 73 by Father Gerrer himself) is open to the public free Sun.–Fri. 2–4. Art objects collected by Father Gerrer from around the world are now in *Oklahoma City*.

Diversified industry now teams with education to keep Shawnee's economy strong. Oldest major business (1906) is the Shawnee Milling Company. Employing 200 persons, it is one of the state's last operating flour mills (tours available). Other Shawnee-made products include electronic tubes, modular homes, work clothes, processed foods.

Two important figures associated with Shawnee: Jim Thorpe, the famed Sac and Fox Indian super athlete (see *Yale, Sacred Heart*), who was born 10 miles northeast of town; and Dr. Brewster Higley, who wrote "Home on the Range," perhaps the favorite song along the cattle trails through Oklahoma. He died in Shawnee in 1911 and is buried in Fairview Cemetery.

Historic buildings of interest include the Santa Fe depot (East Main Street), a be-towered castle of red Bedford stone, built in 1903 and now on the National Register of Historic Places; the Beard Cabin (Woodland Park), said to be town's first residence; and the Bourbonnais Cabin (Shawnee Indian Mission grounds), another early area residence, built of logs in 1882.

Woodland Park provides in-town recreation facilities. Hunting and fishing are added at two municipal reservoirs in the area: Shawnee Twin Lakes (9 mi. W), 2,436 acres in all; and 160-acre Tecumseh (4 mi. SW). Spectator sports fare and a variety of cultural programs are provided throughout the year by OBU and St. Gregory's.

Shawneetown (McCurtain Co., 3 mi. SW of *Idabel*, see Map 6). This area was the first occupied by the Choctaws when they came to present Oklahoma from Mississippi, 1831–34. As early as the 1770's, however, French settlers could be found here. And Shawnee Indians, moving in the very early 1800's, are believed to have tilled the state's first "farm." It was their plowed fields and fences, purchased in the 1830's by Colonel Robert M. Jones, the Choctaw planter, that were expanded into one of Oklahoma's largest plantations (see *Rose Hill*).

A few miles to the south, nearer *Red River*, was Miller Court House, present Oklahoma's first post office, established September 7, 1824. Miller County had been established by the Arkansas legislature in 1820. It included the eastern part of present Oklahoma south of the *Arkansas River*. When the area was ceded to the Choctaw Nation in 1828, the county was abolished. The courthouse itself was promptly destroyed by fire. Miller Court House as post office, however, lingered on the official records in Washington until 1838, which fact could provide smug satisfaction to present-day critics of bureaucratic lethargy.

Sherwood (McCurtain Co., pop. 50, 2 mi. E of US 259, 23 mi. N of *Broken Bow*, see Map 6). A scattered community in one of the state's finest forest areas, it was sufficiently organized in 1912 to rate a post office. However, it was not Robin Hood, but an early settler, one Sherwood Davis, who was honored in the naming.

The adventurous traveler, especially if he is of a naturalist bent, will want to acquire a guide and push on eastward another half a dozen miles, across the upper end of **Broken Bow Reservoir** to the 16,000-acre McCurtain County State Game Refuge. Along with deer and turkeys, a profusion of wildflowers, and a hundred different species of birds, he will find some of the state's finest pine, oak, cypress, gum, holly, sycamore and a dozen other native trees. It is Oklahoma's largest tract of virgin timber.

Shidler (Osage Co., pop. 717, on OK 18, 9 mi. N of US 60, see Map 4). Having popped up on the Osage prairie when oil was discovered in the area in the early 1920's, Shidler today is the epitome of the work-a-day oil camp. At the height of the boom, when it was the Oil Capital of the Osage in fact as well by chamber of commerce slogan, more than 10,000 people got their mail at Shidler. That is ten times more than are now required to care for the area's more settled oil development.

Most of the oil fields, though still productive, are now under waterflood operations to insure maximum secondary recovery. The Shidler-**Webb City** area still produces about two-thirds of Osage County's oil. The town was named for townsite developer E. S. Shidler.

Short (Sequoyah Co., on OK 101, 3 mi. from the Arkansas line, see Map 5). An isolated, almost non-existent rural community that deserves its spot on the map for counter-balancing **Long**, some 12 miles to the southwest—and for giving **Nicut**, almost equally non-existent, the distinction of being "half way between Long and Short."

Skedee (Pawnee Co., pop. 117, off OK 18, 6 mi. NE of **Pawnee**, see Map 4). An isolated rural community named for the Skidi division of the Pawnee tribe. It was the home until he died of Colonel E. Waters, well-known auctioneer during the heyday of the **Osage County**

oil lease sales at **Pawhuska**. Central tourist attraction today is the statue of Chief Bacon Rind, erected in 1926 to symbolize Indian/white man friendship.

Skiatook (Tulsa and Osage Cos., pop. 2,930, at junc. of OK 11 & 20, see Map 5). A one-time Osage Indian camp—originally Skiatooka's Settlement—that has gradually evolved into a pleasantly tree-shaded north-side **Tulsa** suburban community. Its strong farming/ranching background is reflected in its leading annual events: a quarter horse show in June and a rodeo in September. The Osages also have an annual powwow in Skiatook in August.

Skipout Lake (just N of OK 47 some 13 miles W of **Cheyenne**, see Map 3). A recreation facility (fishing, hunting, picnic and camping areas) maintained by the U.S. Forest Service (Hot Springs, Ark.) as part of **Black Kettle National Grasslands**.

Slapout (Beaver Co., pop. 15, on US 270 & OK 3, 18 mi. SW of **Laverne**, see Map 2). Though lacking post office or school, and boasting only a roadside store or two, Slapout lives in Oklahoma folklore for its picturesque name, allegedly derived from the unvarying response of an early-day merchant to every call for an item he didn't have in stock: "I had it yesterday, but I'm slap out today."

Slick (Creek Co., pop. 171, on OK 16, 10 mi. SE of **Bristow**, see Map 4). Its railroad gone, along with its business houses and most of its citizenry, Slick remains on the map, happily, to memorialize one of the Oklahoma petroleum industry's best known—and most successful—wildcatters, Thomas B. Slick.

Smithville (McCurtain Co., pop. 144, at junc. US 259 and OK 4, see Map 6). An old Choctaw community that was first organized in 1886 as Hatobi (Choctaw for "warrior man"). It adopted its present name four years later to honor an intermarried Choctaw resident, Joshua M. Smith. A Methodist boarding school for Indians and whites operated there in the 1920's, and a still impressive white church (its towering steeple only recently toppled by a wind storm) remains with a few other structures to mark the site.

Stretches of US 259 north and south of Smithville are among the most beautiful in Oklahoma. This corner of the county is a sportsman's paradise, and for 10 miles the highway southwestward clings to the north bank of *Mountain Fork River* serving a number of pleasantly located fishing camps. Where Boktukolo Creek flows into the Mountain Fork the highway crosses an old horseback trail used before the Civil War. The route was traced in the 1870's by prospectors searching for silver and copper in the *Kiamichi Mountains* to the north. This cut through "The Narrows" was eventually broadened to where it can now serve adventurous sportsmen and sightseers.

Snowdale Recreation Area. See *Markham Ferry Reservoir*.

Snyder (Kiowa Co., pop. 1,671, at junc. of US 62 and US 183, see Map 8). Established in 1902 with arrival of the Frisco Railroad and named for Bryan Snyder, a railroad official. Conceived in controversy (with nearby *Mountain Park*) over location of the then-all-important rail line, Snyder survived the buffeting of nature and politics to become the center of Oklahoma's important granite industry.

In 1905 a devastating tornado claimed 105 lives, destroyed much of the town. (Storm caves and cellars are now as much a part of the town as Chinese elm trees.) And in 1911, State Supreme Court finally dissolved the abortive Swanson County, of which Snyder was to have been the seat. A few years later, however, the granite industry came into its own near *Mountain Park* and today five different companies produce some 500,000 tons of the stone from various quarries in this area. The distinctive Snyder granite has a pinkish coloration, but gray, black, and blue granites are also cut.

Sod House (Alfalfa Co. on OK 8, 5 mi. N of *Cleo Springs*, see Map 3). An Okla-

homa Historical Society property that dramatizes the way countless thousands of pioneers once lived on the Great Plains. Built in 1894 by homesteader Marshall McCully, the two-room "soddie" is one of the last to stand in Oklahoma on its original site and in something approaching its original condition (though protected now by an outer shell building). Admission is free Tues.–Friday 9–5, Sat.–Sun. 2–5.

Soper (Choctaw Co., pop. 322, on US 70, 12 mi. W of *Hugo*, see Map 6). Another county town born with the building of the Arkansas and Choctaw Railroad (the present Frisco) through this area in 1902. P. L. Soper was an attorney.

South Canadian River, see *Canadian River*.

South Coffeyville (Nowata Co., pop. 646, on US 169 at the Kansas line, see Map 5). A nondescript trading center that shows little indication of having once played Mr. Hyde to the Dr. Jekyll of its bigger and better-known sister city across the state line. When Indian Territory and Kansas were both dry, this settlement was the traditional wild border town that catered for a price to the illicit compulsions of citizens on either side of the border.

When U.S. marshalls arrived, proprietors of the whiskey joints were often able to shuttle their illegal wares out back doors to a safe haven in Kansas. At times frustrated Kansans disregarded legal niceties to cross the border and burn saloons and destroy liquor caches on their own. But South Coffeyville bootleggers were usually back in business within days of these harassments, from whichever side of the line.

The townsite was first named Polson, having been laid out in 1906 on the allotments of Martin and Earl Polson. It took its present name in 1909.

Southard (Blaine Co., pop. 115, at junc. OK 51 and OK 51A, see Map 3). One of Oklahoma's few "company towns." The large U.S. Gypsum Company plant, established in 1905, regularly employs about 250 persons. Formerly known as

Successful fisherman on Spavinaw Lake.

Cherryvale, its name was changed to honor the gypsum mill's developer, Geroge H. Southard.

Spanish American Veterans' Colony (Latimer Co., on OK 2, 10 mi. S of *Wilburton*, see Map 6). A retirement center established in 1936 by Oklahoma's Spanish American War veterans. The 800-acre retreat, on the edge of the scenic *Winding Stair Mountains*, is now open to all veterans.

Sparks (Lincoln Co., pop. 183, on OK 188, 10 mi. SE of *Chandler*, see Map 4).

Another tiny rural community (like *Fallis*) that failed to live up to its early promise of railroad-junction importance. It was founded in 1902 with arrival of the Fort Smith & Western, which crossed the Santa Fe here, and named for George T. Sparks, a FS&W director. Today it has only a SF passing track.

Spavinaw (Mayes Co., pop. 470, on OK 82, 13 mi. N of *Salina*, see Map 5). An old town—established in 1892—that is today an attractive resort center surrounded by some of Oklahoma's best-known fishing waters. To the east is Spavinaw Lake, municipal water supply for Tulsa. *Grand Lake* and *Markham Ferry Reservoir* lie to the west. OK 82 north and south from Spavinaw is one of the state's most pleasant byways.

Spavinaw Recreation Area (on OK 20, 6 mi. S of *Langley*, in Oklahoma, see Map 5). A 35-acre state-maintained playground below the dam that forms 1,647-acre Lower Spavinaw Reservoir. (With *Eucha Reservoir*, Lower Spavinaw is part of the *Tulsa* municipal water supply.) It provides a beach, picnic and camping areas, and a playground. Private developments nearby provide a marina, dock, and limited overnight accommodations. Address: Star Route 2, Spavinaw, OK 74366.

Spencer (Oklahoma Co., pop. 3,603, N of US 62 & 270 at E edge of *Oklahoma City*, see Map 4). A growing residential suburb on the capital city's east side. Started as Munger in 1899, shortly after arrival of the Frisco Railroad, it changed its name in 1903 to honor A. M. Spencer, a railroad developer.

Spencerville (Choctaw Co., pop. 170, on OK 147, see Map 6). An isolated community that owes its birth—and claim to fame—to Spencer Academy, a respected school for Choctaw boys established here in 1841 by the Presbyterians. The name honors John C. Spencer, U.S. Secretary of War 1841–43.

Although the Presbyterians were unhappy with the fact of slavery, the Choctaws had brought the institution with them from Mississippi and a number of Negroes worked in and around the school. One of them, "Uncle Wallace" Willis, is generally credited with first singing "Swing Low, Sweet Chariot" and several other spirituals that a Spencerville official carried back East and helped to popularize. The unmarked grave of "Uncle Wallace" is in a Negro cemetery north of the Academy site, in *Atoka County*.

The school was closed in 1878, reestablished at *Nelson* in 1883. Spencerville as a post office disappeared with the academy. But it re-appeared in 1902, to serve the present community. A large roadside marker notes the academy, all signs of which have now vanished.

Sperry (Tulsa Co., pop. 123, on OK 11, 8 mi. N of *Tulsa*, see Map 5). A tiny agricultural community that dates from 1905. It is best known today as the home of the Oklahoma Farrier's College, the state's only recognized blacksmithing school.

Spiro (LeFlore Co., pop. 2,057, on US 271, see Map 6). This area was one of the first settled in southeastern Oklahoma (see *Scullyville*), but Spiro itself was not founded until about 1895 when the Kansas City Southern Railroad arrived. Today its name is best known for the Spiro Indian Mounds, a highly significant archeological find that was first excavated and studied by professionals in 1936–38. The site itself (not open to visitors) is north of the town. Many of its highly developed artifacts, however, can be viewed at the University of Oklahoma in *Norman*, the Oklahoma Historical Museum in *Oklahoma City*, and Philbrook Museum in *Tulsa*.

Agriculture on the rich *Arkansas River* valley farmlands around Spiro is still dominant. The town's largest employer is a vegetable cannery. Of greater interest to the traveler, however, are the half-dozen small hand-pulled glass novelty plants whose colorful wares dot roadside stands throughout eastern Oklahoma. "Pulling" is a special skill virtually unknown outside this area. The raw glass (often discarded soda bottles) is heated to a molten glob on the end of a pipe. The artisan takes it from the fire, pulls it quickly while still red hot to form vases, swans, and other popular novelty items. The glass is then tempered in baking ovens. All of the plants welcome visitors.

Springer (Carter Co., pop. 256, on US 77, 10 mi. N of *Ardmore*, see Map 7). A tiny ranching community lying on the so-called Sunny (south) Side of the *Arbuckle Mountains*. Rolling rangeland, covered with bluestem and other highly nutritional native grasses and dotted with lakes and spring-fed streams, characterizes the southern and eastern slopes of the Arbuckles. Many of the state's finest ranches have developed in this region, giving it the widely accepted name of "Hereford Heaven." Fittingly enough, W. A. Springer was an early area cattleman when the town sprang up in 1890.

Stephens County (south-central Oklahoma, see Map 7). Area, 893 sq. mi.; pop. 35,902; county seat, *Duncan*. A rich agricultural area that also owes much of its prosperity to the oil industry. Duncan is headquarters for the globe-spanning Halliburton company, pioneer in oil-well cementing. Part of the Chickasaw Nation until 1907, it was named for Texas Congressman John H. Stephens, an advocate for Oklahoma statehood.

Sterling (Comanche Co., pop. 675, at junc. of OK 17 and OK 65, see Map 8). Farming community, established in 1901, when this area was opened to white settlement. Charles Sterling was a captain in the Texas Rangers.

Stidham (McIntosh Co., pop. 53, 11 mi. NW of *Eufaula*, see Map 5). An isolated rural community, settled before the turn of the century and named for the Creek Indian leader, George W. Stidham.

Stigler (Haskell Co. seat, pop. 2,347, at junc. of OK 9 & 82, see Map 6). Established in 1892 as Newman, for a pioneer physician, its name was changed the following year to honor townsite de-

"Old Central," first classroom building at Oklahoma State University in Still-water, is now a museum.

veloper Joseph S. Stigler. Economically hard-pressed for many years following the decline of the coal industry, the Stigler area has benefitted recently from its location between two of Oklahoma's most important bodies of water. *Eufaula Reservoir*, to the west, and the *Arkansas River Navigation System* to the north and east, have stimulated both recreation and coal mining (see *McCurtain*).

Agriculture is still important economically, however, and a cannery is the town's biggest employer. Also reflecting its farming/ranching base is a calendar of annual events heavily weighted with rodeos and livestock shows.

Stillwater (Payne Co. seat, pop. 31,126, at junc. of US 177 and OK 51, see Map 4). In so far as Oklahoma is still an agricultural state, Stillwater can be said to be its capital. The town, named for the *Cimarron River* tributary that skirts it, was laid out immediately after the opening of Old Oklahoma in 1889. Two years later citizens voted unanimously to incorporate their new city and, also unanimously, to issue $10,000 in bonds for "the construction of the Agricultural

and Mechanical College" which the Territorial legislature had just authorized. As Oklahoma State University it continues today to play a strong role in most aspects of life throughout the state.

Points of interest center naturally on the sprawling OSU campus. "Old Central" was the first building erected for classroom use. A handsome pink brick affair, dedicated in 1894, it is on the National Register of Historic Places and has recently been restored for memorial and museum purposes. Also outstanding is the Student Union, a block-long, six-story affair, completed in 1950, and still one of the largest and finest buildings of its type in the nation. Impressive, too, is the OSU Library with its fronting garden mall. Whitehurst Hall houses the on-campus Gardiner Art Gallery (Mon.-Fri. 8-12, 1-5; Sat. 9-12; Sun. 2-5).

Agriculturally oriented gatherings at OSU dominate the Stillwater special events calendar: livestock shows, food festivals, meetings of FFA, FHA, 4-H, and other state-wide organizations. Only in recent years has a drive for industry added some diversification to the town's economy. Rubber and paper products companies are now important employers.

Stilwell (Adair Co. seat, pop. 2,134, at junc. of US 69 with OK 51 and OK 100, see Map 5). The strawberry is king in Stilwell, especially in mid-May when the berries are being harvested and a gala Strawberry Festival draws thousands of visitors from throughout Oklahoma. At the other times the local cannery—the state's largest food freezing and processing plant—handles green beans, spinach, peas, potatoes and other vegetables raised in the area. (One-hour plant tours are available 9-4 weekdays.)

Stilwell began in 1896 when the Flint post office was moved here from a site 3 miles to the north. The name was changed to honor Arthur E. Stilwell, a developer of the Kansas City Southern Railroad. In 1910 the county seat was moved here from *Westville*.

Nearby point of interest for the visitor

is **Bitting Springs Mill**, established before the Civil War and still turning out stone-ground meal.

Stonewall (Pontotoc Co., pop. 650, on OK 3, 13 mi. SE of **Ada**, see Map 7). An historic Chickasaw town that dates back to the Civil War—hence its name honoring Confederate General T. J. "Stonewall" Jackson—although its original site was about 3 miles west of its present location. Pontotoc County was organized in 1856 under the Chickasaw Constitution and Stonewall was its seat from the early 1870's to 1907, when Oklahoma became a state. Only scattered ruins now mark such once important Indian institutions in the area as Collins Institute and the Chickasaw National Academy.

Near Stonewall (inquire locally) is one of the state's last few remaining home sorghum-making operations.

Straight (Texas Co., pop. 240, off OK 136, 16 mi. N of **Guymon**, see Map 2). An isolated, post office-less community near the Kansas line that exists primarily on the strength of a nearby refinery. A by-product of the vast Hugoton Field (see **Hooker**), it justifies the consolidated school that maintains the community's identity.

Strang (Mayes Co., pop. 164, 5 mi. NW of Spavinaw, see Map 5). A rural community on the east bank of **Markham Ferry Reservoir**. From 1905 to 1913 it was known as Lynch for nearby Lynch's Prairie. Strang was the maiden name of the wife of William Kenefic, developer of the Choctaw, Oklahoma and Gulf Railroad. This Kansas, Oklahoma and Gulf line was abandoned in 1962 with the building of Markham Ferry Dam on Grand River.

Stratford (Garvin Co., pop. 1,278, at junc. of US 177 and OK 19, see Map 7). A town laid out on a now abandoned Santa Fe branch line in 1908. The name is apparently a nod in the direction of the Bard of Avon. On Stratford's main street is a noteworthy collection of Indian, pioneer, and historical items assembled by a local resident. Featured

are displays of such pre-1900 frontier enterprises as barber shop, hardware store, doctor's office, telephone exchange, and Wells-Fargo office.

Stringtown (Atoka Co., pop. 397, on US 69, see Map 6). The settlement began as a stage stop on the Butterfield Overland route that sliced across southeastern Indian Territory 1858–61 (see **Red Oak**). Geary Station, now submerged under **Atoka Reservoir**, was two miles to the southwest. The town was known for a time as Sulphur Springs or Springtown, of which the town's present name is believed to be a modification.

The coming of the M-K-T Railroad in 1872 gave Stringtown an economic boost. Lumbering and limestone quarrying have long been important and provide the town with its two largest industrial payrolls today.

For many years Stringtown was best known for the state training school for boys. Though still a correctional institution, the facility is now operated as a vocational school.

Strong City (Roger Mills Co., pop. 40, on OK 33, see Map 3). A small farming community in the fertile **Washita River** valley some 10 miles northeast of **Cheyenne**. Served by a Santa Fe branch line running west from **Clinton** into the Texas Panhandle, it was named for Clinton R. Strong, a railroad developer.

Stroud (Lincoln Co., pop. 2,502, off I 44 at junc. of US 66 & OK 99, see Map 4). As a trading center since the early 1890's (it was named for a pioneer merchant), Stroud over the years has merely changed the nature of its proffered merchandise. Located in "wet" Oklahoma Territory, only 2 miles from "dry" Indian Territory, it prospered initially on the illicit whisky traffic into the nearby Creek lands. Statehood, of course, closed the town's nine flourishing saloons in 1907. But discovery of the Stroud Oil Fields in 1923 gave it a much more dependable industry. Today the town's (and county's) largest employers are two asphalt roofing materials manufacturers.

Establishment of Stroud as midway service center for the pioneering Turner Turnpike (opened in 1953 as the first west of the Mississippi) put the town in the booming travel accommodations business and is contributing considerably to its current growth. Being planned in 1977 for location at the I 44 interchange is a $41 million family entertainment complex in the Disney World or Six Flags mold, to be known as Seven Continents.

Special events in Stroud range from traditional to new and novel. The annual Sac and Fox Indian Powwow is held each July. There are skydiving exhibitions each weekend in March, weather permitting. And for the lover of the unusual there are the International Brick and Rolling Pin Throwing Championships. The mid-July events, with six-person teams (men and women) competing in five categories, feature participants from three other Strouds—in England, Canada, and Australia. Sidewalk sales, flea markets, kid races, and a variety of contests round out the fun and foolishness.

Stuart (Hughes Co., pop. 294, at junc. of US 270 and OK 31A, see Map 7). A small community beside the Rock Island that first saw life as Hoyuby in 1892, changed its name in 1896—perhaps not too surprisingly—to honor territorial jurist Charles B. Stuart.

Sugden (Jefferson Co., off US 81, 5 mi. N of *Ryan*, see Map 7). Little more than a railroad siding today, Sugden began as the Sugg Ranch in the late 1870's, operated by pioneer cattlemen Carl and Ikard Suggs. ("Sugg" was the post office name for nearby *Ryan* from 1888 to 1890.) When Rock Island tracks were laid across the ranch in 1892 the town of Sugden appeared. Serving as ranch headquarters gave it a good start, and until 1912 it contested with *Ryan* and *Waurika* for the county seat. Then it gradually faded to its present near-ghosthood status.

Sulphur (Murray Co. seat, pop. 5,158, at junc. of US 177 and OK 7, see Map 7). A modest health resort that was born in

the late nineteenth century around medicinal springs now included for the most part in *Platt National Park*, adjoining the city on the south. In 1976 Platt was merged into newly created *Chickasaw National Recreation Area*. Indians, of course, knew of and patronized the healing waters of "Sulphur Springs" long before the coming of the white men after the Civil War. This locale was then part of the Chickasaw Nation.

The trading post/spa developed originally around one of the major springs, Pavilion, in the heart of what is now Platt. But in 1902 the Chickasaws transferred this area to the federal government, largely to preserve it from white exploitation. The some 200 people that made up the settlement at that time then moved north to establish the present town.

For the next few decades, while health spas flourished everywhere, Sulphur grew and prospered. Two railroads brought health seekers by the trainload to "take the waters" and frolic in the natural wooded playground of Platt park. Then medicinal baths began to lose favor, and the town's mood and appearance changed gradually into one of relaxed indulgence and somewhat decayed semi-affluence, an atmosphere that persists down to the present.

Even the town's. physical location seems symbolically significant. It is divided by Rock Creek into East and West Sulphur, each with its own business and residential section. In East Sulphur are the city hall and the larger hotels, including the handsome Chickasaw Motor Inn. (Built to replace the historic Artesian Hotel, destroyed by fire in 1964, it has only recently been taken over by the Chickasaws as a tribal project, thereby restoring Indian supervision of at least part of the area's medicinal waters! Now featured occasionally on the menu are such Chickasaw delicacies as fry bread and sofke.) In West Sulphur are the Murray County courthouse and county offices. Although active feuding between the two towns once led to a formal hatchet-burying— in a Rock Creek bridge serving both communities—everything is calm today.

Murray County is still heavily depen-

Old Cherokee National Capitol, the Cherokee County Courthouse in Tahlequah.

dent on agriculture. Most of the town's businesses are farm and ranch oriented, as are the principal annual events: Junior Livestock Show (mid-March); Hereford Heaven Rodeo (early July); and Murray County Fair (mid-September). Also contributing to the town's economy are two state institutions: the Oklahoma School for the Deaf (a constitutional part of the state's free school system) and the Oklahoma State War Veterans Home and Hospital. Nearby Veterans Lake is a well-stocked 115-acre preserve open to public fishing.

In recent years recreation has played an increasingly important roll in the area. Platt has been extensively upgraded, and Arbuckle Recreation Area has been developed around 2,350-acre **Arbuckle Reservoir**. Other nearby playgrounds include the **Arbuckle Mountains** and **Turner Falls Park**.

Summerfield (LeFlore Co., pop. 150, on US 271, 11 mi. SW of **Wister**, see Map 6). Established in 1888 and named for a local sawmill operator, this tiny community sits astride one of the most scenic of all Oklahoma highways (see **Talihina**) at the northern edge of **Ouachita National Forest**. Goat's Bluff

camping area (2 mi. SE) on Holson Creek is a feature of the 17-mile-long Holson Valley Road. Pretty any time of the year, the U.S. Forestry Service road is especially beautiful in spring when the white blossoms of the wild plum and serviceberry mingle profusely with the strong fuchsias of the redbud.

Summit (Muskogee Co., pop. 125, on US 69, 7 mi. S of **Muskogee**, see Map 5). A tiny rural community that owes its name to the fact that it was built on the high point reached by the Katy railroad between the **Arkansas River** and the **North Canadian**.

Sumner (Noble Co., pop. 16, just N of US 64, 12 mi. E of **Perry**, see Map 4). A now almost nonexistent agricultural community on the Frisco in the rich Black Bear Creek valley. The town was started in 1894, a year after the area was opened to settlement, and named for a **Perry** businessman, Henry T. Sumner.

Sweetwater (Beckham and Roger Mills Cos., pop. 70, at junc. of OK 30 & 152, see Maps 3 and 8). A scattered community that maintains its identity largely

Restored Choctaw Chief's House, near Swink.

by virtue of a vast independent school district that embraces this Sweetwater Creek area north of **Red River**'s **North Fork**. The area was settled in 1892, upon opening of the Cheyenne and Arapaho Indian Reservation to white settlement.

Swink (Choctaw Co., pop. 88, on US 70, 18 mi. E of **Hugo**, see Map 6). Another county settlement that owes its founding to the coming of the Arkansas and Choctaw Railroad (present Frisco) shortly after the turn of the century. D. R. Swink was a local merchant.

A mile northeast of the town stands the restored Choctaw Chief's House, dating from about 1832 and believed to be Oklahoma's oldest building. The property is owned by the Oklahoma Historical Society and is open to visitors (Tues.-Fri. 9-5, Sat.-Sun. 2-5, free).

Taft (Muskogee Co., pop. 525, off US 64, 9 mi. W of **Muskogee,** see Map 5). A predominantly Negro community that developed because of the large number of one-time slaves granted allotments in this area by the Creek Nation after the Civil War. The town itself did not begin until 1902, as Twine, taking its present name two years later to honor President William H. Taft.

In 1909, after statehood, Oklahoma established here the State Deaf, Blind and Orphans Institute. Subsequently the State Training School for Negro Girls was also established in Taft, as was the Taft State Hospital. Desegregation of all state institutions after 1954 has led to the conversion of these facilities to a largely state-supported Children's Center, with both a North and a South Campus.

The schools, as well as the community, remain overwhelmingly black. In 1974 Lelia Foley became the first black woman to be elected to the office of mayor in the United States. She was subsequently honored by President Ford in the White House as one of the year's Ten Outstanding Young Women of America. In a sense she was merely upstaging Redd Foxx, the black television star of "Sanford and Son," who had come to Taft a few weeks earlier on behalf of a youth recreation project and been named the town's police chief.

Tahlequah (Cherokee Co. seat, pop. 9,254, on US 62 and junc. of OK 10, 51 & 82, see Map 5). Tahlequah became the capital of the Cherokee Nation on September 6, 1839, and that it remains

Cherokee Village at Tsa-La-Gi, near Tahlequah.

today, in spirit if not in fact. The day is still celebrated as a Cherokee National Holiday. The handsome red-brick Cherokee Capitol, completed in 1869 and now a National Historic Landmark, was until 1978 the Cherokee County Courthouse. Just off the Capitol square are the old Supreme Court Building, dating from 1844, and the one-time Cherokee National Prison, built in 1874. Signs printed in the Cherokee language dot the business district to emphasize even more the strong Indian influence in the town.

The *Park Hill* post office was moved here in 1847, its name changed to Tahlequah (for a Cherokee word variously spelled as Talikwa or Tellico). The year before the Cherokee Male Seminary had been established just south of town and the capital soon developed into a progressive little city.

Tahlequah suffered, with all of Indian Territory, during the tragic Civil War years. But it recovered rapidly. In 1886 a Cherokee citizen, Ed Hicks, built for the town the first commercial telephone system in present Oklahoma. The following year, when the Cherokee Female Seminary in *Park Hill* burned to the ground, the decision was made to rebuild in Tahlequah. The impressively towered and turreted building, now in the National Register of Historic Places, was taken over by the State of Oklahoma in 1909 to become the nucleus of Northeastern Oklahoma State University.

Tahlequah today is surrounded by things to see and do. In addition to spring foliage tours in the nearby woods and the September Cherokee National Holiday (which includes the world championship cornstalk shoot, a recently revived bow-and-arrow competition), the special events calendar includes the National Parachute Championships (in late June, with other competitions throughout the summer), and the "Trail of Tears" musical drama at Tsa-La-Gi Theater (see *Park Hill*).

Special activities for the area would have to include Illinois River float trips. The Chamber of Commerce (Tahlequah, OK 74464) can supply a map and additional details. Other points of visitor

"Trail of Tears" drama at Tsa-La-Gi Theater near Tahlequah.

interest include the Cherokee Indian Weavers (on US 62, 6 mi. E of town); the Cherokee Arts & Crafts Center (and Restaurant of the Cherokees, on US 62, 4 mi. SW of Tahlequah); Northeastern Oklahoma State University Museum (Cherokee artifacts, cultural exhibits, Mon.–Thurs. 1–4, Fri. 1–3); the ambitious Cherokee Cultural Center and the Murrell Home at *Park Hill;* and historic *Bitting Springs Mill.*

Tahlequah also has two highly developed state parks only a few minutes away: *Sequoyah* to the west on OK 51 and *Tenkiller* to the south on OK 82. These two state routes, with OK 10, are among Oklahoma's most scenic byways, which underscores the role of sightseeing in Tahlequah's recreation picture.

Talala (Rogers Co., pop. 163, on US 169, see Map 5). A tiny farming community, established in 1890 and named for Captain Talala, a Cherokee officer in the Civil War.

Talihina (LeFlore Co., pop. 1,227, at junc. of US 271 and OK 1 & 63, see Map 6). Its name the Choctaw word for "iron road," Talihina came into being in 1888 when the Frisco Railroad built through this valley of the *Winding Stair Moun-*

Skyline drive on the Talimena Trail, winding 55 miles to link Talihina with Mena, Arkansas.

tains, on its way from Fort Smith, Ark., to Paris, Texas. The town remained virtually inaccessible, except by rail, until 1919, when convict labor finally helped complete what remains today one of the state's most scenic highways.

A gradually increasing number of roads (see below) has now made Talihina a popular sightseeing mecca and sports center. Nearby streams and lakes are well stocked with game fish, while the surrounding oak, pine, and hickory forests provide dependable fall deer hunting. Along with sports and recreation, the area economy depends on logging, a small clothing factory, and two large public health facilities, one state, the other federal. Eastern Oklahoma Tuberculosis Sanatorium, opened in 1921 (but now closed, at least temporarily), and Talihina Indian Hospital, established by the U.S. Public Health Service in 1916, are both west of town off OK 63-A.

Primary sightseeing road out of Talihina—indeed, the state's No. 1 byway, with the OK 1 tag to prove it—is the new **Talimena Trail.** Western terminus of the scenic road is at the junction with US 271 eight miles northeast of town. US 63, to the east, offers the motorist the mountain-rimmed valley of the **Kiamichi River** from **Whitesboro** to **Big Cedar.** The so-called Indian Road from US 271 south of Talihina to US 259 near Bethel snakes a 33-mile course over the **Kiamichi Mountains** through **Honobia.** Also rewarding is the Holson Valley Road (see **Summerfield**).

Talimena Trail (LeFlore Co., OK 1 from US 271 to the Arkansas Line, see Map 6). This 55-mile-long Skyline Drive was built in the 1960's by the U.S. Forest Service to link **Talihina** with Mena, Arkansas. The $8 million scenic highway follows the crest of the **Kiamichi Mountains** from US 271 to US 259, then the crest of Rich Mountain eastward to US 59 in Arkansas. It's a paved, well marked road, without advertising signs its entire length and offering an unending panorama of seemingly untouched mountains, valleys, forests, and lakes. Deer and other wildlife are not uncommon. Along the way are picnic and camping areas, an embryo arboretum, and numerous turnouts for points of scenic and historic interest. Caution: curves are sometimes sharp and grades as steep as 13 per cent. This is an enjoyable route for the leisure-bent, not a speedway for the hurried or uncaring.

Tallant (Osage Co., pop. 30, on OK 11, 13 mi. SE of **Pawhuska,** see Map 4). A now dwindling oil camp, established in 1921 and named for Ralph K. Tallant, an officer of the Cities Service Oil Company.

Taloga (Dewey Co. seat, pop. 363, on US 183, see Map 3). The smallest of Oklahoma's 77 county seats, Taloga boasts a picturesque setting on the south bank of the **Canadian River.** It is the center of a large stock-farming area. Although several versions of the origin of its name persist, historian George H. Shirk believes it comes from the Creek word for "rock in water," referring to the original boundary of the Creek Nation. Taloga was declared seat of "D" County in 1891 after the U.S. government survey of the Cheyenne and Arapaho reservation, prior to its opening to white settlement the following year. It got its post office March 22,

1892, but the county's name was not changed to Dewey until after the battle of Manila Bay in 1898.

Tamaha (Haskell Co., pop. 83, on county road 13 mi. NE of *Stigler,* see Map 6). One of the oldest towns in Oklahoma, and one of the most picturesquely located. Tamaha (Choctaw for "town") was a steamboat landing on the *Arkansas River* before the Civil War. On June 15, 1864, it witnessed that war's only naval battle fought in present-day Oklahoma, the capture by Confederates of an armed steamboat, the *J. R. Williams.* Only a handful of homes remain in the town today, with a general store and an ancient cemetery on a wooded bluff overlooking *Robert S. Kerr Reservoir.*

Tatums (Carter Co., pop. 150, on OK 7, 4 mi. NE of *Ratliff City,* see Map 7). A rural community dating from before the turn of the century. Lee B. Tatum was first postmaster. Intensive oil development is evident all through this western section of the county, a northern extension of the vast *Healdton* field.

Tecumseh (Pottawatomie Co., pop. 4,451, at junc. of US 177 and OK 9, see Map 7). Though named for the greatest war chief of the Shawnees, Tecumseh lost its most important battle—with nearby *Shawnee* for the county seat—in 1930. It has depended since then for its economic well-being on the sprawling State Industrial School. Now called Girls Town, the training facility for delinquents has its own campus at the south edge of town.

Tecumseh began with the opening of the Pottawatomie Indian lands in 1891. This gave it a four-year head start on *Shawnee* (the Kickapoo lands on the north side of the *North Canadian River* were not opened to settlement until 1895), helped it claim the county seat in 1907 with statehood. Losing it in 1909, Tecumseh regained it in 1913. Attesting to its importance during this period are many substantial red brick downtown business buildings, including a still impressive opera house, now occupied by a feed company.

Temple (Cotton Co., pop. 1,354, at junc. of OK 5 and OK 65, see Map 8). Born in late 1901 as Botsford (for a prominent Indian Territory jurist), the town moved a mile north to the then-building Rock Island Railroad in 1902, changed its name to honor Temple Houston (son of Sam Houston and a famous Oklahoma lawyer in his own right). It quickly acquired a solid economic base, and when Cotton County was separated from *Comanche County* in 1912 it waged a brief struggle for the county seat with *Randlett* and *Walters.* Though Walters eventually won, Temple has continued to prosper.

One remarkable enterprise for such a small town was the Mooney Brothers general store, which opened in 1906 and soon became a true department store, offering everything from lumber to jewelry, groceries to furniture, shoes to ice cream sodas. Other offerings include the ministrations of a doctor, marriage ceremonies, and the services of a traditional funeral "parlor." In 1929 "the store"—as it was referred to over a wide area—was sold to Sears Roebuck and Company, and the giant national chain operated it as a mail order house until 1955. Since 1957 it has housed the town's largest payroll (over 200), a Haggar slacks plant.

Lake Mooney, a 27-acre empoundment just west of Temple, is a popular recreation facility for a wide area.

Tenkiller Reservoir (off I 40, 7 mi. N of *Gore,* in eastern Oklahoma, see Map 5). Among Oklahoma's most scenic, this 12,650-acre lake was formed in 1953 with construction by the U.S. Corps of Engineers of the Tenkiller Ferry Dam. At 197 feet it is Oklahoma's second highest. *Tenkiller State Park* provides its best resort facilities—above the dam on its eastern shore—but 130 miles of wooded shoreline offer water a score of public use areas and extensive private development. OK 82 on the east side of the reservoir, in addition to serving many of the lake's resorts, is one of the state's most scenic byways. There is a 2,590-acre public hunting area on the west side of the lake.

The area offers a wide variety of accommodations and sport and recreational opportunities, provided by both state and federal agencies and private enterprise. Addresses: State Parks Division, 500 Will Rogers Building, Oklahoma City, OK 73105; U.S. Corps of Engineers, Box 61, Tulsa, OK 74102; Lake Tenkiller Association, Cookson, OK 74427.

Tenkiller State Park (off OK 100, 7 mi. NE of *Gore,* see Map 5). One of the state's better-known fishing areas, this 1,190-acre preserve sits beside a pleasantly scenic cove of 12,500-acre *Tenkiller Reservoir.* Although water sports command the most attention, this is the heart of the old Cherokee Nation, and many visitors use Tenkiller as a convenient base for exploring historic sites of interest in *Cherokee* and *Sequoyah* counties.

Facilities: 40 cottages, 10-unit motel, 8 picnic and camp areas, abundant trailer hookups, 6 playgrounds, swimming pool, beach and bathhouse, boat ramps, docks and rentals, enclosed fishing dock, scuba diving supplies. Address: Vian, OK 74962.

Terlton (Pawnee Co., pop. 111, off OK 99, 4 mi. E of *Jennings,* see Map 4). A Frisco railroad-siding community established in 1894 and named for Ira N. Terrell, a member of the first territorial legislature.

Terral (Jefferson Co., pop. 636, on US 81, see Map 7). An agricultural community established in 1892 when the Rock Island completed construction across the state from Kansas to Texas. The town, named for a preacher who laid out the townsite itself, lies less than 2 miles north of *Red River.*

Texanna (McIntosh Co., pop. 25, on a county road 9 mi. NE of *Eufaula,* see Map 5). A rural community near Porum Landing (see *Porum*) on *Eufaula Reservoir,* settled in the 1880's. Its name is believed related to a nearby community of Texas Cherokees.

Texas County (part of the Panhandle in extreme northwestern Oklahoma,

see Map 2). Area, 2,056 sq. mi.; pop., 16,352; county seat, *Guymon.* Occupying the center of the three-county Panhandle-bordering Kansas on the north, Texas on the south—Texas is the second-largest county in the state. High and semi-arid, it was long an area of ranches and marginal farms. Recently, however, deep-well irrigation and improved farming techniques have made it a rich wheat and feed grain producer, and sprawling feed lots now supply a growing meat packing industry. The county has also proved to be a part of a large three-state natural gas field. It was organized in 1907, taking its name from its neighbor to the south.

Top travel lures: No Man's Land Historical Museum at *Goodwell,* the Hitch Ranch and feedlots near *Guymon.*

Texhoma (Texas Co., pop. 921, at junc. of US 54 and OK 95, see Map 2). A Texas/Oklahoma border town, from its combination name and two-state citizenry (mostly Oklahoman) to its grain elevator with line-straddling double doors (one opening to either state) and fence-sitting implement dealer (who, at a time when Texas had no state sales tax, kept his merchandise in Oklahoma and collected for it across the border). The town has two sets of municipal officials. Before the state line was moved 473 feet south in 1934, it went through the depot, and passengers stood in Texas to buy tickets from an agent standing in Oklahoma.

Texhoma came into being in 1902 when the Rock Island completed its main line across the Panhandle. Today towering concrete grain elevators, sprawling feed lots, farm supply houses, and implement and irrigation system dealers mark the course of the railroad and highway along the southeastern edge of the town. The progressive, brick-paved business district, trim, tree-lined residential streets, a large school plant, and several impressive churches (notably the Christian, with an unusual, stained-glass east wall) lie north and west of the tracks, in Oklahoma. Texhoma Museum is in a store building downtown.

Expanded deep-well irrigation has

There are facilities for fishing and all water sports on 89,000-acre Lake Texoma.

Corps of Engineers, Box 61, Tulsa, OK 74102; Lake Texoma Association, Denison, Texas 75020.

Texoma State Park (5 mi. E of *Kingston* on US 70, see Map 7). A 1,883-acre shoreline park, with convention facilities on sprawling *Texoma Reservoir.* As at most of Oklahoma's parks that feature a lodge, recreation facilities are slanted heavily toward water sports of all kinds. Lake excursion cruises are also available. But golf, trap shooting, tennis and other sports have not been overlooked. A Lake Texoma extra: buffalo, longhorn cattle, and deer.

Facilities: 103-room resort lodge, 68 cottages, a 20-room (40-bed) lodge rented as a unit, abundant picnic, camp and trailer areas, 3,000-foot paved air

strengthened an already strong agricultural base in this two-panhandle area. Cattle and grain predominate. The Texhoma cattle auction (every Friday) is noteworthy.

Texoma Reservoir (off US 70 and US 75, SW of *Durant,* in south-central Oklahoma, see Map 7). The Southwest's most popular playground (over ten million visitors a year), 89,000-acre Lake Texoma is Oklahoma's second largest lake and its most highly developed. It was created in 1944 by the U.S. Corps of Engineers as a joint flood control and power project on the **Red River** below the mouth of the flood-prone **Washita.** The $65 million dam is 15,200 feet long and has a maximum height of 165 feet. Its hydroelectric installation is open to visitors. The sprawling reservoir has 580 miles of shoreline and extends into Texas, although the bulk of its recreational developments, public and private, are on the Oklahoma (north) side. Those areas are also served by OK 32 and OK 99.

Facilities: *Texoma State Park* contains 1,884 acres and offers the visitor a fully developed resort; several score additional camps and resorts, public and private, rim the reservoir's many coves and outlets. Addresses: U.S.

One of the countless oil derricks that dot the landscape in Oklahoma—this one in Lake Texoma.

strip, 9-hole golf course, ski school, enclosed fishing dock, complete range of sport and recreation facilities for land and water. Address: Kingston, OK 73439.

Texola (Beckham Co., pop. 144, on US 66 at the Texas line, see Map 8). A dwindling community established in 1902 when the present Rock Island was completed westward as far as the Texas Panhandle. Its name—for a brief time spelled Texokla—memorializes that on-the-border location.

Thackerville (Love Co., pop. 257, on US 77, 10 mi. S of *Marietta,* see Map 7). A dwindling farm community that dates back to 1882, five years before the arrival of the Santa Fe Railroad. The name honors Zachariah Thacker, an early settler in the area, which is actually a long south-projecting spit of land virtually surrounded by the *Red River*—and Texas.

A mile west of US 77, near the river, is the old Refuge Spring (inquire locally), burial ground of many early Texas outlaws. For them, obviously, the "refuge," located among some cedar trees near the Texas-Oklahoma boundary proved quite temporary. Or, depending upon one's point of view, quite permanent.

The Village (Oklahoma Co., pop. 13,695, off OK 74 on the NW edge of *Oklahoma City,* see Map 4). A pleasant middle and upper-middle class residential area on the capital city's north side near Lake Hefner. Just north of *Nichols Hills* and like its more pretentious neighbor a separate municipality, it was incorporated in 1950.

Thomas (Custer Co., pop. 1,336, at junc. of OK 33 & 47, see Map 3). A prosperous agricultural community in the center of some of western Oklahoma's most productive farmlands. Old Thomas came into being (a mile to the southwest) in 1892 with opening of Cheyenne and Arapaho lands to white settlement. William Thomas was an attorney and original homesteader. The post office was in the general store on his farm. When

the Blackwell, Enid and Southwestern Railroad (the "Bess" line, now Frisco) arrived in 1902, the settlement moved to its present location. In 1906 it acquired a second rail line with building of the Kansas City, Mexico and Orient Railway (now Santa Fe).

However, it was the coming of farmers representing the Amish and several other conservative Mennonite groups that gave the area a strong black-buggy appearance for many years. And proved the high productivity of its farmlands. In recent years some of the more conservative of the sects have moved away, but Thomas, with its lacing of tall concrete elevators, progressive fine school plants, and modern business district, attests to their continuing influence.

Three Sands (Noble Co., 6 mi. E of *Billings,* see Map 4). Now a ghost town, this "billion dollar spot" on the prairie mushroomed into existence in June, 1921, with the first oil strike. Almost overnight it became a jumble of derricks and jerry-built shanties, dust-choked one day, a sea of mud the next. At the height of its boom in 1923, more than 500 producing wells were pouring out in excess of 100,000 barrels a day and the town boasted a population of 6,000. Its name recognized the three separate formations from which its wealth came.

Thunderbird Reservoir (off OK 9 E of *Norman,* in Cleveland County, see Map 7). This 6,070-acre lake was created in 1965 by the Bureau of Reclamation as a joint flood control/water supply project on Little River. *Little River State Park* is a 4,010-acre playground that provides excellent recreational facilities on the north shore of the lake. There are other developments. The reservoir's Hog Creek (northern) Arm is included in a 1,280-acre public hunting area.

Facilities: extensive picnic and camping areas, swimming beach, boat ramps, concessions. Address: Bureau of Reclamation, Federal Courthouse, Oklahoma City, OK 73102.

Ti (Pittsburg Co. 11 mi. SW of *Haileyville,* see Map 6). Notable for its name (the shortest in Oklahoma) and its Pine Mountains setting (some of the state's finest, albeit isolated and rugged). Ti boasted a post office from 1896 to 1953. The unique name was created by reversing the initials I. T., for Indian Territory.

Tiawah (Rogers Co., pop. 150, on OK 88, 5 mi. SE of *Claremore,* see Map 5). A tiny community dating from the turn of the century and named for the Tiawah Indian Mound in Georgia.

Tillman County (in far southwestern Oklahoma along the *Red River,* see Map 8). Area, 861 sq. mi.; pop., 12,901; county seat, *Frederick.* Created from part of *Comanche County* at statehood in 1907 and named for Benjamin W. Tillman of South Carolina. It is one of the state's largest cotton producers.

Tipton (Tillman Co., pop. 1,206, at junc. of OK 5 & 5C, see Map 8). A farming/ranching community established in 1909 with arrival of the present M-K-T Railroad. John T. Tipton was a train conductor. Two cotton gins indicate the area's principal crop. The town is best known for the Tipton Children's Home, whose comfortable buildings are scattered over a pleasant, tree-shaded campus on the north edge of town.

Tishomingo (Johnston Co. seat, pop. 2,663, at junc. of OK 22, 78 & 99, see Map 7). Chief Tishomingo got his name from the two words "tishu," meaning servant, and "mingo" (or "minko"), meaning king. He was, literally, the brave warrior who became a servant to the Chickasaw king, or hereditary chief. And Tishomingo, the town, has in its way been a servant to the Chickasaws themselves for over a century.

In 1850 Good Springs was a fine camp site. Jackson Frazier, an Indian, built a home here. Two stores appeared. The Chickasaw Manual Labor School opened in 1851 a few miles to the southeast. And when the Chickasaws won the treaty right to establish their own government, separate from that of the Choctaws, they established their capital in the new settlement. It re-

mained there until the Chickasaw Nation was dissolved with statehood in 1907. A log cabin served as capitol from 1856 until a larger brick structure was completed in 1858. When this second capitol burned, in 1890, an even more imposing stone capitol was erected. It became the Johnston County courthouse in 1907.

On the courthouse grounds is the Chickasaw Council House Museum (Tues.–Fri. 9–5, Sat.–Sun. 2–5, free), maintained by the Oklahoma Historical Society. Exhibits include Chickasaw artifacts, materials pertaining to the Chickasaw Nation, and the restored log cabin capitol.

Another impressive old building of interest is the two-story stone City Hall on West Main. Built by Chickasaw Governor R. M. Harris in 1902, it was originally The Chickasaw Bank. On the second floor is one of the state's oldest Masonic lodges. Among its members have been both Chickasaw Governors Harris and Douglas Johnston (see *Emet*) and Oklahoma Governor William H. "Alfalfa Bill" Murray.

Murray is Tishomingo's best known citizen (his modest frame home still stands on East Main). A colorful lawyer-politician, Murray presided over the Constitutional Convention of 1906–1907, served as governor 1931–35. When he died in 1956, at eighty-six, he had lived to see his son Johnston also serve as governor, 1951–55. The first Oklahoma state legislature, in 1908, authorized establishment at Tishomingo of Murray State Agricultural College. As Murray State College, with an enrollment of about 900 students, its emphasis is now on technology, and "Agricultural" has been dropped. Although the college was named for Bill Murray's brother, Shade, the monument in front of the Administration Building honors the governor. On the campus, too, grounded in a permanent flight position, is the F-11 swept-wing Grumman Tiger of MSC's Blue Angel pilot, Navy Lieutenant Clarence Tolbert, missing in action in Vietnam since 1972.

Indian influence remains strong in Tishomingo. An annual Chickasaw Indian Festival is held in late June. Tishomingo's Daughters, a study club organized in 1903, cooperates actively with the Johnston County Historical Society to preserve the area's heritage and arrange periodic tours of old homes and historic sites. (A fine historical tour map and guide is available from the Daughters for a modest fee.) Of interest to the visitor is Tishomingo Cemetery, one of the state's oldest. Buried here are Governor Bill Murray and many Chickasaw Nation governors.

The Tishomingo area has long been a favorite of sportsmen. Sprawling *Texhoma Reservoir* reaches to the city limits. Other lakes and streams—notably the *Washita* and *Blue* rivers and Pennington Creek, with their tributaries—provide an excellent variety of hunting and fishing opportunities. For more details, see *Tishomingo National Wildlife Refuge, Tishomingo National Fish Hatchery, Blue River Public Fishing and Hunting Area,* and *Devil's Den.*

Tishomingo National Fish Hatchery (Johnston Co., on OK 7, 10 mi. SE of *Mill Creek,* see Map 7). Established in 1929 and enlarged considerably (over 53 ponds for hatching, rearing, and experimental work), this 46-acre facility is now one of the largest and most modern warm-water fish hatcheries operated by the federal government. Water is supplied by spring-fed Pennington Creek, a clear stream that has long been a favorite of sportsmen. The Chickasaw Indians traditionally gathered in this highly scenic area for sports and games. Several private resorts and guest ranches are located in the area.

The hatchery produces largemouth bass, bluegill and redear sunfish, and channel catfish for nearly all of Oklahoma's seventy-seven counties. The station has pioneered research in channel catfish spawning methods, in control of aquatic vegetation by herbicides, and in the development of fish packaging and shipping. Full hatchery tours are available.

Tishomingo National Wildlife Refuge (Johnston Co., 2 mi. SE of *Tishomingo,* see Map 7). Established in 1946, this 16,600-acre refuge on the *Washita River* arm of sprawling *Texoma Reservoir* offers the sportsman a variety of hunting (deer, quail, waterfowl), fishing, boating, and other recreational activities. There are four public use areas. Nida Point is one of the state's three major crow roosts (see *Fort Cobb Reservoir*). Hunting is confined to a 3,170-acre Management Unit.

There are picnic and camping areas, as well as nature observation points (more than 200 species of birds have been recorded in the refuge), and hiking trails. Of historic interest are the substantial homes, barns, silos, and other structures belonging to the pre-refuge Chapman Farms, a depression days cooperative farming project. Write: Refuge Manager, Box 248, Tishomingo, OK 73460.

Tom (McCurtain Co., pop. 200, on OK 3, see Map 6). A scattered community with the southeasternmost post office in Oklahoma. Tom Stewart was an early settler. Four miles east of Tom, just north of OK 3 near the Arkansas Line, is the historic Garland Cemetery. Now owned by the Oklahoma Historical Society, it is on the pre-Civil War plantation of Samuel Garland, principal chief of the Choctaw Nation, 1862–64. Earliest graves are from the late 1830's. One interesting stone bears the inscription "David Crockett, husband of Cynthia Ellen Garland." He is believed to have been the grandson (or grandnephew) of the famed Texas hero. The monument inscribed "Sophia, wife of Major John Pitchlynn" gives her birth as "Dec. 27, 1773," the oldest known birth date on a gravestone in Oklahoma.

Tom Steed Reservoir (off US 183 at *Mountain Park,* see Map 8). A $41 million project constructed by the Bureau of Reclamation to supply municipal water to *Altus, Snyder,* and *Frederick.* The 105-foot dam is on Otter Creek, but a smaller dam and canal will divert Elk Creek waters into the sprawling reservoir, which will in time include extensive sport and recreation facilities. Address: Bureau of Reclamation, Altus, OK 73521.

Tonkawa (Kay Co., pop. 3,347, at junc. of US 60 and US 77 & 177, see Map 4). The fate of this little town—founded in 1894, a year after the Cherokee Outlet was opened to settlement—has been somewhat happier than that of the two Indian tribes most closely associated with it.

The heroic Nez Percés were finally rounded up by the U.S. Army in 1879, brought to Indian Territory as prisoners and exiles. For several unhappy years they lived here, near the Yellow Bull Crossing of the **Salt Fork of the Arkansas River,** just west of the town's main street, before being allowed to return to their homeland in Oregon. Yellow Bull was a Nez Percé chief. The fate of the Tonkawas was even more tragic. Suspected of cannibalism, they were almost exterminated by other Indian tribes during the Civil War, wandered about as the so-called "Ishmaels of the Plains" before finally accepting a small reservation in this area in 1888. Today the tribe has virtually disappeared. The name Tonkawa, ironically, is a Waco term meaning "they all stay together."

In 1901 the Territorial legislature made Tonkawa the site of present Northern Oklahoma Junior College. Greatly expanded and modernized today, it has an enrollment of more than a thousand students. Of special visitor interest is the new A. D. Buck Museum of Science and History (North Pine St. and East North Ave.), also called the Yellow Bull Museum and formerly housed in NOJC's Harold Hall. Featured with Indian and **101 Ranch** materials are outstanding exhibits of wildlife specimens.

Tribbey (Pottawatomie Co., pop. 50, on OK 102, 11 mi. N of **Wanette,** see Map 7). Like nearby **Trousdale,** a rural community dating from the early 1900's and named for its townsite owner (one Alpheus M. Tribbey in this case). It has now dwindled to near-ghosthood.

Trousdale (Pottawatomie Co., off OK 102, 7 mi. N of **Wanette,** see Map 7). An isolated rural community that is now a virtual ghost. Established in the early years of the century, it was named for the townsite owner, William A. Trousdale. In this vicinity in 1859 was located the first Seminole Agency in the Seminole Nation. To the west on Council Creek was the Seminole Council House. No trace of either remains.

Troy (Johnston Co., pop. 80, on OK 12, 7 mi. S of **Mill Creek,** see Map 7). A scattered community, named for the city in New York when first settled before the turn of the century. Sole business today is the Delta Mining Corp. plant (see **Mill Creek**).

Tryon (Lincoln Co., pop. 301, on OK 105, 16 mi. NW of **Chandler,** see Map 4). A small rural community that was laid out in 1899 and given the name of townsite owner Fred S. Tryon. The area's first post office was Fouts, for Byron Fouts, an early settler.

Tullahassee (Wagoner Co., pop. 183, on OK 51-B, 5 mi. NW of **Muskogee,** see Map 5). In Creek the name means "old town," and Tullahassee was established in 1899. But its business district has now been reduced to a post office. The population is largely black, descendants for the most part of Negro freedmen of the Creeks. Tullahassee Mission was established in 1850 by the Rev. R. M. Loughridge (see **Coweta**) and it was the most important educational institution in the Creek Nation. Destroyed by fire in 1880, it was rebuilt by the Creeks and used to educate their one-time slaves. Only foundation stones mark its site on the northeast edge of present Tullahassee.

Tulsa (Tulsa Co. seat, pop. 331,638, at junc. of Turner, Will Rogers & Muskogee turnpikes, US 64, 66, 75 & 169, and OK 11, 33 & 51, see Map 5). Oklahoma's second-largest city—the self-styled Oil Capital of the World—began life as Tulsey Town, for "tallasi," the Creek Indian word for "town." The year was 1836. And the spot, at least according to legend, was a gnarled oak that still stands at 1730 S. Cheyenne Avenue. On the ground beneath it Creeks are said to have scattered ashes, brought with them in an urn from their home-

Tulsa City Hall (photograph by Mike Shelton, Oklahoma Industrial Development and Park Department).

River in **Red Fork,** and the boom was on. When a bond issue for a wagon bridge was turned down, three Tulsa citizens used their own money to build a toll bridge to the new field. Similar pioneer hustle has marked the city's steady development ever since.

An even richer oil discovery was made in 1905 near **Glenpool.** Tulsa soon became home base for the men working in the field. And this led in turn to its preeminence in all phases of the rapidly developing industry. Today more than 850 oil and oil-oriented firms, many of them with national and international headquarters here, employ some 30,000 persons in the area.

Petroleum overshadows Tulsa's economy in many ways. Oil company buildings dominate the city's gleamingly modern skyline (now being altered dramatically by the nine-block, $200 million Williams Center, a privately financed urban renewal project) and handsome tree-lined Main Street Mall, just as the flaming stacks and towers of the Sunoco and Texaco refineries

land in Alabama, before lighting a new council fire.

The Old Council Tree, suitably marked by a bronze tablet, was the traditional meeting place of the Creek busks, or councils. These Indian town meetings—with social and religious, as well as governmental, significance—were held here until the turn of the century.

Until then, however, the settlement's growth was painfully slow. A red granite marker on 41st Street near Sheridan Road notes the site of Tulsa's First Post Office, this in 1879. Then it was in a ranch house, on a newly established post road between Fort Smith, Arkansas, and the Sac and Fox Agency (see **Stroud**). Not until 1882, when the Frisco Railroad arrived, was the post office moved to a store near the present business district.

In the 1900 census, Tulsa boasted no more than 1,390 people. But on June 25, 1901, a highly productive oil well was brought in across the **Arkansas**

Municipal Rose Gardens, Tulsa (photograph courtesy Public Relations Department, Tulsa Chamber of Commerce).

228

dominate the horizon to the southwest. (They are among a score of Tulsa industries to offer conducted tours. See below for where to write or call for advance information.) Tulsa's State Fairgrounds features the sprawling Exposition Center, host every three years (the next one in 1979) to the International Petroleum Exposition, the world's largest industrial trade show. Its symbol is the giant (55-foot) Golden Driller.

Oil has also played a strong cultural role in the city, financing two of the country's finest museums. The Thomas Gilcrease Institute of American History and Art (on the northwest side) has more than 5,000 works of art representing 375 American artists (including the world's largest collections of works by Frederic Remington, Thomas Moran, and Charles Russell). It also has more than 200,000 primitive artifacts and some 60,000 books and manuscripts dealing with the nation's development.

Philbrook Art Center, the former Waite Phillips home, is a 23-acre estate embracing formal gardens, notable col-

Downtown Tulsa, America's newest and westernmost inland water port city (photograph courtesy Public Relations Department, Tulsa Chamber of Commerce).

The Prayer Tower, notable example of the modernistic architecture at Oral Roberts University, Tulsa (photograph courtesy Public Relations Department, Tulsa Chamber of Commerce).

lections of American Indian artifacts, Italian Renaissance paintings and sculpture, Chinese jades. Also noteworthy are the Alexandre Hogue Gallery of Art (on the University of Tulsa Campus, Presbyterian-related and itself interesting), the Rebecca and Gerson Fenster Gallery of Jewish Art (1719 S. Owasso), and the World Museum/Art Centre (1400 E. Skelly Drive, art works from South America, the Pacific area, and the Far East).

Other Tulsa area points of interest: Oral Roberts University with its architecturally interesting Prayer Tower and other fine buildings (the gleamingly modern $55 million campus was opened in 1965); Boston Avenue Methodist Church with its 255-foot tower and summit chapel (the world's first to be built to cathedral scale in modern skyscraper style); the downtown headquarters of the United States Jaycees; the new Port of **Catoosa,** Tulsa's recently opened window on the world, thanks to the

229

"*Golden Driller*," *huge statue in front of Tulsa's Exposition Center, where the International Petroleum Exposition is held.*

Arkansas River Navigation System.

Tulsa cultural fare includes the Tulsa Opera (two productions annually), Tulsa Little Theater, Tulsa Philharmonic, Tulsa Ballet, Broadway Theater league, concert and Town Hall lecture series.

Recreation centers on eighty-eight public parks and playgrounds covering some 3,850 acres. Most noteworthy are Mohawk (on the north) with its zoo, bird sanctuary, and extensive drives; Woodward (23rd Street and Peoria) with its 1000-variety Municipal Rose Garden; and Swan (17th Place and Utica), featuring Swan Lake and resident waterfowl.

The city's special events calendar is highlighted by the International Finals Rodeo (early February), Oklahoma Arts & Crafts Festival (early March), Indian Week and Tulsa Powwow (August), and Tulsa State Fair (late-September to early October). Spectator sports, in addition to those of Tulsa and Oral Roberts Universities, include the Tulsa Oilers (AAA baseball, American Association) and the Tulsa Ice Oilers (Central Hockey League).

For sports schedules, special events calendars, maps, accommodations lists, and information on all aspects of an Oil Capital visit, write the Convention and Tourist Bureau, 616 S. Boston Ave., Tulsa, OK 74119, or call (918) 585-1201.

Tulsa County (in northeastern Oklahoma, see Map 5). Area, 572 sq. mi.; pop.. 401,663; county seat, *Tulsa.* The heart of Oklahoma's early oil development and still one of the world's major oil capitals. The city of *Tulsa* alone headquarters several hundred producing, refining, transporting, and marketing companies active in the petroleum industry. Until organized in 1907, the county was part of the Creek Nation. It took its name from the city, which in turn came from Tulsey Town, a Creek settlement in Alabama.

Top travel lures: *Eucha Reservoir,* Mohawk Park, Thomas Gilcrease Institute of American History and Art, Philbrook Art Center, International Petroleum Exposition grounds, Woodward Park Rose Garden, all in *Tulsa.*

Tupelo (Coal Co., pop. 485, at junc. of OK 3 & 48, see Map 7). Settlement began here in 1900 when the community of Jeffs, established six years earlier, moved to this then railroad junction of the Kansas, Oklahoma & Gulf (now Missouri Pacific) and the Oklahoma City, Ada and Atoka. The present name was adopted in 1904 for the city in Mississippi, homeland of the Choctaw Indians who originally settled this area. Near Tupelo in the years before the coming of the railroads passed the important West Shawnee Trail, up which

World Museum/Art Centre, Tulsa, features art works from South America, the Pacific area, and the Far East.

cattle were herded from Texas to rail-heads in Kansas.

Near Tupelo (inquire locally) is one of the state's last few remaining home sorghum-making operations.

Turkey Ford (Delaware Co., on OK 10 near the Delaware-Ottawa County line, see Map 5). The old town has virtually disappeared, but its name tends to commemorate the nearby Turkey Ford over Elk River, now part of *Grand Lake Reservoir.* Just east of the present highway bridge over the river are the Indian Green Corn Festival Grounds (see *Grove*).

Turley (Tulsa Co., pop. 6,300, on OK 11, 5 mi. N of *Tulsa,* see Map 5). A one-time farming community that dates from 1897. James Turley was a local blacksmith. Today it has been almost completely absorbed into North *Tulsa.*

Turner Falls (Murray Co., off US 77, 6 mi. S of *Davis,* see Map 7). An 850-acre family amusement park, owned by the city of *Davis* and operated by private concessionaire (fee). Mazeppa T. Turner of Virginia is credited by his-torian George H. Shirk as being the discoverer of the 77-foot falls on Honey Creek which is the park's distinguishing scenic feature. Swimming, fishing, boating, hiking trails, spelunking, picnic, and camping facilities are available.

Turpin (Beaver Co., pop. 250, at junc. of US 64 and US 83, see Map 2). A small farm community, its two grain elevators marking the course of the now abandoned M-K-T Railroad (see *Forgan*), its few other businesses tracing the two federal routes to the east and south. Southeast of Turpin near *Beaver River* is the Sharps Creek Crossing site, one of several important archeological finds in the Panhandle (see *Optima*).

Tushka (Atoka Co., pop. 230, on US 69 & 75, 6 mi. S of *Atoka,* see Map 6). A settlement dating from the turn of the century that existed as Peck, Lewis, and Dayton before deciding on its present name—the Choctaw word for warrior—in 1909.

Tuskahoma (Pushmataha Co., pop. 200, on US 271, see Map 6). A rather scattered community that dates from the coming of the Frisco Railroad in 1887.

Scenes at Turner Falls, on Honey Creek near Davis.

By then, however, this immediate area had been extremely important to the Choctaws for more than half a century. A short distance northwest of present Tuskahoma the U.S. government had built for the newly arrived Indians their first National Capitol—a spacious log affair with plastered inner walls and sandstone chimneys. Nunih Wayah (for their ceremonial mound in the Mississippi homeland they had just left) was seat of government for the Choctaw Nation until 1850, when the capital was removed to *Doaksville.*

In 1883 the Choctaws returned tribal government to this area, building the two-story, red brick Council House that still stands just north of present Tuskahoma. Recently restored, the handsome structure with its mansarded third story remained the capitol of the nation until statehood in 1907. Just north of the Council House is an old cemetery where many well-known Choctaw leaders are buried. Nearby only scattered stones remain of Tuskahoma Female Academy, established in 1891 as companion school to Jones Academy for boys at *Hartshorne.*

Biggest annual event at the newly expanded Choctaw Capitol compound is the Choctaw Festival, scheduled for the weekend preceding the regular Labor Day meeting of the Choctaw tribal council. The colorful affair features Indian stick ball, Choctaw Queen contest, Indian supper, arts and crafts displays.

Tuttle (Grady Co., pop. 1,640, on OK 37, 9 mi. E of *Minco,* see Map 7). As a town, Tuttle—for James H. Tuttle, a local rancher—dates from 1902 and the building of the Frisco Railroad southwestward from *Oklahoma City.* But the area was a bustling one for at least thirty-five years before that.

Bronze tablets on a 12-ton boulder beside OK 37 on the east edge of town note the passing over this site of the *Chisholm Trail* and the location (2 mi. N) of now ghosted Silver City, one of the important trading points along that famous route. Listed are the names of the town's 112 pioneer residents between 1873 and 1891. First school in the county was opened here in 1889 (see *Minco*). Beyond Silver City the trail crossed the treacherous *Canadian River,* and trail drovers liked to rest up herds here, buy supplies, and repair equipment before tackling the mile-wide stream bed and its patches of quicksand. No trace of the town remains, but the well-cared-for old cemetery is well worth the drive over an improved dirt road (inquire locally).

In contrast to Silver City, Tuttle has grown over the years. Proximity to *Oklahoma City* and greatly improved highways have made it something of a "bedroom community," doubled its population since 1960.

Twin Bridges Recreation Area. See *Grand Lake of the Cherokees.*

Tyrone (Texas Co., pop. 588, on US 54, 10 mi. NE of *Hooker,* see Map 2). Another agricultural community that owes its founding to construction of the Rock Island Railroad main line across the Panhandle in 1902 (see *Hooker, Goodwell, Texhoma*). Gas and oil has given it a modest population growth, thereby bucking the trend in most rural communities.

An older Tyrone existed in this area as early as 1888. Shade's Well was a well-known watering place on the old Tascosa Trail, up which cattle herds were driven from the Southwest to railheads in Kansas.

U

Uncas (off OK 119 near the. Arkansas River, see Map 4). With "old" *Kaw City,* a casualty of the *Kaw Reservoir,* which will eventually flood both sites. Uncas was laid out in 1902. The name is that of a Mohican Indian chief and means "fox."

Union City (Canadian Co., pop. 306, on US 81, see Map 4). This small farming community on the north-south main line of the Rock Island was platted as Sherman when Old Oklahoma was opened to settlement in 1889. A few months later, Union Post Office superceded it. Union "City" existed only in the ambitious imagination of the developers, although it persists in popular usage to this day.

Upper Spavinaw Recreation Area. See *Eucha Reservoir.*

V

Valliant (McCurtain Co., pop. 840, at junc. of US 70 and OK 98, see Map 6). Started as Fowlerville in the 1890's, this now booming town changed its name in 1902 to honor F. W. Valliant,

chief engineer for the Arkansas and Choctaw Railroad (present Frisco). Until the mid-1960's it was best known for the fertility of its surrounding farmlands and the excellent hunting and fishing to be found in the nearby hills and streams (*Glover* and *Little* rivers).

Today it is home of one of the country's largest containerboard mills. Opened by Weyerhaeuser in 1971, on the west edge of Valliant, the $100 million installation boasts the world's largest paper-making machine, employs 450 workers on a non-stop, 365-day-a-year operation. The mill, with its 600-foot-long main building, required an army of 2,800 men to construct. To date it is the state's largest privately financed industrial project.

OK 98 north of Valliant leads to newly completed *Pine Creek Reservoir* on Little River. Three miles southwest of the town (inquire locally) is the old water-powered Clear Creek grist mill. Built before the turn of the century, it operated until the late 1950's and much of its original equipment remains in the picturesquely crumbling structure.

Vamoosa (Seminole Co., pop. 35, off OK 99, 16 mi. S of *Seminole,* see Map 7). An almost vanished community, established in 1906 and given a corrupted version of the mild Spanish command, "move along." Which is what most of the population has proceeded to do.

Velma (Stephens Co., pop. 611, off OK 7, 17 mi. E of *Duncan,* see Map 7). A scattered community dating from 1886. Velma Dobbins was the daughter of a long-time resident. In recent years development of the rich Sho-Vel-Tum oil producing area revived—and now sustains—both Velma and nearby *Alma.* Nearby is a Skelly gasoline plant.) Consolidation of their two schools into the sprawling Velma-Alma independent district has served further to strengthen the identity of both communities./The 9-hole Velma Wildhorse golf course is open to visitors.

Vera (Washington Co., pop. 215, on county road 7 mi. S of *Ramona,* see Map 5). A small ranching community born in 1900 when the Santa Fe Railroad built a depot here on land donated by W. C. Rogers, last elected chief of the Cherokee Indian Nation. Town builders had previously laid out a site two miles to the north, which was abandoned in favor of the new location.

Verden (Grady Co., pop. 439, on US 62, 9 mi. WNW of *Chickasha,* see Map 7). A small agricultural community in the rich *Washita River* Valley. A. N. Verden was the townsite developer, in 1899. Here in May, 1865, in a cottonwood grove near the river, one of the largest Indian encampments ever held in present Oklahoma was called to discuss problems relating to the Civil War. Assembled at this so-called Camp Napoleon were Confederate-sympathizing members of the Five Civilized Tribes and allied bands of Osages and various of the Plains tribes. Principal conclusion of the council—that if they were to survive in the white man's world, "an Indian shall not spill an Indian's blood"—was largely academic, since the war, which had proved so divisive and destructive to all of the tribes, was virtually at an end. A large marker calling attention to Camp Napoleon stands beside US 62 in the town.

Verdigris (Rogers Co., pop. 200, on US 66, 7 mi. SW of *Claremore,* see Map 5). A small rural community founded in 1880 and named for the nearby river.

Verdigris River. A sluggish, generally undistinguished stream that enters Northeastern Oklahoma north of *Nowata,* flows south-southeastward for 162 miles before entering the *Arkansas River* above *Muskogee* in the historic Three Forks area (see *Fort Gibson*). Its waters make two notable contributions to the work-and-play scene in Oklahoma. Some 50 miles of the Verdigris (literally "green-gray" in descriptive French), from the Arkansas north to the Port of *Catoosa,* now constitute the upper end of the *Arkansas River Navigation System.* And *Oologah Reservoir* helps to maintain the waterway's nine-foot channel.

Vernon (McIntosh Co., pop. 100, off OK 9, 15 mi. S of *Henryetta,* see Map 5). An isolated community settled on this location about 1914 and named for Bishop William T. Vernon.

Vian (Sequoyah Co., pop. 1,135, at junc. of US 64 and OK 82, see Map 5). A town dating back to the 1880's, the name may be a corruption of "viande," French word for "meat." It is currently enjoying a modest boom on the strength of Kerr-McGee Corporation's $25 million Sequoyah facility, a uranium hexafluoride conversion plant.

OK 82 north to *Tahlequah* serves the many *Tenkiller Reservoir* resorts and recreation areas, is one of the state's more popular scenic byways.

Vici (Dewey Co., pop. 694, at junc. of US 60 and OK 34, see Map 3). This cattle and farming center was named in 1900, probably in jest, by a settler familiar with the Latin phrase "veni, vidi, vici." The town is center for the production of bentonite, a clay used in the manufacture of cosmetics. Bentonite is also used in refining crude oil.

Vinco (Payne Co., pop. 50, on US 177, 12 mi. S of *Stillwater,* see Map 4). A rural community first known locally as Main, for the family that donated land in 1952 to start I-O-A Youth Ranch (see *Perkins*). The name is Latin for "I conquer," peculiarly appropriate in view of the I-O-A resolve to give Individuals the Opportunity for Achievement through farm-oriented work in a healthful, family oriented setting.

Vinita (Craig Co. seat, pop. 5,847, on US 60, 66 & 69, see Map 5). An old town that began in 1871 when the Atlantic & Pacific Railroad (Frisco) and the M-K-T Railroad met here, Vinita is now a progressive county seat, its economy buttressed by rich surrounding ranchlands and the increasingly important *Grand Lake* playground to the south and east.

Colonel Elias C. Boudinot, the important Cherokee Indian leader, was one of the promoters of the town. He named it for Vinnie Ream (1850–1914), sculptress of the life-size Abraham Lincoln statue in the Capitol at Washington.

Vinita is another Oklahoma town whose name was made known to the world through the writings of the Sooner State's famed Will Rogers (see *Oologah, Claremore*). It repays the favor with its annual Will Rogers Memorial Rodeo in late August. Will attended secondary school in Vinita, referred to it facetiously as his "college town." He had planned to attend the first rodeo in 1935 when, on August 15, he was killed in the tragic plane crash at Point Barrow, Alaska.

Vinson (Harmon Co., pop. 100, on OK 9, see Map 8). A scattered community that, under a variety of names, dates back to the 1880's when ranchers first began to settle in this area. First post office to be established was Francis, for a local stockman, William P. Francis. The office was then known as Trotter, before townsite owner Henry B. Vinson was honored by the final name change in 1903.

Three miles from Vinson (inquire locally) is a Natural Bridge. The rock formation, nearly 100 feet high, overlooks an area pocked with caves, many of which contain cold springs. In this northern corner of Harmon County, cut by the Salt Fork of *Red River,* a substantial amount of salt is produced from evaporation pans flooded with brine from springs and wells.

W **Wagoner** (Wagoner Co. seat, pop. 4,959, at junc. of US 69 and OK 51, see Map 5). An old and interesting town that booms today largely on the recreational demands of nearby *Fort Gibson Reservoir.* The town was settled in 1886 when the Arkansas Valley and Kansas Railroad (now the Missouri Pacific) met the M-K-T Railroad. The name is believed to have come from that of a popular train dispatcher, "Bigfoot" Wagoner.

Excellent transportation facilities and fine grass in the area made the new town a leading cattle shipping point for many years. (It is still one of the state's busiest rail centers, with as many as thirty-eight freight trains a day passing through the town on the two lines.) A

score of fine homes still survive to recall this prosperous Territorial era when local ranchers and businessmen vied with one another to create the town's showplace. Historical plaques mark these houses—with other noteworthy buildings in the town—and some are open during an annual pilgrimage in early June.

Wagoner County (northeastern Oklahoma, see Map 5). Area, 584 sq. mi.; pop., 22,163; county seat, *Wagoner.* An historically rich corner of the old Creek Nation that is becoming increasingly dependent economically on recreation travel. Established in 1907 at statehood, the county took its name from its largest town, which is believed to honor a popular Parson, Kansas, train dispatcher for the M-K-T Railroad, "Big Foot" Wagoner.

Top travel lure: *Fort Gibson Reservoir.*

Wainwright (Muskogee Co., pop. 135, on OK 56, 18 mi. SW of *Muskogee,* see Map 5). An agricultural community on the Missouri Pacific, established in 1905 and named for a local banker, W. H. Wainwright.

Wakita (Grant Co., pop. 426, on OK 11-A, 16 mi. NW of *Medford,* see Map 4). An isolated little "elevator town" on a lightly used Santa Fe branch line that dates back to 1893 and the opening of this area to settlement. The name is a Cherokee word indicating water collected in an earth depression, such as a buffalo wallow. Today it is best known for the Wakita Clinic, a pioneering cooperative venture whereby the University of Oklahoma Medical School and other agencies assume responsibility for delivering health services to a large, but sparcely populated farming/ranching area. Something of a pilot project, its success or failure could have broad significance for rural areas in all parts of the country.

Walnut Creek State Park (some 10 mi. SE of OK 99 from a point 3 mi. N of *Cleveland,* see Map 4). This 1,429-acre recreation area has been developed on the north shore (**Arkansas River** arm) of sprawling **Keystone Reservoir.**

Facilities: picnic and camping areas, trailer hookups, 2 swimming beaches, boat ramps and rentals. Address: Prue, OK 74060.

Walters (Cotton Co. seat, pop. 2,611, at junc. OK 5 and OK 53, see Map 8). This prosperous farming/ranching community was organized August 6, 1901, the day the Kiowa-Comanche lands were opened to white settlement by drawing. The site was along Cache Creek, half a mile to the north. The move to the present location was prompted by the first head rise to come down the creek. Name adjustments were also called for when the proposed McKnight was pre-empted by a community in another county. The town was then called Walter—by the post office department—and/or Walters. The latter became official in 1917, thereby honoring a city official, Bill Walters.

By that time the town had bested **Temple** and **Randlett** in the battle for the seat of **Cotton County** (separated from **Comanche County** in 1912) and was prospering largely on the strength of wheat and livestock. (Curiously, despite the name of the county, cotton as a crop has never been as important here as in the counties to the west.) Grain elevators dominate the town's "skyline." The biggest employer is the Cotton Electric Cooperative, the state's largest rural co-op, serving some 6,500 customers in nine counties. Additional employment is provided by makers of such disparate products as an oil pipe cleaner and a golf green aerator.

Area recreation is provided by a large natural park on the town's north side and 170-acre Boyer Lake, two miles northwest. The municipal water supply facility offers fishing and boating, a gun club, and a golf course.

Wanette (Pottawatomie Co., pop. 303, on OK 102, see Map 7). An isolated farming community dating from the Pottawatomie/Shawnee Indian lands in 1891. Arrival of the Santa Fe Railroad in 1903 gave it a brief boost. In town is a small, privately operated historical museum in an 1894 log cabin, moved to the site from half a mile north of Wanette by its early-day owner, Henry L. Neal, the retired postmaster. Along with pioneer items it includes a collection of arrowheads and stones from an 800-year-old Indian village site on the nearby **South Canadian River.**

Wann (Nowata Co., pop. 135, on county road W of US 169, see Map 5). Tiny community in isolated farming/ranching area that began life in 1895 as Coon, for nearby Coon Creek, a tributary of the **Verdigris River.** Its present name, taken in 1899, honors Robert F. Wann, a prominent local Cherokee Indian.

Wapanucka (Johnston Co., pop. 425, at junc. of OK 7 & 48, see Map 7). A town best known for Wapanucka Female Manual Labor School, established in 1852 on Delaware Creek, a few miles to the northwest, as one of the first schools in the Chickasaw Nation. But for the Civil War years, the academy operated until 1901, then from 1903 to 1907—when Oklahoma became a state —as a school for boys. Its massive limestone main building is now a picturesque, and virtually inaccessible, ruin.

Wapanucka appeared as a town in 1888. The name is a Delaware Indian word that refers to the tribe as "eastern people." Wide sidewalks mark a business district pocked with empty buildings and vacant lots as the town shares the fate of many non-county-seat communities in predominantly agricultural areas.

Wardville (Atoka Co., pop. 100, on OK 131, 14 mi. NE of **Coalgate,** see Map 6). A dwindling community that began at the turn of the century as Herbert, changed its name in 1907 to honor H. P. Ward, a Territorial jurist. Its rail link with the coal producing areas of **Coal** and **Pittsburg** counties was abandoned by the Rock Island in 1924.

Warner (Muskogee Co., pop. 1,217, at junc. US 64 and US 266, 20 mi. S of **Muskogee,** see Map 5). A farming community, established as Hereford in 1903, that changed its name two years later

Ruins of Wapanucka Academy near Wapanucka in Johnston County (photograph by Larry Marcy, Durant Daily Democrat).

to honor Senator William Warner of Missouri. In 1908 it acquired a preparatory school whose curriculum was extended in 1927 to include junior college courses. Today it is co-educational Connors State Agricultural College, with an enrollment of about 1,000 students.

Warr Acres (Oklahoma Co., pop. 9,887, on US 66 & 270 at the NW edge of *Oklahoma City,* see Map 4). A capital city suburban community incorporated in 1948 by developer C. B. Warr. It is perhaps best known today for its school system, which goes by the older and more historic name of Putnam City.

I. M. Putnam was one of Oklahoma City's early real estate developers. In 1909, when the city was waging its campaign to move the state capital from *Guthrie,* he filed a townsite plat for this area and erected a commodious build-ing he hoped would serve eventually as Capitol. Partially destroyed by fire, rebuilt, and modernized several times, the two-story structure still stands (on NW 39th Street) as part of the extensive Putnam City School plant.

Warren (Jackson Co., pop. 75, on OK 19, 7 mi. E of *Blair,* see Map 8). A scattered farming community in a large horseshoe bend of the *North Fork of Red River.* The district has combined with *Friendship* to build the new *Navajoe* School (1 mi. W, 3 mi. S) and thus preserve the name of that historic old town. Just south of Warren is the Eddie Fisher Southwest Baseball Camp with 25 acres of playing diamonds (7 in all, 3 lighted) and other recreational facilities. It has drawn boys eight to eighteen years old from forty states and two foreign countries.

Warwick (Lincoln Co., pop. 146, at junc. of US 66 & 177, see Map 4). A dwindling rural community that dates from 1892. Its name suggests the English background of some of its early settlers.

Wash Hudson Reservoir See *Markham Ferry Reservoir.*

Washington (McClain Co., pop. 322, on OK 24, 15 mi. NW of *Purcell,* see Map 7). A farming/ranching community named for the Caddo Indian chief, George Washington. Near here, when this was still part of the Chickasaw Nation, Montford T. Johnson, the son of an English actor and a Chickasaw woman, established several ranches. The one just northwest of Washington was put in charge of Negro cowboy Jack Brown. As Johnson's partner, Brown was to receive every fourth calf, thereby becoming what has been called Oklahoma's first sharecropper.

Washington County (in north-central Oklahoma bordering on Kansas, see Map 5). Area, 425 sq. mi.; pop. 42,277; county seat, *Bartlesville.* The second-smallest of Oklahoma's 77 counties, but one of the wealthiest per capita. Fittingly enough, the state's first commercial oil well was completed here in

1897, and **Bartlesville** is headquarters for globe-girdling Phillips Petroleum, as well as many other companies active in the petroleum industry. It was established at statehood and named for George Washington.

Top travel lures: **Woolaroc Museum** southwest of **Bartlesville,** Tom Mix Museum in **Dewey.**

Washita (Caddo Co., pop. 180, off OK 9, 12 mi. NW of **Anadarko,** see Map 7). A scattered farming community in a big northward bend of the **Washita River.** It was established in 1910 on the Mangum branch of the Rock Island Railroad. Near here in 1862 a minor Civil War skirmish took place.

Washita County (southwestern Oklahoma, see Map 8). Area, 1,009 sq. mi.; pop., 12,141; county seat, **Cordell.** A rich cotton producing area that was part of the Cheyenne and Arapaho Indian Reservation until opened to settlement in 1892. The county was organized in 1900 and named for the **Washita River** that meanders through it.

Washita River. The principal drainage system for west-central and south-central Oklahoma and one of the longer (575 miles) rivers in the state. It heads in the Texas Panhandle, enters Oklahoma in **Roger Mills County,** and follows a particularly tortuous southeasterly course to enter the **Red River** between **Marshall** and **Bryan** counties.

The name derives from two Choctaw words, 'owa' and 'chito,' meaning 'big hung.' The English spelling has been given the river, while the French spelling, Ouachita, holds for the national forest in southeastern Oklahoma. The Washita is prone to flooding in the spring, having a generally shallow, narrow bed. Only its upper course, in **Custer County,** has been dammed (see **Foss Reservoir**).

Washunga (Kay Co., just off OK 119 on N bank of the **Arkansas River,** see Map 4). A picturesque near-ghost with an interesting history and a highly uncertain future. Kaw Agency was established in 1873 when the Kaw Indians

were re-located here on the north bank of the **Arkansas River.** A boarding school was soon added, and for many years the little settlement bustled with activity.

Today, with agency and school long since gone, only a handful of ruined native stone buildings remain, half hidden among trees and rank underbrush. And the status of even these broken shells remains in doubt, as backed-up waters of **Kaw Reservoir** approach the site. Already removed to a tract just east of the municipal cemetery of **Newkirk** are approximately 620 Kaw Indian graves, including that of Chief Washunga (Wah-Shun-Gah), the tribe's last hereditary chief, who died in 1911.

Watonga (Blaine Co. seat, pop. 3,696, on US 270-281 and OK 8-33, see Map 3). Established in 1892, when the Cheyenne and Arapaho Reservation was opened to white settlement. The name honors the Arapaho chief, Watonga, or Black Coyote. The town's first newspaper was the "Watonga Rustler," whose editor, Thomas B. Ferguson, was appointed governor of Oklahoma Territory in 1901 by President Theodore Roosevelt. The Ferguson Home (521 N. Weigel) has been restored and is open to the public (Wed.–Sat. 9–5, Sun. & Tues. 1–5).

Blaine Dairy Products, established here in 1941, has a production capability of 10,000 pounds of natural American cheddar per day. It is one of only three cheese plants in the state.

Watova (Nowata Co., pop. 40, on US 169, 7 mi. S of **Nowata,** see Map 5). A tiny settlement established in 1892. The name, that of an Osage chief, means "spider." Principal point of interest to the traveler is likely to be the town's General Store, dating back to Indian Territory days. Although now housed in a modern building (after a fire in 1941), it maintains much of the stock—and atmosphere—of the nineteenth century.

Watson (McCurtain Co., pop. 150, on OK 4, 6 mi. SE of **Smithville,** see Map 6). Community in the rough, wooded country near the Arkansas Line. It dates from the turn of the century.

Watts (Adair Co., pop. 326, on US 59, see Map 5). A small town that serves a popular recreation area. Nearby Lake Francis and the *Illinois River* provide excellent fishing and increasingly popular float trips, the wooded hills dependable fall deer hunting. The name comes from John Watts, a Cherokee chief.

Near Watts is the site of the Cherokee Baptist Mission, commonly referred to as "Breadtown." Established in 1839, it was one of the important educational centers of the early Cherokee Nation. The state's second printing press was set up here to print books and newspapers in the Cherokee language.

Waukomis (Garfield Co., pop. 241, on US 81, 9 mi. S of *Enid,* see Map 4). A small agricultural community in a rich wheat-growing region. It was established in November, 1893, just after opening of the Cherokee Outlet to settlement.

The Waukomis Steam Threshers Association was organized here in 1954, and for the next twenty years it staged an old-fashioned Steam Threshing Bee in late July. As the group of nostalgic steam buffs grew, so did the roster of carefully preserved steam-powered farm equipment. By 1974, with twenty-two members, it had changed its name to the Oklahoma Steam Threshing Association and moved to *Pawnee.*

Waurika (Jefferson Co. seat, pop. 1,833, at junc. of US 70 & 81 and OK 5, see Map 7). A town best known over the years for such disparate items as cows, railroad locomotives, and rattlesnakes. From 1867 to the mid-1880's the site was a favorite of drovers pushing Texas cattle up the *Chisholm Trail* to railheads in Kansas (see *Addington*). After crossing *Red River*, a day's drive to the south, many of the herds were held over on the nutritious buffalo grass of this region to put on fat for the trek northward.

The Rock Island Railroad arrived in 1892, and for many years Waurika—then known as Peery, and later as Moneka—was a bustling rail center, heavily dependent on the line's sprawling shops. (It remains a crew-changing point, but the shops are now gone.) It was a Rock Island official who, in 1902, suggested the last name change, an adapted Indian word meaning "pure water."

It was in 1961 that Waurika joined the present quartet of Oklahoma towns (see *Okeene, Mangum,* and *Waynoka*) in capitalizing on a hardy native "crop" to stage what is now the annual Waurika Rattlesnake Hunt (mid-April). Upwards of 10,000 visitors comb the rugged, rocky rangelands around the town, compete for prizes, and join in the weekend frolic of street dancing, Rattlesnake Queen crowning and other activities.

The rest of the year special events reflect more closely the area's still strong agricultural base: Junior Livestock Show (early March), Jefferson County Fair (mid-September), and Chisholm Trail Stampede. The famed trail blazer is recognized, too, in the newly established Chisholm Trail Museum (on US 70 just east of its junc. with US 81). Recently opened by the Oklahoma Historical Society (Tues.–Fri. 9–5, Sat.–Sun. 1–5), it features materials pertaining to the trail and to the cattle industry in Oklahoma.

In recent years the town has been successful in luring small industries to take up the slack in employment once provided by farming and railroading. Largest employer now is a mobile home manufacturer. Most unusual local "industry" is parakeet raising. Over 300 area residents produce at least a few birds for the market. The largest Waurika dealer handles some 850,000 parakeets a year—about $2,000,000 worth. Oklahoma is now the nation's leading producer and Waurika, thanks to official state legislative proclamation, is "Parakeet Capital of the World!"

Nearing completion northwest of town is *Waurika Reservoir,* a 10-mile-long, multi-purpose lake that will in time offer visitors hunting, fishing, and other sport and recreational facilities.

Waurika Reservoir (off US 81, 6 mi. NW of *Waurika,* see Map 7). A 10,100-

acre empoundment on Beaver Creek, now under construction by the U.S. Corps of Engineers. When filled, the lake will extend west and north from Jefferson into Cotton and Stephens counties. Although primarily a Red River flood control facility, it will provide municipal water for the cities of **Waurika, Lawton, Duncan, Comanche, Temple,** and **Walters.**

Facilities are still under development. Address: U.S. Corps of Engineers, Box 61, Tulsa, OK 74102.

Wayne (McClain Co., pop. 618, at junc. of US 77 and OK 59, see Map 7). Founded in 1890 and named for a town in Pennsylvania, Wayne stands near the crossing point of three important pioneer transportation routes. Between the town and the **South Canadian River** passed the California Road, pioneered by Captain Randolph B. Marcy in 1849 (see **Byars**), and the **Fort Sill** to Fort Smith Military Road (see **Dibble**), laid out in 1869. West of Wayne ran the Fort Arbuckle Road (see **Davis**), used from 1851 to 1861.

Waynoka (Woods Co., pop. 1,444, on US 281 and OK 14, see Map 3). The county's second-largest town began its existence as Keystone, a railroad siding, when the Santa Fe built its main east-west main line through this western section of the Cherokee Outlet in 1886. The name was changed to Waynoka three years later—for the Cheyenne Indian word "winneoka," meaning "good water" or "sweet water." The town was platted in 1893.

As a Santa Fe division point, Waynoka has long been closely involved with transportation. Until recently the yards here contained extensive railway maintenance and repair shops, as well as the state's largest ice plant (for servicing refrigerator cars on long-distance runs). The town also boasted one of the Santa Fe's famed Harvey Houses.

Waynoka's interest in transportation, however, was not limited to surface carriers. In the late 1920's it gained brief fame as a connecting point for transcontinental air travelers. Transconti-

nental Air Transportation, Inc., flew its passengers to Waynoka from Columbus, Ohio, in Ford tri-motor planes. Passengers then boarded the Santa Fe here for an overnight ride to Clovis, New Mexico, where they again boarded a plane for Los Angeles.

The Waynoka area offers visitors two somewhat different travel lures. Just south of town is **Little Sahara Recreation Area** with its camels and dune-buggy rides. And like **Okeene,** Waynoka has capitalized on a "surplus commodity" most communities would choose to ignore—the diamondback rattler. Each year in early April the Waynoka Snake Hunt attracts thousands of hunters and spectators to the area.

Weatherford (Custer Co., pop. 7,959, at junc. of I 40 & US 66 and OK 54, see Map 3). A progressive, fast-growing college town that began in a cornfield on August 6, 1898, with arrival of the present Rock Island Railroad. It boasted a bank the first day. Within two months it had fourteen saloons, five dancehalls, fifteen wagon yards, eight lumber yards—and a reputation as the "wildest and wooliest" town in the area. William J. (Bill) Weatherford had homesteaded just northeast of the settlement in 1892 and the name honored him.

Establishment of present Southwestern State University on the north edge of Weatherford in 1901 gave the town a new focus and future. Enrollment is now approximately 5,500 students. The school's Art Gallery (Mon.–Fri., 8–5) exhibits paintings, sculpture, graphics and ceramics.

Owl Photo Corp. and a large 3M plant, recently located on I 40 just east of Weatherford, also buttress the area's economy. Both offer visitor tours. Five municipal parks provide recreational facilities.

The town's founding is recalled in early August each year with a Pioneer Days celebration, most notable single event of which has been—in an obvious challenge to **Pauls Valley**'s pre-eminence in the field—a World's Championship Watermelon Seed Spitting Competition.

Webb City (Osage Co., pop., 186, off OK 18 just NW of *Shidler,* see Map 4). With *Shidler,* the center of Osage County's still productive oil fields. The two towns, both established in 1922 when the Osage boom began, now share an impressive school plant, live primarily on the servicing of the area's extensive waterflood operations. Horace Webb was the townsite owner.

Webbers Falls (Muskogee Co., pop. 485, on US 64, see Map 5). As a rough spot on the *Arkansas River,* Webber Falls were only a few feet high. But they were significant enough to be noted on maps for over two centuries. The town itself appeared in 1856, the name honoring Walter Webber, a wealthy mixed-blood Cherokee who had operated a salt works and other business enterprises in the area.

In town, just off the highway, is a giant bois d'arc tree whose 15' 1" girth makes it the state's largest and, it is believed, the second largest in the country. It is thought to be as much as 200 years old. The town is perhaps best known today for the nearby Webbers Falls lock and dam on the *Arkansas River Navigation System.*

Webbers Falls Reservoir (off OK 10 N of *Gore,* in Muskogee County, see Map 5). One of Oklahoma's newest major lakes, this 10,900-acre empoundment was created by the U.S. Corps of Engineers in 1970 as an integral part of the *Arkansas River Navigation Project.* Recreational development is only beginning. Address: U.S. Corps of Engineers, Box 61, Tulsa, OK 74102.

Welch (Craig Co., pop. 651, at junc. US 59 and OK 2, see Map 5). Small trading center on the M-K-T Railroad, established in 1892 and named for A. L. Welch, an official of the line.

Weleetka (Okfuskee Co., pop. 1,199, on US 75, see Map 4). Trade center for a *North Canadian River* valley area that still contains many Creek Indian families. (The name means "running water" in the Creek language.) It was estab-

lished in 1902 at the junction of the Frisco and Fort Smith & Western rail lines. Pecans and watermelons are important, but the economic mainstay is the $4 million Public Service Company plant on the river just south of town.

Welling (Cherokee Co., pop. 50, off US 62, 5 mi. SE of *Tahlequah,* see Map 5). An isolated little *Illinois River* valley community in the heart of the Cherokee country. It was established in 1899. Provided one has a good map, the graded roads in this heavily wooded section of the Cherokee Hills offer the byway-lover an interesting alternative route to historic *Bitting Springs Mill.*

Wellston (Lincoln Co., pop. 789, on US 66, see Map 4). The county's first permanent white settlement, Wellston began in 1880 as a trading post opened by Christian T. Wells on the Kickapoo Indian reservation. In 1968 it joined the growing number of Oklahoma towns with at least part of its school system underground. With 3 feet of earth for a roof, the middle school facility also serves as a storm, bomb, and fallout shelter.

Welty (Okfuskee Co., pop. 60, off OK 48, 19 mi. NW of *Okemah,* see Map 4). Rural community that began in 1896 as Creek, the county's first post office. Name was changed in 1905 to honor townsite developer Edwin A. Welty.

Westville (Adair Co., pop. 934, on US 62, 1 mi. E of junc. with US 59, see Map 5). An important lumbering town on the eastern edge of the heavily wooded Cherokee Hills. A post office was established here in 1895 and named for Samuel D. West, a local resident. It was named the seat of *Adair County* at statehood in 1907, but lost that honor to *Stilwell* in 1910.

Wetumka (Hughes Co., pop. 1,687, at junc. of US 75 and OK 9, see Map 7). Spiritual roots of this old Creek Indian town go back to the town of that name in Alabama, from where this faction of the exiled tribe began its long "Trail of Tears" to a new home in the **North Canadian River** valley. A trading post was established here in 1858, a post office in 1881. The name is the Creek word for noisy or tumbling water.

On the Frisco, Wetumka has a clean, prosperous appearance. Nearby, still standing sturdy, though deserted and half-hidden in the brush, is a handsome two-story building that alone represents Levering Mission, a long-important Creek Indian school.

Wewoka (Seminole Co. seat, pop. 5,284, on OK 56, 2 mi. off US 270, see Map 7). In recent years oil has made the word Wewoka (Creek for "roaring water") familiar around the world. But the town itself has boasted a post office since 1867, when it became the capital of the Seminole Nation. The Nation ceased to exist, however, with statehood. And the only physical tie with this aspect of the past is the old pecan tree on the courthouse lawn (204 S. Wewoka Ave.) that served 1899–1907 as the Tribal Whipping Post. It replaced an earlier tree (also used at times for executions), the stump of which is in the Oklahoma Historical Society Building in **Oklahoma City.**

With arrival of the present Rock Island Railroad before the turn of the century, a proper townsite was laid out, and white settlers began to move in. Wewoka became an important Indian trading center, and merchants from a wide area picked up their goods at the new Wewoka siding. Soon it became a convenient excuse for all merchandising shortcomings. "I've got it," the merchant could tell impatient customers, "but it's in the Wewoka Switch."

Then came the **Seminole** oil discovery well, in 1926, and Wewoka doubled its population in sixty days. Boom towns sprang up all over the county, and a flood of oil field goods and supplies poured into the area. Lost freight bills, inadequate telephone service, and a desperate shortage of freighting facilities created monumental tie-ups and congestion. And oil field slang, ever inventive and colorful—promptly picked up the old phrase—and gave it a few new twists. Getting "caught in a We-

Wheelock Mission Church, built in 1846, in McCurtain County near Millerton (photograph courtesy Oklahoma State University).

woka Switch" soon meant finding one's self in a suddenly trying situation, whether commercial, social, or—upon occasion—even anti-social. (Today the town has a Wewoka Switch Motel.)

Although petroleum is still important to Wewoka, as to all Seminole County, diversified small industries play an increasingly strong role. These include metal fabrication, electronics, and half a dozen clothing manufacturers. Three-mile-long Lake Wewoka, a 260-acre municipal reservoir northwest of town, offers recreation and water sports. Biggest annual event is the Pokkecetu golf tournament in June.

Wewoka's rich history, with that of the entire Seminole Nation, white, black, and red, is memorialized in the new Seminole Nation Museum on South Wewoka Street. Opened by the Seminole National Historical Society in 1974, it is housed in the city's picturesque Community and American Legion Building, a native stone and rustic lumber affair dating from the 1930's.

Wheeless (Cimarron Co., pop. 25, on a paved county road 22 mi. W of **Boise City,** see Map 2). The state's newest ghost "town." When the little crossroads community's post office, established in 1907, was finally closed in 1974, the country store that housed it also gave up. A few miles to the northwest are the picturesque ruins of *Camp Nichols.*

Wheelock Church (McCurtain Co., 2 mi. NE of *Millerton*, see Map 6). Handsome old stone church erected in 1846 by a congregation first organized in 1832. The oldest standing church structure in Oklahoma, it is still in use. Wheelock Cemetery, across the road to the south, contains the grave of Missionary Alfred Wright and many other early-day figures, Indian and white, who played important roles in development of the Choctaw Nation. *Wheelock Seminary* is just to the northeast.

Wheelock Seminary (McCurtain Co., 2 mi. NE of *Millerton*, see Map 6). Its complex of white-painted frame buildings now virtually deserted, this important Choctaw educational facility for girls was established in 1844. It did not close until 1955, when its remaining students were sent to Jones Academy (see *Hartshorne*). A caretaker now oversees the vacant property. Near by is *Wheelock Church*.

White Eagle (off US 177, 6 mi. S of *Ponca City*, see Map 4). Settlement began here in 1879 when Colonel George W. Miller of the *101 Ranch* persuaded a small tribe of Ponca Indians living in the extreme northeastern corner of present Oklahoma to accept a reservation on land he had leased from the Osages and then rent it to him for his cattle. White Eagle was a prominent Ponca chief.

The post office, known as Ponca until 1896, was located at the Ponca Indian Agency. Today most of the original stone buildings of the agency and school have been torn down, replaced with modern brick houses for a growing Indian community.

White Eagle died in 1914 and is buried on a hill beside OK 156, several miles to the west of the old agency. The hill once served the Indians as a signal station. The impressive White Eagle

Old Wheelock Seminary, formerly an important school for Choctaw girls. Near Wheelock Church in McCurtain County.

Monument, erected by Colonel Miller's sons, is a native red stone shaft, 12 feet in diameter and 20 feet high, topped by a huge white stone eagle.

Whitefield (Haskell Co., pop. 300, at junc. of OK 2 & 9, see Map 6). Small trading community on the *Canadian River* that began in 1881 as Oklahoma, assumed its present name in 1888—at the request of the Post Office Department—to avoid confusion with Oklahoma Station (see *Oklahoma City*). Though outstripped in population (some 3,000 percent!) by the state capital, tiny Whitefield—for early-day Methodist Bishop George Whitefield—has one distinction: first official use of the word that twenty-six years later was to be adopted as the name for the forty-sixth state of the Union.

Whiteoak (Craig Co., pop. 120, on US 66, 7 mi. W of *Vinita*, see Map 5). Frisco railroad community started in 1898.

Whitesboro (LeFlore Co., pop. 400, on OK 63, 11 mi. ESE of *Talihina*, see Map 6). A *Kiamichi River* Valley ranching community, founded soon after the turn of the century and named for Paul White, an early settler.

Wichita Mountains (Comanche Co., served by OK 49 and various unnum-

Mountain climbing in the rugged Wichita Mountains.

bered roads, see Map 8). Southwestern Oklahoma's most prominent land feature, the Wichitas (for the Wichita Indians; "wia chitoh" is Choctaw for "big arbor") are a series of rough granite peaks rising up rather sharply from a generally level plain. The tops—Mountains Sherman (2207'), McKinley (2035'), Roosevelt (2180'), Elk (2293'), Sunset (2233'), Twin Rock (2183'), Lincoln (2194'), and Scott (2464'), the highest—are actually the crests of buried mountains. Erosion has, in most cases, left little but the bare reddish granite outcroppings.

The region is cut by clear streams, dotted with a series of man-made lakes. Extensive stretches of native range support large numbers of game animals. Much of the northwestern section of the mountains is included in the **Wichita**

Mountains Wildlife Refuge, while much of the eastern and southern parts of the range is now included in the **Fort Sill** Military Reservation. Outstanding scenic feature of the mountains is the looping auto road to the crest of Mt. Scott. Many are the legends of lost Spanish mines and cached treasures. Spanish goldseekers probably probed this area as early as 1650, and prospect holes and abandoned arrastras (see **Meers**) can still be found to mark the extent of the frenzied search for gold and silver. Precise dates are hard to come by, however, and tales of rich strikes, abandoned diggings, and miners murdered by Indians are more a matter of legend than of fact. Most of the mining scars date from the turn of the last century.

Many different Plains Indian tribes roamed the Wichitas over the years. In the extreme northwestern section is Cutthroat Gap, scene of a particularly grisly massacre of a band of Kiowas by Osages, this in 1833. The Kiowa camp was occupied largely by women, children, and old men, as the young braves on this fateful day were away on a hunt. The Osages struck without warning, slitting the throats of their victims and cutting off their heads. These were placed in the Kiowas' buckets, apparently as an offering to the gods. One bucket, found later in the ruined village, is now in the **Fort Sill** Museum.

Wichita Mountains Wildlife Refuge (Comanche Co., 59,020 acres, served by OK 49, see Map 8). When the 2,033,073 acres of Kiowa-Comanche lands were opened to white settlement in 1901, a sizeable chunk of the rugged **Wichita Mountains** was set aside as a forest preserve. In 1905, President Theodore Roosevelt proclaimed the area a game preserve. In 1907, to attack the threatened extinction of the American bison, 8,000 acres of the preserve were fenced and fifteen buffaloes were brought here from the New York Zoological Park for protection. Hundreds of the shaggy beasts now roam the refuge.

Similar protective measures were taken in 1927 on behalf of Texas longhorns, once numbered in the millions. Elk were re-introduced into the Wichitas in 1911 (they'd been exterminated here about 1875) and, in 1938, antelope. The refuge also protects large numbers of white-tailed deer, along with fox squirrels, raccoons, wild turkeys, opossums and many smaller animals. In addition, interestingly enough, the refuge shelters birds from both eastern and western ranges.

With its numerous lakes, ten camp and picnic areas, and 50 miles of scenic access roads, the refuge has recently been attracting over a million visitors a year. Lakes Quanah Parker, Jed Johnson, and Elmer Thomas all have beaches. Boats are allowed on Elmer Thomas, the refuge's largest. But this popularity is producing problems and the Fish and Wildlife Service, which now administers the area, is currently embarked on a policy of severely curtailing swimming, boating, camping, and off-road recreational vehicle use. Access, now virtually unlimited, may well be more restricted in the future. Park headquarters are north of **Cache**. One can pick up the latest refuge folder there, or by writing Refuge Manager, Wichita Mountains Wildlife Refuge, Cache, OK 73527.

Buffaloes grazing in the Wichita Mountains Wildlife Refuge.

Scene in the Wichita Mountains near Lawton.

The refuge has two outstanding special attractions. A three-mile paved highway spirals upward a thousand feet to the 2,467-foot summit of **Mount Scott**. High point of the Wichitas, it offers a 360-degree panorama of rocky lesser peaks, sparkling blue lakes, and vast expanses of level prairie. **Holy City** is a picturesque natural amphitheater at the base of Mount Roosevelt where thousands have gathered for an impressive Easter service each year since 1926. The late Rev. A. M. Wallock was the founder and long-time director of the traditional pageant, a community effort that draws its characters from many towns in this area. Over the years the extensive grounds—permanent stone stage and other structures, handsome memorial chapel, 11-feet-tall "Christ of the Wichitas" statue in white marble, landscaped garden with plants and shrubs associated with Bible times—are visited by thousands throughout the year.

What does Holy City mean to the visitor? A sculptor who visits and works there often, puts it this way: "It is a place where a man can think—and feel the warm sun on his back. It is an outdoor cathedral where all men of all

The birthplace of Will Rogers, restored and maintained as a memorial to the famous humorist.

faiths and creeds can enter and meditate even if they wear rags."

Wilburton (Latimer Co. seat, pop. 2,280, at junc. of US 270 and OK 2, see Map 6). The Choctaw, Oklahoma and Gulf Railroad (present Rock Island) is responsible for the founding of the town, in 1890, and for its naming, although the precise nature of this latter responsibility remains somewhat in doubt. For many years the name was thought to honor Will Burton, a contractor who helped to build the CO&G. More recently the honor has been transferred to Elisha Wilbur, president of the Lehigh Valley Railroad, which probably had a financial hand in CO&G affairs. In any case, railroads played an important role in Wilburton's early years, when coal was still king in this area.

Today, however, education and recreation are the principal economic stimulators. Eastern Oklahoma State College was established on the west edge of town in 1909 as a School of Mines and Metallurgy. It drifted into agricultural and mechanical fields as the nature of the area's economy changed. Today it is a fully accredited coeducational state junior college,

awarding associate degrees in a score of academic programs and a dozen occupational fields. The school strongly influences the community's sports and cultural fare, and is largely responsible for the recently launched Belle Starr Festival, a light-hearted early summer affair that combines folk arts and historical pageantry for a week of community fun.

In the fertile valley of the Fourche Maline, between the San Bois Mountains on the north (see *Robbers Cave State Park*) and the *Winding Stairs* on the south, Wilburton is profiting increasingly from recreation travel. OK 2 is one of the state's more scenic secondary routes.

Wildcat (Okmulgee Co., pop. 142, off US 266, 10 mi. NE of *Henryetta*, see Map 5). A community that prospered for a time with the booming coal industry, then declined when that fuel lost favor. Founded in 1897, it took the more dignified name of Grayson in 1902 (for Creek tribal leader George W. Grayson). With loss of its post office in 1929 the town has drifted back to Wildcat.

Will Rogers State Park (3 mi. NE of *Oologah*, see Map 5). A 993-acre playground on the west shore of *Oologah Reservoir* near the original birthplace site of Oklahoma's best-known native son, Will Rogers. When the *Verdigris River* was dammed, its backed-up waters flooded the original site. The two-story white frame birthplace was moved here to higher ground, restored and opened to the public as a memorial to the world-famed humorist.

Facilities: picnic and camping areas, beach, boat ramps. Address: Route 1, Oologah, OK 74053.

Willis (Marshall Co., pop. 10, on OK 99, 16 mi. S of *Madill*, see Map 7). A scattered community—established in 1886 and named for a local resident, Bret Willis—with an importance far greater than its official population would imply.

Just east of Willis on the Buncombe Creek arm of *Texoma Reservoir* is the twenty-two-building complex that comprises the University of Oklahoma Biological Station, established in 1950. The facility includes an aquarium and offers regular summer session work in botany and zoology to both graduate and undergraduate students. In a recent two-year period a total of thirty-six theses, dissertations, and published papers came from students and professors attending the station.

Willis Bridge is a long, gracefully arching span, immediately south of the community, that carries OK 99 across the *Red River* arm of Lake Texoma into Texas.

Willow (Greer Co., pop. 188, off US 283 and OK 34, see Map 8). Like *Brinkman*, a small farming community on the now-abandoned M-K-T rail line built across western Oklahoma in 1910 as the Wichita Falls and Northwestern. Settlement in this area, however, began just before 1900. The town's name probably came from that of Will O'Connell, the first postmaster.

Wilson (Carter Co., pop. 1,569, off US 70, 17 mi. W of *Ardmore*, see Map 7). Yet another product of the great *Healdton* oil field that opened in 1913. When *Ardmore* oilman Jake L. Hamon found production in the area, he persuaded his friend, circus owner John Ringling, to build a railroad to serve it (see *Ringling*). Wilson was laid out on the new line (now the Santa Fe) in 1914 and named for Ringling's secretary, Charles Wilson. A clean, progressive town, it still serves the continuing oil development and rich surrounding ranchlands.

Winding Stair Mountains, see *Ouachita Mountains*.

Wirt (Carter Co., 2 mi. W of *Healdton*, see Map 7). Now boasting a post office but no official population, Wirt roared into existence in 1913 with the Franklin No. 1 discovery well that opened the fabulously rich *Healdton* field. As news of the oil strike spread, throngs of oilmen and their camp followers poured into the area. Rag Town, as the boom camp was promptly dubbed, sprang up almost over night. It has been said

that the town, consisting mostly of tents, could burn to the ground on Saturday night and be completely rebuilt by Sunday night. Those boom days are over now, but the area is dotted with the bobbing "grasshopper" pumping units of still-producing wells. Officially the settlement honors famed oil producer Wirt Franklin.

Wister (LeFlore Co., pop. 927, at junc. of US 270 & US 271, see Map 6). A town that began in 1890 as Wister Junction, where the westward-building Choctaw Coal and Railway Company (the present Rock Island) crossed the Texas-bound Frisco Railroad. Today, however, railroading is far less important locally than recreation (see *Wister Reservoir* and *Lake Wister State Park*).
U.S. Corps of Engineers in 1949 as a

Wister Reservoir (off US 270 S of *Wister*, in southeastern Oklahoma, see Map 5). A 4,000-acre lake formed by the means of controlling floods on the *Poteau River*. There is a waterfowl refuge on the lake and a 16,316-acre public hunting area around the reservoir's western end. Much of the recreational development is to be found around the dam and at *Lake Wister State Park*. At the Wister Lake Project office near the dam is the Garner Collection of archeological artifacts representing some 10,000 years of human history in this area. It consists of about 5,000 stone shells, pottery pieces, and other Indian items from four distinct culture groups. They were collected by Lynn Garner Sr. and given to the Corps for public display (Mon.–Fri. 8:00–4:30).

Facilities: cottages, picnic and camping areas, swimming beaches, boat ramps and boat rentals, concessions. Address: U.S. Corps of Engineers, Box 61, Tulsa, OK 74102.

Wolco (Osage Co., on OK 11, 5 mi. SE of *Barnsdall*, see Map 4). Another Osage County oil camp named, like *Barnsdall* and *Carter Nine*, for the oil company that gave it birth—the Wolverine Oil Company, in this case—in 1922.

Woods County (in northwestern Oklahoma bordering on Kansas, see Map 3). Area, 1,271 sq. mi.; pop. 11,920; county seat, **Alva**. A lightly populated farming/ranching area north of the **Cimarron River** that was part of the Cherokee Outlet until opened to settlement in 1893. The county was organized in 1900 and honors Kansas politician, Sam Wood. (The "s" was added by mistake and never corrected.)

Top travel lures: **Little Sahara State Recreation Area**, extensive salt mining operations along the **Cimarron** near **Freedom**, Northwestern State College and Cherokee Strip Museum, both in **Alva**.

Woodward (Woodward Co. seat, pop. 8,710, on US 183-270 and OK 15, see Map 3). One of the principal cities of northwestern Oklahoma and the trade center of a wide farming/ranching area that is turning more and more to processing and manufacturing. Free one-hour plant tours are available weekdays (advance notice required) at Fenimore Manufacturing Co. (bindery equipment) and Trego's Westwear (western-style clothing).

Town was established officially on September 16, 1893, when the Cherokee Strip was opened to white settlement. It had its post office several months before, however, named for Brinton W. Woodward, a Santa Fe Railroad director. And the area was well known to whites as early as 1868, when **Camp Supply** was established as a base of army operations against the Plains Indians. In 1876 the first herd of Texas cattle came through the present town site. The new route became known as the Western Trail and soon carried the bulk of the cattle headed north for railheads in Kansas.

A physical tie with old Fort Supply exists in Woodward today. The original chapel at the old post was moved to the corner of 11th and Texas streets in 1894. Now Woodward's oldest building, it has served as St. John's Episcopal church ever since.

Ironically, Woodward is perhaps best known outside Oklahoma for the devastating April 9, 1947, tornado that flat-

Entrance to the Woolaroc Museum grounds.

tened more than a hundred city blocks, leaving behind 107 dead and more than 700 wounded. One of the most savage ever analyzed by the U.S. Weather Bureau (its destructive core was 1.8 miles wide), it caused property damage in excess of $8 million. A three-scene bronze memorial plaque in the reception room of the Woodward Memorial Hospital recalls the tragic event. Otherwise few physical scars remain.

Crystal Beach Park at the southeast corner of the city features a 15-acre lake, golf course, swimming pool, fishing, or other sport and recreation facilities. Park is scene of the town's two principal annual events: American Legion horse races (July 2–4) and the four-day Elk's Rodeo (late July).

Cultural scene is highlighted by the Oklahoma Northwest Pioneer Museum and Art Center, opened on the south edge of Woodward in 1966. (Open Tues. through Sat., 12–5; Sun. 2–5.)

Visitor attractions in the area: Great Plains Field Station (SW edge of town) with interesting landscaped grounds, **Boiling Springs State Park** (6 mi. NE), **Alabaster Caverns State Park** (40 mi. NE), old military buildings at **Fort Supply** (15 mi. NW), and nearby **Fort Supply Reservoir**.

Of special interest to rail buffs is the 4-mile-long Northwestern Oklahoma

Indian pottery in the Woolaroc Museum near Bartlesville.

Railroad, the state's newest—and shortest—carrier. Actually, the line was constructed in 1912 as part of the Missouri-Kansas-Texas (Katy) Railroad that served the **Oklahoma Panhandle** until abandoned in 1973. Rail Buff Frank Pollock, a Florida salesman, then bought 12 miles of track (with sidings and house tracks) in the Woodward area to establish "The Red Carpet Line" (Oklahoma tourism's name for the 17 counties of northwestern Oklahoma). Pollock and two crewmen now provide freight service to 14 industries on their short line, hope to acquire a steam locomotive so they can start carrying nostalgic passengers as well.

Woodward County (northwestern Oklahoma, see Map 3). Area, 1,232 sq. mi.; pop., 15,537; county seat, **Woodward**. A prosperous ranching area astride the **North Canadian River**. It was organized in 1893, when the Cherokee Outlet was opened to settlement. The name was that of the town, which honored Brinton W. Woodward, director of the Santa Fe Railroad, whose Chicago-to-Los An-

geles main line slices through the county.

Top travel lures: **Alabaster Caverns State Park**, **Boiling Springs State Park**, **Fort Supply Reservoir**, Pioneer Museum in **Woodward**.

Woolaroc Museum (Osage Co., on OK 123, 14 mi. SW of **Bartlesville**, see Map 4). Named for "woods," "lake," and "rock," this 4,000-acre ranch was the one-time country home of Frank Phillips, co-founder of Phillips Petroleum Co. (see **Bartlesville**). It is owned and operated by the Frank Phillips Foundation for ". . . the boys and girls of today, the fathers and mothers of tomorrow . . ." There is no charge for admission to the sprawling grounds with their convenient picnic areas, nor to the rustic Phillips Lodge (built in 1927) and the handsome museum.

Woolaroc Museum itself is a 300-foot-long stone building containing some 55,000 items. These include a priceless archeological collection, an outstanding gallery of western paintings and sculptures (Remington, Rus-

249

Extensive collections of paintings, sculptures, artifacts and fine Indian blankets are housed in the Woolaroc Museum.

screen on which is staged "Arrows Skyward," a 20-minute presentation of Indian cultural history.

Wright City (McCurtain Co., pop. 1,068, on OK 198, see Map 6). A 100 per cent lumber town, established by the Dierks Lumber Company in 1910 as Bismark, apparently to honor the German Chancellor. World War I changed the mood of the community. William W. Wright was the first county soldier to lose his life in that conflict, and the name change to honor him became effective September 13, 1918, less than two months before the Armistice.

Wright City remained a company town until 1966, when its sprawling lumber mill became part of the Dierks Division of the Weyerhaeuser Company. Now a self-governing city, it still lives off the mill, currently being expanded to boost its present level of 425 jobs.

sell, Leigh, and many others), and one of the world's finest collections of Indian blankets.

Among artifacts and ornaments of seven different prehistoric cultures of the Southwest are some outstanding pieces from the famed **Spiro Mounds** of southeastern Oklahoma. Woolaroc's sculptures include the twelve original models from which the Pioneer Woman at **Ponca City** was chosen, and the original model of the Lincoln Memorial in Washington.

The lake-studded grounds are looped by a meandering scenic road. Along the way may be seen the preserve's buffalo (American bison, actually), elk, deer, and other animals. Nearby is the new National Y-Indian Guide Center, dedicated in 1972 to serve the nation-wide 500,000-strong membership of the YMCA's Indian branch.

The building, opposite the museum itself, is a massive sandstone replica of an Indian long house. Topped by an ornamental iron observation tower, the Long House is divided into two sections: Heritage Hall and Talent Tepee. The latter features a 60-foot wrap-around

Wyandotte (Ottawa Co., pop. 297, on US 60, see Map 5). Like **Peoria** and **Quapah**, Wyandotte commemorates another small Indian tribe settled in the extreme northeast corner of Indian Territory in the nineteenth century. The Wyandottes came to Oklahoma in 1855, moved to this area in 1867 when it was given up by the Senecas.

Numbering less than a thousand, the Wyandottes last made newspaper headlines in 1956, when an Act of Congress returned to them an ancient 2-acre tribal cemetery they had ceded to the government when they left Kansas. In downtown Kansas City, it is now valued at over a million dollars.

Dominating the small town from a hill immediately to the north, the Seneca Indian School was founded by the Quakers in 1869. Starting with a single log cabin, the school now includes a dozen well-maintained brick and frame structures scattered over a neat, tree-shaded campus. A large brick Friends church is in the town itself, which sits beside the Lost Creek arm of **Grand Lake**. The town was known as Grand River from 1876 until 1894, when it became Wyandotte.

Wynnewood (Garvin Co., pop. 2,374, at junc. of US 77 and OK 29, see Map 7). Settlement here began in 1886 as Walner. With the coming of the Santa Fe Railroad the next year the name was changed to Wynnewood for the Pennsylvania town of that name. With *Pauls Valley*, Wynnewood is one of central Oklahoma's best native pecan markets, and visitors may tour the local pecan shelling plant. But the town now depends primarily not on the soil, but what lies under it.

The $20 million Kerr-McGee industrial complex, beside US 77 south of town, is the town's largest employer. The sprawling refinery—which now includes a vast tank farm, asphalt plants, and other facilities—was established in the early 1940's. Its 225 employees represent a $3 million annual payroll for the area. Plant tours are available.

Two historic structures in Wynnewood are currently being developed as museums: the three-story Eskridge Hotel, built in the statehood year of 1907, and the William F. Moore House, a one-time showplace dating from about 1897. With its three-story tower and encircling veranda, the old home is being restored to its former Victorian grandeur. The hotel, Wynnewood's largest commercial structure, was at one time a favorite stop on the Santa Fe between Oklahoma City and Dallas. Extensively converted to historic displays, it is now open only in the summer months (Fri.–Sat. 10–5).

Wynona (Osage Co., pop. 547, on OK 99, 10 mi. S of *Pawhuska*, see Map 4). A small community, dating from 1903, with impressive brick business buildings—now empty, for the most part—that attest to the vigor of the shallow well oil boom of the 1920's. Sturdy black "walking beams" of producing oil wells still dot the town.

The name Wynona is Sioux for "first born daughter."

Y

Yale (Payne Co., pop. 1,239, on OK 51, see Map 4). A small community established in 1895, sustained by Oklahoma's two principal industries, agriculture

and petroleum, and named—if historian George H. Shirk is to be believed—with a complete lack of romanticism. Was the first postmaster perhaps a graduate of the famed Ivy League school? No, the first post office was protected by a Yale lock.

In Yale (at 706 East Boston) is the modest frame house once owned and lived in, from 1917 to 1923, by Oklahoma's best-known—and one of the world's greatest—athletes, Jim Thorpe. Now restored by the Oklahoma Historical Society, it displays the medals won by the famed Sac and Fox Indian while he attended Carlisle Institute. If and when the charge of professionalism against him is dropped and his Olympic medals returned (as recent moves by the U.S. Olympic Committee would appear to make likely), it is hoped they, too, can be displayed in the only piece of property Thorpe ever owned. The home is open Tues.–Fri. 9–5, Sat.–Sun. 1–5.

Yanush (Latimer Co., pop. 100, on OK 2, 20 mi. S of *Wilburton*, see Map 6). A scattered community in the mountain-rimmed valley of Buffalo Creek, the Choctaw word for which was given it when postal service was established in 1911. The office was abandoned in 1925, but the community itself lingers on, in its picturesquely isolated setting.

Yewed (Alfalfa Co., pop. 10, off US 64, 5 mi. S of *Cherokee*, see Map 3). A tiny community that has long since lost its post office and is notable today primarily for the fact that the date of its founding, 1898, dictated it should honor Manila Bay hero Admiral George Dewey. The name was spelled backward to create Yewed, presumably because the state had two other towns (present *Weatherford* and *Dewey* itself) with similar designs on the name. At last report the "town" was down to a single track-side elevator/store and two people.

Yuba (Bryan Co., pop. 60, on OK 78, 12 mi. E of *Achille*, see Map 6). A scattered settlement that serves as trade and school center for a sprawling area along

Street dancing at the annual Czech Festival in Yukon.

the **Red River** that also includes such one-time post office communities as Yarnaby, Karma, and Romia.

Yukon (Canadian Co., pop. 8,411, on US 66 & 270, see Map 4). Twin mill and elevator complexes of concrete form something of a giant entrance gateway to this town from the east, indicate dramatically the abundance of rich winter wheat that has long underlaid its economy. But in recent years the town's essential nature has shifted from that of prosperous farming community to one of booming bedroom suburb of nearby **Oklahoma City**. **North Canadian River** farmlands not covered with housing developments and shopping centers still produce generously. But the mills are closed, and the town itself is becoming increasingly residential in nature.

This area was opened to settlement in 1889 and many Bohemian farmers were successful in filing claims. Czech influence is still strong. As at **Prague**, east of **Oklahoma City**, cries of "*Vitame vas*" welcome visitors to an annual Czech Festival (early October) of parades, colorful native costumes, folk dancing in the street, and concession stands featuring kolaches (sweet rolls with fruit centers) and other old-country delicacies. A Czech Hall south of Yukon serves as a year-round culture and recreation center.

Yukon was founded in 1891 (within 7 miles of the geographical center of Oklahoma) and apparently took its name from the Alaskan river. It was laid out astride the old **Chisholm Trail**, just a mile north of a cold spring long used by the trail riders. The spring can still be seen in Yukon City Park.

APPENDIX

Readers wanting more information may write to:

Oklahoma Tourism Department, 500 Will Rogers Building, Oklahoma City, Okla. 73105.

Department of Wildlife Conservation, Box 53465, Oklahoma City, Okla. 73105.

Oklahoma City Convention & Tourism Center, 3 Santa Fe Plaza, Oklahoma City, Okla. 73102

Tulsa Convention & Tourist Bureau, 616 S. Boston Avenue, Tulsa, Okla. 74119.

Platt National Park, Box 201, Sulphur, Okla. 73086.

Ouachita National Forest, address the District Ranger at Talihina, Okla. 74571, Heavener, Okla. 74937, or Idabel, Okla. 74745.

United States Corps of Engineers, Box 61, Tulsa, Okla. 74102.

Grand Lake Association, Grove, Okla. 74344.

Lake Texoma Association, Box 700, Denison, Texas 75020.

Spectators at '89ers Day Celebration, Guthrie (photograph by Fred W. Marvel, courtesy of Oklahoma Department of Tourism).

INDEX